CONSTRUCTING THE AMERICAN PAST

A SOURCEBOOK OF A PEOPLE'S HISTORY
VOLUME TWO FROM 1865

Elliott J. Gorn
Randy Roberts
Susan Schulten
Terry D. Bilhartz

NEW YORK   OXFORD
OXFORD UNIVERSITY PRESS

Oxford University Press is a department of the University of Oxford.
It furthers the University's objective of excellence in research, scholarship,
and education by publishing worldwide. Oxford is a registered trade mark
of Oxford University Press in the UK and certain other countries.

Published in the United States of America by
Oxford University Press
198 Madison Avenue, New York, NY 10016,
United States of America.

Library of Congress Cataloging-in-Publication Data

Names: Gorn, Elliott J., 1951- editor of compilation. | Roberts, Randy, 1951-
    editor of compilation. | Schulten, Susan, editor of compilation.
Title: Constructing the American past : a sourcebook of a people's history /
    Elliot J. Gorn, Randy Roberts, Susan Schulten.
Other titles: Sourcebook of a people's history
Description: Eighth edition. | New York, NY : Oxford University Press, [2018]
    | Audience: "Constructing the American Past asks students to become
    historians. This volume-volume sourcebook is a series of "case studies" of
    particular episodes or events in American History."—Provided by publisher.
Identifiers: LCCN 2017026453 | ISBN 9780190280956 (v. 1 : pbk.)/9780190280963 (v. 2 : pbk.)
Subjects: LCSH: United States—History—Sources. | United
    States—History—Textbooks.
Classification: LCC E173 .C69 2018 | DDC 973—dc23 LC record available at https://lccn.loc.
gov/2017026453

9 8 7 6 5 4 3 2
Printed by Sheridan Books, Inc., United States of America

TABLE OF CONTENTS

CHAPTER 3   Cultures Collide at Wounded Knee   44

CHAPTER 4   New Americans: The Immigrants   69

CHAPTER 13 **The Freedom Struggle: States' Rights Versus Federal Intervention** *265*

CHAPTER 14   **Vietnam: The Tipping Point**   *290*

CHAPTER 15   **Turning Left**   *313*

ABOUT THE EDITORS

ELLIOTT J. GORN

Elliott J. Gorn is Joseph Gagliano Professor of History at Loyola University Chicago. After taking his bachelor's degree from UC Berkeley and PhD from Yale, he taught at Alabama, Miami of Ohio, Purdue, Brown, and the University of Helsinki. He is author of *The Manly Art: Bare-Knuckle Prize Fighting in America*, *Mother Jones: The Most Dangerous Woman in America*, and *Dillinger's Wild Ride: The Year that Made Public Enemy Number One*. Gorn's research has been supported by grants from the Guggenheim Foundation, the National Endowment for the Humanities, the Stanford Humanities Center and the Huntington Library. He is finishing a book about the 1955 murder of Emmett Till.

RANDY ROBERTS

Randy Roberts is Distinguished Professor of History at Purdue University. He took his bachelor's degree from Mansfield University in Pennsylvania and his PhD at Louisiana State University. He is author or co-author of ten books, including *Blood Brothers: The Fatal Friendship Between Muhammad Ali and Malcolm X*, *Where the Domino Fell: America and Vietnam, 1945–1990*, *Papa Jack: Jack Johnson and the Era of White Hopes*, and *John Wayne, American*. Roberts has won numerous teaching awards, including the Carnegie Foundation's "Professor of the Year Award" for the state of Indiana. He specializes in teaching military history, sports history, and popular culture. He has served frequently as a consultant and on-camera commentator for PBS, HBO, and the History Channel.

SUSAN SCHULTEN

Susan Schulten is professor of history at the University of Denver, where she has taught since 1996. She earned her B.A. from U.C. Berkeley and PhD from University of Pennsylvania. Schulten is the author of *Mapping the Nation: History and Cartography in Nineteenth-Century America* (www.mappingthenation.com) and *The Geographical Imagination in America,*

1880–1950. From 2010 to 2014, she contributed regularly to the *New York Times* "Disunion" series, which commemorated the sesquicentennial of the American Civil War. Her work has been supported by the Guggenheim Foundation and the National Endowment for the Humanities. Her current project—a history of America through 100 maps—is forthcoming from the University of Chicago Press.

TERRY D. BILHARTZ

Terry Bilhartz taught at Sam Houston State University for nearly forty years. A graduate of Dallas Baptist College, he took a Master's degree from Emory University and his PhD from George Washington University, then began full-time teaching in 1977. He conducted research at Vanderbilt, Stanford, and the University of Connecticut, and in the course of his career he authored or co-authored over fifty books and articles, including *Urban Religion and the Second Great Awakening*, *Francis Asbury's America*, *Images of Texas in the Nation*, and *Sacred Words: A Source Book on the Great Religions of the World*. Terry passed away unexpectedly on December 12, 2014. He was 64. Terry was always a joy to work with, and we hope this new edition of *Constructing the American Past* continues to reflect his passion for teaching history.

INTRODUCTION

What was it like back then? What did people think and believe? What motivated them to laugh and cry, fight and die? How did people live? Were their homes comfortable? Were their workdays long? Were their diets sufficient? How did they worship, if at all? These questions and hundreds more surface instantly when historians and students ponder the past. Indeed, the question "What was it like back then?" is fundamental to any person with a sense of curiosity. It also lies at the core of the historical profession. Using a wide range of sources, historians try to "construct" what life was like in the past.

The process of construction is challenging. Since the sources needed to answer any important historical question are frequently incomplete, contradictory, or evasive, the writing of history can never be as precise as we would like. Imagine putting together a picture puzzle that is supposed to contain 1,000 pieces, but half of them have been lost. With effort and imagination, you might be able to reconstruct the general outlines of the picture. The process is roughly akin to historical inquiry. Hard work, analytical ability, and imagination—these come into play in both ventures.

Constructing the American Past asks you to become your own historian. This volume is a series of "case studies" of particular episodes or events in American history. The "Historical Context" essay that introduces each chapter sets the stage for the issue at hand. The essay is followed by a selection of primary documents, including maps, broadsides, diaries, letters, newspaper articles, trial records, memoirs, political pamphlets—the basic stuff that historians use to construct the past, the materials on which historians base their interpretations and build their narratives.

All historical sources have biases, but some are more reliable than others. The historian's task—your task—is to sort through contradictory evidence and come up with a plausible account of what happened and why. But equally important, documents come from people, and people disagree in their fundamental values and beliefs. You want to get "underneath" the sources, think about what sorts of assumptions their authors made, consider why people believed and acted as they did, and ponder why history is so frequently contested ground. Remember above all that being a historian—constructing the past—is interpretive work; history is more an art than a science.

That's what makes doing history exciting. Every historian has a story of working in an archive, feeling sleepy and bored, when something leaps off the page. Maybe a paragraph written by someone who has been dead 100 years boldly states a new idea, or a diary turns up and reveals the inner life of someone who seemed so unknowable, or an eyewitness account of clashing armies makes the battlefield come alive. Doing history can be as exciting as any act of discovery and exploration. And as you will see, *everything* has a history.

Take lunch for example. We assume today that the food we eat is safe and pure, but that expectation came only after a national debate in the early twentieth century about how to make mass-produced food fit for human consumption. The meatpacking industry in Chicago was a flashpoint for this controversy, and Chapter 6 takes you into that debate through the words and images of journalists, novelists, scientists, satirists, workers and businessmen. The result of the conflict over how to assure public safety was the Pure Food and Drug Act, a landmark piece of legislation.

That battle over food regulation was part of a much larger trend in early twentieth century America called progressivism. Debates about all sorts of things people took for granted sprang up during the Progressive Era—should voters be allowed to recall inept or corrupt politicians, should corporations be reduced in size, how can city streets be made safer, should women be allowed to practice birth control (which we take up in Chapter 8). *Constructing the American Past* lets you explore how people debated such issues in their own day, what they wrote and thought about them.

This eighth edition of *Constructing the American Past*, Volume 2, includes our most extensive revisions to date. Nearly every chapter has been strengthened with material—both textual and visual—that illuminates the central problem under question. We have maintained the original structure, so there are still chapters on the Great Depression, World War 2, the Cold War, and the Civil Rights Movement, for example. But much of our content is fresh, so those same chapters have many new documents that tell new stories. Throughout the text, new images have been included to provoke discussion and convey the visual dimension of the past. Above all, our overriding goal is to stimulate conversation and critical thinking about key issues in American history. Note that the language in some of these documents is powerful, even offensive, but we have preserved as it originally appeared so that the sources may speak for themselves.

Since the last edition of *Constructing the American Past* was published, one of our co-editors, Terry Bilhartz passed away. For over twenty years, Terry, Elliott and Randy worked together, edited, argued, and constructed these volumes together. We miss Terry. He was a fine historian and a great collaborator. But we welcome our new co-editor, Susan Schulten of the University of Denver. Susan has brought enormous energy and great ideas to this latest edition of *Constructing the American Past*. She truly has revitalized this project.

We have had considerable help preparing this eighth edition. First Brian Wheel and then Charles Cavaliare at Oxford University Press guided us through the editorial process. Katherine Schnakenberg at Oxford gave us thorough and prompt help negotiating permission to reprint primary sources from countless archives. Patricia Berube carefully supervised the final stages of editing. Three graduate students at Loyola University Chicago served as research assistants: Chelsea Denault, Hope Shannon, and Sebastian Wuepper; editorial assistance was also provided by Sam Anderson.

Several outside readers have strengthened our work. We acknowledge with gratitude the comments we received from Cindy Hahamovitch, University of Georgia, Louis Haas at Middle Tennessee State University, Damon Eubank at Cambellsville University, and two reviewers who wished to remain anonymous.

Many of the events and documents in this collection were first used in our own classrooms. In that spirit, we dedicate this collection to our students, past, present, and future, who have taught us so much about teaching.

Elliott. J. Gorn
Randy Roberts
Susan Schulten
Terry D. Bilhartz

CHAPTER 1

RECONSTRUCTION AND THE RISE OF THE KU KLUX KLAN

HISTORICAL CONTEXT

In a letter to the House of Representatives dated April 19, 1872, President Ulysses S. Grant described a "grand system of criminal associations pervading most of the Southern States." Investigations by the attorney general, by the Joint Committee of Congress upon Southern Outrages, and by local officials all revealed that a terrorist organization known as the Ku Klux Klan, or KKK, exercised enormous influence in the South and worked in defiance of federal Reconstruction. Grant alleged that members swore oaths of obedience and secrecy that they considered more binding than their allegiance to the United States. "They are organized and armed," the president declared. "They effect their objects by personal violence, often extending to murder. They terrify witnesses, they control juries in the State courts, and sometimes in the courts of the United States." Klansmen spied on, murdered, and intimidated their enemies and thereby destroyed the rule of law. Their goals, according to Grant, were

> by force and terror, to prevent all political action not in accord with the views of the members, to deprive colored citizens of the right to bear arms, and of the right of a free ballot, and to suppress the schools in which colored children were taught, and to reduce the colored people to a condition closely allied to that of slavery.[1]

The KKK, in other words, threatened the very hallmarks of democratic citizenship, as it attempted to seize by terror what the South had lost on the battlefield.

The KKK originated in informal organizations that Confederate men joined immediately after the Civil War. The agenda of these organizations became increasingly political, as Andrew Johnson's Reconstruction policies were replaced by the more stringent ones of the so-called radical Republicans in Congress. The South was now occupied by enemy troops, its cities burned, farms barren, elected officials disgraced, and population decimated. Those who had been slaves, black men and women stigmatized as ineradicably inferior, were now to be treated as equal citizens of a democracy. There was even talk of confiscating southern agricultural land and redistributing it so that blacks and poor whites could become independent farmers. This plan, as it turned out, was too radical for most Republicans, whose devotion to private property—even that of former rebels—brooked few exceptions.

For African Americans, the era of Reconstruction was a time of relative freedom. Many took the opportunity to leave the land they had been bound to and sought opportunity in southern cities and even in the North. Certainly, whites feared the possible loss of their labor force. Equally threatening, the former slaves were more free to worship, work, learn, and acquire power and money than ever before. Many whites alleged that blacks were incapable of handling freedom—that black politicians were corrupt; black workers, slothful; and black masses, ignorant. But the unspoken and perhaps deeper fear was that African Americans were indeed capable of good citizenship and would compete with their former masters. In other words, the comforting idea of white superiority no longer held. If radical Reconstruction failed to secure real economic opportunity for the former slaves, it did insist that African Americans be treated as equal citizens under the law, an idea antithetical to the old southern economic and social structure, indeed to white southern identity.

But it was not just the new position of blacks that threatened white southerners. Republican rule included policies for changing the region to conform more with the tone of northern society. The "carpetbaggers" (northerners who came south after the war) and "scalawags" (southerners sympathetic to the north) generally were not corrupt individuals but people who genuinely believed that the South's salvation would come through railroads, new industries, and public schools—in short, institutions associated with economic progress in the free-labor North. Radical Reconstruction not only proposed to change racial mores but also aimed to replace the old slave system with northern-style free labor capitalism. Such drastic changes, imposed, as it appeared to many white southerners, by upstart blacks and alien Yankees, were terrifying.

The Ku Klux Klan was a response to the social, cultural, and economic changes that many white southerners found so disturbing. It might best be seen as the extreme wing of the "redeemers," those whites who sought the end of federal Reconstruction and the restoration of their wealth and power. African Americans and southern Unionists, with the aid of the federal government and the Republican Party, were able to govern several states for a few years after the Civil War, but eventually the political experience, popularity, and just plain brutality of the redeemers won the day. The Klan specialized in the latter.

Klansmen typically dressed in white robes and hoods, and they tried to convince their black victims that they were the ghosts of the Confederate dead. Blacks were intimidated, not by the transparent ghostly ruse but by the Klansmen's violence. By the late 1860s, their pattern was clear: several Klansmen would surround a victim's house at night, shoot into the windows, set fire to the structure, poison livestock, or simply drag the inhabitants out and shoot, whip, or hang them. Usually the victims were individuals who had stood up for their rights, blacks who voted, ran for office, or refused to take whites' insults. Occasionally there was open warfare between Klansmen and black militias. White citizens, too,

Image 1.1 Frank Bellew, "Visit of the Ku-Klux"

Frank Bellew's stark depiction of the Klan's use of violence against African-American freedmen stunned northern readers of *Harper's Weekly* and contributed to the crackdown on this lawless and terroristic organization.

Source: Harper's Weekly, February 24, 1872, v.16 n.791

who dared support blacks or expressed Unionist sympathies were terrorized by the night riders.

It is impossible to know how many southern men ever joined the Klan given that it was a secret organization. Yet through the late 1860s and into the early 1870s, it successfully intimidated both blacks and whites. When the federal government outlawed the organization and began prosecuting its members, the Klan lost some of its effectiveness. But by that point, violence, along with social ostracism and economic coercion, had become part of the arsenal of redeemer politics, which aimed to restore white Democratic rule to the former slave states. Redemption came to state and local government but succeeded only because the federal government lost its resolve to make sure that all citizens were treated, as promised in the Constitution, with equality. Slowly, African

Americans' rights to vote, speak out freely, and participate equally in social life were stripped away.

Just as the political disenfranchisement of African Americans that followed Reconstruction was their reduction to economic peonage. Slavery died at Appomattox, but new forms of economic and political servitude soon took its place, and they lasted for a century. In the years following the Civil War, most blacks became tenant farmers with no land of their own, and most of these sharecropped, work that offered little more freedom or material comfort than slavery. As a sharecropper, a former slave might farm a white man's land; buy tools, supplies, and food from him; and rent a shack for the family from him. Owner and renter would split the proceeds of the harvest, but the black farmer's debt for the goods that the white man had furnished would almost certainly exceed any profit. Indebted to the white planter, former slaves would be unable to leave; year after year they would have to stay on the land, trying to pay off a debt that grew ever larger.

The following documents reveal the Ku Klux Klan from various points of view. The initiation oath of the Knights of the White Camelia (a part of the Klan) reveals the style and purposes of this organization. Despite the Klan's high-toned rhetoric defending southern honor, the narratives of former slaves and their testimony in congressional hearings reveals how the Klan used violence to accomplish its goals. Note here the reasons for which the victims felt they were being attacked. Congressman Stevenson's speech summarizes the federal findings on the scope of Klan activities and shows the conflict over values and ideology between southern redeemers and northern agents of Reconstruction. Finally, *Experience of a Northern Man among the Ku-Klux* gives a good sense of how northerners viewed the South and how some of them even visualized colonizing it and remaking its society to conform to northern norms. As you read these selections, ask yourself how and why ideas about race intermingled with issues of ideology, labor, and politics.

INTRODUCTION TO DOCUMENT 1

The initiation oath of the Knights of the White Camelia reveals the appeal of such organizations. The Knights originated during the early days of the Klan in the late 1860s. Note the claims to religious faith and patriotism and the chivalric mandate: to protect the weak and defenseless against the outrages of "lawless" blacks. There was a sense of white southern manhood in this; defending home and family was the manly thing to do. Aside from the reassertion of crude white supremacy, the KKK must have been very popular for its sense of mystery, pageantry, and ritual; individuals were made to feel that they belonged to something splendid and grand.

1. INITIATION OATH OF THE KNIGHTS OF THE WHITE CAMELIA

I do solemnly swear, in the presence of these witnesses, never to reveal, without authority, the existence of this Order, its objects, its acts, and signs of recognition; never to reveal or publish, in any manner whatsoever, what I shall see or hear in this Council; never to divulge the names of the members of the Order, or their acts done in connection therewith; I swear to maintain and defend the social and political superiority of the White Race on this Continent; always and in all places to observe a marked distinction between the White and African races; to vote for none but white men for any office of honor, profit or trust; to devote my intelligence, energy and influence to instill these principles in the minds and hearts of others; and to protect and defend persons of the White Race, in their lives, rights and property, against the encroachments and aggressions of an inferior race.

I swear, moreover, to unite myself in heart, soul and body with those who compose this Order; to aid, protect and defend them in all places; to obey the orders of those, who, by our statutes, will have the right of giving those orders. . . .

The oath having been taken by the candidate, the C[ommander] shall now say:

Brother, by virtue of the authority to me delegated, I now pronounce you a Knight of the [White Camelia]. . . .

Brothers: You have been initiated into one of the most important Orders, which have ever been established on this continent: an Order, which, if its principles are faithfully observed and its objects diligently carried out, is destined to regenerate our unfortunate country and to relieve the White Race from the humiliating condition to which it has lately been reduced in this Republic. It is necessary, therefore, that before taking part in the labors of this Association, you should understand fully its principles and objects and the duties which devolve upon you as one of its members.

As you may have already gathered from the questions which were propounded to you, and which you have answered so satisfactorily, and from the clauses of the Oath which you have taken, our main and fundamental object is the *maintenance of the supremacy of the white race* in this Republic. History and physiology teach us that we belong to a race which nature has endowed with an evident superiority over all other races, and that the Maker, in thus elevating us above the common standard of human creation, has intended to give us over inferior races, a dominion from which no human laws can permanently derogate. The experience of ages demonstrates that, from the origin of the world, this dominion has always remained in the hands of the Caucasian Race; whilst all the other races have constantly occupied a subordinate and secondary position; a fact which triumphantly confirms this great law of nature. Powerful nations have succeeded each other in the face of the world, and have marked their passage by glorious and memorable deeds; and among those who have thus left on this globe indelible traces of their splendor and greatness, we find none but descended from the Caucasian stock. We see, on the contrary, that most of the countries inhabited by the other races have remained in a state of complete barbarity; whilst the small number of those who have advanced beyond this savage existence, have, for centuries, stagnated in a semi-barbarous condition, of which there can be no progress or improvement. And it is a remarkable fact that as a race of men is more remote from the Caucasian and approaches nearer to the black African, the more fatally that stamp of inferiority is affixed to its sons, and irrevocably dooms them to eternal imperfectibility and degradation.

Convinced that we are of these elements of natural ethics, we know, besides, that the government of our Republic was established by white men, for white men alone, and that it never was in the contemplation of its founders that it should fall into the hands of an inferior and degraded race. We hold, therefore, that any attempt to wrest from the white race the management of its affairs in order to transfer it to control of the black population, is an invasion of the sacred prerogatives vouchsafed to us by the Constitution, and a violation of the laws established by God himself; that such encroachments are subversive of the established institutions of our Republic, and that no individual of the white race can submit to them without humiliation and shame.

It, then, becomes our solemn duty, as white men, to resist strenuously and persistently those attempts against our natural and constitutional rights, and to do everything in our power in order to maintain, in this Republic, the supremacy of the Caucasian race, and restrain the black or African race to that condition of social and political inferiority for which God has destined it. This is the object for which our Order was instituted; and, in carrying it out, we intend to infringe no laws, to violate no rights, and to resort to no forcible means, except for purposes of legitimate and necessary defense.

As an essential condition of success, this Order proscribes absolutely all social equality between the races. If we were to admit persons of African race on the same level with ourselves, a state of personal relations would follow which would unavoidably lead to political equality; for it would be a virtual recognition of *status*, after which we could not consistently deny them an equal share in the administration of our public affairs. The man who is good enough to be our familiar companion, is good enough also to participate in our political government; and if we were to grant the one, there could be no good reason for us not to concede the other of these two privileges.

There is another reason, Brothers, for which we condemn this social equality. Its toleration would soon be a fruitful source of intermarriages between individuals of the two races; and the result of this *miscegenation* [*sic*] would be gradual amalgamation and the production of a degenerate and bastard offspring, which would soon populate these States with a degraded and ignoble population, incapable of moral and intellectual development and unfitted to support a great and powerful country. We must maintain the purity of the white blood, if we would preserve for it that natural superiority with which God has ennobled it.

To avoid these evils, therefore, we take the obligation *to observe a marked distinction between the two races*, not only in the relations of public affairs, but also in the more intimate dealings and intercourse of private life which, by the frequency of their occurrence, are more apt to have an influence on the attainment of the purposes of the Order.

Now that I have laid before you the objects of this Association, let me charge you specially in relation to one of your most important studies as one of its members. Our statutes make us bound to respect sedulously the rights of the colored inhabitants of this Republic, and in every instance, to give to them whatever lawfully belongs to them. It is an act of simple justice not to deny them any of the privileges to which they are legitimately entitled; and we cannot better show the inherent superiority of our race than by dealing with them in that spirit of firmness, liberality and impartiality which characterizes all superior organizations. Besides, it would be ungenerous for us to undertake to restrict them to the narrowest limits as to the exercise of certain rights, without conceding to them, at the same time, the fullest measure of those which we recognize as theirs; and a fair construction of a white man's duty towards them would be, not only to respect and observe their acknowledged rights, but also to see that these are respected and observed by others.[2]

INTRODUCTION TO DOCUMENTS 2 AND 3

Despite the Klan's lofty rhetoric, the following testimonies by its victims reveal the terrorism for which the organization was renowned. Ask yourself who became Klan victims and why. The three statements in Document 2 were made by former slaves looking back on their experiences from a distance of several decades; the statements are taken from oral histories collected during the 1930s by the Federal Writers Project (note how the former slaves' words were rendered in heavy "Negro dialect"). The two statements in Document 3 come from testimony before a congressional committee investigating Klan violence in the early 1870s and transcribed in standard English.

2. TESTIMONY OF VICTIMS OF THE KU KLUX KLAN (1871)

PIERCE HARPER

After de colored people was considered free an' turned loose de Klu Klux broke out. Some of de colored people commenced to farming like I tol' you an' all de ol' stock dey could pick up after de Yankees left dey took an' took care of. If you got so you made good money an' had a good farm de Klu Klux'd come an' murder you. De gov'ment built de colored people school houses an' de Klu Klux went to work an' burn 'em down. Dey'd go to de jails an' take de colored men out an' knock dere brains out an' break dere necks an' throw 'em in de river.

Dere was a man dat dey taken, his name was Jim Freeman. Dey taken him an' destroyed his stuff an' him 'cause he was making some money. Hung him on a tree in his front yard, right in front of his cabin. Dere was some young men who went to de schools de gov'ment opened for de colored folks. Some white widder woman said someone had stole something she own', so dey put these young fellers in jail 'cause dey suspicioned 'em. De Klu Kluxes went to de jail an' took 'em out an' kill 'em. Dat happen de second year after de War.

After de Klu Kluxes got so strong de colored men got together an' made a complaint before de law. De Gov'nor told de law to give 'em de ol' guns in de commissary what de Southern soldiers had use, so dey issued de colored men old muskets an' told 'em to protect theirselves.

De colored men got together an' organized the 'Malicy [Militia]. Dey had leaders like regular soldiers, men dat led 'em right on. Dey didn't meet 'cept when dey heard de Klu Kluxes was coming to get some of de colored folks. Den de one who knowed dat tol' de leader an' he went 'round an' told de others when an'

where dey's meet. Den dey was ready for 'em. Dey'd hide in de cabins an' when de Klu Kluxes come dere dey was. Den's when dey found out who a lot of de Klu Kluxes was, 'cause a lot of 'em was killed. Dey wore dem long sheets an' you couldn't tell who dey was. Dey even covered dere horses up so you couldn't tell who dey belong to. Men you thought was your friend was Klu Kluxes. You deal wit' 'em in de stores in de day time an' at night dey come out to your house an' kill you.

SUE CRAFT

My teacher's name Dunlap—a white teacher teachin de cullud. De Ku Klux whupped him fo' teachin' us. I saw de Ku Klux ridin' a heap dem days. Dey had hoods pulled ovah dere faces. One time dey come to our house twict. Fus' time dey come quiet. It was right 'fore de 'lection o' Grant jus' after slavery. It was fus' time cullud people 'lowed t' vote. Dey ast my father was he goin' to vote for Grant. He tell 'em he don' know he goin' vote. After 'lection dey come back, whoopin' an' hollerin. Dey shoot out de winder lights. It was 'cause my father voted for Grant. Dey broke de do' open. My father was a settin' on de bed. I 'member he had a shot gun in his han'. Well, dey broke de do' down, an' then father he shoot, an' dey scattered all ovah de fence.

MORGAN RAY

. . . I heard a lot about the Klu Klux, but it warn't till long afterwards dat I evan see 'em. It was one night after de work of de day was done and I was takin' a walk near where I worked. Suddenly I hear the hoof beats of horses and I natcherly wuz curious and waited beside de road to see what was comin'. I saw a company of men hooded and wearin' what looked like sheets. Dey had a young cullud man as dere prisoner. I wuz too skairt to say anything or ask any questions. I just went on my sweet way. Later I found out dey acclaimed de prisoner had assaulted a white woman. Dey strung him up when he wouldn't confess, and shot him full of holes and threw his body in de pond.[3]

3. CONGRESSIONAL INQUIRY INTO KLAN ACTIVITIES (1871)

ATLANTA, GEORGIA, OCTOBER 25, 1871

Joseph Addison (White) Sworn and Examined by the Chairman:

QUESTION: What is your age, where were you born, where do you live, and what is your present occupation?

ANSWER: I am about twenty-four years old; I was born in Muscogee County, and now live in Haralson County; I have been living there ever since I was a little bit of a boy; I am a farmer.

QUESTION: During the war which side were you on?

ANSWER: I never fought a day in the rebel army; I was not in it at all.

QUESTION: Which side were your feelings on?

ANSWER: My feelings were on the side of what you call the radical party now.

QUESTION: What did they call it then?

ANSWER: I was what you call a Union man then.

QUESTION: Were your opinions well known?

ANSWER: Yes, sir; I reckon I am well known.

QUESTION: Have you seen any people, or do you know of any, in your county, called Ku-Klux?

ANSWER: Yes, sir.

QUESTION: Tell us what you know about them.

ANSWER: Do you want me to state just about all how they did?

QUESTION: Yes.

ANSWER: I will tell you how they did me. . . . My wife looked out and said, "Lord have mercy! Joe, it is the Ku-Klux." I jumped out of the door and ran. One of them was right in the back yard, and he jabbed the end of his six-shooter almost against my head, and said, "Halt! God damn you." I said, "I will give up." I asked them what they were doing that for; they said that I had been stealing. I said, "You men here know I have not." They said, "We gave you time once to get away, and, God damn you, you have not gone; now, God damn you, you shall not go, for we allow to kill you." I said, "If you do not abuse me or whip me, I will go the next morning." They said they would not abuse me or whip me, but they would kill me. I said, "Let me go and see my wife and children." They said, "No, God damn you." I turned away from the man; he jammed his pistol in my face, and said, "God damn you, go on, or I will kill you." They took me about eighty or ninety yards from there into a little thicket. The man on my right was a high, tall man; the one on my left was a low, chunky fellow. The man on my right stepped back, and said to the little fellow on my left, "Old man, we have got him here now; do as you please with him." There were some little hickories near him; he looked at them, but did not take them. They were all standing right around me with their guns pointing at me. Just as he turned around, I wheeled and run; but before I had run ten yards I heard a half a dozen caps bursted at me. Just as I made a turn to go behind some buildings and little bushes, I heard two guns fired. I must have gone seventy or eighty yards, and then I heard what I thought was a pistol fired. I heard a bullet hit a tree. I run on eight or ten steps further, and then I heard a bullet hit a tree just before me. Every one of them took after me, and run me for a hundred and fifty yards. I ran down a little bluff and ran across a branch. When I got across there, I could not run any further, for my shoes were all muddy. I cut the strings of my old shoes, and left them there. I stopped to listen, but I never saw anything more of them. I then went around and climbed up on the fence, and sat there and watched until dark. I then went to the house and got some dry clothes, and then went back where I had fixed a place in the woods to sleep in, and went to bed. That was the last I heard of them that night. They came back Sunday night before court commenced on Monday, in Haralson County. My wife would not stay there by herself, but went to her sister-in-law's, Milton Powell's wife. They came in on them on Sunday night, or about two hours and a half before day Monday morning. They abused her and cursed her powerfully, and tried to make her tell where I was. They said that if she did not tell them they would shoot her God-damned brains out. I was laying out close by there, and I stood there and heard them. They shot five or six shots in the yard; some of them said they shot into the house. They scared my wife and sister-in-law so bad that they took the children and went into the woods and staid there all night. That was the last time they were there. . . .

QUESTION: Have they ever molested you since then?

ANSWER: No, sir; they have never been on me any more since then.

QUESTION: Do you still stay there?

ANSWER: No, sir; I have done moved now. I moved off, and left my hogs and my crop and everything there, what little I made. I did not make much crop this year, for I was afraid to work, and now I am afraid to go back there to save anything.

ATLANTA, GEORGIA, OCTOBER 26, 1871

Thomas M. Allen (Colored) Sworn and Examined by the Chairman:

QUESTION: What is your age, where were you born, and where do you now live?

ANSWER: I am now thirty-eight years old. I was born in Charleston, South Carolina, and I am living here at present; that is, my family is here; I am pastor of the Baptist church at Marietta, Jasper County.

QUESTION: How long have you been living in this State?

ANSWER: I came to this State the year that James K. Polk died, about 1849.

QUESTION: How do you connect your coming here with his death?

ANSWER: I landed in Savannah at the time they were firing cannon there, and asked what was the matter.

QUESTION: Were you a slave?

ANSWER: Partly so. My father was a white man and he set us free at his death. They stole us from Charleston and run me and my brother and mother into this State. He left us ten thousand dollars each to educate us, and give us trades, and for that money they stole us away.

QUESTION: Were you kept in slavery until the time of emancipation?

ANSWER: Yes, sir; I was held as a slave; I hired my time.

QUESTION: You never were able to assert your freedom before emancipation?

ANSWER: No, sir, I could not do it. . . .

QUESTION: Have you been connected with political affairs in this State since the war?

ANSWER: Yes, sir. When the constitutional convention was called, I took an active part, and did all I could, of course. Afterwards I ran for the legislature and was elected.

QUESTION: In what year?

ANSWER: I was elected in 1868; the colored members were expelled that year.

QUESTION: From what county were you elected?

ANSWER: From Jasper County.

QUESTION: Were you reinstated in your seat in the legislature?

ANSWER: Yes, sir.

QUESTION: Have you witnessed any violence towards any of your race, yourself or any others?

ANSWER: Yes, sir. After we were expelled from the legislature, I went home to Jasper County; I was carrying on a farm there. On the 16th of

October, a party of men came to my house; I cannot say how many, for I did not see them. . . .

About 2 o'clock my wife woke me up, and said that there were persons all around the house; that they had been there for half an hour, and were calling for me. I heard them call again, and I asked them what they wanted, and who they were. . . .

They asked me to come out. At this time my brother-in-law waked up and said, "Who are they, Thomas?" I said, "I do not know." . . .

He put on his shoes and vest and hat; this was all he was found with after he was killed. He opened the door and hollered, "Where are you?" He hollered twice, and then two guns were fired. He seemed to fall, and I and my wife hollered, and his wife hollered. I jumped up, and ran back to the fire-place, where I started to get a light, and then started to go over the partition to him. I threw a clock down, and then I thought of the closet there, and went through it to him, and my wife closed the door. I hollered for Joe, a third man on the place, to come up and bring his gun, for Emanuel was killed. He did not come for some time, and then I was so excited that I could not recognize his voice. After a time I let him in. We made up a light, and then I saw my brother-in-law laying on his back as he fell. I examined him; there were four or five number one buck-shot in his breast. . . .

QUESTION: What do you know about this organization of men they call Ku-Klux?

ANSWER: I have never seen one in my life; I have seen a great many people who have seen them. I have a Ku-Klux letter here that I got on the day of the election for the constitution.

QUESTION: Will you read it?

ANSWER: Yes, sir; this is it.

To Thomas Allen:

Tom, you are in great danger; you are going heedless with the radicals, against the interest of the conservative white population, and I tell you if you do not change your course before the election for the ratification of the infernal constitution, your days are numbered, and they will be but few. Just vote or use your influence for the radicals or for the constitution, and you go up certain. My advice to you, Tom, is to stay at home if you value your life, and not vote at all, and advise all of your race to do the same thing. You are marked and closely watched by K.K.K. (or in plain words Ku-Klux.)

Take heed; a word to the wise is sufficient.

By order of Grand Cyclops.

QUESTION: Where did you get this?

ANSWER: It was dropped in the shop the morning of the election, when I was running for the legislature. I showed it to a great many men in town; I showed it to Colonel Preston, a friend of mine. He asked where I got it, and I told him. He said, "Tear it up." I said, "No, it may be of service to my children if not to me." He said, "You need not talk so slack about it; there may be heaps of Ku-Klux in the State, and they might get hold of your talk. . . ."

QUESTION: What is the feeling of your people in regard to their personal safety?

ANSWER: They do not consider that they have any safety at all, only in the cities; that is the truth. In a great many places the colored people call the white people master and mistress, just as they ever did; if they do not do it they are whipped. They have no safety at all except in a large place like this. If I could have stayed at home I would not have been here. I left all my crops and never got anything for them. My wife had no education, and when I came away everything went wrong. There are thousands in my condition.

QUESTION: Is that the reason so many of your people come to the large cities?

ANSWER: Yes, sir, that is the reason. Mr. Abram Turner, a member of the legislature, from Putnam County, the county adjoining mine, was shot down in the street in open day. He was a colored man. They have elected another in his place, a democrat.

QUESTION: When was he elected?

ANSWER: Last fall.

QUESTION: He has been killed since?

ANSWER: Yes, sir, shot down in broad open day. . . .

QUESTION: Was he a republican?

ANSWER: Yes sir, I knew him very well; he was a good man, a harmless man; I married him to his wife.

QUESTION: Do the people of your race feel that they have the protection of the laws?

ANSWER: By no means.

QUESTION: What is their hope and expectation for the future?

ANSWER: They expect to get protection from the Federal Government at Washington; that is all. You ask any one of my people out there, even the most ignorant of them, and they will tell you so. . . . I believe that many of the jurymen, and lawyers too, are members of the Ku-Klux; I believe it positively; I would say so on my deathbed.

QUESTION: How much have you been over the State?

ANSWER: I have traveled all over the State.

QUESTION: Have you communicated pretty freely with the people of your own race?

ANSWER: Yes, sir.

QUESTION: Have you received information from them about the Ku-Klux?

ANSWER: Yes, sir, occasionally.

QUESTION: In how large a portion of the State do you find reports of Ku-Klux operations?

ANSWER: I find it in the counties of what is known among us as the Black Belt. Wherever the negroes are in the majority, there the Ku-Klux range more than in any other places. Up in Cobb County they are very peaceable. The democrats are always elected there to the general assembly. The whites have about seven hundred majority. The colored people get along splendidly there. In those counties where the whites are largely in the majority, the colored people get along very well; but go into the counties where the negroes are in the majority, and there is always trouble; for instance, in

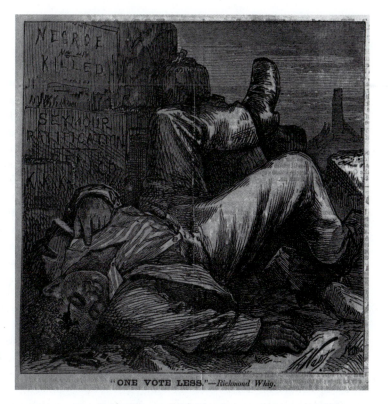

"ONE VOTE LESS."—*Richmond Whig.*

Image 1.2 Thomas Nast, "One Vote Less"

The famous cartoonist Thomas Nast drew this image to publicize the violence used to keep blacks from the ballot box throughout the South. The words "Seymour Ratification" refer to the presidential election between Republican Ulysses S. Grant and New York Democratic governor Horatio Seymour, who supported state rights and resisted the Fourteenth Amendment's guarantee of black citizenship. The image proved so powerful with audiences that *Harper's Weekly* used it in both the 1868 and 1872 elections.

Source: Harper's Weekly, August 6, 1868

Monroe County, or Warren County, or anywhere in the Black Belt, there is always trouble between the whites and the colored people.

QUESTION: Are the colored people riotous in disposition? Are they inclined to make trouble?

ANSWER: I suppose the colored people are as peaceable as any people in the world. The colored people of Madison, when the white people went to the jail and murdered a man there, could have burned up the town and killed all the white people there.[4]

INTRODUCTION TO DOCUMENT 4

As Thomas Allen's testimony above revealed, Klan violence grew not just out of hatred and bigotry—it had particular political goals in mind. Congressman Job E. Stevenson from Ohio delivered the following address in the House of Representatives on May 30, 1872, less than half a year from the coming presidential election. Stevenson argued that the Klan was not merely brutal; it was a political conspiracy to overthrow Reconstruction and re-enslave African Americans. As you read the excerpts from his speech, note his characterization of the newly conquered South. Why did he believe that the North must stop the Klan? What arguments did he make? Note that Stevenson mentions General Forrest. He refers to General Nathan Bedford Forrest, a Confederate general notorious in the North first for the Fort Pillow Massacre in which his troops butchered hundreds of black Union troops in the act of surrendering and also for his early leadership of the Ku Klux Klan.

4. SPEECH TO THE HOUSE OF REPRESENTATIVES (1872)

HON. JOB E. STEVENSON OF OHIO

Mr. Speaker: The gravest question before Congress is the Kuklux Conspiracy, its origin and extent, character and actions, plans and purposes, condition and prospects.

ORIGIN

It originated in hostility to the Government, in enmity against the Union. It is the successor of the southern confederacy, rebellion in disguise, war at midnight. It rose like an exhalation from the unsodden grave of the "lost cause." . . .

A POLITICAL CONSPIRACY

Such being the origin . . . of this great conspiracy, we may well inquire against whom its terrors are aimed. It strikes exclusively at the Unionists of the South, principally at the freedmen. No man can deny that it is political. The oath swears the member to oppose Radicalism, to oppose the Radical party, to oppose the political equality of the races.

General Forrest said: "It is a protective political military organization. Its objects originally were protection against Loyal Leagues and the Grand Army of the Republic; but after it became general, it was found that political matters and interests could best be promoted within it, and it was then made a political organization, giving its support, of course, to the Democratic party." . . .

It appears that in the States of Georgia, Louisiana, Tennessee, and South Carolina from the spring election in 1868 to the election for President in 1868, the Republican vote was reduced eighty-five thousand by intimidation and violence.

COMMANDERS

The forces of the conspiracy are controlled by such men as Generals Gordon, Hampton, and Forrest, and under them by inferior officers, running down from grade to grade, to captains of companies, or chiefs of klans or cyclops of dens. The organization begins at the den and extends to the precinct, the county, the congressional district, the State, the South. It is compact, connected, consistent, moving as a perfect body from the head to the humblest member, as an army in the field, with sterner discipline than that of an army. . . .

AUTHORITY

These commands bind the members by an oath enforced by fear; administered with strange ceremonies, emphasized by penalty of death. At midnight the member is led blindfold to the den, and there, on his knees, hears the ritual and takes the oath. And as the bandage drops from his eyes he sees circles of men in frightful disguises armed with revolvers leveled on his head, and the Grand Cyclops says: "And this you do under penalty of a traitor's doom, which is death! death! death!" . . .

Thus members are sworn to obey their superior officers on penalty of death, and under that oath they are compelled to take the field at the command and to do any deed he may order, even to murder. Scores of members have confessed and testified that they have committed outrages and murders at the command of their officers.

OUTRAGES

The outrages vary from threats and intimidations to scourging, wounding, maiming, and killing by shooting, drowning, hanging, and burning. If we could know the whole truth it would appear that since the war this conspiracy has outraged more than thirty thousand men, women, and children—peaceful, innocent, defenseless citizens of the Republic. . . .

EXCUSES

Among the excuses made by those who control and defend this organization is that they feared the negroes; yet all Southern men of intelligence testify that the negroes of the South have behaved better than any other people ever did under similar circumstances. . . . They pretend that the Government of the United States has oppressed them, yet that Government, to which they had forfeited property, liberty, and life, spared their lives, allowed them their liberty, and returned them their property. No confiscated estates are withheld from their owners; although some abandoned property was taken, the only rebel estate remaining in the hands of the Government is Arlington [Robert E. Lee's estate], and gentlemen in both Houses of Congress propose to remove the remains of our soldiers and give that cemetery back to its rebel owners. No life has been taken for treason. Jefferson Davis is as free as the air, a citizen of the Republic. Few political privileges are denied, few leaders are unamnestied. . . .

FINANCIAL RESULTS OF RECONSTRUCTION

What has been the financial result of reconstruction? The Government and the peoples of the North forgave the people of the South and caused them to repudiate debts amounting to more than twenty-five hundred million dollars. We relieved them by constitutional amendments, and by the generosity of our people, of debts nearly double the property their own crimes had left. If the Government and the people of the North had merely withheld their hands from the South, and left the conquered rebels to their own financial devices, the South would have sunk in bankruptcy and ruin as a man thrown into the sea with a millstone at his neck. The Government and people of the North rescued them, fed them, advanced money and property, restored peace and order, and gave them the opportunity to revive their fortunes.

The white people of the South continually upbraid the colored people, saying, "The negro will not work." Yet wherever you go you see scores of white men lounging on the piazzas of the hotels, shifting their chairs to keep out of the sun, moving only to get "refreshments," while freedmen are laboring in the fields earning money to enable the whites to lounge. The laborers of the South have produced in cotton and other agricultural products since the war nearly $4,000,000,000, more than double the value of property in 1865. That is the financial result of reconstruction.

FINANCIAL EFFECTS OF KU KLUX CONSPIRACY

. . . The Kuklux conspiracy is fatal to values. It disturbs business, disorganizes labor, paralyzes industry and commerce. . . . The Kuklux conspiracy has cost the South more than all the carpet-baggers of all the States (including the Louisiana leader of the new movement), have been able to misappropriate.

DEPOPULATION

The conspiracy is driving away the people. Here is a copy of the *Freedmen's Repository*, giving an account of the emigration from this country to Liberia, showing that last fall a ship took out of the country from Virginia one passenger; from Florida, five; from North Carolina, five; from Georgia, sixty-six; and from Clay Hill, York county, South Carolina, one hundred and sixty-six. And at the head of this South Carolina party was Rev. Elias Hill, a description of whom is given here, a Baptist preacher, a cripple, whom the Kuklux scourged because he preached the gospel, taught school, and belonged to the Republican Party. He was driven with a colony of one hundred and sixty-six souls out of South Carolina, out of the United States of America, even to Liberia.

Here were two hundred and thirty-eight industrious people driven at once from the United States to Africa.

Before the war these colored people—men, women, and children—were valued by their owners at $500 each. Now they are driven out of the country by outrage, scourging, and murder; and we are told that the United States Government must not interfere to protect them. Imagine Elias Hill in the wilds of Africa, telling the bushmen how the great American Republic protects its citizens . . .

Image 1.3 Thomas Nast, "Let Us Clasp Hands over the Bloody Chasm"

Artist Thomas Nast frequently satirized political corruption in the Reconstruction era after the Civil War. Here he skewers Horace Greeley, the 1872 presidential candidate, for joining with conservative and anti-Reconstruction southerners to win the White House. Note that the alliance of these two camps is forged at the expense of both African Americans and the American flag, a symbol of the recent Union victory in the Civil War.

Source: Harper's Weekly, October 19, 1872. Penrose Library, University of Denver.

PRESENT CONDITION OF THE CONSPIRACY

In South Carolina the members of this organization raided in 1868, outraged and murdered Union people, and changed votes by scores of thousands. From that time until 1870 they were quiet, and then they raided again until more than three thousand outrages were committed in less than six months. The conspiracy is so organized that it may remain quiescent for a year or for two years, ready to be called into the field by the blast of the bugle, or by the click of the telegraph. Within one week this "military political" organization could throw into action a quarter of a million men, armed with the revolver, the bowie-knife, . . . with bayonets captured from State militia, and revolving rifles furnished from New York city.

ITS POWER

Shall we trust them? Are we blind—blind to the red rivers of blood they have shed; deaf to the cries of their thousands of victims? Are we mad to forget our own interests and safety? These conspirators have power, if they dare—and they are men who have dared death at the cannon's mouth—to sweep the whole South at the next presidential election; and if the result depends on the South, they can seat their candidate in the presidential chair. . . . *Whoever shall be the Democratic candidate will be the candidate of the Kuklux conspiracy. If the Democrats elect the next President it will be by Kuklux votes and violence; and the man thus elected will be the Kuklux President.*[5]

INTRODUCTION TO DOCUMENT 5

Benjamin Bryant's *Experience of a Northern Man among the Ku-Klux* argues that, while the South had been defeated, the region's way of life remained stubbornly unchanged. Bryant began with the problem of education, stating that the southern aristocracy kept both African Americans and poor whites in ignorance. The Klan had arisen to maintain this situation. Keeping the masses poor and ignorant, according to Bryant, was the Klan's main goal. Document 5 consists of excerpts from his book.

5. FROM *EXPERIENCE OF A NORTHERN MAN AMONG THE KU-KLUX* (1872)

BENJAMIN BRYANT

In order to better inform my readers of my intention for writing a book, I will say before entering into the main body of the work, that I have just returned from a long visit in the South, and have witnessed things which have occurred in the States late in Rebellion, and have kept a record of all, for the interest of the Northern people, and also, to give in detail the present situation of the people who are living there. . . .

As education is the great aim of every true American citizen, I will first inform you of its progress. The South has not had the advantages to aid in the development of education like the people of the North; but it has always been discouraged by the aristocracy of the South; and in so doing they have deprived the poor white people of education and other intelligences, as well as the black man. . . .

A great many freedmen are working on shares with their former masters, and are generally doing well, but are working for one-half, one-third, or one-fourth of their former pay, and are working under their master's hand, calling their former masters, "master," and denouncing the Proclamation of Emancipation. They hate that "old Northern woman" who is teaching the "nigger school," and resist all aid to free schools, and say, "I can live without education; I don't want it and will not have it."

"You are a good negro, and you may live on my land all your life-time."

That black man will work there for some time, and make one or two bales of cotton and give it to his master, as he calls him, to sell; and he will sell it and bring Tom, the good and smart negro, what he has a mind to.

Well, some day Tom will walk by the school-house and have a word or two with the teacher. Tom will tell him about his cotton. The teacher will say, "How much cotton did you have?"

"So much."

"How much money did you get?"

Tom says, "I got fifty dollars."

The school teacher will say, "Is that all? You should have more than that."

"How much more?"

"You should have twenty-five dollars more."

Tom says, "I am going to see him." . . .

[Tom's former master asked who told him he deserved more money.]

"The school teacher told me so."

"Who, that damn'd Yankee?"

"Yes sir."

"He told you that you could get more pay if you should go North, did he?"

"Yes sir. He told John, that black boy that lives with Mr. Brown, that he was free and should go to school. Yes, master, he told all the colored people to send their children and let them learn something." . . .

"Where is he from?"

"Massachusetts."

"We will fix him," says Tom's master. "Hitch up my horse; I am going away."

He will then go to the fork of the roads and tell everybody about what the damn'd Yankee school teacher told his niggers. If he stays here long he will have every nigger in the place think that he is as good as a white man. Well, we must run him away. Send him word to leave by Monday. If not, we will fix him.

Monday has come—Tuesday has come. The nigger-school teacher has not gone yet. We must get together. (This is not talked in the presence of Tom, but Tom is in the next room and hears it all.)

"Tom, you go and tell Mr. Brown and Mr. Bond to come here, and on your way back go round by the Pugh Place and tell Mr. Pollock to come, too, and bring every one that he can."

They will all meet and talk the matter over, and agree to meet on Wednesday night at 10 o'clock, all dressed in uniform, ready to commence their secret midnight demonstration. They went to his house and took him out, and tied a large rope round his neck, and he was seen down on his knees praying. But the party who saw him was a colored man (in the woods), and he says that he could go to the spot where he was hung with his feet up, tied to the branch of an oak tree, and a log of wood round his neck, and his tongue from five to seven inches out of his mouth. This punishment will be applied to that class of Northern people who will go South and settle and have not received full information how to act. You know it is an old saying, and a good one too, when you are in Rome, act as a Roman, and when you are in the South, you must act as a Southern man. What are these actions? First, I will say, you must act with the majority, let their actions be good or bad. You must denounce all free schools for white or black children. You must not come South and pay more for labor than the established price, which is all the way from five to ten dollars per month, but an extra good hand, who has always been farming, may in some cases get from fifteen to sixteen dollars per month. Never give a black man, or a poor white man who cannot read, any advice to post themselves upon matters pertaining to their own welfare. Never speak a good word for New England, because her States demand human rights before the law, for all men. Never say anything about Bunker Hill, because that is in Massachusetts. Never express your political opinion, let it be Republican or Democratic, for we know that both parties wanted to maintain the Union. And, above all, you must hate niggers. There has been many a good enterprising Northern man driven from the newly established homestead because he did not know the existing circumstances. This organization, known as the "Invisible Empire," or Ku-Klux, does exist in the Southern States. There is a number of Northern people in both of the political parties that have manifested a strong unbelief in regard to the Ku-Klux Klans, but I will say a word on a verified fact, and truth, which is today being witnessed by every peace-loving and upright citizen.[6]

INTRODUCTION TO DOCUMENT 6

In *The Grand Army of the Republic Versus the Ku Klux Klan,* W. H. Gannon proposed that 100,000 former Union soldiers be allowed to colonize the South. These men would be given land and money, and, presumably, their example would show Southerners the value of northern industriousness and the free-labor system. Such a plan would also help alleviate the unemployment caused by swings of the business cycle. Note, however, how unspecific Gannon is. For example, would he confiscate land from southern owners? The following excerpts are taken from the chapter "How to Extirpate Ku-Kluxism from the South" in Gannon's book.

6. "HOW TO EXTIRPATE KU-KLUXISM FROM THE SOUTH" (1872)

W. H. GANNON

. . . In view of the fact, that the present phase [Reconstruction] of the difficulty between the North and the South has already continued for eight long and dreary years, whereas half that time sufficed in which to annihilate the whole of rebel armies, the conclusion is inevitable that the Northern People are making some very serious mistakes in conducting their case in its present form; and consequently, that they must make some radical change in their Southern policy, before they can hope to gain their cause at the South. . . .

(1.) That the fatal mistake of the Northern People in their Southern policy since the dispersion of the rebel armies, has been their reliance upon United States Marshals and United States soldiers, almost exclusively, to represent them at the South; (2.) that their true course to pursue towards the South is to colonize it with at least One Hundred Thousand (100,000) intelligent, respectable, and industrious Northern Working Men; (3.) that, inasmuch as the Federal Government found no very great difficulty, any time during the late war, in inducing a million of Northern men to exchange the security, peace, and enjoyment of their homes for the dangers and privations of prolonged active warfare in the face of a determined and powerful enemy at the South and to remain there year after year, until the overthrow of their antagonists left them free to return to their homes,—there are 100,000 of those same men who would gladly return South now with the implements of peace in their hands, to make their homes there, provided they had the means to enable them to do so; (4.) that One Thousand (1000) Dollars per man would be all sufficient to establish them comfortably there; (5.) that the required funds would readily enough be forthcoming, were the proper parties to ask the public for them; and (6.) that the proper parties to collect the required funds, and to select the proposed colonists, and superintend the suggested undertaking, generally, are the GRAND ARMY OF THE REPUBLIC, and the various WORKING MEN'S SOCIETIES throughout the North. . . .

All purely patriotic considerations aside, the success of this plan would, in a mere speculative and economic point of view, prove highly beneficial to the industrial and business interests of the North. Its operations, if extended to anything like National proportions, would necessarily open a vast field for utilizing the immense mass of well disposed and intelligent, but adventurous young energy now wandering aimless about the North; they would provide acceptable and remunerative employment, at the South, for multitudes of Northern working people who find it impossible to secure the means of a decent support for themselves and their families in their present abodes. For, while individual Northern enterprise in that direction is not just now advisable, yet throughout the whole civilized world, there is not another so favorable an opening for co-operative Northern enterprise, if it be united, systematic, and of a legitimate character, as the South, in its present condition, offers to it. Every associated enterprise, such as this plan suggests, if judiciously located and properly managed for developing the natural resources of the South, instead of (as some have done) plunging into mad attempts at competition with great Northern industries, would handsomely compensate the laborer for his work, besides, after the first year, paying cent-per-cent, per annum on every dollar of capital invested in it. Once settled at the South, the colonist, amidst congenial social surroundings that this plan would secure to him, could not, with a tithe of the industry, fail to secure an ample competency for themselves and their dependents, without that incessant toil which, for even a scanty and precarious support, the North exacts from every person who depends solely upon manual labor, for their livelihood within its great centers of population. Thus they would materially benefit themselves in all the relations of life, and, at the same time, leave a freer field to, and open a new market for, the industry of those of their fraternity who are established at the North. It would, also, give a new and lasting impetus to legitimate business of all kinds throughout the whole country. Therefore, leaving Southern interests and political considerations out of the question altogether, this plan deserves the serious attention of the Working men and the Business men of the North.[7]

INTRODUCTION TO DOCUMENTS 7 AND 8

The violence against southern blacks and whites engaged with Reconstruction had a deeply political character. The Democratic Party became the stronghold against Reconstruction policy, resisting reforms and working to end military occupation. The pervasive violence was extremely effective in this regard, as the following documents reveal. In Document 7 we hear form Adelbert Ames, a northerner appointed as governor of Mississippi. Ames wrote directly to President Grant, D.C. on September 8, and again on September 11, 1875, to detail the violence that had become so common against blacks in his state, particularly as a way to discourage black men from voting. Ames begged for federal assistance in the form of troops to protect the citizens, insisting that the violence was politically motivated.

The day after Ames's first letter. The chairman of the Democratic State Executive Committee telegraphed the Attorney General to declare that "Peace prevails throughout the State," arguing against federal intervention. Document 8 is the response of Grant's Attorney General, Edwards Pierrepont to Governor Ames, expressing sympathy but refusing his request. Pierrepont's letter quoted President Grant, who expressed his frustration at the extent of violence, but also underscored Ames's own responsibility as Governor for addressing it. The Mississippi election in 1875 resulted in a landslide for Democrats.

7. LETTER OF MISSISSIPPI GOVERNOR ADELBERT AMES TO PRESIDENT U.S. GRANT

SEPTEMBER 8, 1875

Domestic violence prevails in various parts of this State, beyond the power of the State authorities to suppress. The Legislature cannot be convened in time to meet the emergency. I therefore, in accordance with section 4, Article IV of the Constitution of the United States, which provides that the United States shall guarantee to every State in this Union a republican form of government, and shall protect each of them against invasion, and on application of the Legislature, or of the Executive when the Legislature cannot be convened, against domestic violence, make this my application for such aid from the Federal Government as may be necessary to restore peace to the State and protect its citizens.

SEPTEMBER 11, 1875

The violence is incident to a political contest preceding the pending election. Unfortunately, the question of race, which has been prominent in the South since the war, has assumed magnified importance at this time in certain localities. In fact, the race feeling is so intense that protection for the colored people by white organizations is despaired of. A political contest made on the white line forbids it.

8. RESPONSE OF ATTORNEY-GENERAL PIERREPONT

DEPARTMENT OF JUSTICE, WASHINGTON, D.C.

SEPTEMBER 14, 1875

To Governor Ames, Jackson, Miss.
This hour I have had dispatches from the President. I can best convey to you his ideas by extracts from his dispatches:

The whole public are tired out with these annual outbreaks in the South, and the great majority are ready now to condemn any interference on the part of the Government. I heartily wish that peace and good order may be restored without issuing the proclamation, but if it is not the proclamation must be issued.

But if it is, I shall instruct the commander of the forces to have no child's play. If there is a necessity for military interference there is justice in such interference, to deter evil-doers. I would suggest the sending of a dispatch or letter, by means of a private messenger, to Governor Ames, urging him to strengthen his own position by exhausting his own resources in restoring order before he receives Government aid. . . .

You see by the mind of the President—with which I, and every member of the cabinet who has been consulted, are in full accord. You see the difficulties, you see the responsibilities which you assume. We cannot understand why you do not strengthen yourself in the way the President suggests. Nor do we see why you do not call the Legislature together and obtain from them whatever power, and money, and arms, you need.

. . .I suggest that you take all lawful means and all needed measures to preserve the peace by the forces in your own State, and let that country see that citizens of Mississippi, who are largely favorable to good order, and who are largely Republican, have the courage and the manhood to fight for their rights, and to destroy the bloody ruffians who murder the innocent and unoffending freedmen. Everything is in readiness. Be careful to bring yourself strictly within the Constitution and the laws, and if there is such

Image 1.4   A.B. Frost, "Of Course He Wants to Vote the Democratic Ticket"

Artist A. B. Frost captured the dynamics of southern Democratic political violence just weeks before the presidential election of 1876, which effectively ended Reconstruction. The caricature reveals the degree to which the freedmen had been left to their own devices, unprotected from southern white violence and political coercion.

Source: Harper's Weekly, October 21, 1876

resistance to your State authorities as you cannot by all the means at your command suppress, the President will quickly aid you in crushing these lawless traitors to human rights.

Telegraph me on receipt of this, and state explicitly what you need.

Very respectfully yours,

(signed) Edwards Pierrepont[8]

POSTSCRIPT

The violence in Mississippi achieved its aim: in the 1875 election Democrats regained power, effectively ending the Reconstruction government. The Republican Party's razor-thin victory in the election of 1876 included a "compromise" with the South to end Reconstruction and return political control in those states to the Democratic Party. Many of these state and local governments regained control through terrorism, as depicted in Image 1.4. With this shift, life for African Americans continued to deteriorate, subject as they were to political disfranchisement, violence, and—ultimately—segregation. Not until the civil rights movement of the 1960s would the nation's attention fully return to the plight of African Americans in the South.

QUESTIONS

1. How did the Klan choose its victims? Why were whites sometimes attacked by the Klan in addition to African Americans? Which blacks were singled out?
2. What political circumstances contributed to the Klan's formation?
3. Is the Ku Klux Klan best characterized as a political organization, a terrorist organization, both, or something else entirely? Was the Klan based in race hatred? Ideology? Political power? How do you sort out its means and ends, the rational from the irrational?
4. Who were the Klan's opponents? Was stopping racism their only aim, or did they have an additional agenda?
5. What do the images reveal about the nature of violence during Reconstruction and its aftermath? Did Governor Ames, for instance, have ways of combating this threat to civic life in Mississippi?
6. Ultimately, was the Klan successful? Why or why not?

ADDITIONAL READING

On the conclusion of the war, see Elizabeth Varon, *Appomattox: Victory, Defeat, and Freedom at the End of the Civil War* (2013). On the Ku Klux Klan, see Allen Trelease, *White Terror: The Ku Klux Klan Conspiracy and Southern Reconstruction* (1971), and David Mark Chalmers, *Hooded Americanism: The History of the Ku Klux Klan* (1981). On the violence of politics in this era see Douglas Egerton, *The Wars of Reconstruction* (2015). For various interpretations of Reconstruction, see John Hope Franklin, *Reconstruction After the Civil War* (1961); Kenneth M. Stampp, *The Era of Reconstruction, 1865–1877* (1965); Eric Foner, *Reconstruction: America's Unfinished Revolution, 1863–1877* (1988); and Gregory P. Downs, *After Appomattox: Military Occupation and the Ends of War* (2015). On African Americans during emancipation, see W. E. B. DuBois, *Black Reconstruction* (1935), and Leon F. Litwack, *Been in the Storm So Long: The Aftermath of Slavery* (1979). On gender in the postemancipation South, see Amy Dru Stanley, *From Bondage to Contract* (1998), and Laura F. Edwards, *Gendered Strife and Confusion* (1997). For the era's legacy, see Jay R. Mandle, *Not Slave, Not Free: The African American Economic Experience Since the Civil War* (1992), and David Blight, *Race and Reunion: The Civil War in American Memory* (2002). On the reborn Klan of the 1920s, see Leonard Moore, *Citizen Klansmen* (1992), and Nancy MacLean, *Behind the Mask of Chivalry; The Making of the Second Ku Klux Klan* (1994).

ENDNOTES

1. President Grant, "Condition of Affairs in the Southern States," message to the House of Representatives, April 19, 1872, in House Executive Document No. 268, 42d Congress, Second Session.
2. Walter L. Fleming, ed., *The Constitution and the Ritual of the Knights of the White Camelia* (Morgantown: West Virginia University, 1904), pp. 21–29.
3. George Rawick, ed., *The American Slave: A Composite Autobiography* (Westport, CT: Greenwood Press, 1977, 1979), Supp. 1, v.5, p. 426; Supp. 2, v.4, part 3, p. 957; Supp. 2, v.5, part 4, pp. 1648–1659.
4. *Testimony Taken by the Joint Select Committee to Inquire into the Condition of Affairs in the Late Insurrectionary States* (Washington, D.C.: U.S. Government Printing Office, 1872), v.6, pp. 545–546; v.7, pp. 607–611.
5. *Congressional Record*, May 30, 1872, pp. 1–7.
6. Benjamin Bryant, *Experience of a Northern Man Among the Ku-Klux, or The Condition of the South* (Hartford, CT, 1872).
7. W. H. Gannon, *The Grand Army of the Republic Versus the Ku Klux Klan* (Boston: W. F. Brown & Company, 1872).
8. *Appletons' Annual Cyclopaedia and Register of Important Events of the Year 1875* (New York: D. Appleton & Company, 1877), p. 516.

CHAPTER 2

THE GREAT STRIKE OF 1877

HISTORICAL CONTEXT

The year 1876 was one of celebration. The centennial of the Declaration of Independence was heralded with speeches, fireworks, and prayers. In Philadelphia, a great exhibition made palpable the nation's progress in technology and the arts. Self-congratulation seemed in order, for the Union had been preserved, the railroad now linked both coasts, and new inventions like the telephone and the Corliss engine promised a bright and prosperous future.

Yet these were not altogether happy times. Reconstruction in the South seemed more and more tortured as the Ku Klux Klan continued its rampage of violence and whites found ways to limit blacks' newly won freedom. In the summer of 1876, word came from the West that General George Armstrong Custer and over 200 cavalrymen had been wiped out at the battle of the Little Bighorn, and during the following year, Chief Joseph and his Nez Percés tribe gave the army all it could handle. Moreover, corruption tainted business and government at the highest levels, as a series of scandals rocked the Grant administration, Wall Street, and especially the nation's largest business, the railroads.

Worst of all, a severe economic depression continued into its fourth year. Millions were unemployed, and many who had jobs experienced severe wage cuts. In New York City, roughly one-quarter of the labor force was out of work, and police brutally dispersed angry crowds of the unemployed. Some workers questioned the logic of celebrating a hundred years of freedom when families went hungry in the streets, and a handful of laborers even began calling for a second American Revolution. The concentration of wealth in the hands of relatively few entrepreneurs raised questions in many workers' minds. Beneath the celebrations of the centennial, there was a haunting sense among working-class Americans that they were not living in the best of times.

Labor organizing and militancy had a long history in America. Before the Civil War, as the old artisan system broke down, as the division of labor grew more specialized, and as manufacturing wealth began to concentrate—in other words, as the dividing line between employers and employees grew ever sharper—labor unions formed in several crafts and industries. Their record was spotty; sometimes they succeeded in gaining worker control over wages, hours, and hiring practices; sometimes they failed. Some workers and labor

Image 2.1 Souvenir ribbon from the 1876 Centennial Exposition

The nation's centennial was marked by an extraordinarily ambitious exposition, designed to celebrate technological progress and the victory of free labor in the Civil War. Yet the commemoration occurred amidst a terrible economic depression that precipitated the great railroad strike of 1877.

Source: Susan H. Douglas Political Americana Collection, #2214. Division of Rare and Manuscript Collections, Cornell University Library.

leaders criticized the system of production and distribution itself, asking why a relative handful of individuals should own so much wealth while most families barely scratched out a living.

But nothing on the scale of the Great Strike of 1877 had ever happened before. In the middle of that year, most of the nation's vast new transcontinental railroad system—the very symbol of American progress, wealth, and modernity—was shut down by angry employees. Tracks, engines, and switching yards were destroyed, related businesses were forced to close, and workers in other industries organized themselves for strikes. Rather suddenly, America looked less like a special land of opportunity for all and more like the London of Charles Dickens, where poverty ground down the working class, or like Paris, where the masses organized themselves for bloody revolution.

The strike began on July 16, in the town of Martinsburg, West Virginia. The Baltimore & Ohio (B&O) Railroad on that day announced a 10 percent wage cut for all employees, the second such cut in eight months and part of the policy for all railroads across the country. Workers grumbled that companies continued to pay generous dividends to stockholders during the depression but that those who labored were forced to take starvation wages. Men gathered and talked through the day. When the crew of one train abandoned their posts, other men refused to replace them, and soon everyone threw down their tools. Workers then rode all of the engines into the roundhouse and announced to B&O officials that no trains would move through Martinsburg until their pay was restored.

Local sheriffs and militia were powerless to get the engines running, for the strikers grew too numerous. As they left Wheeling, state troops sent by the governor of West Virginia were met by angry workers, and when they got to Martinsburg, they found themselves overwhelmed by an orderly but determined crowd. Equally important, the soldiers themselves came mostly from laboring families and were sympathetic to the strikers. Finally, at the urging of the governor of West Virginia and the president of the B&O line, President Hayes dispatched 300 federal troops, who guarded strikebreakers sent from Baltimore. But by now thousands had gathered, including miners and canal workers, all angered by the conditions of labor in their industries. The federal soldiers managed to get trains moving out of Martinsburg, but soon strikers were ambushing these, side-railing and detaining them. Worse, the strike was spreading. Workers, one Baltimore leader declared,

> know what it is to bring up a family on ninety cents a day, to live on beans and cornmeal week in and week out, to run in debt at the stores until you cannot get trusted any longer, to see the wife breaking down under privation and distress, and the children growing up sharp and fierce like wolves day after day because they don't get enough to eat.

The incidents begun in Martinsburg were repeated across the country. The strike was not well organized; during the depression, the small gains made by unions in previous years had been nearly wiped out, and the workers' organizations that did exist tended to be very conservative. The faith of many workers in equal opportunity meant that unions generally were not terribly strong, and as the need for labor solidarity in the face of ever larger companies grew apparent, owners used lockouts, blacklists, scabs, espionage, firings, and prosecutions to keep unions out of their shops. The lack of organization and preparation for a major strike gave the upheaval considerable spontaneity, as workers in various communities responded to local situations and did their best to control events. But sometimes things got out of hand.

The strike reached its climax in Pittsburgh. The Pennsylvania Railroad was America's largest private enterprise, controlling 6,000 miles of track and creating over 20,000 jobs. Three days after the Martinsburg incident began, Pennsylvania Railroad managers ordered that all trains running east from Pittsburgh be "doubleheaders," meaning that two engines pull twice the usual number of cars. Doubleheaders meant harder work, increased danger of accidents, and more layoffs. Brakemen, conductors, flagmen, and others walked off the job, and they were joined by angry workers from other industries. Once again, the state militia was called in, but as an officer explained, "The sympathy of the people, the sympathy of the troops, my own sympathy, was with the strikers proper. We all felt that those men were not receiving enough wages." Soon the soldiers laid down their weapons and fraternized with the strikers. But then 600 fresh troops from Philadelphia were called in; since they were not from the local area, they had less sympathy for the workers. A crowd of 6,000, including women and children there to support their husbands and fathers, began jeering and throwing rocks, the militia opened fire and, in five minutes, killed twenty people. When the soldiers retreated to the roundhouse, strikers armed themselves and

Images 2.2 and 2.3 Photographs of the 1877 Pittsburgh strike

The Pennsylvania Railroad transported Philadelphia militiamen to Pittsburgh to quell the strike of 1877. When the militia fired into the crowd, killing twenty strikers, the protesters—rather than fleeing—attacked the troops and the rail yards. The month of violence that ensued was the worst of the strike, and ended only when President Hayes called in other federal troops.

Source: Pennsylvania Historical and Museum Commission, Pennsylvania State Archives.

attacked them, burned the roundhouse, tore up tracks, and destroyed over 2,000 cars and 100 engines.

And so the upheaval rolled across the country; in St. Louis, Chicago, Cincinnati, Buffalo, and countless other towns, workers from various industries refused to accept low wages, authoritarian owners, or armed coercion. For a few days, workers stopped the wheels of business and rejected the sovereignty of management. The general strike that had begun with the railroads gripped all parts of industry.

But the strike ended as quickly as it began. Lacking organization, the workers failed to make their demands clear, and the ability of laborers to counter management quickly eroded. The federal government mobilized thousands of troops, and cities reorganized their police forces. Soldiers moved into a town, drove off strikers, secured management's property, allowed strikebreakers to restart businesses, and then traveled on to the next town. Occasionally workers won concessions from management; more often, not. In all, over 100 laborers were killed.

The strikes threw disturbing new features of American life into bold relief. At the time of the uprising, about fifty corporations controlled 80,000 miles of line and employed hundreds of thousands of workers. As companies competed and sometimes drove each other out of business, the railroads were concentrated in fewer and fewer hands. A handful of men enjoyed private fortunes and paid themselves dividends even during depressions, but most of their employees would be wage laborers for life and would never rise to become independent entrepreneurs, that status so exalted by journalists and orators. And the railroads, it was clear, had merely led the way, for America now was less than ever a land of small shopkeepers and apprentices, but rather a nation of capitalists and workers.

The notion that America had escaped the curse of class conflict—Europe's blight of a rich upper class and an oppressed working class—seemed no longer plausible, if it had ever been true. The events of 1877 made it abundantly clear that a deep chasm divided and would continue to divide the rich and the poor in America. The Great Strike also gave a glimpse of how government would respond to this state of affairs. In the past, civic officials often took the part of the workers, for they represented local control rather than the distant power of faceless corporations. But in 1877, as in future conflicts (and there would be many intense labor struggles in the coming decades, in steel, mining, and textiles, indeed, in hundreds of trades, at thousands of job sites, involving tens of thousands of workers), state and federal power were the creatures of the rich and powerful. When the government intervened, it was to protect private property against the claims of workers.

INTRODUCTION TO DOCUMENTS 1, 2, AND 3

The documents in this section are as much about how individuals responded to the strike as about the strike itself. Document 1 is a proclamation issued by the sheriff of Harrisburg, Pennsylvania, during the strike. It is followed by the sheriff's testimony one year later about his experience in those tense days of July 1877. Note not only the urgency and disorder brought by the strike but also his testimony that many of the rioters were not railroad men. Document 2 appeared in a leading journal of the day, the *North American Review*, in September 1877. It is a letter written by an anonymous striker justifying the actions of those who had taken part in the uprising. Document 3 is an article that the *North American Review* solicited from Colonel Thomas Scott, the president of the Pennsylvania Railroad. Note how both identified their own interests with those of the nation. Compare the striker's assumption that all value is created by labor with the railroad president's belief that the best interests of his company and of the nation were one. How did each writer define patriotism? How did they differ on what constitutes fairness? Did they share any common ground?

1. PROCLAMATION AND TESTIMONY OF SHERIFF WILLIAM JENNINGS (1877)

PROCLAMATION

Sheriff's Office, Harrisburg, PA.

WHEREAS, For the past two days the peace and good order of the country have been disturbed and grave apprehensions exist lest injury be done;

And whereas, The duty rests upon me to preserve the peace and promote tranquility;

Now, therefore, I William W. Jennings, high Sheriff of the county of Dauphin, do hereby enjoin all persons to remain quietly at their homes or places of business, to avoid gathering upon the streets and highways, thus by their presence keeping alive the excitement which pervades the community, and to further the restoration of good order, I charge upon parents to prevent the half grown lads over whom they have control from frequenting the streets.

And I hereby announce my resolute determination, with the aid of special deputies whom I have appointed, and the posse which I have summoned to preserve the peace and protect the person and property of the people within my bailiwick, and I hereby call upon all good and law abiding citizens to assist me and those acting with me to enforce the law and maintain good order.

Given under my hand this 23d day of July, A.D. 1877.

Wm. W. Jennings, Sheriff

Image 2.4 Frank Bellew, The American Frankenstein

Anxiety about the sheer power and size of the railroads permeated America in the 1870s. Frank Bellew captured that fear by portraying an "American Frankenstein" that ran destroyed small communities and families. The caption beneath reads "Agriculture, Commerce, and Manufacture are all in my Power; My Interest is the Higher Law of American Politics." The tattered robe of "Judicial Ermine" refers to the corruption of the courts by big business.

Source: New York Daily Graphic, April 14, 1874.

TESTIMONY

Harrisburg, March 12, 1878
W.W. Jennings:
By Mr. Lindsey:

Q. You were sheriff of Dauphin county in July last?

A. Yes, sir.

Q. Still sheriff?

A. Yes, sir.

Q. Were you at home at the time of the first distur-bance that broke out in Harrisburg[?]

A. . . . I arrived home Monday evening, July 23, about half-past six or seven o'clock.

Q. Just state how you found the city as to order and quietness when you arrived home?

A. I found the city under a great deal of excitement. The trains, I was informed, had been stopped from running, and I immediately went to my counsel, Mr. Wise, for instructions in regard to my powers and duties, and met a number of the prominent citizens, and went to work at once under advice of my counsel to prepare a proclamation, and I was informed by the major and other citizens, that the citizens had been notified to assemble at two strokes of the court-house bell. I went around town and endeavored to get parties together, until about ten or eleven o'clock, as near as I can recollect, and spent sometime preparing a proclamation and advis-ing with the prominent citizens, and one came to me at the Lochiel Hotel and said that the rioters were breaking into the stores on Market street. I called upon the good citizens for the preservation of law and order to go with me and suppress the riot. I suppose about one hundred or one hundred and fifty went with me, and went down Market street, and we dispersed the mob. We arrested a couple of the rioters there. Afterwards came back, and I sent squads out. I then organized the party into companies, and I sent squads out to arrest and take these men out of bed who had been prominent and active as rioters, who I was informed had been prominent and active as rioters, and we put those in jail. The next morning I had my proclamation out, and also orders organizing companies. The citizens responded promptly. We organized some ten or eleven companies, and we ran the town on military principles for about one week. We had an officer of the day detailed to patrol the town at night, and we had the fire department under command, and everything in readiness if there would be any further trouble. . . .

Q. Did you have any difficulty in raising a posse of citizens?

A. No, sir; I cannot say that I had any great difficulty.

Q. They joined cheerfully.

A. They responded to my call. I arrived here at seven o'clock on Monday evening, and on Tuesday evening I paraded in the streets about nine or ten hundred men, organized as a regiment. My proclamation in the morning—that was issued on Tuesday morning. I had it printed during the night, and I had it posted all around town by day-light almost, and one of my proclamations called for them to assemble at the court-house, at two o'clock in the afternoon, and I supposed there were six or eight hundred men at two o'clock that afternoon there organized into companies. . . .[1]

2. A STRIKER DESCRIBES "FAIR WAGES" (1877)

The newspapers have fallen into line to defend the railway companies, who thus have brought all the great guns of public opinion to bear on one side of the fight, so the strikers have got the worst of it before the community. We have been so handled that if a workingman stands out to speak his mind, the public have theirs so full of pictures of him and his doings in the illustrated papers, that he is listened to as if he was a convicted rough pleading in mitigation of penalty, instead of an honest and sincere man asking for a fair show. I would not have any one mistake what my principles are and have been. I don't envy any man his wealth, whether it is ill-gotten or not. I am a workingman, therefore an honest one, and would refuse a dollar I did not earn, for I am neither a beggar to accept charity nor a thief to take what belongs to another, however he came by it. If it be his according to law, I, for one, am ready to protect him in his legal rights, and in return I want to be protected in what I believe to be mine.

Forty years ago my father came over to this country from Sweden. He had a small business and a large family. In Europe business does not grow as fast as children come, and poverty over there is an inheritance. He heard that North America was peopled and governed by workingmen, and the care of the States was mainly engaged in the welfare and prosperity of labor. That moved him, and so I came to be born here. He, and millions like him, made this country their home, and their homes have mainly made this country what it is. Until lately the States kept their faith and promise to the people, and we, the people, showed ours when trouble came; an assessment of blood was made on our shares of liberty, and we paid it. That is our record. We did not fight for this party or that party, but for the country and against all that were against the United States. . . .

So it was before the war, but since then, it seems to me, the power has got fixed so long in one set of hands that things are settling down into a condition like what my father left behind him in Europe forty years ago, and what stands there still. I mean the slavery of labor. The landed aristocracy over there made the feudal system, just as the moneyed men of this continent are now making a ruling class. As the aristocracy used to make war on each other, so in our time the millionaires live on each other's ruin. As the feudal lords hired mercenary soldiers to garrison their strongholds and to prey on the common people, so the railway lords and stock-exchange barons hire a mercenary press to defend their power, the object

of both being the same: the spoils of labor. It looks very like as though this country was settling down into the form and system we fled from in Europe. . . .

We are sick of this game, we are soul-weary of looking around for some sympathy or spirit of justice, and, finding none, we turn to each other and form brotherhoods and unions, depots of the army of labor, officered by the skilled mechanic.

This organized force is now in process of formation, and prepared to meet the great questions of the age: Has labor any rights? If so, what are they? Our claim is simple. We demand *fair wages*.

We say that the man able and willing to work, and for whom there is work to do, is entitled to wages sufficient to provide him with enough food, shelter, and clothing to sustain and preserve his health and strength. We contend that the employer has no right to speculate on starvation when he reduces wages below a living figure, saying, if we refuse that remuneration, there are plenty of starving men out of work that will gladly accept half a loaf instead of no bread.

We contend that to regard the laboring class in this manner is to consider them as the captain of a slave-ship regards his cargo, who throws overboard those unable to stand their sufferings. Let those who knew the South before the war go now amongst the mining districts of Pennsylvania, and compare the home of the white laborer with the quarters of the slave; let them compare the fruits of freedom with the produce of slavery!

. . . Let me put this matter in a plain way, as we understand it, and use round numbers instead of fractions, as we have to deal with hundreds of millions,—dividing the subject into sections.

1. In the United States the amount of capital invested in railway property last year was $4,470,000,000, made up of $2,250,000,000 capital stock and $2,220,000,000 bonded debt. The gross earnings were $500,000,000, or about eight and a half per cent on the capital. The running expenses (of which the bulk was for labor) were $310,000,000, leaving $185,000,000 as [profit] interest to the capitalist, or barely four per cent on his investment.

Labor is admitted into this enterprise as a preferential creditor, to be paid out of gross earnings before the most preferred mortgagee or bond holder receives a dollar. For as capital could not build the roads nor equip them without labor, so the enterprise, when complete, cannot be run without labor.

Capital, therefore, takes a back seat when it comes to the push, and acknowledges not only that labor has the largest interest in the concern, but takes the first fruits.

I take the railroad as a sample out of all enterprises, and if we could get at figures, there is no doubt it is a fair sample of the crowd. If, then, labor is the more important and essential factor in the result, when it comes to the question which of the two shall suffer in moments of general distress, the capitalist in his pocket or the laborer in his belly, we think the answer has been already settled by the rights assumed by one and acknowledged by the other

2. It is manifestly unjust that the workingman should be subject to under wages in bad times, if he has not the equivalent of over wages in good times. If railroad companies in concert with the laboring class had established a tariff of labor, and paid a bonus on wages at every distribution of dividends, that bonus being in proportion to the profits of the road, so that each man becomes a shareholder in his very small way, then he would have submitted to bear his share of distress when all were called on to share trouble, but to share it equally and alike.

3. When folks say that labor and capital must find, by the laws of demand and supply, their natural relations to each other in all commercial enterprises, and neither one has any rights it can enforce on the other, they take for granted that the labor "market" is, like the produce market, liable to natural fluctuations. If that were so, we should not complain. But it is not. The labor market has got to be like the stock and share market; a few large capitalists control it and make what prices they please. This sort of game may ruin the gamblers in stocks, and injure those who invest, but the trouble is confined mostly to those who deserve to lose or those who can afford it.

But not so when the same practice operates in the labor market. The capitalist must not gamble with the bread of the workingman, or if he does, let him regard where that speculation led France one hundred years ago, when the financiers made a corner in flour, and the people broke the ring with the axe of the guillotine.

4. When the railway companies obtained privileges and rights over private property, and became by force of law the great landowners of the state, holding its movable property as well, and controlling every avenue and department of business, public and private, they became powerful monopolies. The state endowed them with powers to frame laws of their own and deprived citizens of their property, means, facilities of transport, to vest it all in these corporations. Thus endowed, they cannot pretend they are no more than ordinary commercial enterprises. They are responsible to the state for the result of their operations, if they disturb fatally the order of our concerns. They are not independent. The state has claims upon them it has not on private concerns. They may not accept liabilities and then decline responsibility. It behooves the state to decide what the people are entitled to in return for all they have conceded to these companies, and to enforce such claims.

5. The English Parliament legislated on the question of the number of hours a workingman should labor. It limits them to so many. It legislates for his health and supply of light and water. In all these matters the capitalist has an interest. (He does as much for his horse.) But when it comes to the question of a proper amount of food and clothing, of warmth and shelter, the government declines to interfere. It leaves the question of fair wages to be adjusted between employer and employed.

And so I leave it, fearing I have put the matter in rough language, but not intentionally rude, having a deep and loyal faith in the humanity and justice that abide in the hearts of all this community, and wishing that God had given me the power to touch them.

A "Striker"[2]

3. "THE RECENT STRIKES" (1877)

BY THE PRESIDENT OF THE PENNSYLVANIA RAILROAD

PHILADELPHIA AUGUST 13, 1877

Allen Thorndike Rice, Esq.,
Editor of the *North American Review*
My Dear Sir,
On the 16th of July it became known that the firemen and freight brakemen of the Baltimore and Ohio Railroad were on a strike at Martinsburg, West Virginia, and that no freight trains were allowed to pass that point in either direction. This proved to be the beginning of a movement which spread with great rapidity from New York to Kansas, and from Michigan to Texas, which placed an embargo on the entire freight traffic of more than twenty thousand miles of railway, put passenger travel and the movement of the United States mails at the mercy of a mob, subjected great commercial centres like Chicago and St. Louis to the violent disturbance of all their business relations, and made the great manufacturing city of Pittsburgh for twenty-four hours such a scene of riot, arson, and bloodshed as can never be erased from the memory of its people. . . .

I do not wish, and happily it is not necessary, to fill your pages with the mere recital of the distressing cases of violence and outrage which marked the course of these riots unexampled in American history. Suffice it to say that the conduct of the rioters is entirely inconsistent with the idea that this movement could have been directed by serious, right-minded men bent on improving the condition of the laboring classes. How wages could be improved by destroying property, the existence of which alone made the payment of any wages at all possible, it is difficult to understand. Nothing but the insanity of passion, played upon by designing and mischievous leaders, can explain the destruction of vast quantities of railroad equipment absolutely necessary to the transaction of its business, by men whose

complaint was that the business done by the full equipment in possession of the railways did not pay them sufficient compensation for their labor. . . .

It must not for a moment, however, be understood that the greatest portion, or, indeed, any considerable portion, of the outrages upon life and property which have disgraced our recent history were actually committed by railway employés. It is not true that the majority, or even any large portion, of these men have been disloyal to the trust reposed in them. Probably ninety per cent of the men on all the important lines of the country where strikes occurred were faithful to their duties, and either remained at work, or stood ready to resume it as soon as they were relieved from the actual intimidation to which they were subjected by the rioters and their leaders. It was the dissatisfied element—which exists in that branch of industry as in all others—which perpetrated or allowed the perpetration of most of the overt acts of violence, such as stopping trains, forcing men therefrom, uncoupling cars, disconnecting engines, and other lawless doings of the kind, and which made itself amenable also to the charge of directly attacking the interests of the government and society at large as well as of the railway companies.

As General Hurlbut of Illinois so forcibly expresses it, in a paper recently published, "they permitted themselves to be the nucleus around which the idle, vicious, and criminal element could gather. Reinforced by these dark and disreputable allies, they destroyed property, stopped commerce, deranged the mails, burned great public buildings, broke up tracks, and thus paralyzed the natural circulation of the Commonwealth." It is in the menace to the general interests of society involved in these disturbances that the real gravity of the situation with which this country is now called to deal exists. "The railroad system is today a supreme necessity to maintain life, furnish ready markets, and to bring about the enormous interchange of products which makes the country one. Stop it, and in ten days many parts of the country would near the starvation-point, and within a month there would be no hamlet in the vast territory drained by these channels but would feel to the core of its business the effects of the stoppage of this regular and unusual circulation."

The enormous mechanical changes and progress of the past century have brought about a complete revolution, so gradual that perhaps it has not been generally apprehended, in the very condition of things in the United States. The water lines, which, at the date of the framing of the Constitution, were our important channels of internal commerce, have been almost superseded by the new iron highways. Upon these is borne a traffic so essentially national, so closely interwoven with the interests not only of our own but other countries, that it demands the most efficient and speedy protection against all unlawful interference. . . .

It is well known that the government uses the railway lines of the country, both as postal and military highways, in such form as its interests may require. The Constitution of the United States imposes upon the government the duty of thoroughly protecting inter-State commerce. When it is considered that the stock and bond holders of the various railway companies, whenever the interests of the government required it, paid taxes upon their coupons, their dividends, and their gross receipts, that they promptly met every call made by the Federal authorities, and that the entire equipment of the various lines was often placed at the disposal of the government for the prompt movement of the national forces and their supplies, to the exclusion often of other and more profitable traffic, it would seem but a matter of equity that the government should insure such protection to these railways as would preserve their usefulness and keep them always in condition to render similar services when they may be required. But over and beyond such considerations as these, the absolute dependence of the whole community upon this great system of railways for almost its very existence as a civilized body would seem to impose upon the Federal government in the last resort the supreme duty of preventing any lawless and violent interference with the regular and certain operation of every railway in the United States.

This insurrection, which extended through fourteen States, and in many cases successfully defied the local authorities, presents a state of facts almost as serious as that which prevailed at the outbreak of the Civil War. Unless our own experience is to differ entirely from other countries,—and it is not easy to see why it should, with the increasing population of our large cities and business centres, and the inevitable assemblage at such points of the vicious and evil-disposed,—the late troubles may be but the prelude to other manifestations of mob violence, with this added peril, that now, for the first time in American history, has an organized mob learned its power to terrorize the law-abiding citizens of great communities. With our recent experience before us, it is believed that no thoughtful man can argue in favor of delay by the proper authorities in dealing with lawless and riotous assemblages. Delay simply leads to destruction of property, and may lead in the end to the destruction of life. . . .

With the approach of winter, and the loss of outdoor employment which severe weather even in the most prosperous times entails, the country will have to deal not only with the deserving among the unemployed, who can be reached and helped through local organizations, but with vast numbers of idle, dangerous, and in many cases desperate men, who have been allowed unfortunately to catch a glimpse of their possible power for mischief. Such men, unless confronted by a thorough organization in the cities, States, and other communities, backed by the power of the Federal government and an unmistakable public opinion, will need but little urging to renew the scenes which have already brought such disgrace upon the American name. . . .

My own railway experience, extending over a period of thirty years, leads me to believe that the managers of American railways in general may fearlessly appeal to their past relations with the faithful among their employés, to prove that they at least have always endeavored to treat the interests of employers and employed as identical, and have never failed to take into prompt and respectful consideration every grievance which has been fairly and properly presented to them.

I am sure that it has been the purpose of the company with which I am connected to at all times pay its employés the best compensation that the business of the country would warrant; and I have no doubt that this will be the policy of the company for all future time, as it is founded on sound business principles no less than upon the instincts of humanity.

Very truly yours,
Thomas A. Scott[3]

INTRODUCTION TO DOCUMENTS 4 AND 5

The next two documents come from Allan Pinkerton and Terence Powderly. Pinkerton became famous as a private detective. During the Civil War, his company provided the federal government with (often incorrect) intelligence reports of Confederate troop strength and movements. After the war, Pinkerton's agency sold its services to private businesses, providing industrial espionage, guards, strikebreakers, and agents provocateurs. Pinkerton assumed that the Great Strike of 1877 was part of a much larger conspiracy, imported to the United States from Europe and designed to destroy the country. The excerpt reprinted here is from a book entitled *Strikers, Communists, Tramps and Detectives* (1878).

Terence Powderly, on the other hand, was an early member of one of the first nationwide unions, the Knights of Labor. Founded in Philadelphia in 1869, it remained a small and secret organization until the convulsions of the 1877 railroad strike broadened its reach and appeal to 800,000 members by 1887. Perhaps more important was the influence the strike had on the goals of the Knights. The violence and failure of the strike led many to embrace a more conciliatory approach to capital and labor. Here Powderly stresses the ideals of solidarity and brotherhood in the Knights, and the persistent hope of reconciliation and arbitration as a way to avoid strikes. How do the principles of the Knights compare to those articulated by the striker in Document 2? How would you characterize the aims of the Knights? Of Pinkerton?

4. FROM *STRIKERS, COMMUNISTS, TRAMPS AND DETECTIVES* (1878)

ALLAN PINKERTON

It was everywhere; it was nowhere. A condition of sedition which can be located, fixed, or given boundaries, may, by any ordinary community or government, be subdued. This uprising, in its far-reaching extent, was so alarmingly sudden that it seemed like the hideous growth of a night. It was as if the surrounding seas had swept in upon the land from every quarter, or some sudden central volcano had upraised its hideous head and belched forth burning rivers that coursed out upon the country in every direction. No general action for safety could be taken. Look where we might, some fresh danger was presented. No one had prophesied it; no one could prevent it; no one was found brave enough or wise enough to stop its pestilential spread. Its birth was spontaneous; its progress like a hurricane; its demise a complete farce.

But, looking over the destruction wrought, the consideration of the now clearly established fact, that our country has arrived at such an age and condition that it contains the dormant elements which require only a certain measure of turbulent handling to at any moment again bring to the surface even a stronger and more concentrated power of violence and outlawry, becomes not only a most wise policy, but an urgent necessity. . . .

The great strike has left everybody poorer. Who has been bettered? Who can point to a single instance where a body of workingmen has been benefited by their participation?

Who shall pay for the enforced idleness of millions; the ruin to vast business interests; the misery brought upon innocent working men and women; and for the hundreds of lives sacrificed upon this altar of human ignorance, blindness, and frenzy?

Looking at the matter from any point of consideration, no good thing can be seen in it, unless it may be judged a good thing to know that we have among us a pernicious communistic spirit which is demoralizing workingmen, continually creating a deeper and more intense antagonism between labor and capital, and so embittering naturally restless elements against the better elements of society, that it must be crushed out completely, or we shall be compelled to submit to greater excesses and more overwhelming disasters in the near future.

The "strike" is essentially an institution of continental Europe, and, like all other good and bad emanations from that part of the world, gradually but surely found its way into England, Scotland, and Ireland, and from thence was transplanted to this country. Riot, which has always existed, has become the constant companion of the strike everywhere. Through my Scotch and English experiences I have become well acquainted with the characteristics of strikes in those countries. One marked difference in them there is in the fact that women, in almost every instance after the strike is inaugurated, seem the most savage in preventing the breaking of the strike by the employment of "nobs," as the "scabs" are called there, and in both inciting and participating in riots. . . .

A good deal has been written and said regarding the causes of our great strike of '77. To my mind they seem clear and distinct. For years, and without any particular attention on the part of the press or the public, animated by the vicious dictation of the International Society, all manner of labor unions and leagues have been forming. No manufacturing town, nor any city, has escaped this baleful influence. Though many of these organizations have professed opposition to communistic principles, their pernicious influence has unconsciously become powerful among them. Other organizations have openly avowed them. They have become an element in politics. The intelligent workingmen, not being altogether ready for the acceptance of these extreme doctrines, have given them no political support, and their violent propagators have been obliged to fall back upon agitation of subjects which would antagonize labor and capital. For years we have been recovering from the extravagances of the war period. Labor has gradually, but surely, been becoming cheaper, and its demand less. Workingmen have not economized in the proportion that economy became necessary. Want and penury followed. Workingmen consequently have become discontented and embittered. They have been taught steadily, as their needs increased, that they were being enslaved and robbed, and that all that was necessary for bettering their condition was a general uprising against capital. So that when, under the leadership of designing men, that great class of railroad employees— than whom no body of workingmen in America were ever better compensated—began their strike, nearly every other class caught the infection, and by these dangerous communistic leaders were made to believe that the proper time for action had come.[4]

5. "THE THOROUGH UNIFICATION OF LABOR" (1878)

TERENCE POWDERLY

Three years ago it was suggested to the author that he write a book on the labor question. The stirring events of that year, in labor circles attracted the attention of all classes toward the labor problem, and for the first time in the history of America did the industrial question assume such proportions as to become the theme of conversation in public and private. . . .

The necessity for organization among producers becomes clearly discernible when one takes note of the tendencies toward centralization of power in the hands of those who control the wealth of the country. Combinations, monopolies, trusts, and pools, make it easy for a few to absorb the earnings of the workers, and limit their earnings to the lowest sum on which they can sustain life. Combination, in America, is heartless in the extreme, and has reached a point where it hesitates about going still farther only through the fear of crowding the poor to a condition "where the brute takes the place of the man." And yet these combinations and pools are educators; they are teaching the American people that if a few men may successfully corner the results of labor, and the wealth to purchase them, there is no just reason why the many may not do so for the benefit of all, through agents of their own selection. . . . .

The recent alarming development and aggression of aggregated wealth, which, unless checked, will invariably lead to the pauperization and hopeless degradation of the toiling masses, render it imperative, if we desire to enjoy the blessings of life, that a check should be placed upon its power and upon unjust accumulation, and a system adopted which will secure to the laborer the fruits of his toil; and as this much-desired object can only be accomplished by the thorough unification of labor, and the united efforts of those who obey the divine injunction that "In the sweat of thy brow shalt thou eat bread," we have formed the ***** with a view of securing the organization and direction, by co-operative effort, of the power of the industrial classes; and we submit to the world the objects sought to be accomplished by our organization, calling upon all who believe in securing 'the greatest good to the greatest number' to aid and assist us:—

I.   To bring within the folds of organization every department of productive industry, making knowledge a stand-point for action, and industrial and moral worth, not wealth, the true standard of individual and national greatness.

II. To secure to the toilers a proper share of the wealth that they create; more of the leisure that rightfully belongs to them; more societary advantages; more of the benefits, privileges, and emoluments of the world; in a word, all those rights and privileges necessary to make them capable of enjoying, appreciating, defending, and perpetuating the blessings of good government.

III. To arrive at the true condition of the producing masses in their educational, moral, and financial condition, by demanding from the various governments the establishment of bureaus of Labor Statistics.

IV. The establishment of co-operative institutions, productive and distributive.

V. The reserving of the public lands—the heritage of the people—for the actual settler;—not another acre for railroads or speculators.

VI. The abrogation of all laws that do not bear equally upon capital and labor, the removal of unjust technicalities, delays, and discriminations in the administration of justice, and the adopting of measures providing for the health and safety of those engaged in mining, manufacturing, or building pursuits.

VII. The enactment of laws to compel chartered corporations to pay their employes weekly, in full, for labor performed during the preceding week, in the lawful money of the country.

VIII. The enactment of laws giving mechanics and laborers a first lien on their work for their full wages.

IX. The abolishment of the contract system on national, State, and municipal work.

X. The substitution of arbitration for strikes, whenever and wherever employers and employes are willing to meet on equitable grounds.

XI. The prohibition of the employment of children in workshops, mines and factories before attaining their fourteenth year.

XII. To abolish the system of letting out by contract the labor of convicts in our prisons and reformatory institutions.

XIII. To secure for both sexes equal pay for equal work

XIV. The reduction of the hours of labor to eight per day, so that the laborers may have more time for social enjoyment and intellectual improvement, and be enabled to reap the advantages conferred by the labor-saving machinery which their brains have created.

XV. To prevail upon governments to establish a purely national circulating medium, based upon the faith and resources of the nation, and issued directly to the people, without the intervention of any system of banking corporations, which money shall be a legal tender in payment of all debts, public or private.[5]

INTRODUCTION TO DOCUMENTS 6 AND 7

Documents 6 and 7 are contemporary commentaries on the conflict between labor and capital. Document 6 is an 1882 cartoon satirizing the growing gulf between the two. Drawn by Joseph Keppler, "The First Annual Picnic of the Knights of Labor" paints a despairing view of the apparent indifference of industrial and financial elites to the plight of workers, who fail to make progress despite their efforts. Note the presence of both the Knights of Labor and sympathizers with the Pittsburgh strikers.

Document 7 comes from a *New York Times* report on the sermons of Reverend Henry Ward Beecher during the strike. Beecher's congregation, Plymouth Church in Brooklyn, was very wealthy, and Beecher was one of the most famous clergymen in America. Beecher's harsh judgment of the strikers grew out of his attachment to the Social Darwinist assumption that the law of living is survival of the fittest, which just happened to flatter his very successful congregants.

6. "THE FIRST ANNUAL PICNIC OF THE KNIGHTS OF LABOR" (1882)

JOSEPH KEPPLER

FIRST ANNUAL PICNIC OF THE "KNIGHTS OF LABOR"— MORE FUN FOR THE SPECTATORS THAN FOR THE PERFORMERS.

Image 2.5 *Puck* (1882).

Austrian immigrant Joseph Keppler used his satirical magazine to critique the conflict between labor and capital. Here he shows the financial giants Cornelius Vanderbilt and Jay Gould riding past a worker and his impoverished family who try to ascend a "Monopoly Greased" pole to reach better wages, food, and wine. The Knights of Labor had grown significantly in the years since the strike of 1877 to become— briefly—the most powerful labor organization in the country. As the Knights began to embrace and initiate strikes, Keppler became much less sympathetic.

Source: New York: Published by Keppler & Schwarzmann, June 21, 1882. Courtesy Library of Congress.

7. "THERE IS NO RICH CLASS AND NO WORKING CLASS UNDER THE LAW" (1877)

HENRY WARD BEECHER

THE PULPIT ON THE SITUATION

REV. HENRY WARD BEECHER CONDEMNS THE STRIKE AND DECLARES THAT A FAMILY CAN LIVE ON A DOLLAR A DAY

What right had the working men, the members of those great organizations, to say to any one, 'You shall not work for wages which we refuse.' They had a perfect right to say to the employers, 'We shall not work for you,' but they had no right to tyrannize over their fellow-men. They had put themselves in an attitude of tyrannical opposition to all law and order and they could not be defended. The necessities of the great railroad companies demanded that there should be a reduction of wages. There must be continual shrinkage until things come back to the gold standard, and wages, as well as greenbacks, provisions, and property, must share in it. It was true that $1 a day was not enough to support a man and five children, if a man would insist on smoking and drinking beer. Was not a dollar a day enough to buy bread! Water costs nothing. [Laughter.] Man cannot live by bread, it is true; but the man who cannot live on bread and water is not fit to live. [Laughter.] When a man is educated away from the power of self-denial, he is falsely educated. A family may live on good bread and water in the morning, water and bread at midday, and good water and bread at night. [Continued laughter.] Such may be called the bread of affliction, but it was fit that man should eat of the bread of affliction. Thousands would be glad of a dollar a day, and it added to the sin of the men on strike for them to turn round and say to those men, 'You can do so, but you shall not.' There might be special cases of hardship, but the great laws of political economy could not be set at defiance.

COMMUNISM DENOUNCED

HENRY WARD BEECHER'S OPINION ON THE LABOR QUESTION

We look upon the importation of the communistic and like European notions as abominations. Their notions and theories that the Government should be paternal and take care of the welfare of its subjects and provide them with labor, is un-American. It is the form in which oppression has had its most disastrous scope in the world. The American doctrine is that it is the duty of the Government merely to protect the people while they are taking care of themselves—nothing more than that. "Hands off," we say to the Government; "see to it that we are protected in our rights and our individuality. No more than that." The theories of Europe in regard to the community of property we reject because they are against natural law and will never be practicable. God has intended the great to be great, and the little to be little. No equalization process can ever take place until men are made equal as productive forces. It is a wild vision, not a practicable theory. The European theories of combinations between workmen and trades-unions and communes destroy the individuality of the person, and there is no possible way of preserving the liberty of the people except by the maintenance of individual liberty, intact from Government and intact from individual meddling. Persons have the right to work when or where they please, as long as they please, and for what they please, and any attempt to infringe on this right, and to put good workmen on a level with poor workmen—any such attempt to regiment labor is preposterous. . . .

Our theory is that the Government protects men in their rights, and not Government, but God, gave them those rights. The Government gave me no right of liberty, but God did. The Government protects me in that right. All that the Government has the right to say is, you shall use your rights so as not to injure another's; to secure to every man the liberty that God gave him. Clear the arena! Let each man go into it for what he is! Let him reap what he can sow! Let the Government see that there is fair play between man and man and citizen and citizen! When I hear men say that the Government shall take charge of the railroads, of the telegraphs, and of other forms of industry, and that the proceeds shall be distributed equally among the working men, I say that if all citizens were angels this would be folly. But as men are, only a theorist insane by nature and thrown by meditation into delirium tremens could have invented such a theory. No human being on earth has any rights resulting from the fact that he belongs to a class. In the eye of the law we have rights, but simply of men. The law rubs out all the European distinctions of class and says all men are born equal. We hear of the rich class being arrayed against the working class. There is no rich class and no working class before the law. The way in which these terms are coming now to be used is undemocratic, unphilosophical, and false in fact. It is an American doctrine that every man is to have the full ownership of himself, and the right to develop himself if he can do it.[6]

INTRODUCTION TO DOCUMENTS 8 AND 9

Unlike the prior selections in this chapter, Documents 8 and 9 come from two individuals remembering the strike many decades later. Samuel Gompers worked as a cigar maker in New York City during the strike. He eventually rose from worker to local union leader and finally to president of the American Federation of Labor, a coalition of craft unions founded in 1886. In his later life, Gompers always insisted that organized labor must stay out of politics, must eschew socialism, and must not question owners' rights to hold property and manage it; unions existed to improve wages and working conditions, not to make workers co-owners or managers. Gompers's passage was written fifty years after the Great Strike and published in his memoirs.

Similarly, Mary Harris "Mother" Jones was a labor organizer and, in the following excerpt from her autobiography, also remembers the strike from a distance of fifty years. Unlike Gompers, Jones was not a political moderate but a socialist known for her militant oratory. She was over forty years old when the strike broke out, and it was her first direct involvement in a labor action. She would be at the eye of the storm as an organizer for another half century. Like Gompers, she accused company agents of fomenting the violence and destruction. Note also her point that local businessmen as well as laborers resented big national corporations like the Pennsylvania Railroad.

8. "A DECLARATION OF PROTEST IN THE NAME OF AMERICAN MANHOOD" (1925)

SAMUEL GOMPERS

During the summer of 1876 the unemployment situation grew steadily worse. A feeling of desperation was growing as week after week slipped by and still the unemployed had no dependable means of earning a livelihood. The city authorities selected that time to suspend improvements on public works.

The workingmen protested against this course as a harmful, cruel policy. Our next effort was in the form of demonstrations. First, we called a mass meeting in Tompkins Square early in August. Crowds met quietly on the appointed day. We had police protection instead of police aggression. . . .

Mass meetings for organization and as unemployment demonstrations continued. We tried to organize discontent for constructive purposes. Mayor Ely paid no more attention to our needs than other Mayors had done, but wage earners did heed our gospel of organization and solidarity. I am recounting in some detail a picture of cumulative misery in order to bring out why revolt brought a whisper of hope. The crash that broke the months of strain came in the revolt of the railroad workers in July, 1877. That was in the pioneer period of railroading. The Union Pacific had been completed but a short time before, uniting the eastern and western coasts in a new effort to conquer distance. The railway unions were but fledglings. In fierce competitive fights, railroad managements cut passenger and freight rates far below the maintenance level. They were preparing to shift the resulting losses upon their employes by wage cuts. In 1873, wages of railroad workers had been reduced ten per cent; a similar wage reduction was announced for June 1, 1877. Railroad officials had organized and united upon a uniform policy. They did not even consider consultation with their employes. They handed down an order that meant another ten-per-cent reduction in the standards of living of their employes. Although both employment and pay on the railroads were irregular, unemployment was general in all other lines of work, and railroad workers were obliged either to accept conditions, bad as they were, or join the already large ranks of tramps. In addition to cutting wages, the railroads announced employes were to be required to use company hotels which still further reduced real wages.

Made desperate by this accumulation of miseries, without organizations strong enough to conduct a successful strike, the railway workers rebelled. Their rebellion was a declaration of protest in the name of American manhood against conditions that nullified the rights of American citizens. The railroad strike of 1877 was the tocsin that sounded a ringing message of hope to us all.

The railroad rebellion was spontaneous. In those days before the establishment of collective bargaining as an orderly system for presenting grievances to employers as the preliminary to securing an adjustment based on mutuality, the only way the workers could secure the attention of employers was through some demonstration of protest in the form of a strike. The strike grew steadily until it surpassed in numbers and importance all previous industrial movements. Strikers and sympathetic workmen crowded into the streets. The New York papers said at the time that so far as the arguments were concerned, the workers had the best of the situation, but that they could not win because of the weakness of the unions. The authorities grew apprehensive and asked for military protection. Then the fight was on. Long pent-up resentment found vent in destruction. The primitive weapons, fire and violence, were labor's response to arbitrary force. . . .

When the co-operative factory was abandoned with the close of the strike, I could have continued to work there, but, of course, I had neither the desire nor the willingness to act as superintendent or foreman for the factory although requested by them to do so, so I applied to Hirsch for my old job. That had been filled and there was really no opportunity for work with him. The Cigar Manufacturers' Association had declared that under no circumstances would any leaders of the strike be employed for at least six months. As a consequence, for nearly four months I was out of employment. I had parted with everything of any value in the house, and my wife and I were every day expecting a newcomer in addition to the five children we already had. . . .[7]

9. THE GREAT UPRISING (1925)

MARY HARRIS "MOTHER" JONES

One of the first strikes that I remember occurred in the Seventies. The Baltimore and Ohio Railroad employees went on strike and they sent for me to come help them. I went. The mayor of Pittsburgh swore in as deputy sheriffs a lawless, reckless bunch of fellows who had drifted into that city during the panic of 1873. They pillaged and burned and rioted and looted. Their acts were charged up to the striking workingmen. The governor sent the militia.

The Railroads had succeeded in getting a law passed that in case of a strike, the train-crew should bring in the locomotive to the roundhouse before striking. This law the strikers faithfully obeyed. Scores of locomotives were housed in Pittsburgh.

One night a riot occurred. Hundreds of box cars standing on the tracks were soaked with oil and set on fire and sent down the tracks to the roundhouse. The roundhouse caught fire. Over one hundred locomotives, belonging to the Pennsylvania Railroad Company, were destroyed. It was a wild night. The flames lighted the sky and turned to fiery flames the steel bayonets of the soldiers.

The strikers were charged with the crimes of arson and rioting, although it was common knowledge that it was not they who instigated the fire; that it was started by hoodlums backed by the business men of Pittsburgh who for a long time had felt that the Railroad Company discriminated against their city in the matter of rates.

I knew the strikers personally. I knew that it was they who had tried to enforce orderly law. I knew they disciplined their members when they did violence.

I knew, as everybody knew, who really perpetrated the crime of burning the railroad's property. Then and there I learned in the early part of my career that labor must bear the cross for others' sins, must be the vicarious sufferer for the wrongs that others do.

These early years saw the beginning of America's industrial life. Hand and hand with the growth of factories and the expansion of railroads, with the accumulation of capital and the rise of banks, came anti-labor legislation. Came strikes. Came violence. Came the belief in the hearts and minds of the workers that legislatures but carry out the will of the industrialists.[8]

Image 2.6 Convention of the Knights of Labor (1886)

By the time of the 1886 convention the Knights of Labor had achieved national stature and a membership of 800,000. This breadth of membership included Frank Farrell, an African-American delegate, pictured here introducing Grand Master Workman Terence Powderly, who led the Knights.

Source: Frank Leslie's Illustrated Newspaper, October 16, 1886. Courtesy Library of Congress.

QUESTIONS

1. Who were the strikers? What were their goals? How do accounts differ? Whom do you believe?
2. How did the law and government react to the crisis? Were they consistent? Evenhanded?
3. What did Gompers mean by "American manhood"? Why did he use that phrase? Did Powderly share Gompers's outlook on the future of American labor?
4. If they could argue with Powderly, Gompers, Jones, and the anonymous striker, what do you think Scott, Pinkerton, and Beecher would say? How would Gompers, Jones, and the striker respond? Do you see any shared values between these camps?
5. What patriotic appeals did each side make? How did they differ?
6. Do you view the uprisings of 1877 as a strike? A riot? A rally? A terrorist attack? How did you decide?

ADDITIONAL READING

On the 1877 strike, see Philip Foner, *The Great Labor Uprising of 1877* (1977); David O. Stowell, *Street Railroads and the Great Strike of 1877* (1999); and Robert V. Bruce, *1877: Year of Violence* (1959). For discussions of particular aspects of labor in this era, see Melvyn Dubofsky, *Industrialism and the American Worker, 1865–1920* (1985); Herbert Gutman, *Work, Culture and Society in Industrializing America* (1976); Gutman, *Power and Culture: Essays on the American Working Class* (1987); David Montgomery, *The Fall of the House of Labor: The Workplace, the State, and American Labor Activism, 1865–1925* (1987); and James Greene, *Death in the Haymarket* (2007). An international perspective is provided by Eric Hobsbawm, *The Age of Capital, 1848–1875* (1975) and *The Age of Empire* (1987). On the poor, see Jacqueline Jones, *The Dispossessed: America's Underclass from the Civil War to the Present* (1992). For politics in the era of rapid economic growth, see Richard Franklin Bensel, *The Political Economy of American Industrialization* (2000). For a discussion on workers in American fiction, see Laura Hapke, *Labors Text* (2001). For an overview of the era, see Alan Trachtenberg, *The Incorporation of America* (2007); H. W. Brands, *American Colossus* (2011), and Rebecca Edwards, *New Spirits: Americans in the Gilded Age* (2005).

ENDNOTES

1. Commonwealth of Pennsylvania, *Legislative Documents Comprising the Department and other Reports, made to the Senate and House of Representatives of Pennsylvania.* V. 5 (Harrisburg: Lane S. Hart, State Printer, 1878), testimony pp. 646–647, proclamation p. 839.
2. The *North American Review*, v.124(257), pp. 332–326.
3. The *North American Review*, v.125(258), pp. 351–362.
4. Allan Pinkerton, *Strikers, Communists, Tramps and Detectives* (New York: C. W. Carleton & Co., 1878), pp. 13–21.
5. Terence Powderly, *Thirty Years of Labor* (Columbus, Ohio: Excelsior Publishing House, 1889), pp. 243–245.
6. *The New York Times*, July 23 and July 30, 1877.
7. Samuel Gompers, *Seventy Years of Life and Labor* (New York: E. P. Dutton & Company, 1925), pp. 134–135, 137–141, 155–157.
8. Mary Harris Jones, *The Autobiography of Mother Jones*, ed., Mary Field Parton (Chicago: Charles H. Kerr, 1925), pp. 14–16.

CHAPTER 3

CULTURES COLLIDE
AT WOUNDED KNEE

HISTORICAL CONTEXT

"The 'Great American Desert,'" Charles Nordhoff wrote in 1873, "has disappeared at the snort of the iron horse. . . . The very desert becomes fruitful, and in the midst of the sage-brush and alkali country, you will see corn, wheat, potatoes, and fruits of different kinds growing luxuriantly." For Nordhoff, as for his fellow Americans, settling the West was a poetic ideal, a hymn of progress:

> One can not help but speculate upon what kind of men we Americans shall be when all these now desolate plains are filled; when cities shall be found where now only the lonely depot or the infrequent cabin stands; when the iron and coal of these regions shall have become, as they soon must, the foundation of great manufacturing populations; and when, perhaps, the whole continent will be covered by our Stars and Stripes.

Americans' prose soared as they contemplated their prosperous and powerful republic stretching from sea to shining sea.

In the most concrete sense, the expansion of white settlers westward was part of the same set of processes transforming the rest of society. Imagine, for example, a Nebraska farmer purchasing a Currier and Ives lithograph for his home in 1875, perhaps a scene of pioneers making their way across the continent. He buys the lithograph from a store in Omaha, where the pictures just came off the train from New York. He sells his wheat in the same city, and some of it may find its way onto the tables of railroad workers, who at that moment are worried about rumors of an impending wage cut. Or perhaps our farmer looks at the lithograph and chooses not to buy it, because the low price he will get for his wheat means another lean year in these troubled economic times. He wonders for a moment how he will ever pay off the bank for the new threshing machine that allowed him to grow more wheat. Farmers mechanize, he muses, and grow bigger crops, and, as a result, prices go down. The point, of course, is that industrialization, urbanization, and commercial exchange were all related. The railroad was one of the ties that bound western farmers to eastern laborers. And underlying the entire transformation—manufacturing, shipping, growing, processing, and financing—was the market economy.

As the quotation from Nordhoff reveals—and as Currier and Ives lithographs of westward expansion made palpable—prosperity, progress, productivity, and individual betterment were highly charged ideals. The marketplace was not just a system of exchange; it generated its own ideology. But shining visions of progress usually did not include those whose land was taken; rather, the myth of progress justified the taking.

When white colonists first came to British North America, there were already millions of native people living in this "uninhabited" land, this "desert," as some colonists called it. European diseases, to which the indigenous peoples had no immunity, quickly wiped out many of them. As whites colonized the new lands, then, they faced greatly weakened tribes that, when not outnumbered, were outgunned. Some groups, after resisting the whites, were simply destroyed, such as the Pequots of New England. The large southeastern tribes—the Creeks, Cherokees, Choctaws, and Chickasaws—were finally conquered during the presidency of Andrew Jackson and forced to relocate west to lands that would be theirs "forever."

Image 3.1 Fanny Palmer, "Across the Continent, Westward the Course of Empire Takes Its Way" (1868)
The title of this popular lithograph captured the sense of many Americans that the West was a natural extension of their nation. Note virtuous labor and public education in the left foreground, Indians on the verge of disappearing into railroad smoke at right, and glorious open land in the distance.
Source: New York: Currier and Ives, 1868. Courtesy Library of Congress.

By the late nineteenth century, the Sioux of the northern plains were one of the largest and most powerful tribal cultures remaining. During the colonial era, they had occupied lands between Lake Superior and the headwaters of the Mississippi River, but the Ojibwas, armed by the French, drove them west to the plains. The Sioux adapted well to the new environment, cultivating their skills as horsemen and hunters and following the enormous herds of buffalo that roamed the western prairies. Until the Civil War, they ranged from Minnesota to the Rockies and from the Yellowstone River to the Platte, and, with millions of buffalo and thousands of horses, they were masters of these lands.

In 1868, with the acceleration of white settlement on the plains, the federal government sought direct control over the native inhabitants. The Sioux agreed to a treaty granting them the western half of the present state of South Dakota and portions of Nebraska and Wyoming, "for their absolute and undisturbed use and occupation," along with rights to hunt for buffalo beyond reservation boundaries. The treaty seemed to provide not only an endless supply of food but also peace. "From this day forth," the treaty stated, "all wars between the parties of this agreement shall cease forever." In a few years, however, marksmen and trappers had hunted the buffalo to near extinction, while white settlers had poured in on the new railroads. When gold—"the yellow metal that they worship and that makes them crazy," as one Sioux called it—was discovered on the tribal reservation in the Black Hills, a massive influx of whites into the region commenced.

Bands of Sioux resisted the occupation of their lands, but as sporadic violence broke out on both sides, the government sent in the army to round up the "hostiles." George Armstrong Custer led the Seventh Cavalry into the Sioux country as part of a larger expedition under the command of General Alfred Terry. In the spring of 1876, Custer divided his forces into three groups to assault the enemy near the Little Bighorn. The entire regiment—over 250 men—was killed by a force of at least 2,500 Indians. The government promptly sent in more troops, who arrested several chiefs and chased the main leader of the uprising, Sitting Bull, and his people into Canada.

Government officials from the military and from the Bureau of Indian Affairs (under the Department of the Interior) now drew up a new treaty, and an accommodating chief, Red Cloud, signed for the tribe. The Sioux lost one-third of their reservation, including the sacred Black Hills. A people who had been hunter-gatherers, with no experience, habits, or capital for agriculture, were left on poor land, without the buffalo herds that had provided food, shelter, clothes, and goods for barter. After another decade of land speculators greedy for profits, railroad owners coveting rights of way, and squatters clamoring for land, the federal government in 1889 seized half of the remaining Sioux territory and, in the process, divided the one large reservation into five separate units.

In exchange for all of these concessions, the government promised to supply food (which often never came), clothing (which always arrived after the arctic cold), schools for Indian children (where tribal ways were demeaned), and reservation administrators (who were often incompetent political hacks). The old way of life was undermined: Agents of the federal government forbade warrior societies and honors; usurped the powers of the chiefs; and banned tribal religious customs, holidays, and ceremonies. The Sioux and other tribes were forced to trade the freedom of the plains for broken promises and confinement to the reservation.

In the midst of this crisis, a new religion swept through the tribes of the western United States, a religion containing both Christian and Native American elements, as seen in the two names given to the movement: the Messiah Craze, as whites called it, and the Ghost Dance. By 1890, word had spread to the plains of a Paiute chief in Nevada named Wavoka who claimed to be "the Christ," returned to earth as an Indian. Throughout the western territories, Native Americans of various tribes listened to Wavoka's message and followed his advice. He promised to renew the earth to what it had been before the coming of the whites. In the spring of 1891, when the grass grew knee-high, the earth would be covered with fresh soil, running water, trees, and buffalo. And all of the old Indians who had died would return as young men and women. Those who did the Ghost Dance would be lifted into the sky, and the new soil would roll over the old and bury the whites; the dancers would then descend to earth and dwell there with their ancestors.

Native Americans across the West donned ghost shirts, painted with symbols that allegedly made them impervious to white men's bullets, and they danced the Ghost Dance. For the Sioux—starved and humiliated, their numbers depleted—the promise of living in peace and plenty was irresistible. Widows would be reunited with their husbands, hunting bands would once again be able to provide food, and an *Indian* messiah would take revenge

Image 3.2: The Oglala Sioux Ghost Dance at Pine Ridge Agency, Dakota, by Frederic S. Remington Frederick Remington, who became famous depicting western scenes, here portrayed the Ghost Dance for the large national audience of *Harper's Weekly magazine*.
Source: Harper's Weekly, December 6, 1890. Courtesy Penrose Library, University of Denver.

on the white oppressors. With promises like these, the reservations resounded with the sacred dance.

Reports of the "Messiah Craze" greatly alarmed whites. There is no doubt that the new religion gave Native Americans the confidence to assert themselves in ways that reservation agents and white citizens saw as threatening. Certainly, the idea of a Native American messiah offered tribal members a sense of pride and a new militancy. Many whites, on the other hand, jumped to the conclusion that the Ghost Dance merely proved how wild and barbaric the Indians were and that the new religion was a cover for a treacherous attack. Soon army troops were again streaming west, and Native American bands, feeling threatened, began leaving the reservations. The scene was set for tragedy.

INTRODUCTION TO DOCUMENT 1

Anthropologists call phenomena like the Ghost Dance *revitalization movements.* In times of social stress, people often go back to important elements of their culture and reshape them in powerful new ways. The rejuvenated customs or beliefs become a focus of group solidarity and cultural revival. Z. A. Parker, a teacher on the Pine Ridge reservation in South Dakota, described the Ghost Dance she witnessed at White Clay Creek, June 20, 1890.

1. "THE GHOST DANCE OBSERVED" (1890)

Z. A. PARKER

We drove to this spot about 10.30 oclock on a delightful October day. We came upon tents scattered here and there in low, sheltered places long before reaching the dance ground. Presently we saw over three hundred tents placed in a circle, with a large pine tree in the center, which was covered with strips of cloth of various colors, eagle feathers, stuffed birds, claws, and horns—all offerings to the Great Spirit. The ceremonies had just begun. In the center, around the tree, were gathered their medicine-men; also those who had been so fortunate as to have had visions and in them had seen and talked with friends who had died. A company of fifteen had started a chant and were marching abreast, others coming in behind as they marched. After marching around the circle of tents they turned to the center, where many had gathered and were seated on the ground.

I think they wore the ghost shirt or ghost dress for the first time that day. I noticed that these were all new and were worn by about seventy men and forty women. The wife of a man called Return-from-scout had seen in a vision that her friends all wore a similar robe, and on reviving from her trance she called the women together and they made a great number of the sacred garments. They were of white cotton cloth. The women's dress was cut like their ordinary dress, a loose robe with wide, flowing sleeves, painted blue in the neck, in the shape of a three-cornered handkerchief, with moon, stars, birds, etc., interspersed with real feathers, painted on the waist and sleeves. While dancing they wound their shawls about their waists, letting them fall to within 3 inches of the ground, the fringe at the bottom. In the hair, near the crown, a feather was tied. I noticed an absence of any manner of head ornaments, and, as I knew their vanity and fondness for them, wondered why it was. Upon making inquiries I found they discarded everything they could which was made by white men.

The ghost shirt for the men was made of the same material—shirts and leggings painted in red. Some of the leggings were painted in stripes running up and down, others running around. The shirt was painted blue around the neck, and the whole garment was fantastically sprinkled with figures of birds, bows and arrows, sun, moon, and stars, and everything they saw in nature. Down the outside of the sleeve were rows of feathers tied by the quill ends and left to fly in the breeze, and also a row around the neck and up and down the outside of the leggings. I noticed that a number had stuffed birds, squirrel beads, etc., tied in their long hair. The faces of all were painted red with a black half-moon on the forehead or on one cheek.

As the crowd gathered about the tree the high priest, or master of ceremonies, began his address, giving them directions as to the chant and other matters. After he had spoken for about fifteen minutes they arose and formed in a circle. As nearly as I could count, there were between three and four hundred persons. One stood directly behind another, each with his hands on his neighbor's shoulders. After walking about a few times, chanting, "Father, I come," they stopped marching, but remained in the circle, and set up the most fearful, heart-piercing wails I ever heard—crying, moaning, groaning, and shrieking out their grief, and naming over their departed friends and relatives, at the same time taking up handfuls of dust at their feet, washing their hands in it, and throwing it over their heads. Finally, they raised their eyes to heaven, their hands clasped high above their heads, and stood straight and perfectly still, invoking the power of the Great Spirit to allow them to see and talk with their people who had

died. This ceremony lasted about fifteen minutes, when they all sat down where they were and listened to another address, which I did not understand, but which I afterwards learned were words of encouragement and assurance of the coming messiah.

When they rose again, they enlarged the circle by facing toward the center, taking hold of hands, and moving around in the manner of school children in their play of "needle's eye." And now the most intense excitement began. They would go as fast as they could, their heads moving from side to side, their bodies swaying, their arms, with hands gripped tightly in their neighbors', swinging back and forth with all their might. If one, more weak and frail, came near falling, he would be jerked up and into position until tired nature gave way. The ground had been worked and worn by many feet, until the fine, flour-like dust lay light and loose to the depth of two or three inches. The wind, which had increased, would sometimes take it up, enveloping the dancers and hiding them from view. In the ring were men, women, and children; the strong and the robust, the weak consumptive, and those near to death's door. They believed those who were sick would be cured by joining in the dance and losing consciousness. From the beginning they chanted, to a monotonous tune, the words—

Father, I come;
Mother, I come;
Brother, I come;
Father, give us back our arrows.

All of which they would repeat over and over again until first one and then another would break from the ring and stagger away and fall down. One woman fell a few feet from me. She came toward us, her hair flying over her face, which was purple, looking as if the blood would burst through; her hands and arms moving wildly; every breath a pant and a groan; and she fell on her back, and went down like a log. I stepped up to her as she lay there motionless, but with every muscle twitching and quivering. . . .

They kept up dancing until fully 100 persons were lying unconscious. Then they stopped and seated themselves in a circle, and as each one recovered from his trance he was brought to the center of the ring to relate his experience. Each told his story to the medicine-man and he shouted it to the crowd. Not one in ten claimed that he saw anything. I asked one Indian—a tall, strong fellow, straight as an arrow—what his experience was. He said he saw an eagle coming toward him. It flew round and round, drawing nearer and nearer until he put out his hand to take it, when it was gone. I asked him what he thought of it. "Big lie," he replied. I found by talking to them that not one in twenty believed it. After resting for a time they would go through the same performance, perhaps three times a day. They practiced fasting, and every morning those who joined in the dance were obliged to immerse themselves in the creek.[1]

INTRODUCTION TO DOCUMENT 2

The Ghost Dance spread, and by autumn of 1890, government officials in the West had made their fears known in Washington. The following letters were sent by agents on the reservations to their superiors in the Office of Indian Affairs. The letters give a sense of the anxiety that the Ghost Dance was engendering among whites. It was on the basis of such information that military forces were dispatched to prevent a Sioux "outbreak."

2. LETTERS FROM RESERVATIONS AGENTS

COMMISSIONER OF INDIAN AFFAIRS, WASHINGTON, D.C.

UNITED STATES INDIAN SERVICE, OFFICE OF INDIAN AGENT PINE RIDGE AGENCY, S. DAK., OCTOBER 12, 1890

Sir:

. . . These ghost dances have assumed such proportions that they become very serious. . . . The mistake was made by not nipping it in the bud four months ago when it was in its infancy. They have been permitted to continue in these foolish and harmful practices until they are entirely beyond the control of the police. As yet I have taken no definite action in the matter, my object being to thoroughly acquaint myself with the situation, so that I could act intelligently and wisely when I did make a move. . . .

It is useless for me to undertake to describe the foolish manner in which they conduct themselves during these dances. I can only say it injures them physically, mentally, and morally, and undoes all the Department has done for them in the past. What makes the situation so serious is that every Indian on the reservation is armed with a Winchester rifle, and when they are requested to stop these dances they strip themselves and are ready to fight. Why any Indian on the reservation is permitted to have a gun I am not informed. They certainly have no use for them except to endanger the lives of those who try to suppress them in some wrongdoing. If it were not for this fact alone, we would not have any trouble in controlling them with the police. . . .

Very respectfully,
D. F. Royer
United States Indian Agent

HON. T. F. MORGAN
COMMISSIONER OF INDIAN AFFAIRS,
WASHINGTON, D.C.

UNITED STATES INDIAN SERVICE
ROSEBUD AGENCY, S. DAK.,
NOVEMBER 2, 1890

Sir:

I deem it my duty to call the attention of the Department to the extremely disaffected and troublesome state of a portion of the Indians on this and other Sioux agencies.

The coming new order of things as preached to this people during the past seven months is the return to earth of their forefathers, the buffalo, elk, and all other game, the complete restoration of their ancient habits, customs, and power, and the annihilation of the white man. This movement, which some three weeks ago it was supposed had been completely abandoned, while not so openly indulged in, is continually gaining new adherents, and they are daily becoming more threatening and defiant of the authorities.

This latter phase of the case may in a measure be attributed to the scant supply of rations, to which my attention has been almost daily called by the Indians, and especially to the reduction in the quantity of beef as compared to the issue of former years. They kill cows and oxen issued to them for breeding and working purposes, make no secret of doing so, and openly defy arrest. They say that the cattle were issued to them by the Great Father and it is their right to do as they please with them. . . . During the past week it is reported to me that two Indians in the Red Leaf Camp on Black White Creek had killed their cows for a feast at the ghost dance. I sent a policeman to bring them in; they refused to come.

The following day I sent two officers and eight policemen, and they returned without the men, reporting that after they arrived at the camp they were surrounded by seventy-five or more Indians, well armed and with plenty of ammunition, and they unanimously agreed that an attempt to arrest the offenders would have resulted in death to the entire posse. On Friday I sent the chief of police, with an interpreter, to explain matters and endeavor to bring the men in. They positively refused to come, and the chief of police reports that the matter is beyond the control of the police. . . .

The religious excitement aggravated by almost starvation is bearing fruits in this state of insubordination; Indians say they had better die fighting than to die a slow death of starvation, and as the new religion promises their return to earth, at the coming of the millennium, they have no great fear of death. To one not accustomed to the Indians, it is a hard matter to believe the confident assurance with which they look forward to the fulfillment of their Prophet's promise.

The time first set for the inauguration of the new era was next spring, but I am reliably informed that it has since and only lately been advanced to the new moon after the next one, or about December 11.

The indications are unmistakable; these Indians have within the past three weeks traded horses and everything else they could trade for arms and ammunition, and all the cash they became possessed of was spent in the same way.

One of the traders here reports that Indians within the last few days have come to his store and offered to sell receipts for wood delivered at the agency, and for which no funds are on hand to pay them for one-third the value *in cash*. When asked what urgent necessity there was for such a sacrifice of receipts for less than their face value, they answered that they wanted *the cash* to buy ammunition. . . .

To me, there appears to be but one remedy . . . and that is a sufficient force of troops to prevent the outbreak which is imminent, and which any one of a dozen unforeseen causes may precipitate.

Very respectfully, your obedient servant,
E. B. Reynolds
Special United States Indian Agent

THE COMMISSIONER OF INDIAN AFFAIRS WASHINGTON, D.C.

UNITED STATES INDIAN SERVICE WESTERN SHOSHONE AGENCY, NEV., NOVEMBER 8, 1890

Sir:

The Indians of this reservation and vicinity have just concluded their second medicine dance, the previous one taking place in August last. They are looking for the coming of the Indian Christ, the resurrection of the dead Indians, and consequent supremacy of the Indian race. Fully one thousand people took part in the dance. While the best of order prevailed, the excitement was very great as morning approached, when the dancers were worn out mentally and physically. The medicine-men would shout that they could see the faces of departed friends and relatives moving about the circle. No pen can paint the picture of wild excitement that ensued; all shouted in a chorus, "Christ has come!" and then danced and sung until they fell in a confused and exhausted mass on the ground. The more intelligent ones freely admit that it is all foolishness, but dare not disobey the order of the medicine-men to attend. I apprehend no trouble beyond the loss of time and the general demoralizing effect of these large gatherings of people.

Several of the leading men have gone to Walker Lake to confer with a man that calls himself Christ; others have gone to Fort Hall to meet Indians from Montana and Dakota, to get the news from that section; in fact, the astonishing part of the business "is the fact that" all the Indians in the country seem to possess practically the same ideas and expect about the same result. So universal is this that I can not think but some designing white man or men are at the bottom of the whole matter, and yet there seems to be nothing beyond the merest suspicion to base that opinion on. . . .

Very respectfully,
William I. Plumb
United States Indian Agent

THE COMMISSIONER OF INDIAN AFFAIRS WASHINGTON, D.C.

UNITED STATES INDIAN SERVICE, OFFICE OF INDIAN AGENT PINE RIDGE AGENCY, S. DAK., NOVEMBER 12, 1890

Sir:

The condition of affairs at this agency when I took charge, whether intentional or not, were to render my administration a failure. Orders of constitutional authority are daily violated and defied, and I am powerless to enforce them. The condition of affairs is going from bad to worse. Yesterday in attempting to arrest an Indian for violation of regulations the offender drew a butcher knife on the police and in less than two minutes he was reënforced by two hundred ghost dancers all armed and ready to fight, consequently the arrest was not made. To-day I received a communication from the offender stating that the policeman who attempted to enforce my orders must be discharged or I could expect trouble, and I was given four weeks to do it.

The police force are overpowered and disheartened; we have no protection; are at the mercy of these crazy dancers.

The situation is serious. I urgently request that I be permitted to proceed to Washington at once and confer with you personally, as a correct idea of the situation can not be conveyed otherwise. The Indians have received their beef and rations, and are going home, and there is no immediate danger until next big issue (four weeks from to-day). I can leave now without the service being injured, and I do hope you will grant my request, or let the blame rest where it belongs. I have no other object in view save the best interest of the service.

Royer, Agent

COMMISSIONER OF INDIAN AFFAIRS

WASHINGTON, D.C.

PINE RIDGE AGENCY, S. DAK.,

NOVEMBER 15, 1890

Indians are dancing in the snow and are wild and crazy. I have fully informed you that employés and Government property at this agency have no protection and are at the mercy of these dancers. Why delay by further investigation? We need protection and we need it now. The leaders should be arrested and confined in some military post until the matter is quieted, and this should be done at once.

Royer, Agent[2]

INTRODUCTION TO DOCUMENT 3

William T. Selwyn was a full-blooded Sioux who worked for the U.S. government on the Yankton reservation as a policeman. When he learned that a man named Kuwapi from the Rosebud reservation was at Yankton teaching the Ghost Dance, Selwyn arrested him. He then interviewed his prisoner and reported his findings to Colonel E. W. Foster on November 22, 1890. Compare this account of the Ghost Dance to Z. A. Parker's in Document 1. How and why do they differ?

3. WILLIAM SELWYN'S INTERVIEW WITH KUWAPI (1890)

Do you believe in the new messiah?—*A.* I somewhat believe it.

What made you believe it?—*A.* Because I ate some of the buffalo meat that he (the new messiah) sent to the Rosebud Indians through Short Bull.

Did Short Bull say that he saw the living herd of roaming buffaloes while he was with the son of the Great Spirit?—*A.* Short Bull told the Indians at Rosebud that the buffalo and other wild game will be restored to the Indians at the same time when the general resurrection in favor of the Indians takes place.

You said a "general resurrection in favor of the Indians takes place"; when or how soon will this be?—*A.* The father sends word to us that he will have all these caused to be so in the spring, when the grass is knee high.

You said "father;" who is this father?—*A.* It is the new messiah. He has ordered his children (Indians) to call him "father."

You said the father is not going to send the buffalo until the resurrection takes place. Would he be able to send a few buffaloes over this way for a sort of a sample, so as to have his children (Indians) to have a taste of the meat?—*A.* The father wishes to do things all at once, even in destroying the white race. . . .

What other object could you come to by which you are led to believe that there is such a new messiah on earth at present?—*A.* The ghost dancers are fainted whenever the dance goes on.

Do you believe that they are really fainted?—*A.* Yes.

What makes you believe that the dancers have really fainted?—*A.* Because when they wake or come back to their senses they sometimes bring back some news from the unknown world, and some little trinkets, such as buffalo tail, buffalo meat, etc.

What did the fainted ones see when they get fainted?—*A.* They visited the happy hunting ground, the camps, multitudes of people, and a great many strange people. . . .

Were the people at Rosebud agency anxiously waiting or expecting to see all of their dead relatives who have died several years ago?—A. Yes.

We will have a great many older folks when all the dead people come back, would we not?—A. The visitors all say that there is not a single old man nor woman in the other world—all changed to young.

Are we going to die when the dead ones come back?—A. No; we will be just the same as we are today.

Did the visitor say that there is any white men in the other world?—A. No; no white people.

If there is no white people in the other world, where did they get their provisions and clothing?—A. In the other world, the messenger tells us that they have depended altogether for their food on the flesh of buffalo and other wild game; also, they were all clad in skins of wild animals.

Did the Rosebud agency Indians believe the new messiah, or the son of the Great Spirit?—A. Yes. . . .

Do you faithfully believe in the new messiah?—A. I did not in the first place, but as I became more acquainted with the doctrines of the new messiah. . . . I really believe in him.

How many people at Rosebud, in your opinion, believe this new messiah?—A. Nearly every one.

Did not the Rosebud people prepare to attack the white people this summer? While I was at Pine Ridge agency this summer the Oglalla Sioux Indians say they will resist against the government if the latter should try to put a stop to the messiah question. Did your folks at Rosebud say the same thing?—A. Yes. . . .

You do not mean to say that the Rosebud Indians will try and cause an outbreak?—A. That seems to be the case. . . .[3]

INTRODUCTION TO DOCUMENTS 4 AND 5

The following petitions were submitted by citizens' committees to the federal government. The first, addressed to the President of the United States from Mandan, North Dakota, makes clear the contest over resources between white settlers and native peoples. How did the issues of safety, economics, race, and culture merge together? The second petition, from Chadron, Nebraska, insists that all Sioux be disarmed and that their horses be taken away. Under what justification did the citizens of these towns expect government intervention in their behalf?

4. "PETITION TO THE FEDERAL GOVERNMENT"

Mandan, N. Dak.,
November 18, 1890

Dear Sir:

. . . The settlers who live in the country surrounding Mandan desire to urge strongly that the Indian Department from henceforth deny to Indians the right to carry arms or ammunition off their reservations. Game off the reservations belongs to the white men anyway. . . .

While this is being written there are camped within the city limits of Mandan over one hundred Indians, armed to the teeth, and our wives and our children are asking why these red men are allowed to molest and overawe and annoy us. Our people have stood the ravages of prairie fires, drought, and blizzards for a number of years and are still hopeful; but if, added to their other troubles, they are to be subjected to the depredations of Indians who are supposed to be under the control and subject to the Government they will have to leave the country.

The most conservative men in this community will be powerless to suppress the determination of the majority of the settlers to kill off every Indian that presents his face in this county in the future unless the Government does something to protect us. There are scores of men in this immediate neighborhood who were sufferers by the Minnesota massacres in 1862, and they don't propose to be annoyed and harassed any longer.

Their property has been destroyed and their children and wives frightened by these worthless nomads, who are permitted by a lax Government to prowl over the country with arms that would not be allowed on the person of a white man. They will stand it no longer, and we ask that something be done to tighten the rules and regulations governing the actions of the Indians who are under the Indian agents of this locality.

R. M. Tuttle, Chairman
Jesse Ayers
P. B. Wickham
Joseph Miller[4]

5. "PETITION TO THE FEDERAL GOVERNMENT"

Chadron, Nebr.,
November 26, 1890
Secretary of the Interior
Washington, D.C.

"Resolved, That we respectfully demand of the Government that such steps be taken at this opportune time as shall effectually dispose of the Indian outbreak subject on the Sioux Reservation, and restore to the citizens the confidence the Government may demand of him.

"Resolved, That the allowing of thousands of savages to be armed to the teeth in the center of a sparsely settled agrarian State is a condition improvident and unreasonable.

"Resolved, That the leaders and instigators of criminality in savages should receive at the hands of the Government the punishment the law provides for traitors, anarchists, and assassins.

"Resolved, That in our judgment the exigencies of the occasion demand nothing short of the complete disarming of the Indian and making it a crime for any person to furnish him with arms or implements of war, and we respectfully suggest that the shortest route to the satisfactory settlement of the question would be to deprive the savages of their horses, substituting therefor oxen trained to the plow.[5]

INTRODUCTION TO DOCUMENTS 6, 7, AND 8

The violence exploded as the year 1890 ended. Military forces that were sent to round up hostile Sioux engaged a band under Chief Big Foot camped at Wounded Knee Creek. Document 6 is an account taken from the Annual Report of the Commissioner of Indian Affairs for 1891. Document 7 is a set of three letters written by military leaders in the field; it is taken from the same congressional report as Document 2. Document 8 is a series of eyewitness reports from Indians who were interviewed by the Office of Indian Affairs. How do the accounts in Documents 6 through 8 differ from each other? Which do you find most believable, and why? Parsing these documents, tell what happened on December 29, 1890 at Wounded Knee Creek.

6. ANNUAL REPORT OF THE COMMISSIONER OF INDIAN AFFAIRS, 1891

THE "MESSIAH CRAZE"

Early in November reports received from the agents at Pine Ridge, Rosebud, and Cheyenne River showed that the Indians of those agencies, especially Pine Ridge, were arming themselves and taking a defiant attitude towards the Government and its representatives, committing depredations, and likely to go to other excesses, and November 13 this office recommended that the matter be submitted to the War Department, with request that such prompt action be taken to avert an outbreak as the emergency might be found by them to demand. . . .

DEATH OF SITTING BULL

At daybreak, December 15, 39 Indian police and 4 volunteers went to Sitting Bull's cabin and arrested him. He agreed to accompany them to the agency, but while dressing caused considerable delay, and during this time his followers began to congregate to the number of 150, so that when he was brought out of the house they had the police entirely surrounded. Sitting Bull then refused to go and called on his friends, the ghost dancers, to rescue him. At this juncture one of them shot Lieutenant Bullhead. The lieutenant then shot Sitting Bull, who also received another shot and was killed outright. Another shot struck Sergeant Shavehead and then the firing became general. In about two hours the police had secured possession of Sitting Bull's house and driven their assailants into the woods. . . . The losses were six policemen killed (including Bullhead and

Shavehead who soon died at the agency hospital) and one wounded. The attacking party lost eight killed and three wounded.

INDIANS CONCENTRATE IN THE BAD LANDS

Groups of Indians from the different reservations had commenced concentrating in the "bad lands," upon or in the vicinity of the Pine Ridge Reservation. Killing of cattle and destruction of other property by these Indians almost entirely within the limits of Pine Ridge and Rosebud reservations occurred, but no signal fires were built, no warlike demonstrations were made, no violence was done to any white settler, nor was there cohesion or organization among the Indians themselves. Many of them were friendly Indians who had never participated in the ghost dance but had fled thither from fear of soldiers, in consequence of the Sitting Bull affair, or through the over persuasion of friends. The military gradually began to close in around them, and they offered no resistance, and a speedy and quiet capitulation of all was confidently expected.

FIGHT AT WOUNDED KNEE CREEK

Among them was Big Foot's band belonging to the Cheyenne River Agency, numbering with others who had joined him, about 120 men and 230 women and children. They had escaped to the bad lands, after arrest by the military at Cheyenne River, but soon started from the bad lands for the Pine Ridge Agency, and with a flag of truce advanced into the open country and proposed a parley with the troops whom they met. This being refused they surrendered unconditionally, remained in camp at Wounded Knee Creek over night, expecting to proceed next morning under escort of the troops to Pine Ridge, whither most of the quondam bad-land Indians were moving. The next day, December 29, when ordered to turn in their arms, they surrendered very few. By a search in the teepees 60 guns were obtained. When the military—a detachment of the Seventh Cavalry (Custer's old command), with other troops—began to take the arms from their persons a shot was fired and carnage ensued. According to reports of military officers, the Indians attacked the troops as soon as the disarmament commenced. The Indians claim that the first shot was fired by a half crazy, irresponsible Indian. At any rate, a short, sharp, indiscriminate fight immediately followed, and, during the fighting and the subsequent flight and pursuit of the Indians, the troops lost 25 killed and 35 wounded, and of the Indians, 84 men and boys, 44 women, and 18 children were killed and at least 33 were wounded, many of them fatally. Most of the men, including Big Foot, were killed around his tent where he lay sick. The bodies of women and children were scattered along a distance of two miles from the scene of the encounter.

Frightened and exasperated, again the Indians made for the bad lands. Indians en route thence to the agency turned back and others rushed away from Pine Ridge.[6]

Image 3.3 Corporal Paul Weinert and gunners of Battery "E" 1st Artillery, 1891
Lakota scouts and four U.S. soldiers pose behind a Hotchkiss gun, the same that was used in the at Wounded Knee just months earlier.
Source: John Grabill, Deadwood, South Dakota. Courtesy John C. H. Grabill Collection, Library of Congress.

7. THREE LETTERS BY MILITARY LEADERS

CAMP PINE RIDGE AGENCY
DECEMBER 31, 1890
ACTING ASSISTANT ADJUTANT GENERAL
HEADQUARTERS DEPARTMENT OF THE PLATTE
IN THE FIELD

Sir:

I have the honor to report the following in connection with the movements of my command on the night of December 28th and during the following day. Pursuant to verbal orders from the Commanding General of the Department, I moved my command from this point to the crossing of the Wounded Knee by the main trail to the Rosebud Agency, leaving here at 4:40 P.M., and arriving there at about 8:30 P.M. Major Whitside's battalion of the 7th Cavalry and detachment Light Battery E, 1st Artillery, had that day captured Big Foot's band of Indians, and when I arrived had them in his camp. My command, consisting of Regimental Headquarters and the second battalion, detachment of Light Battery E, 1st Artillery, went into camp for the night. At about 7:30 the next morning, after considerable trouble, the bucks of Big Foot's band, numbering 106 were collected away from their camp, and after explaining to them that having surrendered they would be treated as prisoners of war, but that as such they must surrender their arms. Squads of twenty were cut off, and told to bring them to a designated place. The result of this was very unsatisfactory, but few arms being brought. Keeping the bucks collected, details of soldiers were made under officers to search the Indian camp. While this was in progress, one Indian separated a little from the rest, and in ghost dance costumes, began an address, to which I paid no attention, as the interpreter said he was telling the Indians to be quiet and submit. After a short while, however, the interpreter told me that he was talking of wiping out the whites. I then made him cease his address. Just after this, the search through their camp having proved almost fruitless, I gave orders to search the persons of the bucks, again telling them that they must do as white men always do when surrendering, that is, give up their arms.

At the first move to carry out the order last referred to, the bucks made a break, which at once resulted in terrific fire and a hot fight, lasting about twenty minutes, followed by skirmish firing of about one hour. From the first instant the squaws parted for the hills and it is my belief that comparatively few of them were injured. Some bucks succeeded in getting away and three troops were sent in pursuit. They overtook and captured five bucks (all badly wounded), nineteen squaws and children, and killed one buck. Very soon after the force was attacked by about 125 bucks, supposed to be from the agency. . . . As accurate estimate as could be made of the dead Indians, bucks in and near the camp, was 83, which added to the 7 before mentioned, makes 90 as the number of bucks killed. . . .

Our loss was one officer (Captain Wallace), six non-commissioned officers and eighteen privates killed, and two officers (Lieuts. Garlington and Gresham, the latter slightly, 7th Cavalry, and Lieut. Hawthorn, 2d Artillery), eleven non-commissioned officers and twenty-two privates wounded. . . .

In closing this report, I desire to express my admiration of the gallant conduct of my command in an engagement with a band of Indians in desperate condition, and crazed by religious fanaticism. . . .

Very respectfully,
Your obedient servant,
James W. Forsyth
Colonel 7th Cavalry Commanding

HEADQUARTERS DIVISION OF THE MISSOURI
IN THE FIELD, PINE RIDGE, S.D.
JANUARY 21, 1891
TO THE ASSISTANT ADJUTANT GENERAL
HEADQUARTERS DIVISION OF THE MISSOURI
PINE RIDGE, S.D.

Sir:

I have the honor to report that in obedience to verbal orders of the Division Commander, I proceeded this morning at 7 A.M., under escort of a detachment of the 1st Infantry, mounted, to White Horse Creek, about eleven miles distant, where I found the bodies of one woman, adult, two girls, eight and seven years old, and a boy of about ten years of age.

They were found in the valley of White Horse Creek, in the brush, under a high bluff, where they had evidently been discovered and shot. Each person had been shot once, the character of which was necessarily fatal in each case. The bodies had not been plundered or molested. The shooting was done at so close a range that the person or clothing of each was powder-burned.

The location of the bodies was about three miles westward of the scene of the Wounded Knee battle. All of the bodies were properly buried by the troops of my escort.

From my knowledge of the facts, I am certain that these people were killed on the day of the Wounded Knee fight, and no doubt by the troop of the 7th Cavalry, under command of Captain Godfrey. Tracks of horses shod with the Goodenough shoes were plainly visible and running along the road passing close by where the bodies were found. . . .

Very respectfully,
Your obedient servant,
Frank D. Baldwin
Captain 5th Infantry, A.A.I.G.

HEADQUARTERS DIVISION
OF THE MISSOURI
CHICAGO, ILLINOIS, JANUARY 31, 1891
RESPECTFULLY FORWARDED TO THE
ADJUTANT GENERAL OF THE ARMY . . .

Certain features of the affair at Wounded Knee Creek were so unusual and extraordinary, and such injurious reports were current immediately thereafter, so to imperatively demand an investigation in order to ascertain and record as accurately as possible all the facts, so that an intelligent opinion might guide in the bestowal of commendation or censure. The testimony elicited shows the following facts: First, that Colonel Forsyth had received repeated warnings as to the desperate and deceitful character of Big Foot's band of Indians, and repeated orders as to the exercise of constant vigilance to guard against surprise or disaster under all circumstances.

Secondly, that these warnings and orders were unheeded and disregarded by Colonel Forsyth, who seemed to consider an outbreak of the Indians as being beyond the pale of possibility, in the presence of the large force of troops at hand. The disasters that have occurred to our troops in the past from the desperation of the Indian nature are known to all who are familiar with our history. In addition to this it was well known and Colonel Forsyth had been warned that this particular band contained many of the most desperate and deceitful characters in the Sioux nation, and that a religious excitement nearly approaching frenzy had made them peculiarly dangerous. Under these circumstances the apparent indifference and security of the officer in command of the troops at Wounded Knee Creek is incomprehensive and inexcusable.

Thirdly. An examination of the accompanying map and testimony shows conclusively that at the beginning of the outbreak not a single company of the troops was so disposed as to deliver its fire upon the warriors without endangering the lives of some of their own comrades. It is in fact difficult to conceive how a worse disposition of the troops could have been made. It will be noticed that it would have been perfectly practicable for the entire command of upwards of four hundred and fifty men to have been placed between the warriors and the women and children, with their backs toward the latter and their faces toward the warriors, where they might have used their weapons effectively if required. The testimony goes to show that most of the troops were forced to withhold their fire, leaving the brunt of the affair to fall upon two companies until such warriors as had not been killed broke through or overpowered the small force directly about them and reached the camp occupied by their women and children. The battery of four Hotchkiss guns had until then been useless, the friction primers having been removed from the guns by order of the Captain commanding the battery, lest the gunners might in their excitement discharge the pieces and destroy their own comrades. These guns were now opened upon the Indian camp, even at that time placing in peril Troops C and D, 7th Cav., which were obliged to retreat for some distance owing to the fire from these guns and from the small arms of other portions of the command. The fact that a large number of the one hundred and six warriors were without fire arms when the outbreak occurred is shown by the evidence that forty-eight guns had been taken from the tepees and that a personal search of twenty or more warriors resulted in finding them unarmed. This fact taken in connection with the extremely injudicious disposition of the troops, and the large number of casualties among them, constrains the belief that some of these casualties were suffered at the hands of our own men. The fatal disposition of the troops was such as at the outset to counteract in great measure the immense disparity of strength, and would have been inexcusable in the face of an armed and desperate foe, even had no special warnings and orders been received from higher authority. . . .

Nelson A. Miles[7]

Image 3.4 General Miles and staff viewing the largest hostile Indian Camp in the US, near Pine Ridge, January 16, 1891
General Nelson Miles and his men overlook the Lakota encampment just two weeks after the Wounded Knee massacre.
Source: John Grabill, Deadwood, South Dakota. Courtesy John C. H. Grabill Collection, Library of Congress.

8. EYEWITNESS REPORTS OF INDIANS INTERVIEWED BY THE OFFICE OF INDIAN AFFAIRS

TURNING HAWK, PINE RIDGE (MR. COOK, INTERPRETER)

. . . At first we thought that Pine Ridge and Rosebud were the only two agencies where soldiers were sent, but finally we heard that the other agencies fared likewise. We heard and saw that about half our friends at Rosebud agency, from fear at seeing the soldiers, began the move of running away from their agency toward ours (Pine Ridge), and when they had gotten inside of our reservation they there learned that right ahead of them at our agency was another large crowd of soldiers, and while the soldiers were there, there was constantly a great deal of false rumor flying back and forth. The special rumor I have in mind is the threat that the soldiers had come there to disarm the Indians entirely and to take away all their horses from them. That was the oft-repeated story. . . .

They were met by the soldiers and surrounded and finally taken to the Wounded Knee creek, and there at a given time their guns were demanded. When they had delivered them up, the men were separated from their families, from their tipis, and taken to a certain spot. When the guns were thus taken and the men thus separated, there was a crazy man, a young man of very bad influence and in fact a nobody, among that bunch of Indians fired his gun, and of course the firing of a gun must have been the breaking of a military rule of some sort, because immediately the soldiers returned fire and indiscriminate killing followed.

Spotted Horse. This man shot an officer in the army; the first shot killed this officer. I was a voluntary scout at that encounter and I saw exactly what was done, and that was what I noticed; that the first shot killed an officer. As soon as this shot was fired the Indians immediately began drawing their knives, and they were exhorted from all sides to desist, but this was not obeyed. Consequently the firing began immediately on the part of the soldiers.

Turning Hawk. All the men who were in a bunch were killed right there, and those who escaped that first fire got into the ravine, and as they went along up the ravine for a long distance they were pursued on both sides by the soldiers and shot down, as the dead bodies showed afterwards. The women were standing off at a different place from where the men were stationed, and when the firing began, those of the men who escaped the first onslaught went in one direction up the ravine, and then the women, who were bunched together at another place, went entirely in a different direction through an open field, and the women fared the same fate as the men who went up the deep ravine.

American Horse. The men were separated, as has already been said, from the women, and they were surrounded by the soldiers. Then came next the village of the Indians and that was entirely surrounded by the soldiers also. When the firing began, of course the people who were standing immediately around the young man who fired the first shot were killed right together, and then they turned their guns, Hotchkiss guns, etc., upon the women who were in the lodges standing there under a flag of truce, and of course as soon as they were fired upon they fled, the men fleeing in one direction and the women running in two different directions. So that there were three general directions in which they took flight.

There was a woman with an infant in her arms who was killed as she almost touched the flag of truce, and the women and children of course were strewn all along the circular village until they were dispatched. Right near the flag of truce a mother was shot down with her infant; the child not knowing that its mother was dead was still nursing, and that especially was a very sad sight. The women as they were fleeing with their babes

Image 3.5 "What's Left of Big Foot's Band" (1891)
Source: John C. Grabill, Deadwood, South Dakota. Courtesy Grabill Collection, Library of Congress.

were killed together, shot right through, and the women who were very heavy with child were also killed. All the Indians fled in these three directions, and after most all of them had been killed a cry was made that all those who were not killed or wounded should come forth and they would be safe. Little boys who were not wounded came out of their places of refuge, and as soon as they came in sight a number of soldiers surrounded them and butchered them there. . . .[8]

INTRODUCTION TO DOCUMENT 9

The following two reports try to assess what happened at Wounded Knee Creek and why. Dr. V. T. McGillycuddy had been the agent at the Pine Ridge reservation but had left months before the bloodshed. He wrote his report two weeks after the incident as a letter to General L. W. Colby. General Nelson A. Miles was in charge of the overall military operation on the plains. His report was printed in the Annual Report of the Secretary of War for 1891. Rather than just the details of what happened at the end of 1890, both McGillycuddy and Miles take a longer view and provide much context. How do the two reports agree or disagree as to what happened and why? How do you explain the violence at Wounded Knee Creek?

---

9. GOVERNMENT AND MILITARY STATEMENTS ON WOUNDED KNEE

EX-AGENT MCGILLYCUDDY'S STATEMENT

Sir:

In answer to your inquiry of a recent date, I would state that in my opinion to no one cause can be attributed the recent so-called outbreak on the part of the Sioux, but rather to a combination of causes gradually cumulative in their effect and dating back through many years—in fact to the inauguration of our practically demonstrated faulty Indian policy.

There can be no question but that many of the treaties, agreements, or solemn promises made by our government with these Indians have been broken. Many of them have been kept by us technically, but as far as the Indian is concerned have been misunderstood by him through a lack of proper explanation at time of signing, and hence considered by him as broken.

It must also be remembered that in all of the treaties made by the government with the Indians, a large portion of them have not agreed to or signed the same. Noticeably was this so in the agreement secured by us with them the summer before last, by which we secured one-half of the remainder of the Sioux reserve, amounting to about 16,000 square miles. This agreement barely carried with the Sioux nation as a whole, but did not carry at Pine Ridge or Rosebud, where the strong majority were against it; and it must be noted that wherever there was the strongest opposition manifested to the recent treaty, there, during the present trouble, have been found the elements opposed to the government.

The Sioux nation, which at one time, with the confederated bands of Cheyennes and Arapahos, controlled a region of country bounded on the north by the Yellowstone, on the south by the Arkansas, and reaching from the Missouri river to the Rocky mountains, has seen this large domain, under the various treaties, dwindle down to their now limited reserve of less than 16,000 square miles, and with the land has disappeared the buffalo and other game. The memory of this, chargeable by them to the white man, necessarily irritates them.

There is back of all this the natural race antagonism which our dealings with the aborigine in connection with the inevitable onward march of civilization has in no degree lessened. It has been our experience, and the experience of other nations, that defeat in war is soon, not sooner or later, forgotten by the coming generation, and as a result we have a tendency to a constant recurrence of outbreak on the part of the weaker race. It is now sixteen years since our last war with the Sioux in 1876—a time when our present Sioux warriors were mostly children, and therefore have no memory of having felt the power of the government. It is but natural that these young warriors, lacking in experience, should require but little incentive to induce them to test the bravery of the white man on the war path, where the traditions of his people teach him is the only path to glory and a chosen seat in the "happy hunting grounds." For these reasons every precaution should be adopted by the government to guard against trouble with its disastrous results. Have such precautions been adopted? Investigation of the present trouble does not so indicate. . . .

By the fortunes of political war, weak agents were placed in charge of some of the agencies at the very time that trouble was known to be brewing. Noticeably was this so at Pine Ridge, where a notoriously weak and unfit man was placed in charge. His flight, abandonment of his agency, and his call for troops have, with the horrible results of the same, become facts in history.

Now, as for facts in connection with Pine Ridge, which agency has unfortunately become the theater of the present "war," was there necessity for troops? My past experience with those Indians does not so indicate. For seven long years, from 1879 to 1886, I, as agent, managed this agency without the presence of a soldier on the reservation, and none nearer than 60 miles, and in those times the Indians were naturally much wilder than they are to-day. To be sure, during the seven years we occasionally had exciting times, when the only thing lacking to cause an outbreak was the calling for troops by the agent and the presence of the same. As a matter of fact, however, no matter how much disturbed affairs were, no matter how imminent an outbreak, the progressive chiefs, with their following, came to the front enough in the majority, with the fifty Indian policemen, to at once crush out all attempts at rebellion against the authority of the agent and the government.

Why was this? Because in those times we believed in placing confidence in the Indians; in establishing, as far as possible, a home-rule government on the reservation. We established local courts, presided over by the Indians, with Indian juries; in fact, we believed in having the Indians assist in working out their own salvation. We courted and secured the friendship and support of the progressive and orderly element, as against the mob element. Whether the system thus inaugurated was practicable, was successful, comparison with recent events will decide. . . .

As for the ghost dance, too much attention has been paid to it. It was only the symptom or surface indication of deep-rooted, long-existing difficulty: as well treat the eruption of smallpox as the disease and ignore the constitutional disease.

As regards disarming the Sioux, however desirable it may appear, I consider it neither advisable nor practicable. I fear that it will result as the theoretical enforcement of prohibition in Kansas, Iowa, and Dakota; you will succeed in disarming the friendly Indians, because you can, and you will not so succeed with the mob element, because you can not. If I were again to be an Indian agent and had my choice, I would take charge of 10,000 armed Sioux in preference to a like number of disarmed ones: and,

furthermore, agree to handle that number, or the whole Sioux nation, without a white soldier.

Respectfully, etc.
V. T. McGillycuddy

STATEMENT OF GENERAL MILES

Cause of Indian dissatisfaction. The causes that led to the serious disturbance of the peace in the northwest last autumn and winter were so remarkable that an explanation of them is necessary in order to comprehend the seriousness of the situation. The Indians assuming the most threatening attitude of hostility were the Cheyennes and Sioux. . . .

The commanding officer at Fort Yates, North Dakota, under date of December 7, 1890, at the time the Messiah delusion was approaching a climax, says, in reference to the disaffection of the Sioux Indians at Standing Rock agency, that it is due to the following causes:

1. Failure of the government to establish an equitable southern boundary of the Standing Rock agency reservation.

2. Failure of the government to expend a just proportion of the money received from the Chicago, Milwaukee and St. Paul railroad company, for right of way privileges, for the benefit of the Indians of said agency. Official notice was received October 18, 1881, by the Indian agent at the Standing Rock agency, that the said railroad company had paid the government under its agreement with the Sioux Indians, for right of way privileges, the sum of $13,911. . . . No portion of the money had been expended up to that time (December, 1890) for the benefit of the Indians of the agency, and frequent complaints had been made to the agent by the Indians because they had received no benefits from their concessions to the said railroad companies.

3. Failure of the government to issue the certificates of title to allotments, as required by article 6 of the treaty of 1868.

4. Failure of the government to provide the full allowance of seeds and agricultural implements to Indians engaged in farming, as required in article 8, treaty of 1868.

5. Failure of the government to issue to such Indians the full number of cows and oxen provided in article 10, treaty of 1876.

6. Failure of the government to issue to the Indians the full ration stipulated in article 5, treaty of 1876. (For the fiscal year beginning July 1, 1890, the following shortages in the rations were found to exist: 485,275 pounds of beef [gross], 761,212 pounds of corn, 11,937 pounds of coffee, 281,712 pounds of flour, 26,234 pounds of sugar, and 39,852 pounds of beans.) . . .

7. Failure of the government to issue to the Indians the full amount of annuity supplies to which they were entitled under the provisions of article 10, treaty of 1868.

8. Failure of the government to have the clothing and other annuity supplies ready for issue on the first day of August of each year. Such supplies have not been ready for issue to the Indians, as a rule, until the winter season is well advanced. . . . Such supplies for the present fiscal year, beginning July 1, 1890, had not yet reached (December, 1890) the nearest railway station, about 60 miles distant, from which point they must, at this season of the year, be freighted to this agency in wagons. It is now certain that the winter will be well advanced before the Indians at this agency receive their annual allowance of clothing and other annuity supplies.)

9. Failure of the government to appropriate money for the payment of the Indians for the ponies taken from them, by the authority of the government, in 1876.

In conclusion, the commanding officer says: "It, however, appears from the foregoing, that the government has failed to fulfill its obligations, and in order to render the Indians law-abiding, peaceful, contented, and prosperous it is strongly recommended that the treaties be promptly and fully carried out, and that the promises made by the commission in 1889 be faithfully kept."[9]

INTRODUCTION TO DOCUMENT 10

In 1910 Congress passed the Pine Ridge Act, opening large portions of the Pine Ridge reservation just west of the Rosebud reservation to non-Indian settlement. Document 10 is the advertisement and promotional map designed to attract homesteaders to the newly created Bennett County. Despite the enthusiastic and promising language used to describe the land, it remained difficult to farm throughout the twentieth century.

10. "FREE HOMESTEAD SETTLEMENT" (1910)

GOVERNMENT LAND OPENING:
THE HOMESEEKERS OPPORTUNITY

Several thousand acres of the richest portion of Pine Ridge Reservation, Bennett County, surrounding Lacreek, S. Dak., thrown open to settlement, offers wonderful opportunities to Homesteaders and for big profit from investment in lands and town lots. The incoming of settlers during the next few months, will increase values enormously. The immense success of those who settled in the Rosebud country some years ago, and have become independent, has been the means of arousing wide-spread interest in this, the first opening on Pine Ridge Reservation.

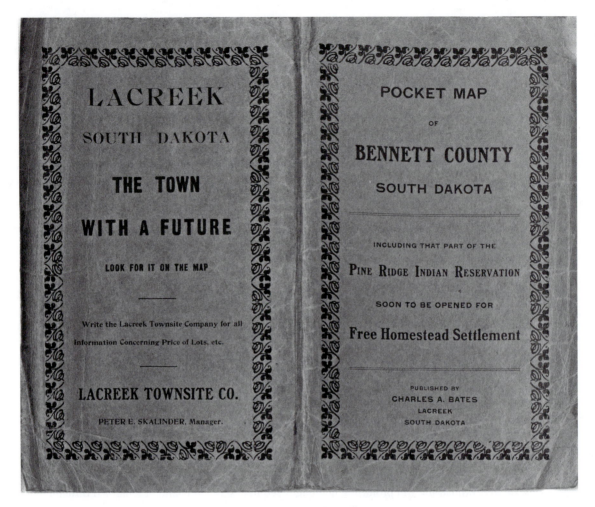

Image 3.6 Cover of landownership map for Bennett County, South Dakota, 1910
Source: (Lacreek, SD: Charles A. Bates, c. 1910). Courtesy Library of Congress.

The great agricultural wealth of this portion of So. Dakota, its fine climate, productive soil, and abundant supply of pure soft water, is just becoming known to the people further east. The onrush of settlers, and extension of railroad lines into this new empire of wealth points out the easy path to independence.

To secure the best bargains, come early.

BUY A LOT IN LACREEK

If you have missed former openings, where lot buyers and land buyers made fortunes, get in at Lacreek. The big profit will be made by securing allotment now. With thousands of homeseekers coming into this district within the next 90 days, every lot should be sold, and prices will advance rapidly.

INTERSTATE LAND CO.

Offices: Merriman, NEB   Lacreek, S.D.[10]

POSTSCRIPT

Ten days before the bloodletting at Wounded Knee, an editorial appeared in the Aberdeen, South Dakota, *Pioneer*. The author declared that Sitting Bull's death marked the final passing of the "proud spirit" of these "wild" and "untamed" people. The best thing for whites to do now was to exterminate the remaining thousands:

> . . . The nobility of the Redskin is extinguished, and what few are left are a pack of whining curs who lick the hand that smites them. The Whites, by law of conquest, by justice of civilization, are masters of the American continent, and the best safety of the frontier settlements will be secured by the total annihilation of the few remaining Indians. Why not annihilation? Their glory has fled, their spirit broken, their manhood effaced; better that they should die than live the miserable wretches that they are. History would forget these latter despicable beings, and speak, in latter ages of the glory of these grand Kings of the forest and plain. . . .[11]

The author's belief in the Indians' former nobility was no bar to his calling for their elimination. Rather, by romanticizing their past, he was able to condemn them in the present. Two weeks after the editorial appeared, just four days after Wounded Knee, the editor concluded: "Having wronged them for centuries we had better, in order to protect our civilization, follow it up by one more wrong and wipe these untamed and untamable creatures from the face of the earth. . . . Otherwise, we may expect future years to be as full of trouble with the redskins as those have been in the past." The author of these editorials was L. Frank Baum, who in 1900 became famous for writing *The Wizard of Oz*.

QUESTIONS

1. Describe the "Messiah Craze" and the Ghost Dance. How did whites react to it?
2. What evidence is there that the Sioux were armed and preparing to attack?
3. How do you think whites and Native Americans differed in their ideas about progress?
4. Why do you think so many Indians became interested in the Ghost Dance?
5. Could Wounded Knee have been avoided? How?
6. Was Wounded Knee a battle or a massacre?

ADDITIONAL READING

For the Plains wars, see Dee Brown, *Bury My Heart at Wounded Knee* (1971), and Colin Calloway, *Our Hearts Fell to the Ground: Plains Indian Views of How the West Was Lost* (1996). A Native American perspective is provided in John G. Neihardt, *Black Elk Speaks* (1932), and multiple perspectives are provided in William S.E. Coleman, *Voices of Wounded Knee* (2000). On the history of white-Indian relations, see Wilcomb Washburn, *The Indian in America* (1975), and Robert M. Utley, *The Indian Frontier of the American West, 1846–1890* (1984). For the legends that whites constructed about their confrontations with the Indians, see Richard Slotkin, *Regeneration Through Violence: The Mythology of the American Frontier, 1600–1860* (1973) and *The Fatal Environment: The Myth of the Frontier in the Age of Industrialization, 1800–1890* (1985). Also see Richard White, *"It's Your Misfortune and None of My Own": A New History of the American West* (1991); Donald Worster, *Under*

Western Skies (1992); Janet A. McDowell, *The Dispossession of the American Indian* (1991); and Patricia Limerick, *The Legacy of Conquest* (1987). For the Sioux, see Catherine Price, *The Oglala People* (1996); on armed conflict, see John McDermott, *A Guide to the Indian Wars of the West* (1998); and on gender, see Theda Perdue, ed. *Sisters: Native American Women's Lives* (2001). For more primary sources, see William S. E. Coleman, *Voices of Wounded Knee* (2000). For more contemporary histories of the same region, see Mary Crow Dog *Lakota Woman* (1991), and Stewart Magnuson, *The Death of Raymond Yellow Thunder* (2008).

ENDNOTES

1. From James Mooney, *The Ghost Dance Religion and the Sioux Outbreak*, Part 2. 14th Annual Report of the Bureau of Ethnology (Washington, D.C.: Government Printing Office, 1896), pp. 916–917.
2. From *The Wounded Knee Massacre: Hearings Before the Committee on the Judiciary*, United States Senate, 94th Congress, Second Session (Washington, D.C.: Government Printing Office, 1976), a reprint of "Report of Investigation into the Battle at Wounded Knee Creek, South Dakota, Fought December 29, 1890," pp. 156–173.
3. From James Mooney, *The Ghost Dance Religion and the Sioux Outbreak*, Part 2. 14th Annual Report of the Bureau of Ethnology (Washington, D.C.: Government Printing Office, 1896), pp. 798–801.
4. From *The Wounded Knee Massacre: Hearings Before the Committee on the Judiciary*, United States Senate, 94th Congress, Second Session (Washington, D.C.: Government Printing Office, 1976), a reprint of "Report of Investigation into the Battle at Wounded Knee Creek, South Dakota, Fought December 29, 1890," pp. 173–190.
5. Ibid.
6. Ibid.
7. Ibid.,
8. From James Mooney, *The Ghost Dance Religion and the Sioux Outbreak*, Part 2. 14th Annual Report of the Bureau of Ethnology (Washington, D.C.: Government Printing Office, 1896), pp. 884–886.
9. Both reports are reprinted from James Mooney, *The Ghost Dance Religion and the Sioux Outbreak*, Part 2. 14th Annual Report of the Bureau of Ethnology (Washington, D.C.: Government Printing Office, 1896), pp. 831–835.
10. Charles A. Bates, surveyor, *Pocket Map of Bennett County, South Dakota, including That Part of the Pine Ridge Indian Reservation Soon to Be Opened for Free Homestead Settlement* (Lacreek, S.D.: Charles A. Bates, *c.* 1910).
11. From the *Aberdeen Saturday Pioneer*, Aberdeen, South Dakota, December 20, 1891.

CHAPTER 4

NEW AMERICANS:
THE IMMIGRANTS

HISTORICAL CONTEXT

One day in August 1921, the artist Joseph Pennell was walking in the Lower East Side of New York City. He wandered into a street of houses that were trimmed with ornate carvings, mouldings, and ironwork, all products of old craft traditions. Pennell was at once taken with the beauty of the architecture and disturbed by the people in the neighborhood. He wrote to his friend Cass Gilbert, a renowned architect, that the beauty of the buildings was "destroyed by the tribe of mongrels, the spewings out of niggers, dagoes, Chinese, and Greeks who herd in them and make by millions the new Americans." Nonetheless, Pennell advised Gilbert to go there: "If you can stand the stink and sight of your fellow countrymen and women though they aren't mostly naturalized and can get a police permit to see the dens where they herd and breed, *you might get some marble pieces.*" An architect like Gilbert, in other words, could extract artwork from these people's homes and reuse it in buildings located in more respectable neighborhoods. Pennell added as an afterthought that there was no danger that anyone in the neighborhood might object; "as there are no Jews there, these people don't know the things have any value."

It was not uncommon for Americans in this era to think of those from other lands as "spewings," to comment on how they smelled, or to mention their "herding" and "breeding," terms usually reserved for animals. The inscription on the newly erected Statue of Liberty, after all, referred to immigrants as "wretched refuse," hardly a compliment to the parents, grandparents, and great-grandparents of so many of us. Nativism, racism, and xenophobia have been long and enduring in American culture. Pennell's letter merely tapped into resurgent prejudices.

Nevertheless, it would be a mistake to see such attitudes as fixed and immutable. Ethnic stereotypes may range from tasteless jokes to vicious images that are used to justify violence. The intensity of prejudice varies with such circumstances as economic conditions, competition for jobs, the degree of closeness in which people of different groups live to each other, and the amount of contact over time they share with each other. By 1880, for example, few Americans had encountered Polish people, but nearly everyone was familiar with the racist stereotypes of African Americans that infused popular culture. Prejudice may be enduring, but its pervasiveness, intensity, and consequences change dramatically across time and place.

To read Pennell's letter as part of an unvarying climate of hatred for strangers is to imply that there were no alternatives. The logic is circular: everyone harbored ugly prejudices because that was how everyone felt. Such a position absolves individuals from responsibility, for it makes them seem powerless before the ideas that control them. But to say "everybody thought that way back then" simply is not true; the history of ideas is never so clear or uniform. For example, Pennell's last remark derives from the age-old stereotype of Jews' alleged obsession with money, their stinginess, wealth, power, and so forth. In the stereotype, an entire people's history, traditions, and religion are reduced to a simple and pernicious cluster of prejudices.

Not everyone believed such nonsense. To cite an alternative (and history is the study of alternatives, of roads taken and not taken), Hutchins Hapgood, a man from an old American family, wrote an extraordinarily sensitive and complex book about the cultural life of the Jewish neighborhoods of New York City. Hapgood walked on the same streets as Pennell (though he had walked through them twenty years earlier) and saw something very different. "The Jewish quarter of New York," Hapgood wrote in the preface to his *Spirit of the Ghetto* (1902), "is generally supposed to be a place of poverty, dirt, ignorance, and immorality. . . . But the unpleasant aspect is not the subject of the following sketches." Philanthropists, sociologists, and reformers might enter ethnic neighborhoods to document the immigrants' debasement, but Hapgood was attracted by "the charm [he] felt in men and things there." By not reducing Jewish immigrant culture to poverty, depravity, or stereotypes, Hapgood could explore the rich cultural life that Jews created in America.

The history of America, of course, is the history of immigrants. But the half-century between the late 1870s and the late 1920s—by which date new legal restrictions and economic depression had ended the influx of foreign peoples—witnessed unprecedented immigration. Roughly 30 million newcomers entered the country in those years, sometimes at a rate of over 1 million per year. They came less from western and northern Europe than from southern and eastern Europe, and they came too from Asia, so that, taken together, Italians, Jews, Poles, Russians, and other Slavic and Mediterranean peoples, as well as Chinese, arrived in numbers far exceeding the legions of Irish, German, and Scandinavian immigrants who dominated earlier in the nineteenth century.

The newcomers tended to settle north of the Ohio and east of the Mississippi Rivers in burgeoning urban centers like Chicago, Cleveland, and New York. Industrialization and the expansion of the worldwide market economy caused massive shifts in the supply of goods and the demand for labor, so that millions found themselves in motion. The vagaries of weather or falling prices in international markets might leave Italian or Slavic farmworkers on the edge of starvation, but the demand for laborers to dig the subways of New York City or to man the steel mills of Pittsburgh offered them a chance to survive. Some people migrated within their native countries; others moved through Europe or Asia;

many went overseas to Latin America, Canada, or especially the United States; but immigration was an international phenomenon rooted in economic dislocations that left millions without the means to make a living.

The majority of the new immigrants were men; they came in search of jobs while their families stayed behind. (Jews, more than other ethnic groups, migrated as whole families because political persecution in eastern Europe gave them little hope of a decent life there; Chinese women, on the other hand, were forbidden to enter the United States, so Chinese men often settled in all-male work camps to mine gold or to build the railroads in the West.) Many intended to remain in America—or in whatever country they found work—only long enough to send money home to secure the survival of their families in the old country. In some years, half as many people returned to Europe as came to America. Moreover, immigrants tended to come in patterns that demographers call *chain migrations*. The decision to go was not made randomly by individuals; rather, extended families, neighbors, and even whole towns migrated within a few years of each other, sold their labor together, and settled into new communities together. The Chinatowns, Little Italys, and other ethnic neighborhoods were the result of people's need to help one another economically, to maintain their language and culture, and to defend themselves from prejudice.

Despite occasional recessions, America's economy boomed during this era, providing plenty of work to lure the newcomers. But immigrants were mostly unskilled, exploitable labor, easily replaced by others if they started to organize and make demands. In New York sweatshops, Jews sewed garments for the ready-to-wear industry; in Pittsburgh mills, Poles poured steel; on California ranches, Mexicans picked the crops; and in downtown Chicago, Greeks shined businessmen's shoes. Most worked brutally long hours to make a bit more or less than subsistence wages. All lived with the fear that new workers might undercut their wages, and they labored in horrid conditions that caused tens of thousands to die prematurely every year. Epidemics swept the crowded slums, mines caved in, explosions rocked the mills, construction workers fell from shoddy scaffoldings, and tenements burned to the ground. Prejudice and fear prevented many Americans from recognizing the human tragedy before their eyes. The relative powerlessness of immigrants—their difficulties communicating across ethnic boundaries, their need to keep jobs, and their sheer exhaustion from overwork—too often kept them from organizing effectively to resist oppression.

All of their hardships notwithstanding, the immigrants made a life for themselves and their children. Perhaps it is more accurate to say that, to survive the hardships, they knew that they must stick together and cling to their old ways. In ethnic communities, they sang the songs, played the games, and told the stories of the old country. Extended families reinforced distinctive gender roles, foodways, languages, and other cultural patterns. The new immigrants built churches, especially Catholic churches, since the majority of them were of that faith. They worshiped in their own unique ways; Polish Catholicism differed markedly from Italian Catholicism, as did the Greek Orthodox from the Russian

Orthodox church. Politics engaged many immigrants' attention, and community leaders helped to develop local resources, to accomplish goals for their people, and, in the process, to become powerful individuals. Many groups also came with well-developed traditions of economic protest, so socialist, communist, trade unionist, and anarchist organizations flourished.

But there were always tensions. The children of immigrants were divided in their loyalties between the ways of their parents and those of the American culture. Wealthier foreigners were embarrassed by their poor compatriots but often not too embarrassed to exploit them. Patriotic feelings toward the new country that fed them vied with hatred of America's prejudice and exploitation. The experiences of migrating to a strange land, settling, making a living, establishing communities, and deciding whether to stay and for how long were difficult challenges that individuals negotiated for themselves day by day.

INTRODUCTION TO DOCUMENTS 1–6

The documents in this chapter give a sense of the complexity of the immigrant experience. There are interviews with three immigrants—one Italian, one Chinese, and one Jewish—that appeared in the reform magazine *The Independent* just after the beginning of the twentieth century. While we cannot know what questions were asked by the representative of the magazine or how the interviews were edited, these pieces give us the rare opportunity to hear the immigrants' own voices and to glimpse how they viewed themselves. Preceding each interview is a portion of Jacob Riis's famous book *How the Other Half Lives* (1890). Riis was a Danish immigrant who became a journalist and a social reformer. Before his success and fame in middle age, however, he had suffered severe poverty and alienation shortly after he migrated to America. During the economic depression of the 1870s, when he was in his twenties, Riis wandered the streets of New York unemployed, homeless, and suicidal. He was saved by a job as a police reporter for the *New York Tribune.* For the rest of the century, he wrote about the city's impoverished lower Manhattan wards.

Despite his own experience of immigration and poverty, Riis was by no means wholly sympathetic to the people he wrote about and photographed. He hated the dirt and the anarchy, the stink and the poverty of lower Manhattan, but he hated these things as a man running from something in himself. He saw mostly the immigrants' degradation, barely the people themselves, so he readily fastened onto ethnic stereotypes to describe them and focused on the material environment as a remedy to their problems. Compare Riis's characterization of the Chinese with what Lee Chew says about himself and his people. Are there similarities between Riis's description of Italians and the picture we get from Rocco Corresca? Can you square Riis's characterization of Jews as obsessed with money with Rose Schneiderman's commitment to labor organizing?

1. "LITTLE ITALY" (1890)

JACOB RIIS

Certainly a picturesque, if not very tidy, element has been added to the population in the "assisted" Italian immigrant who claims so large a share of public attention, partly because he keeps coming at such a tremendous rate, but chiefly because he elects to stay in New York, or near enough for it to serve as his base of operations, and here promptly reproduces conditions of destitution and disorder which, set in the frame-work of Mediterranean exuberance, are the delight of the artist, but in a matter-of-fact American community become its danger and reproach. The reproduction is made easier in New York because he finds the material ready to hand in the worst of the slum tenements; but even where it is not he soon reduces what he does find to his own level, if allowed to follow his natural bent. The Italian comes in at the bottom, and in the generation that came over the sea he stays there. In the slums he is welcomed as a tenant who "makes less trouble" than the contentious Irishman or the order-loving German, that is to say: is content to live in a pig-sty and submits to robbery at the hands of the rent-collector without murmur. Yet this very tractability makes of him in good hands, when firmly and intelligently managed, a really desirable tenant. . . .

Recent Congressional inquiries have shown the nature of the "assistance" he receives from greedy steamship agents and "bankers," who persuade him by false promises to mortgage his home, his few belongings, and his wages for months to come for a ticket to the land where plenty of work is to be had at princely wages. The padrone—the "banker" is nothing else—having made his ten per cent. out of him en route, receives him at the landing and turns him to double account as a wage-earner and a rent-payer. In each of these roles he is made to yield a profit to his unscrupulous countryman, whom he trusts implicitly with the instinct of utter helplessness. The man is so ignorant that, as one of the sharpers

who prey upon him put it once, it "would be downright sinful not to take him in." His ignorance and unconquerable suspicion of strangers dig the pit into which he falls. He not only knows no word of English, but he does not know enough to learn. Rarely only can he write his own language. Unlike the German, who begins learning English the day he lands as a matter of duty, or the Polish Jew, who takes it up as soon as he is able as an investment, the Italian learns slowly, if at all. Even his boy, born here, often speaks his native tongue indifferently. He is forced, therefore, to have constant recourse to the middle-man who makes him pay handsomely at every turn. He hires him out to the railroad contractor, receiving a commission from the employer as well as from the laborer, and repeats the performance monthly, or as often as he can have him dismissed. In the city he contracts for his lodging, subletting to him space in the vilest tenements at extortionate rents, and sets an example that does not lack imitators. The "princely wages" have vanished with his coming, and in their place hardships and a dollar a day, [along] with the padrone's merciless mortgage, confront him. Bred to even worse fare, he takes both as a matter of course, and, applying the maxim that it is not what one makes but what he saves that makes him rich, manages to turn the very dirt of the streets into a hoard of gold, with which he either returns to his Southern home, or brings over his family to join in his work and in his fortunes the next season. . . .

Like the Chinese, the Italian is a born gambler. His soul is in the game from the moment the cards are on the table, and very frequently his knife is in it too before the game is ended. No Sunday has passed in New York since "the Bend" became a suburb of Naples without one or more of these murderous affrays coming to the notice of the police. As a rule that happens only when the man the game went against is

Image 4.1 Jacob Riis, "In the Home of an Italian Ragpicker, Jersey Street" (*c*. 1890)
Source: Museum of the City of New York. 90.13.2.128.

either dead or so badly wounded as to require instant surgical help. As to the other, unless he be caught red-handed, the chances that the police will ever get him are slim indeed. The wounded man can seldom be persuaded to betray him. He wards off all inquiries with a wicked "I fix him myself," and there the matter rests until he either dies or recovers. If the latter, the community hears after a while of another Italian affray, a man stabbed in a quarrel, dead or dying, and the police know that "he" has been fixed, and the account squared.

With all his conspicuous faults, the swarthy Italian immigrant has his redeeming traits. He is as honest as he is hot-headed. There are no Italian burglars in the Rogues' Gallery; the ex-brigand toils peacefully with pickaxe and shovel on American ground. . . . The women are faithful wives and devoted mothers. Their vivid and picturesque costumes lend a tinge of color to the otherwise dull monotony of the slums they inhabit. The Italian is gay, light-hearted and, if his fur is not stroked the wrong way, inoffensive as a child. . . .[1]

2. "THE BIOGRAPHY OF A BOOTBLACK" (1902)

ROCCO CORRESCA

[The story of Rocco Corresca is presented almost as he told it to a representative of *The Independent*. There are changes of language and some suppressions, but no change of meaning has been made. The ideas and statements of fact are all his, and, astonishing as it may seem to Americans, much of the experience is typical of thousands of Italians who come to this country penniless and make their fortunes, though beginning as low down in the scale as the narrator. Rocco is known to many people as "Joe." He claims that he has always been known as Rocco but that the name Corresca was given him when he went aboard the ship that brought him here. It was entered on the books. He has since kept it for official purposes and proposes to be known by it in the future. —*Editor*.]

When I was a very small boy I lived in Italy in a large house with many other small boys, who were all dressed alike and were taken care of by some nuns. It was a good place, situated on the side of the mountain, where grapes were growing and melons and oranges and plums.

They taught us our letters and how to pray and say the catechism, and we worked in the fields during the middle of the day. We always had enough to eat and good beds to sleep in at night, and sometimes there were feast days, when we marched about wearing flowers.

Those were good times and they lasted till I was nearly eight years of age. Then an old man came and said he was my grandfather. He showed some papers and cried over me and said that the money had come at last and now he could take me to his beautiful home. He seemed very glad to see me and after they looked at his papers he took me away and we went to the big city—Naples. He kept talking about his beautiful house, but when we got there it was a dark cellar that he lived in and I did not like it at all. Very rich people were on the first floor. They had

carriages and servants and music and plenty of good things to eat, but we were down below in the cellar and had nothing. There were four other boys in the cellar and the old man said they were all my brothers. All were larger than I and they beat me at first till one day Francisco said that they should not beat me any more, and then Paulo, who was the largest of all, fought him till Francisco drew a knife and gave him a cut. Then Paulo, too, got a knife and said that he would kill Francisco, but the old man knocked them both down with a stick and took their knives away and gave them beatings.

Each morning we boys all went out to beg and we begged all day near the churches and at night near the theatres, running to the carriages and opening the doors and then getting in the way of the people so that they had to give us money or walk over us. The old man often watched us and at night he took all the money, except when we could hide something. . . .

Then the old man said to me: "If you don't want to be a thief you can be a cripple. That is an easy life and they make a great deal of money."

I was frightened then, and that night I heard him talking to one of the men that came to see him. He asked how much he would charge to make me a good cripple like those that crawl about the church. They had a dispute, but at last they agreed and the man said that I should be made so that people would shudder and give me plenty of money.

I was much frightened, but I did not make a sound and in the morning I went out to beg with Francisco. I said to him: "I am going to run away. I don't believe 'Tony is my grandfather . . . and I don't want to be a cripple, no matter how much money the people may give."

"Where will you go?" Francisco asked me.

"I don't know," I said; "somewhere."

He thought awhile and then he said: "I will go, too."

So we ran away out of the city and begged from the country people as we went along. We came to a village down by the sea and a long way from Naples and there we found some fishermen and they took us aboard their boat. We were with them five years, and tho it was a very hard life we liked it well because there was always plenty to eat. Fish do not keep long and those that we did not sell we ate.

The chief fisherman, whose name was Ciguciano, had a daughter, Teresa, who was very beautiful, and tho she was two years younger than I, she could cook and keep house quite well. She was a kind, good girl and he was a good man. When we told him about the old man who told us he was our grandfather, the fisherman said he was an old rascal who should be in prison for life. Teresa cried much when she heard that he was going to make me a cripple. Ciguciano said that all the old man had taught us was wrong—that it was bad to beg, to steal and to tell lies. He called in the priest and the priest said the same thing and was very angry at the old man in Naples, and he taught us to read and write in the evenings. He also taught us our duties to the church. . . .

We grew large and strong with the fisherman and he told us that we were getting too big for him, that he could not afford to pay us the money that we were worth. He was a fine, honest man—one in a thousand.

Now and then I had heard things about America—that it was a far off country where everybody was rich and that Italians went there and made plenty of money, so that they could return to Italy and live in pleasure ever after. One day I met a young man who pulled out a handful of gold and told me he had made that in America in a few days. . . .

The young man took us to a big ship and got us work away down where the fires are. We had to carry coal to the place where it could be thrown on the fires. Francisco and I were very sick from the great heat at first and lay on the coal for a long time, but they threw water on us and made us get up. We could not stand on our feet well, for everything was going around and we had no strength. We said that we wished we had stayed in Italy no matter how much gold there was in America. We could not eat for three days and could not do much work. Then we got better and sometimes we went up above and looked about. There was no land anywhere and we were much surprised. How could the people tell where to go when there was no land to steer by? . . .

We were all landed on an island and the bosses there said that Francisco and I must go back because we had not enough money, but a man named Bartolo came up and told them that we were brothers and he was our uncle and would take care of us. He brought two other men who swore that they knew us in Italy and that Bartolo was our uncle. I had never seen any of them before, but even then Bartolo might be my uncle, so I did not say anything. The bosses of the island let us go out with Bartolo after he had made the oath.

We came to Brooklyn to a wooden house in Adams Street that was full of Italians from Naples. Bartolo had a room on the third floor and there were fifteen men in the room, all boarding with Bartolo. He did the cooking on a stove in the middle of the room and there were beds all around the sides, one bed above another. It was very hot in the room, but we were soon asleep, for we were very tired.

The next morning, early, Bartolo told us to go out and pick rags and get bottles. He gave us bags and hooks and showed us the ash barrels. On the streets where the fine houses are the people are very careless and put out good things, like mattresses and umbrellas, clothes, hats and boots. We brought all these to Bartolo and he made them new again and sold them on the sidewalk; but mostly we brought rags and bones. The rags we had to wash in the back yard and then we hung them to dry on lines under the ceiling in our room. The bones we kept under the beds till Bartolo could find a man to buy them.

Most of the men in our room worked at digging the sewer. Bartolo got them the work and they paid him about one quarter of their wages. Then he charged them for board and he bought the clothes for them, too. So they got little money after all.

Bartolo was always saying that the rent of the room was so high that he could not make anything, but he was really making plenty. He was what they call a padrone and is now a very rich man. The men that were living with him had just come to the country and could not speak English. They had all been sent by the young man we met in Italy. Bartolo told us all that we must work for him and that if we did not the police would come and put us in prison.

He gave us very little money, and our clothes were some of those that were found on the street. Still we had enough to eat and we had meat quite often, which we never had in Italy. Bartolo got it from the butcher—the meat that he could not sell to the other people—but it was quite good meat. Bartolo cooked it in the pan while we all sat on our beds in the evening. Then he cut it into small bits and passed the pan around, saying:

"See what I do for you and yet you are not glad. I am too kind a man, that is why I am so poor."

We were with Bartolo nearly a year, but some of our countrymen who had been in the place a long time said that Bartolo had no right to us and we could get work for a dollar and a half a day, which, when you make it *lire* (the Italian currency) is very much. So we went away one day to Newark and got work on the street. Bartolo came after us and made a great noise, but the boss said that if he did not go away soon the police would have him. Then he went, saying that there was no justice in this country.

We paid a man five dollars each for getting us the work and we were with that boss for six months. He was Irish, but a good man and he gave us our money every Saturday night. We lived much better than with Bartolo, and when the work was done we each had nearly $200 saved. Plenty of the men spoke English and they taught us, and we taught them to read and write. That was at night, for we had a lamp in our room, and there were only five other men who lived in that room with us. . . .

When the Newark boss told us that there was no more work Francisco and I talked about what we would do and we went back to Brooklyn to a saloon near Hamilton Ferry, where we got a job cleaning it out and slept in a little room upstairs. There was a bootblack named Michael on the corner and when I had time I helped him and learned the business. Francisco cooked the lunch in the saloon and he, too,

worked for the bootblack and we were soon able to make the best polish.

Then we thought we would go into business and we got a basement on Hamilton avenue, near the Ferry, and put four chairs in it. We paid $75 for the chairs and all the other things. We had tables and looking glasses there and curtains. We took the papers that have the pictures in and made the place high toned. Outside we had a big sign that said: *The Best Shine for Ten Cents.* Men that did not want to pay ten cents could get a good shine for five cents, but it was not an oil shine. We had two boys helping us and paid each of them fifty cents a day. The rent of the place was $20 a month, so the expenses were very great, but we made money from the beginning. We slept in the basement, but got our meals in the saloon till we could put a stove in our place, and then Francisco cooked for us all. That would not do, tho, because some of our customers said that they did not like to smell garlic and onions and red herrings. I thought that was strange, but we had to do what the customers said. So we got the woman who lived upstairs to give us our meals and paid her $1.50 a week each. She gave the boys soup in the middle of the day—five cents for two plates. . . .

We had said that when we saved $1,000 each we would go back to Italy and buy a farm, but now that the time is coming we are so busy and making so much money that we think we will stay. We have opened another parlor near South Ferry, in New York. We have to pay $30 a month rent, but the business is very good. The boys in this place charge sixty cents a day because there is so much work.

There are plenty of rich Italians here, men who a few years ago had nothing and now have so much money that they could not count all their dollars in a week. The richest ones go away from the other Italians and live with the Americans. . . .

I am nineteen years of age now and have $700 saved. Francisco is twenty-one and has about $900. We shall open some more parlors soon. I know an Italian who was a bootblack ten years ago and now bosses bootblacks all over the city, who has so much money that if it was turned into gold it would weight more than himself. . . .[2]

3. "CHINATOWN" (1890)

JACOB RIIS

... Whatever may be said about the Chinaman being a thousand years behind the age on his own shores, here he is distinctly abreast of it in his successful scheming to "make it pay." It is doubtful if there is anything he does not turn to a paying account, from his religion down, or up, as one prefers. At the risk of distressing some well-meaning, but, I fear, too trustful people, I state it in advance as my opinion, based on the steady observation of years, that all attempts to make an effective Christian of John Chinaman will remain abortive in this generation; of the next I have, if anything, less hope. Ages of senseless idolatry, a mere grub-worship, have left him without the essential qualities for appreciating the gentle teachings of a faith whose motive and unselfish spirit are alike beyond his grasp.... There is nothing strong about him, except his passions when aroused. I am convinced that he adopts Christianity, when he adopts it

Image 4.2 Jacob Riis, "The Official Organ of Chinatown" (*c.* 1890)

Source: Museum of the City of New York. 90.13.2.128

at all, as he puts on American clothes, with what the politicans would call an ulterior motive, some sort of gain in the near prospect—washing, a Christian wife perhaps, anything he happens to rate for the moment above his cherished pigtail.

Stealth and secretiveness are as much part of the Chinaman in New York as the cat-like tread of his felt shoes. His business, as his domestic life, shuns the light, less because there is anything to conceal than because that is the way of the man. Perhaps the attitude of American civilization toward the stranger, whom it invited in, has taught him that way. At any rate, the very doorways of his offices and shops are fenced off by queer, forbidding partitions suggestive of a continual state of siege. The stranger who enters through the crooked approach is received with sudden silence, a sullen stare, and an angry "Vat you vant?" that breathes annoyance and distrust.

. . . The average Chinaman, the police will tell you, would rather gamble than eat any day, and they have ample experience to back them. Only the fellow in the bunk smokes away, indifferent to all else but his pipe and his own enjoyment. . . . Not a Chinese home or burrow there but has its bunk and its layout, where they can be enjoyed safe from police interference. The Chinaman smokes opium as Caucasians smoke tobacco, and apparently with little worse effect upon himself. But woe unto the white victim upon which his pitiless drug gets its grip! . . .

From the teeming tenements to the right and left of [Chinatown] come the white slaves of its dens of vice and their infernal drug, that have infused into the "Bloody Sixth" Ward a subtler poison than ever the stale-beer dives knew, or the "sudden death" of the Old Brewery. There are houses, dozens of them, in Mott and Pell Streets, that are literally jammed, from the "joint" in the cellar to the attic, with these hapless victims of a passion which, once acquired, demands the sacrifice of every instinct of decency to its insatiate desire. . . . I came across a company of them [young Caucasian prostitutes] "hitting the pipe" together, on a tour through their dens one night with the police captain of the precinct. The girls knew him, called him by name, offered him a pipe, and chatted with him about the incidents of their acquaintance, how many times he had "sent them up,"

and their chances of "lasting" much longer. There was no shade of regret in their voices, nothing but utter indifference and surrender.

One thing about them was conspicuous: their scrupulous neatness. It is the distinguishing mark of Chinatown, outwardly and physically. It is not altogether by chance the Chinaman has chosen the laundry as his distinctive field. He is by nature as clean as the cat, which he resembles in his traits of cruel cunning and savage fury when aroused. On this point of cleanliness he insists in his domestic circle, yielding in others with crafty submissiveness to the caprice of the girls, who "boss" him in a very independent manner, fretting vengefully under the yoke they loathe, but which they know right well they can never shake off, once they have put the pipe to their lips and given Mott Street a mortgage upon their souls for all time. . . .

The frequent assertions of the authorities that at least no girls under age are wrecked on this Chinese shoal, are disproved by the observation of those who go frequently among these dens, though the smallest girl will invariably, and usually without being asked, insist that she is sixteen, and so of age to choose the company she keeps. Such assertions are not to be taken seriously. Even while I am writing, the morning returns from one of the precincts that pass through my hands report the arrest of a Chinaman for "inveigling little girls into his laundry," one of the hundred outposts of Chinatown that are scattered all over the city, as the outer threads of the spider's web that holds its prey fast. . . .

Withal the police give the Chinese the name of being the "quietest people down there," meaning in the notoriously turbulent Sixth Ward; and they are. The one thing they desire above all is to be let alone, a very natural wish perhaps, considering all the circumstances. If it were a laudable or even an allowable ambition that prompts it, they might be humored with advantage, probably, to both sides. But the facts show too plainly that it is not, and that in their very exclusiveness and reserve they are a constant and terrible menace to society. . . . The severest official scrutiny, the harshest repressive measures are justifiable in Chinatown, orderly as it appears on the surface. . . .[3]

4. "THE BIOGRAPHY OF A CHINAMAN" (1903)

LEE CHEW

[Mr. Lee Chew is a representative Chinese business man who expresses with much force views that are generally held by his countrymen throughout America. The interview that follows is strictly as he gave it, except as to detail of arrangement and mere verbiage. Mr. Lee was assisted by the well-known Chinese interpreter, Mr. Joseph M. Singleton, of 24 Pell Street. —*Editor.*]

The village where I was born is situated in the province of Canton, on one of the banks of the Si-Kiang River. It is called a village, altho it is really as big as a city, for there are about 5,000 men in it over eighteen years of age—women and children and even youths are not counted in our villages.

All in the village belonged to the tribe of Lee. They did not intermarry with one another, but the men went to other villages for their wives and brought them home to their fathers' houses, and men from other villages—Wus and Wings and Sings and Fongs, etc.—chose wives from among our girls. . . .

My father's house is built of fine blue brick, better than the brick in the houses here in the United States. It is only one story high, roofed with red tiles and surrounded by a stone wall which also incloses the yard. There are four rooms in the house, one large living room which serves for a parlor and three private rooms, one occupied by my grandfather, who is very old and very honorable; another by my father and mother, and the third by my oldest brother and his wife and two little children. There are no windows, but the door is left open all day.

All the men of the village have farms, but they don't live on them as the farmers do here; they live in the village, but go out during the day time and work their farms, coming home before dark. My father has a farm of about ten acres, on which he grows a great abundance of things—sweet potatoes, rice, beans, peas, yams, sugar cane, pineapples, bananas, lychee nuts and palms. The palm leaves are useful and can be sold. Men make fans of the lower part of each leaf near the stem, and water proof coats and hats, and awnings for boats, of the parts that are left when the fans are cut out. . . .

In spite of the fact that any man may correct them for a fault, Chinese boys have good times and plenty of play. We played games like tag, and other games like shinny and a sort of football called yin. . . . It was not all play for us boys, however. We had to go to school, where we learned to read and write and to recite the precepts of Kong-foo-tsze and the other Sages, and stories about the great Emperors of China, who ruled with the wisdom of gods and gave to the whole world the light of high civilization and the culture of our literature, which is the admiration of all nations.

I went to my parents' house for meals, approaching my grandfather with awe, my father and mother with veneration and my elder brother with respect. I never spoke unless spoken to, but I listened and heard much concerning the red haired, green eyed foreign devils with the hairy faces, who had lately come out of the sea and clustered on our shores. They were wild and fierce and wicked, and paid no regard to the moral precepts of Kong-foo-tsze and the Sages; neither did they worship their ancestors, but pretended to be wiser than their fathers and grandfathers. They loved to beat people and to rob and murder. In the streets of Hong Kong many of them could be seen reeling drunk. Their speech was a savage roar, like the voice of the tiger or the buffalo, and they wanted to take the land away from the Chinese. Their men and women lived together like animals, without any marriage or faithfulness, and even were shameless enough to walk the streets arm in arm in daylight. So the old men said.

All this was very shocking and disgusting, as our women seldom were on the street, except in the evenings, when they went with the water jars to the three wells that supplied all the people. Then if they met a man they stood still, with their faces turned to the wall, while he looked the other way when he passed them. A man who spoke to a woman on the street in a Chinese village would be beaten, perhaps killed.

My grandfather told how the English foreign devils had made wicked war on the Emperor, and by means of their enchantments and spells had defeated his armies and forced him to admit their opium, so that the Chinese might smoke and become weakened and the foreign devils might rob them of their land.

My grandfather said that it was well known that the Chinese were always the greatest and wisest among men. They had invented and discovered everything that was good. Therefore the things which the foreign devils had and the Chinese had not must be evil. Some of these things were very wonderful, enabling the red haired savages to talk with one another, tho they might be thousands of miles apart. They had suns that made darkness like day, their ships carried earthquakes and volcanoes to fight for them, and thousands of demons that lived in iron and steel houses spun their cotton and silk, pushed their boats, pulled their cars, printed their newspapers and did other work for them. They were constantly showing disrespect for their ancestors by getting new things to take the place of the old.

I heard about the American foreign devils, that they were false, having made a treaty by which it was agreed that they could freely come to China, and the Chinese as freely go to their country. After this treaty was made China opened its doors to them and then they broke the treaty that they had asked for by shutting the Chinese out of their country. . . .

I worked on my father's farm till I was about sixteen years of age, when a man of our tribe came back from America and took ground as large as four city blocks and made a paradise of it. He put a large stone wall around and led some streams through and built a palace and summer house and about twenty other structures, with beautiful bridges over the streams and walks and roads. Trees and flowers, singing birds, water fowl and curious animals were within the walls.

The man had gone away from our village a poor boy. Now he returned with unlimited wealth, which he had obtained in the country of the American wizards. After many amazing adventures he had become a merchant in a city called Mott Street, so it was said.

When his palace and grounds were completed he gave a dinner to all the people who assembled to be his guests. One hundred pigs roasted whole were served on the tables, with chickens, ducks, geese and such an abundance of dainties that our villagers even now lick their fingers when they think of it. He had the best actors from Hong Kong performing, and every musician for miles around was playing and singing. At night the blaze of the lanterns could be seen for many miles.

Having made his wealth among the barbarians this man had faithfully returned to pour it out among his tribesmen, and he is living in our village now very happy, and a pillar of strength to the poor.

The wealth of this man filled my mind with the idea that I, too, would like to go to the country of the wizards and gain some of their wealth, and after a long time my father consented, and gave me his blessing, and my mother took leave of me with tears, while my grandfather laid his hand upon my head and told me to remember and live up to the admonitions of the Sages, to avoid gambling, bad women and men of evil minds, and so to govern my conduct that when I died my ancestors might rejoice to welcome me as a guest on high.

My father gave me $100, and I went to Hong Kong with five other boys from our place and we got steerage passage on a steamer, paying $50 each. . . . Of the great power of these people I saw many signs. The engines that moved the ship were wonderful monsters, strong enough to lift mountains. When I got to San Francisco, which was before the passage of the Exclusion act [1882], I was half starved, because I was afraid to eat the provisions of the barbarians, but a few days' living in the Chinese quarter made me happy again. A man got me work as a house servant in an American family, and my start was the same as that of almost all the Chinese in this country.

The Chinese laundryman does not learn his trade in China; there are no laundries in China. The women there do the washing in tubs and have no washboards or flat irons. All the Chinese laundrymen here were taught in the first place by American women just as I was taught.

When I went to work for that American family I could not speak a word of English, and I did not know anything about housework. The family consisted of husband, wife and two children. They were very good to me and paid me $3.50 a week, of which I could save $3.

I did not know how to do anything, and I did not understand what the lady said to me, but she showed me how to cook, wash, iron, sweep, dust, make beds, wash dishes, clean windows, paint, and brass, polish the knives and forks, etc., by doing the things herself and then overseeing my efforts to imitate her. She would take my hands and show them how to do things. She and her husband and children laughed at me a great deal, but it was all good natured. I was not confined to the house in the way servants are confined here, but when my work was done in the morning I was allowed to go out till lunch time. People in California are more generous than they are here.

In six months I had learned how to do the work of our house quite well, and I was getting $5 a week and board, and putting away about $4.25 a week. I had also learned some English, and by going to a Sunday school I learned more English and something about Jesus, who was a great Sage, and whose precepts are like those of Kong-foo-tsze.

It was twenty years ago when I came to this country, and I worked for two years as a servant, getting at the last $35 a month. I sent money home to comfort my parents, but tho I dressed well and lived well and had pleasure, going quite often to the Chinese theater and to dinner parties in Chinatown, I saved $50 in the first six months, $90 in the second, $120 in the third and $150 in the fourth. So I had $410 at the end of two years, and I was now ready to start in business.

When I first opened a laundry it was in company with a partner, who had been in the business for some years. We went to a town about 500 miles inland, where a railroad was building. We got a board shanty and worked for the men employed by the railroads. Our rent cost us $10 a month and food nearly $5 a week each, for all food was dear and we wanted the best of everything—we lived principally on rice, chickens, ducks and pork, and did our own cooking. The Chinese take naturally to cooking. It cost us about $50 for our furniture and apparatus, and we made close upon $60 a week, which we divided between us. We had to put up with many insults and some frauds, as men would come in and

claim parcels that did not belong to them, saying they had lost their tickets, and would fight if they did not get what they asked for. Sometimes we were taken before Magistrates and fined for losing shirts that we had never seen. On the other hand, we were making money, and even after sending home $3 a week I was able to save about $15. When the railroad construction gang moved on we went with them. The men were rough and prejudiced against us, but not more so than in the big Eastern cities. It is only lately in New York that the Chinese have been able to discontinue putting wire screens in front of their windows, and at the present time the street boys are still breaking the windows of Chinese laundries all over the city, while the police seem to think it a joke.

We were three years with the railroad, and then went to the mines, where we made plenty of money in gold dust, but had a hard time, for many of the miners were wild men who carried revolvers and after drinking would come into our place to shoot and steal shirts, for which we had to pay. One of these men hit his head hard against a flat iron and all the miners came and broke up our laundry, chasing us out of town. They were going to hang us. We lost all our property and $365 in money, which members of the mob must have found.

Luckily most of our money was in the hands of Chinese bankers in San Francisco. I drew $500 and went East to Chicago, where I had a laundry for three years, during which I increased my capital to $2,500. After that I was four years in Detroit. I went home to China in 1897, but returned in 1898, and began a laundry business in Buffalo. But Chinese laundry business now is not as good as it was ten years ago. American cheap labor in the steam laundries had hurt it. So I determined to become a general merchant, and with this idea I came to New York and opened a shop in the Chinese quarter. . . .

The ordinary laundry shop is generally divided into three rooms. In front is the room where the customers are received, behind that a bedroom and in the back the work shop, which is also the dining room and kitchen. The stove and cooking utensils are the same as those of the Americans.

Work in a laundry begins early on Monday morning—about seven o'clock. There are generally two men, one of whom washes while the other does the ironing. The man who irons does not start in till Tuesday, as the clothes are not ready for him to begin till that time. So he has Sundays and Mondays as holidays. The man who does the washing finishes up on Friday night, and so he has Saturday and Sunday. Each works only five days a week, but those are long days—from seven o'clock in the morning till midnight.

During his holidays the Chinaman gets a good deal of fun out of life. There's a good deal of gambling and some opium smoking, but not so much as Americans imagine. Only a few of New York's Chinamen smoke opium. The habit is very general among rich men and the officials in China, but not so much among poor men. I don't think it does as much harm as the liquor that the Americans drink. There's nothing so bad as a drunken man. Opium doesn't make people crazy. . . .

The fights among the Chinese and the operations of the hatchet men are all due to gambling. Newspapers often say that there are feuds between the six companies, but that is a mistake. The six companies are purely benevolent societies, which look after the Chinaman when he first lands here. They represent the six southern provinces of China, where most of our people are from, and they are like the German, Swedish, English, Irish and Italian societies which assist emigrants. When the Chinese keep clear of gambling and opium they are not blackmailed, and they have no trouble with hatchet men or any others.

About 500 of New York's Chinese are Christians, the others are Buddhists, Taoists, etc., all mixed up. These haven't any Sunday of their own, but keep New Year's Day and the first and fifteenth days of each month, when they go to the temple in Mott Street.

In all New York there are only thirty-four Chinese women, and it is impossible to get a Chinese woman out here unless one goes to China and marries her there, and then he must collect affidavits to prove that she really is his wife. That is in case of a merchant. A laundryman can't bring his wife here under any circumstances, and even the women of the Chinese Ambassador's family had trouble getting in lately.

Is it any wonder, therefore, or any proof of the demoralization of our people if some of the white women in Chinatown are not of good character?

What other set of men so isolated and so surrounded by alien and prejudiced people are more moral? Men, wherever they may be, need the society of women, and among the white women of Chinatown are many excellent and faithful wives and mothers. . . .

I have found out, during my residence in this country, that much of the Chinese prejudice against Americans is unfounded, and I no longer put faith in the wild tales that were told about them in our village, tho some of the Chinese, who have been here twenty years and who are learned men, still believe that there is no marriage in this country, that the land is infested with demons and that all the people are given over to general wickedness.

I know better. Americans are not all bad, nor are they wicked wizards. Still, they have their faults, and their treatment of us is outrageous.

The reason why so many Chinese go into the laundry business in this country is because it requires little capital and is one of the few opportunities that are open. Men of other nationalities who are jealous of the Chinese, because he is a more faithful worker than one of their people, have raised such a great outcry about Chinese cheap labor that they have shut him out of working on farms or in factories or building railroads or making streets or digging sewers. He cannot practice any trade, and his opportunities to do business are limited to his own countrymen. So he opens a laundry when he quits domestic service.

The treatment of the Chinese in this country is all wrong and mean. It is persisted in merely because China is not a fighting nation. The Americans would not dare to treat Germans, English, Italians or even Japanese as they treat the Chinese, because if they did there would be a war.

There is no reason for the prejudice against the Chinese. The cheap labor cry was always a falsehood. Their labor was never cheap, and is not cheap now. It has always commanded the highest market price. But the trouble is that the Chinese are such excellent and faithful workers that bosses will have no others when they can get them. If you look at men working on the street you will find an overseer for every four or five of them. That watching is not necessary for Chinese. They work as well when left to themselves as they do when some one is looking at them.

It was the jealousy of laboring men of other nationalities—especially the Irish—that raised all the outcry against the Chinese. No one would hire an Irishman, German, Englishman or Italian when he could get a Chinese, because our countrymen are so much more honest, industrious, steady, sober and painstaking. Chinese were persecuted, not for their vices, but for their virtues. There never was any honesty in the pretended fear of leprosy or in the cheap labor scare, and the persecution continues still, because Americans make a mere practice of loving justice. They are all for money making, and they want to be on the strongest side always. They treat you as a friend while you are prosperous, but if you have a misfortune they don't know you. There is nothing substantial in their friendship. . . .

Irish fill the almshouses and prisons and orphan asylums, Italians are among the most dangerous of men, Jews are unclean and ignorant. Yet they are all let in, while Chinese, who are sober, or duly law abiding, clean, educated and industrious, are shut out. There are few Chinamen in jails and none in the poor houses. There are no Chinese tramps or drunkards. Many Chinese here have become sincere Christians, in spite of the persecution which they have to endure from their heathen countrymen. More than half the Chinese in this country would become citizens if allowed to do so, and would be patriotic Americans. But how can they make this country their home as matters now are! They are not allowed to bring wives here from China, and if they marry American women there is a great outcry.

All Congressmen acknowledge the injustice of the treatment of my people, yet they continue it. They have no backbone.

Under the circumstances, how can I call this my home, and how can any one blame me if I take my money and go back to my village in China?[4]

5. "JEWTOWN" (1890)

JACOB RIIS

Thrift is the watchword of Jewtown, as of its people the world over. It is at once its strength and its fatal weakness, its cardinal virtue and its foul disgrace. Become an overmastering passion with these people who come here in droves from Eastern Europe to escape persecution, from which freedom could be bought only with gold, it has enslaved them in bondage worse than that from which they fled. Money is their God. Life itself is of little value compared with even the leanest bank account. In no other spot does life wear so intensely bald and materialistic an aspect as in Ludlow Street. Over and over again I have met with instances of these Polish or Russian Jews deliberately starving themselves to the point of physical exhaustion, while working night and day at a tremendous pressure to save a little money. An avenging Nemesis pursues this headlong hunt for wealth; there is no worse paid class anywhere. . . .

Penury and poverty are wedded everywhere to dirt and disease, and Jewtown is no exception. It could not well be otherwise in such crowds, considering especially their low intellectual status. The managers of the Eastern Dispensary, which is in the very heart of their district, told the whole story when they said: "The diseases these people suffer from are not due to intemperance or immorality, but to ignorance, want of suitable food, and the foul air in which they live and work." The homes of the Hebrew quarter are its workshops also. Reference will be made to the economic conditions under which they work in a succeeding chapter. Here we are concerned simply with the fact. You are made fully aware of it before you have travelled the length of a single block in any of these East Side streets, by the whir of a thousand sewing-machines, worked at high pressure from earliest dawn till mind and muscle give out together. Every member of the family, from the youngest to the oldest, bears a hand, shut in the qualmy rooms, where meals are cooked and clothing washed and dried besides, the live-long day. It is not unusual to find a dozen persons—men, women, and children—at work in a single small room. . . .

Oppression, persecution, have not shorn the Jew of his native combativeness one whit. He is as ready to fight for his rights, or what he considers his rights, in a business transaction—synonymous generally with his advantage—as if he had not been robbed of them for eighteen hundred years. One strong impression survives with him from his days of bondage: the power of the law. On the slightest provocation he rushes off to invoke it for his protection. . . .

In all matters pertaining to their religious life that tinges all their customs, they stand, these East Side Jews, where the new day that dawned on Calvary left them standing, stubbornly refusing to see the light. A visit to a Jewish house of mourning is like bridging the gap of two thousand years. The inexpressibly sad and sorrowful wail for the dead, as it swells and rises in the hush of all sounds of life, comes back from the ages like a mournful echo of the voice of Rachel "weeping for her children and refusing to be comforted, because they are not."

Attached to many of the synagogues, which among the poorest Jews frequently consist of a scantily furnished room in a rear tenement, with a few wooden stools or benches for the congregation, are Talmudic schools that absorb a share of the growing youth. The school-master is not rarely a man of some

Image 4.3 Jacob Riis, "Knee Pants" at forty five cents a dozen—A Ludlow Street Sweater's Shop
Source: Museum of the City of New York. 90.13.4.151.

attainments who has been stranded there, his native instinct for money-making having been smothered in the process that has made of him a learned man. . . . But the majority of the children seek the public schools, where they are received sometimes with some misgivings on the part of the teachers, who find it necessary to inculcate lessons of cleanliness in the worst cases by practical demonstration with wash-bowl and soap. "He took hold of the soap as if it were some animal," said one of these teachers to me after such an experiment upon a new pupil, "and wiped three fingers across his face. He called that washing." . . .

As scholars, the children of the most ignorant Polish Jew keep fairly abreast of their more favored playmates, until it comes to mental arithmetic, when they leave them behind with a bound. It is surprising to see how strong the instinct of dollars and cents is in them. They can count, and correctly, almost before they can talk.[5]

6. "A CAP MAKER'S STORY" (1905)

ROSE SCHNEIDERMAN

[Miss Schneiderman led the women capmakers in their recent successful strike for the union shop. She is a small, quiet, serious, good looking young woman of twenty years, already a member of the National Board, and fast rising in the labor world. —*Editor*.]

My name is Rose Schneiderman, and I was born in some small city of Russian Poland. I don't know the name of the city, and have no memory of that part of my childhood. When I was about five years of age my parents brought me to this country and we settled in New York.

So my earliest recollections are of living in a crowded street among the East Side Jews, for we also are Jews.

My father got work as a tailor, and we lived in two rooms on Eldridge Street, and did very well, though not so well as in Russia, because mother and father both earned money, and here father alone earned the money, while mother attended to the house. There were then two other children besides me, a boy of three and one of five.

I went to school until I was nine years old, enjoying it thoroughly and making great progress, but then my father died of brain fever and mother was left with three children and another one coming. So I had to stay at home to help her and she went out to look for work.

A month later the baby was born, and mother got work in a fur house, earning about $6 a week and afterward $8 a week, for she was clever and steady.

I was the house worker, preparing the meals and looking after the other children—the baby, a little girl of six years, and a boy of nine. I managed very well, tho the meals were not very elaborate. I could cook simple things like porridge, coffee and eggs, and mother used to prepare the meat before she went away in the morning, so that all I had to do was to put it in the pan at night. . . .

When the other children were sent away mother was able to send me back to school, and I stayed in this school (Houston Street Grammar) till I had reached the Sixth Grammar Grade.

Then I had to leave in order to help support the family. I got a place in Hearn's as a cash girl, and after working there three weeks changed to Ridley's, where I remained for two and a half years. I finally left because the pay was so very poor and there did not seem to be any chance of advancement, and a friend told me that I could do better making caps.

So I got a place in the factory of Hein & Fox. The hours were from 8 A.M. to 6 P.M., and we made all sorts of linings—or, rather, we stitched in the linings—golf caps, yachting caps, etc. It was piece work, and we received from 3 1/2 cents to 10 cents a dozen, according to the different grades. By working hard we could make an average of about $5 a week. We would have made more but had to provide our own machines, which cost us $45, we paying for them on the installment plan. We paid $5 down and $1 a month after that.

I learned the business in about two months, and then made as much as the others, and was consequently doing quite well when the factory burned down, destroying all our machines—150 of them. This was very hard on the girls who had paid for their machines. It was not so bad for me, as I had only paid a little of what I owed.

The bosses got $500,000 insurance, so I heard, but they never gave the girls a cent to help them bear their losses. I think they might have given them $10, anyway.

Soon work went on again in four lofts, and a little later I became assistant sample maker. This is a position which, tho coveted by many, pays better in glory than in cash. It was still piece work, and tho the pay per dozen was better the work demanded was of a higher quality, and one could not rush through samples as through the other caps. So I still could average only about $5 per week.

After I had been working as a cap maker for three years it began to dawn on me that we girls needed an organization. The men had organized already, and had gained some advantages, but the bosses had lost nothing, as they took it out of us.

We were helpless; no one girl dare stand up for anything alone. Matters kept getting worse. The bosses kept making reductions in our pay, half a cent a dozen at a time. It did not sound important, but at the end of the week we found a difference.

We didn't complain to the bosses; we didn't say anything except to each other. There was no use. The bosses would not pay any attention unless we were like the men and could make them attend. . . .

A new girl from another shop got in among us. She was Miss Bessie Brout, and she talked organization as a remedy for our ills. She was radical and progressive, and she stimulated thoughts which were already in our minds before she came.

Finally Miss Brout and I and another girl went to the National Board of United Cloth Hat and Cap Makers when it was in session, and asked them to organize the girls. . . .

We were told to come to the next meeting of the National Board, which we did, and then received a favorable answer, and were asked to bring all the girls who were willing to be organized to the next

meeting, and at the next meeting, accordingly, we were there twelve strong and were organized.

When Fox found out what had happened he discharged Miss Brout, and probably would have discharged me but that I was a sample maker and not so easy to replace. In a few weeks we had all the girls in the organization, because the men told the girls that they must enter the union or they would not be allowed to work in the shop.

Then came a big strike. Price lists for the coming season were given in to the bosses, to which they did not agree. After some wrangling a strike was declared in five of the biggest factories. There are 30 factories in the city. About 100 girls went out.

The result was a victory, which netted us—I mean the girls—$2 increase in our wages on the average.

All the time our union was progressing very nicely. There were lectures to make us understand what trades unionism is and our real position in the labor movement. I read upon the subject and grew more and more interested, and after a time I became a member of the National Board, and had duties and responsibilities that kept me busy after my day's work was done.

But all was not lovely by any means, for the bosses were not at all pleased with their beating and had determined to fight us again.

They agreed among themselves that after the 26th of December, 1904, they would run their shops on the "open" system.

This agreement was reached last fall, and soon notices, reading as follows, were hung in the various shops:

Notice
After the 26th of December, 1904, this shop will be run on the open shop system, the bosses having the right to engage and discharge employees as they see fit, whether the latter are union or nonunion.

Of course, we knew that this meant an attack on the union. The bosses intended gradually to get rid of us, employing in our place child labor and raw immigrant girls who would work for next to nothing.

On December 22d the above notice appeared, and the National Board, which had known about it all along, went into session prepared for action.

Our people were very restive, saying that they could not sit under that notice, and that if the National Board did not call them out soon they would go out of themselves.

At last word was sent out, and at 2:30 o'clock all the workers stopped, and, laying down their scissors and other tools, marched out, some of them singing the "Marseillaise."

We were out for thirteen weeks, and the girls established their reputation. They were on picket duty from seven o'clock in the morning till six o'clock in the evening, and gained over many of the nonunion workers by appeals to them to quit working against us.

Our theory was that if properly approached and talked to few would be found who would resist our offer to take them into our organization. No right thinking person desires to injure another. We did not believe in violence and never employed it.

During this strike period we girls each received $3 a week; single men $3 a week, and married men $5 a week. This was paid us by the National Board.

We were greatly helped by the other unions, because the open shop issue was a tremendous one, and this was the second fight which the bosses had conducted for it.

Their first was with the tailors, whom they beat. If they now could beat us the outlook for unionism would be bad.

Some were aided and we stuck out, and won a glorious victory all along the line. That was only last week. The shops are open now for all union hands and for them only. . . .

The bosses try to represent this open shop issue as tho they were fighting a battle for the public, but really it is nothing of the sort. The open shop is a weapon to break the unions and set men once more cutting each other's throats by individual competition.

Why, there was a time in the cap trade when men worked fourteen hours a day, and then took the heads of their machines home in bags and setting them up on stands, put mattresses underneath to deaden the sound and worked away till far into the morning.

We don't want such slavery as that to come back.

The shops are open now for all union people, and all nonunion people can join the union. In order to take in newcomer foreigners we have for them cut the initiation fees down to one-half what we Americans have to pay, and we trust them till they get work and their wages.

In order to give the newcomers a chance we have stopped night work, which doesn't suit the bosses, because it causes them to pay more rent when they can't use their buildings night and day. It costs them the price of another loft instead of costing the workers their health and lives as in the old days.

Our trade is well organized, we have won two victories and are not going backward.

But there is much to be done in other directions. The shop girls certainly need organization, and I think that they ought to be easy to organize, as their duties are simple and regular and they have a regular scale of wages.

Many saleswomen on Grand and Division streets, and, in fact, all over the East Side, work from 8 A.M. till 9 P.M. week days, and one-half a day on Sundays for $5 and $6 a week; so they certainly need organization.

The waitresses also could easily be organized, and perhaps the domestic servants. I don't know about stenographers. I have not come in contact with them.

Women have proved in the late strike that they can be faithful to an organization and to each other. The men give us the credit of winning the strike.

Certainly our organization constantly grows stronger, and the Woman's Trade Union League makes progress.

The girls and women by their meetings and discussions come to understand and sympathize with each other, and more and more easily they act together.

It is the only way in which they can hope to hold what they now have or better present conditions.

Certainly there is no hope from the mercy of the bosses.

Each boss does the best he can for himself with no thought of the other bosses, and that compels each to gouge and squeeze his hands to the last penny in order to make a profit.

So we must stand together to resist, for we will get what we can take—just that and no more.[6]

POSTSCRIPT

In 1921, 1924, and 1927, Congress passed a series of laws to restrict the flow of immigrants. The legislation targeted southern and eastern Europeans as well as Asians. These laws were woven out of several ideological strands: Resurgent fundamentalist Protestantism perceived Catholics as a major threat; immigrants were viewed (with some justification) as major participants in the strikes and radical movements of the post-World War I period and so were accused of being un-American; and citizens from old families grew increasingly concerned about the so-called dilution of American stock, upholding their Anglo-Saxon ancestry as the key to national greatness. This last was a particularly insidious form of racism and was uppermost in Joseph Pennell's thinking as he wandered the streets of Lower Manhattan in 1921. Whereas Jacob Riis would reform the immigrants into Americans, the new trend was toward exclusion. By the late 1920s, total immigration was capped at about 250,000 per year, with western and northern Europe receiving much higher quotas than countries from the east or the south. Immigration did not reemerge as a vital factor in American life until the last decades of the twentieth century, when new laws made it possible for migrants, especially from Latin America and Asia, to come to the United States in numbers comparable to those of the late nineteenth and early twentieth centuries. Then in the early twenty-first century came a resurgence of nativism.

QUESTIONS

1. Compare Riis's narrative and visual depictions of immigrant groups with the interviews.
2. How do you think these three immigrants would have defined success? Had they achieved it by their own standards? By the standards of the larger society?
3. To what extent did these immigrants consider themselves American? To what extent Chinese, Italian, or Jewish? Do you think it is possible to combine an American identity with some other affiliation?
4. How were the three immigrants whose life stories you read typical or atypical?
5. How did Corresca, Lee, and Schneiderman differ in their memories of their homelands? In their attitudes toward America? In their desciptions of work? What do you think accounted for the differences? How did they feel about other immigrants?
6. How are today's conflicts over immigration similar or different from those a century ago?

ADDITIONAL READING

The classic work on nativism is John Higham's *Strangers in the Land: Patterns of American Nativism, 1860–1925* (1955). Oscar Handlin's *The Uprooted: The Epic Story of the Great Migration That Made the American People* (1951) remains a moving study of the pressures immigrants felt to abandon their native cultures, but also see John Bodnar's *The Transplanted* (1987). Other studies have emphasized ethnic groups' success in community building. For examples, see Irving Howe, *World of Our Fathers* (1976), and Ronald Takaki, *Strangers from a Different Shore: A History of Asian Americans* (1989). For a marvelous immigrant autobiography, see Marie Hall Ets, ed., *Rosa: The Life of an Italian Immigrant* (1970). For a survey of diverse immigrant experiences, see Stephan Thernstrom, ed., *The Harvard Encyclopedia of American Ethnic Groups* (1980). For a fine anthology of women's writings, see Ellen Dubois and Vicki Ruiz, eds., *Unequal Sisters* (1990). More recent studies emphasize the connections between ethnicity and race, such as Matthew Frye Jacobson, *Whiteness of a Different Color* (1999); Thomas Guglielmo, *White on Arrival: Italians, Race, Color, and*

Power in Chicago, 1890-1945 (2004); and David Roediger, *Working Toward Whiteness: How America's Immigrants Became White* (2006). On recent immigration, see David Reimers, *Still the Golden Door: the Third World Comes to America* (1992), and especially Mae Ngai, *Impossible Subjects: Illegal Aliens and the Making of Modern America* (2005).

ENDNOTES

1. Jacob Riis, *How the Other Half Lives; Studies among the Tenements of New York* (New York: Charles Scribner's Sons, 1890), pp. 48–53.
2. *The Independent*, v.54 (December 4, 1902).
3. Riis, *How the Other Half Lives*, pp. 93–102.
4. *The Independent*, v.55 (February 19, 1903).
5. Riis, *How the Other Half Lives*, pp. 106–114.
6. *The Independent*, v.58 (April 27, 1905).

CHAPTER 5

THE RISE OF AN AMERICAN OVERSEAS EMPIRE

HISTORICAL CONTEXT

Woodrow Wilson once declared Theodore Roosevelt "the most dangerous man of the age." Mark Twain called him "clearly insane" and added that Roosevelt was "insanest upon war and its supreme glories." Yet Roosevelt exercised an almost magical pull on the imagination of Americans. He was the very personification of energy. Even as president, he boxed and wrestled in the White House, took grueling cross-country hikes, and, after he stepped down from the presidency in 1909, went on a long hunting safari in Africa. Small and anemic as a child, he whipped his body into shape with strenuous rounds of swimming, calisthenics, and gymnastics. At Harvard in the 1870s, he was known for his sheer doggedness, if not his raw talent, as an athlete. Descriptions of his speeches as governor of New York in the 1890s refer endlessly to the way that his hands chopped the air, his body danced, his voice bristled, and his eyeglasses flashed. If, as the historian John Higham claims, there was a vigorous new spirit and an upbeat tempo in turn-of-the-century America, then Theodore Roosevelt was its embodiment.

One thing Roosevelt was not, however, was an example of the rags-to-riches mythology of American culture. He was born in 1858 to one of the wealthiest families in New York City, heir to a Dutch fortune as old as the colony itself. Yet wealth did not confer ease. Like many men and women born to elite, or Brahmin, families, as they were known, privilege meant responsibility, a Calvinist sense of stewardship in which the "elect" must help take care of the less fortunate. Roosevelt grew up in a family of jurists, public servants, and philanthropists, and he was imbued early with a powerful sense of social duty.

The selection by Roosevelt in this chapter is from an essay that he wrote in the years just before he became president. Read carefully, it reveals his underlying assumptions and values, what we might call his *ideology*. Ideology includes a person's or a society's fundamental beliefs about how the world is structured and what the relationship of individuals or nations to each other should be; it also includes their beliefs about the uses of power and the very nature of the social order.

For example, a simple statement such as "In America, any man can become president" is ideological. In the most literal sense, it is a true statement, for any native-born male who is not a felon and is over the age of thirty-five *can* run for the office of president; no legal barriers stand in his way. But when people use this phrase, they mean something more. They are expressing an ideal of equality, the faith that a person's own drive and talent are the keys to advancement in this society. To say that any man can become president is short-hand for the American dream, the belief that this nation offers equal and virtually unlimited opportunity for all and that such openness is one of the greatest things about our country. Yet ideological statements, even as they purport to describe reality, tend to confuse the way things are with the way we would like them to be.

American foreign policy at the end of the nineteenth century became a focus of deep ideological tensions. As the country grew increasingly involved in overseas business and military ventures, Americans debated the proper place of a democracy in a world divided between imperial powers and their colonies. Just as in the war between the United States and Mexico fifty years earlier, the conflicts at the end of the nineteenth century had been shaped by the presence of the old Spanish Empire in the western hemisphere.

Cuba lies less than 100 miles off the Florida coast. Before the Civil War, southerners coveted the island as an extension of the slave empire. For decades, the Cuban people had sought their independence from Spain in a series of rebellions, and a new round of insurgency and repression beginning in 1895 brought a wave of American sympathy for the rebels. American newspapers whipped up sentiment for the underdog Cubans, as Spain moved to crush the uprising. Moreover, large American companies had invested millions of dollars in Cuban sugar plantations, and these companies wanted to secure stable markets against political upheaval. President William McKinley resisted calls for American intervention until 1898. The revelation of a secret cable by the Spanish minister to the United States calling McKinley weak and hypocritical, followed by the mysterious blowing up of the U.S. battleship *Maine*, docked in Havana harbor (262 sailors perished on the ship sent to Cuba to protect Americans), made the pressure for American intervention irresistible. McKinley asked Congress for a declaration of war.

The war was popular, quick, and glorious. The Spanish colonies of Cuba, Guam, Puerto Rico, and the Philippines all fell with only a few hundred American battle deaths (though over 5,000 died of tropical diseases). Naval confrontations in Santiago Bay and Manila Bay were even more decisive, as American ships destroyed the Spanish fleet while sustaining minimal damage and casualties.

With victory came the controversial question about what to do with Spain's former colonies. By August 1898, an armistice had ended hostilities, but within half a year, Filipinos and Americans—former allies—were locked in combat with each other. The Treaty of Paris ceded all 7,000 islands of the Philippine archipelago to the United States, in exchange for $20 million. But Philippine rebels were not willing to trade Spain's domination for America's. By February 1899, Congress had approved the treaty with Spain, McKinley was on the verge of calling for Philippine annexation, and a bloody two-year struggle had begun. Before it was over, more than 100,000 Americans served in the Philippines; over 4,000 of them died, and another 3,000 were wounded. Nearly 20,000 Filipinos were killed in combat, and ten times that number died of starvation and disease, as the American military pursued a policy of burning villages and destroying farms.

View of wreck of "*Maine*" from aft. 19 – 9 – 21

Image 5.1 View of the wreck of the *Maine* in Havana Harbor, 1898

The sinking of the *Maine* sparked widespread anger among Americans, and the incident eventually became a justification for war with Spain.

Source: Courtesy U.S. Naval History and Heritage Command, NH 46774.

Those Americans who opposed annexation were never a majority, but they were very vocal and included such diverse people as Andrew Carnegie, Jane Addams, William Jennings Bryan, Mark Twain, Samuel Gompers, and former presidents Harrison and Cleveland. Their arguments ranged widely. Friends of unions worried that new territories meant a cheap source of labor for business, undercutting American workers. Prejudiced men like Senator Ben Tillman of South Carolina declared that freeing Spain's colonies was a patriotic act but that annexing those territories to the United States would not only defy our democratic principles but contaminate American blood with "inferior" racial stock. Still others argued that an empire would overextend an already troubled American economy or that it would dangerously expand the powers of the presidency, or that a colonial empire simply could not be reconciled with deep American principles of freedom and self-determination. Proponents of overseas expansion argued that other imperial powers would seize the islands if the United States failed to, that America was obliged to civilize and Christianize "inferior" peoples, that an empire would open new markets and bring prosperity to all, and that overseas expansion meant glory and honor for the military.

Image 5.2 Advertisement, "Uncle Sam Is Expanding" (1898)

The quick victory over Spain led many Americans to marvel at their nation's extended new reach into the Pacific and the Caribbean. Even commercial advertisers traded on the nation's nationalistic fervor.

Source: Courtesy Library of Congress.

The following documents are filled with ideological positions on politics, foreign policy, labor, gender, race, and ethnicity. As you read these selections, try to uncover their authors' underlying ideological assumptions. What were their social ideals? How did they believe groups interacted or ought to interact? With what tone did they address their audience, and who was that audience?

INTRODUCTION TO DOCUMENTS 1 AND 2

Albert J. Beveridge was elected Republican senator from Indiana in 1898, when he was just thirty-six years old. The following speech, "The March of the Flag," was delivered first in Indianapolis in September 1898, after the victory over Spain but before the Treaty of Paris ceded the Philippines to the United States. Beveridge's speech became a kind of manifesto of American expansionism during this era, and it was widely reprinted. Note how seamlessly he merged America's God-given mission in the world to elevate those less "civilized" than ourselves, the almost mystical spread of freedom wherever the American flag waved, the need for the United States to compete with other imperial powers, and the benefits (moral as well as economic) of opening up new overseas markets. All were part of a historical pageant of progress from Bunker Hill to Manila Bay. Beveridge gave this speech countless times.

William Graham Sumner, on the contrary, viewed recent events as a betrayal of all that America stood for. Sumner was a professor of sociology at Yale and one of the best-known intellectuals of his day. He had popularized the concept of "social Darwinism" in America, which held that social groups—nations, classes, and businesses—competed for resources, and that, on balance, the most fit among them lived and the weakest perished, ensuring progress through the survival of the strong. Sumner's assumption was that social evolution, like natural selection, created the greatest good for the greatest number, cruel as that process might appear.

Sumner's was an austere view of history's unfolding, but since he assumed that people would wield force in hurtful ways, he advocated limiting the power of institutions. He believed that different peoples had their own values, beliefs, and patterns of interacting—their own folkways, as he called them—and that social life ran as smoothly as possible when these local ways were respected and kept uncontaminated by others. Sumner's ideas could lead in two directions: to an acceptance of provincialism, and even racism and nativism, but also to a hands-off policy toward foreign lands, based on the argument that colonization could only contaminate both cultures and bring on the hatred of those whom we subjugate. Sumner was deeply suspicious of government's tendency to acquire more and more power, and many conservative politicians, especially in the South and the West, agreed with him. The speech "The Conquest of the United States by Spain" was a Phi Beta Kappa address at Yale given in 1898, almost simultaneously with Beveridge's address. Had they met face to face, how might these two men have engaged in a debate over America's role abroad?

1. "THE MARCH OF THE FLAG" (1898)

ALBERT J. BEVERIDGE

It is a noble land that God has given us; a land that can feed and clothe the world; a land whose coastlines would inclose half the countries of Europe; a land set like a sentinel between the two imperial oceans of the globe, a greater England with a nobler destiny.

It is a mighty people that He has planted on this soil; a people sprung from the most masterful blood of history; a people perpetually revitalized by the virile, man-producing working-folk of all the earth; a people imperial by virtue of their power, by right of their institutions, by authority of their Heaven-directed purposes—the propagandists and not the misers of liberty.

It is a glorious history our God has bestowed upon His chosen people; a history heroic with faith in our mission and our future. . . .

. . . Shall the American people continue their march toward the commercial supremacy of the world? Shall free institutions broaden their blessed reign as the children of liberty wax in strength, until the empire of our principles is established over the hearts of all mankind?

Have we no mission to perform, no duty to discharge to our fellow-man? Has God endowed us with gifts beyond our deserts and marked us as the people of His peculiar favor, merely to rot in our own selfishness, as men and nations must, who take cowardice for their companion and self for their deity—as China has, as India has, as Egypt has? . . .

The Opposition tells us that we ought not to govern a people without their consent. I answer, The rule of liberty that all just government derives its authority from the consent of the governed, applies only to those who are capable of self-government. We govern the Indians without their consent, we govern our territories without their consent, we govern our children without their consent. How do they know that our government would be without their consent? Would not the people of the Philippines prefer the just, humane, civilizing government of this Republic to the savage, bloody rule of pillage and extortion from which we have rescued them?

And, regardless of this formula of words made only for enlightened, self-governing people, do we owe no duty to the world? Shall we turn these peoples back to the reeking hands from which we have taken them? Shall we abandon them, with Germany, England, Japan, hungering for them? Shall we save them from those nations, to give them a self-rule of tragedy? . . .

The march of the flag! In 1789 the flag of the Republic waved over 4,000,000 souls in thirteen states, and their savage territory which stretched to the Mississippi, to Canada, to the Floridas. The timid minds of that day said that no new territory was needed, and, for the hour, they were right. But Jefferson, through whose intellect the centuries marched; Jefferson, who dreamed of Cuba as an American state; Jefferson, the first Imperialist of the Republic—Jefferson acquired that imperial territory which swept from the Mississippi to the mountains, from Texas to the British possessions, and the march of the flag began!

The infidels to the gospel of liberty raved, but the flag swept on! The title to that noble land out of which Oregon, Washington, Idaho and Montana have been carved was uncertain; Jefferson, strict constructionist of constitutional power though he was, obeyed the Anglo-Saxon impulse within him, whose watchword then and whose watchword throughout the world to-day is, "Forward!": another empire was added to the Republic, and the march of the flag went on!

Those who deny the power of free institutions to expand urged every argument, and more, that we hear, to-day; but the people's judgment approved the command of their blood, and the march of the flag went on!

A screen of land from New Orleans to Florida shut us from the Gulf, and over this and the Everglade Peninsula waved the saffron flag of Spain; Andrew Jackson seized both, the American people stood at his back, and, under Monroe, the Floridas came under the dominion of the Republic, and the march of the flag went on! The Cassandras prophesied every prophecy of despair we hear, to-day, but the march of the flag went on!

Then Texas responded to the bugle calls of liberty, and the march of the flag went on! And, at last, we waged war with Mexico, and the flag swept over the southwest, over peerless California, past the Gate of Gold to Oregon on the north, and from ocean to ocean its folds of glory blazed.

And, now, obeying the same voice that Jefferson heard and obeyed, that Jackson heard and obeyed, that Monroe heard and obeyed, that Seward heard and obeyed, that Grant heard and obeyed, that Harrison heard and obeyed, our President to-day plants the flag over the islands of the seas, outposts of commerce, citadels of national security, and the march of the flag goes on! . . .

But the Opposition is right—there is a difference. We did not need the western Mississippi Valley when we acquired it, nor Florida, nor Texas, nor California, nor the royal provinces of the far northwest. We had no emigrants to people this imperial wilderness, no money to develop it, even no highways to cover it. No trade awaited us in its savage fastnesses. Our productions were not greater than our trade. There was not one reason for the land-lust of our statesmen from Jefferson to Grant, other than the prophet and the Saxon within them. But, to-day, we are raising more than we can consume, making more than we can use. Therefore we must find new markets for our produce.

And so, while we did not need the territory taken during the past century at the time it was acquired, we do need what we have taken in 1898, and we need it now. The resources and the commerce of these immensely rich dominions will be increased as much as American energy is greater than Spanish sloth. In Cuba, alone, there are 15,000,000 acres of forest unacquainted with the ax, exhaustless mines of iron, priceless deposits of manganese, millions of dollars' worth of which we must buy, to-day, from the Black Sea districts. There are millions of acres yet unexplored.

The resources of Porto Rico have only been trifled with. The riches of the Philippines have hardly been touched by the finger-tips of modern methods. And they produce what we consume, and consume what we produce—the very predestination of reciprocity—a reciprocity "not made with hands, eternal in the heavens." They sell hemp, sugar, cocoanuts, fruits of the tropics, timber of price like mahogany; they buy flour, clothing, tools, implements, machinery and all that we can raise and make. Their trade will be ours in time. Do you endorse that policy with your vote?

Cuba is as large as Pennsylvania, and is the richest spot on the globe. Hawaii is as large as New Jersey; Porto Rico half as large as Hawaii; the Philippines larger than all New England, New York, New Jersey and Delaware combined. Together they are larger than the British Isles, larger than France, larger than Germany, larger than Japan. . . .

So Hawaii furnishes us a naval base in the heart of the Pacific; the Ladrones another, a voyage further on; Manila another, at the gates of Asia—Asia, to the trade of whose hundreds of millions American merchants, manufacturers, farmers, have as good right as those of Germany or France or Russia or England; Asia, whose commerce with the United Kingdom alone amounts to hundreds of millions of dollars every year; Asia, to whom Germany looks to take her surplus products; Asia, whose doors must not be shut against American trade. Within five decades the bulk of Oriental commerce will be ours. . . .

Wonderfully has God guided us. Yonder at Bunker Hill and Yorktown His providence was above us. At New Orleans and on ensanguined seas His hand sustained us. Abraham Lincoln was His minister and His was the altar of freedom the Nation's soldiers set up on a hundred battle-fields. His power directed Dewey in the East and delivered the Spanish fleet into our hands, as He delivered the elder Armada into the hands of our English sires two centuries ago. . . . We can not fly from our world duties; it is ours to execute the purpose of a fate that has driven us to be greater than our small intentions. We can not retreat from any soil where Providence has unfurled our banner; it is ours to save that soil for liberty and civilization.[1]

2. "THE CONQUEST OF THE UNITED STATES BY SPAIN" (1898)

WILLIAM GRAHAM SUMNER

. . . Spain was the first, for a long time the greatest, of the modern imperialistic states. The United States, by its historical origin, its traditions, and its principles, is the chief representative of the revolt and reaction against that kind of state. I intend to show that, by the line of action now proposed to us, which we call expansion and imperialism, we are throwing away some of the most important elements of the American symbol and are adopting some of the most important elements of the Spanish symbol. We have beaten Spain in a military conflict, but we are submitting to be conquered by her on the field of ideas and policies. Expansionism and imperialism are nothing but the old philosophies of national prosperity which have brought Spain to where she now is. Those philosophies appeal to national vanity and national cupidity. They are seductive, especially upon the first view and the most superficial judgment, and therefore it cannot be denied that they are very strong for popular effect. They are delusions, and they will lead us to ruin unless we are hard-headed enough to resist them. . . .

There is not a civilized nation which does not talk about its civilizing mission just as grandly as we do. The English, who really have more to boast of in this respect than anybody else, talk least about it, but the Phariseeism with which they correct and instruct other people has made them hated all over the globe. The French believe themselves the guardians of the highest and purest culture, and that the eyes of all mankind are fixed on Paris, whence they expect oracles of thought and taste. The Germans regard themselves as charged with a mission, especially to us Americans, to save us from egoism and materialism. . . . Now each nation laughs at all the others when it observes these manifestations of national vanity. You may rely upon it that they are all ridiculous by virtue of these pretensions, including ourselves. The point is that each of them repudiates the standards of the others, and the outlying nations, which are to be civilized, hate all the standards of civilized men. . . .

We assume that what we like and practice, and what we think better, must come as a welcome blessing to Spanish-Americans and Filipinos. This is grossly and obviously untrue. They hate our ways. They are hostile to our ideas. Our religion, language, institutions, and manners offend them. They like their own ways, and if we appear amongst them as rulers, there will be social discord in all the great departments of social interest. The most important thing which we shall inherit from the Spaniards will be the task of suppressing rebellions. If the United States takes out of the hands of Spain her mission, on the ground that Spain is not executing it well, and if this nation in its turn attempts to be school-mistress to others, it will shrivel up into the same vanity and self-conceit of which Spain now presents an example. To read our current literature one would think

that we were already well on the way to it. Now, the great reason why all these enterprises which begin by saying to somebody else, "We know what is good for you better than you know yourself and we are going to make you do it," are false and wrong is that they violate liberty; or, to turn the same statement into other words, the reason why liberty, of which we Americans talk so much, is a good thing is that it means leaving people to live out their own lives in their own way, while we do the same. If we believe in liberty, as an American principle, why do we not stand by it? Why are we going to throw it away to enter upon a Spanish policy of dominion and regulation? . . .

There are plenty of people in the United States to-day who regard negroes as human beings, perhaps, but of a different order from white men, so that the ideas and social arrangements of white men cannot be applied to them with propriety. Others feel the same way about Indians. This attitude of mind, wherever you meet with it, is what causes tyranny and cruelty. . . . The doctrine that all men are equal has come to stand as one of the corner-stones of the temple of justice and truth. It was set up as a bar to just this notion that we are so much better than others that it is liberty for them to be governed by us.

The Americans have been committed from the outset to the doctrine that all men are equal. We have elevated it into an absolute doctrine as a part of the theory of our social and political fabric. It has always been a domestic dogma in spite of its absolute form, and as a domestic dogma it has always stood in glaring contradiction to the facts about Indians and negroes and to our legislation about Chinamen. In its absolute form it must, of course, apply to Kanakas, Malays, Tagals, and Chinese just as much as to Yankees, Germans, and Irish. It is an astonishing event that we have lived to see American arms carry this domestic dogma out where it must be tested in its application to uncivilized and half-civilized peoples. At the first touch of the test we throw the doctrine away and adopt the Spanish doctrine. We are told by all the imperialists that these people are not fit for liberty and self-government; that it is rebellion for them to resist our beneficence; that we must send fleets and armies to kill them if they do it; that we must devise a government for them and administer it ourselves;

that we may buy them or sell them as we please, and dispose of their "trade" for our own advantage. What is that but the policy of Spain to her dependencies? What can we expect as a consequence of it? Nothing but that it will bring us where Spain is now.

But then, if it is not right for us to hold these islands as dependencies, you may ask me whether I think that we ought to take them into our Union, at least some of them, and let them help to govern us. Certainly not. . . . It is unwisdom to take into a State like this any foreign element which is not congenial to it. Any such element will act as a solvent upon it. Consequently we are brought by our new conquests face to face with this dilemma: we must either hold them as inferior possessions, to be ruled and exploited by us after the fashion of the old colonial system, or we must take them in on an equality with ourselves, where they will help to govern us and to corrupt a political system which they do not understand and in which they cannot participate. From that dilemma there is no escape except to give them independence and to let them work out their own salvation or go without it. . . .

Everywhere you go on the continent of Europe at this hour you see the conflict between militarism and industrialism. You see the expansion of industrial power pushed forward by the energy, hope, and thrift of men, and you see the development arrested, diverted, crippled, and defeated by measures which are dictated by military considerations. . . . It is militarism which is eating up all the products of science and art, defeating the energy of the population and wasting its savings. It is militarism which forbids the people to give their attention to the problems of their own welfare and to give their strength to the education and comfort of their children. It is militarism which is combating the grand efforts of science and art to ameliorate the struggle for existence. . . .

Now what will hasten the day when our present advantages will wear out and when we shall come down to the conditions of the older and densely populated nations? The answer is: war, debt, taxation, diplomacy, a grand governmental system, pomp, glory, a big army and navy, lavish expenditures, political jobbery—in a word, imperialism. . . .

Expansion and imperialism are at war with the best traditions, principles, and interests of the American people. . . . They will plunge us into a network of difficult problems and political perils, which we might have avoided, while they offer us no corresponding advantage in return. . . . Three years ago we were on the verge of a law to keep immigrants out who were not good enough to be in with us. Now we are going to take in eight million barbarians and semi-barbarians, and we are paying twenty million dollars to get them. . . . That is the great fundamental cause of what I have tried to show throughout this lecture, that we cannot govern dependencies consistently with our political system, and that, if we try it, the State which our fathers founded will suffer a reaction which will transform it into another empire just after the fashion of all the old ones. That is what imperialism means. That is what it will be; and the democratic republic, which has been, will stand in history, like the colonial organization of earlier days, as a mere transition form. . . .

My patriotism is of the kind which is outraged by the notion that the United States never was a great nation until in a petty three months' campaign it knocked to pieces a poor, decrepit, bankrupt old state like Spain. To hold such an opinion as that is to abandon all American standards, to put shame and scorn on all that our ancestors tried to build up here, and to go over to the standards of which Spain is a representative.[2]

INTRODUCTION TO DOCUMENT 3

Theodore Roosevelt was one of the most aggressive advocates of overseas empire. He was part of a group of like-minded men who pushed for expansion—men such as Senator Henry Cabot Lodge, Admiral Alfred Thayer Mahan, and historian Brooks Adams, all of whom were from powerful and wealthy families. Roosevelt became the most prominent spokesman for liberating Cuba and the Philippines from Spanish rule, annexing Hawaii, and asserting American military might around the world. Moreover, as assistant secretary of the Navy in the late 1890s, he was in a position to build up American sea power and beat the drums of war from inside the government. When the Spanish–American War began, Roosevelt resigned his job, obtained a commission as colonel, raised a regiment known as the Rough Riders, and led his men in a charge up San Juan Hill in Cuba. Document 3 is taken from Roosevelt's speech "The Strenuous Life," given to an audience of businessmen and local leaders at the Hamilton Club in Chicago on April 10, 1899. The very phrase "the strenuous life" became an emblem for the age of Roosevelt.

3. "THE STRENUOUS LIFE" (1899)

THEODORE ROOSEVELT

In speaking to you, men of the greatest city of the West, men of the State which gave to the country Lincoln and Grant, men who preeminently and distinctly embody all that is most American in the American character, I wish to preach, not the doctrine of ignoble ease, but the doctrine of the strenuous life, the life of toil and effort, of labor and strife; to preach that highest form of success which comes, not to the man who desires mere easy peace, but to the man who does not shrink from danger, from hardship, or from bitter toil, and who out of these wins the splendid ultimate triumph.

A life of slothful ease, a life of that peace which springs merely from lack either of desire or of power to strive after great things, is as little worthy of a nation as of an individual. I ask only that what every self-respecting American demands from himself and from his sons shall be demanded of the American nation as a whole. Who among you would teach your boys that ease, that peace, is to be the first consideration in their eyes—to be the ultimate goal after which they strive? . . . We do not admire the man of timid peace. We admire the man who embodies victorious effort; the man who never wrongs his neighbor, who is prompt to help a friend, but who has those virile qualities necessary to win the stern strife of actual life. . . . A mere life of ease is not in the end a very satisfactory life, and, above all, it is a life which ultimately unfits those who follow it for serious work in the world.

In the last analysis a healthy state can exist only when the men and women who make it up lead clean, vigorous, healthy lives; when the children are so trained that they shall endeavor, not to shirk difficulties, but to overcome them; not to seek ease, but to know how to wrest triumph from toil and risk. The man must be glad to do a man's work, to dare and endure and to labor; to keep himself, and to keep those dependent upon him. The woman must be the housewife, the helpmeet of the homemaker, the wise and fearless mother of many healthy children. . . . When men fear work or fear righteous war, when women fear motherhood, they tremble on the brink of doom; and well it is that they should vanish from the earth, where they are fit subjects for the scorn of all men and women who are themselves strong and brave and high-minded.

As it is with the individual, so it is with the nation. It is a base untruth to say that happy is the nation that has no history. Thrice happy is the nation that has a glorious history. Far better it is to dare mighty things, to win glorious triumphs, even though checkered by failure, than to take rank with those poor spirits who neither enjoy much nor suffer much, because they live in the gray twilight that knows not victory nor defeat. If in 1861 the men who loved the Union had believed that peace was the end of all things, and war and strife the worst of all things, and had acted up to their belief, we would have saved hundreds of thousands of lives, we would have saved hundreds of millions of dollars. Moreover, besides saving all the blood and treasure we then lavished, we would have prevented the heartbreak of many women, the dissolution of many homes, and we would have spared the country those months of gloom and shame when it seemed as if our armies marched only to defeat. We could have avoided all this suffering simply by shrinking from strife. And if we had thus avoided it, we would have shown that we were weaklings, and that we were unfit to stand among the great nations of the earth. Thank God for the iron in the blood of our fathers, the men who upheld the wisdom of Lincoln, and bore sword or rifle in the armies of Grant! Let us, the children of the men who proved themselves equal to the mighty days, let us, the children of the men who carried the great Civil War to a triumphant conclusion, praise the God of our fathers that the ignoble counsels of peace were rejected; that the suffering and loss, the blackness of sorrow and despair, were unflinchingly faced, and the years of strife endured; for in the end the slave was freed, the Union restored, and the mighty American republic placed once more as a helmeted queen among nations.

We of this generation do not have to face a task such as that our fathers faced, but we have our tasks, and woe to us if we fail to perform them! . . . We cannot avoid meeting great issues. All that we can determine for ourselves is whether we shall meet them well or ill. In 1898 we could not help being brought face to face with the problem of war with Spain. All we could decide was whether we should shrink like cowards from the contest, or enter into it as beseemed a brave and high-spirited people; and, once in, whether failure or success should crown our banners. So it is now. We cannot avoid the responsibilities that confront us in Hawaii, Cuba, Porto Rico, and the Philippines. All we can decide is whether we shall meet them in a way that will redound to the national credit, or whether we shall make of our dealings with these new problems a dark and shameful page in our history. To refuse to deal with them at all merely amounts to dealing with them badly. We have a given problem to solve. If we undertake the solution, there is, of course, always danger that we may not solve it aright; but to refuse to undertake the solution simply renders it certain that we cannot possibly solve it aright. The timid man, the lazy man, the man who distrusts his country, the over-civilized man, who has lost the great fighting, masterful virtues, the ignorant man, and the man of dull mind, whose soul is incapable of feeling the mighty lift that thrills "stern men with empires in their brains"—all these, of course, shrink from seeing the nation undertake its new duties; shrink from seeing us build a navy and an army adequate to our needs; shrink from seeing us do our share of the world's work, by bringing order out of chaos in the great, fair tropic islands from which the valor of our soldiers and sailors has driven the Spanish flag. These are the men who fear the strenuous life, who fear the only national life which is really worth leading. They believe in that cloistered life which saps the hardy virtues in a nation, as it saps them in the individual; or else they are wedded to that base spirit of gain and greed which recognizes in commercialism the be-all and end-all of national life, instead of realizing that, though an indispensable element, it is, after all, but one of the many elements that go to make up true national greatness. No country can long endure if its foundations are not laid deep in the material prosperity which comes from thrift, from business energy and enterprise, from hard, unsparing effort in the fields of industrial activity; but neither was any nation ever yet truly great if it relied upon material prosperity alone. All honor must be paid to the architects of our material prosperity, to the great captains of industry who have built our factories and our railroads, to the strong men who toil for wealth with brain or hand; for great is the debt of the nation to these and their kind. But our debt is yet greater to the men whose highest type is to be found in a statesman like Lincoln, a soldier like Grant. They showed by their lives that they recognized the law of work, the law of strife; they toiled to win a competence for themselves and those dependent upon them; but they recognized that there were yet other and even loftier duties— duties to the nation and duties to the race.

We cannot sit huddled within our own borders and avow ourselves merely an assemblage of well-to-do hucksters who care nothing for what happens beyond. Such a policy would defeat even its own end; for as the nations grow to have ever wider and wider interests, and are brought into closer and closer contact, if we are to hold our own in the struggle for naval and commercial supremacy, we must build up our power without our own borders. We must build the isthmian canal, and we must grasp the points of vantage which will enable us to have our say in deciding the destiny of the oceans of the East and the West.

So much for the commercial side. From the standpoint of international honor the argument is even stronger. The guns that thundered off Manila and Santiago left us echoes of glory, but they also left us a legacy of duty. If we drove out a mediæval tyranny only to make room for savage anarchy, we had better not have begun the task at all. It is worse than idle to say that we have no duty to perform, and can leave to their fates the islands we have conquered. Such a course would be the course of infamy. It would be followed at once by utter chaos in the wretched islands themselves. Some stronger, manlier power would have to step in and do the work, and we would have shown ourselves weaklings, unable to carry to successful completion the labors that great and high-spirited nations are eager to undertake. . . .

The problems are different for the different islands. Porto Rico is not large enough to stand alone. We must govern it wisely and well, primarily in the interest of its own people. Cuba is, in my judgment, entitled ultimately to settle for itself whether it shall be an independent state or an integral portion of the mightiest of republics. But until order and stable liberty are secured, we must remain in the island to insure them, and infinite tact, judgment, moderation, and courage must be shown by our military and civil representatives in keeping the island pacified, in relentlessly stamping out brigandage, in protecting all alike, and yet in showing proper recognition to the men who have fought for Cuban liberty. The Philippines offer a yet graver problem. Their population includes half-caste and native Christians, warlike Moslems, and wild pagans. Many of their people are utterly unfit for self-government, and show no signs of becoming fit. Others may in time become fit but at present can only take part in self-government under a wise supervision, at once firm and beneficent. We have driven Spanish tyranny from the islands. If we now let it be replaced by savage anarchy, our work has been for harm and not for good. I have scant patience with those who fear to undertake the task of governing the Philippines, and who openly avow that they do fear to undertake it, or that they shrink from it because of the expense and trouble; but I have even scanter patience with those who make a pretense of humanitarianism to hide and cover their timidity, and who can't about "liberty" and the "consent of the governed," in order to excuse themselves for their unwillingness to play the part of men. Their doctrines, if carried out, would make it incumbent upon us to leave the Apaches of Arizona to work out their own salvation, and to decline to interfere in a single Indian reservation. Their doctrines condemn your forefathers and mine for ever having settled in these United States.

England's rule in India and Egypt has been of great benefit to England, for it has trained up generations of men accustomed to look at the larger and loftier side of public life. It has been of even greater benefit to India and Egypt. And finally, and most of all, it has advanced the cause of civilization. So, if we do our duty aright in the Philippines, we will add to that national renown which is the highest and finest part of national life, will greatly benefit the people of the Philippine Islands, and, above all, we will play our part well in the great work of uplifting mankind.... As for those in our own country who encourage the foe, we can afford contemptuously to disregard them; but it must be remembered that their utterances are not saved from being treasonable merely by the fact that they are despicable. . . .

I preach to you, then, my countrymen, that our country calls not for the life of ease but for the life of strenuous endeavor. The twentieth century looms before us big with the fate of many nations. If we stand idly by, if we seek merely swollen, slothful ease and ignoble peace, if we shrink from the hard contests where men must win at hazard of their lives and at the risk of all they hold dear, then the bolder and stronger peoples will pass us by, and will win for themselves the domination of the world. Let us therefore boldly face the life of strife, resolute to do our duty well and manfully; resolute to uphold

Image 5.3 Joseph Keppler, "The Rough Riders"

Theodore Roosevelt's exuberant yet brief participation in the Spanish-American War generated enthusiasm and no little patriotism in American culture.

Source: Puck, 1898. Courtesy Library of Congress.

righteousness by deed and by word; resolute to be both honest and brave, to serve high ideals, yet to use practical methods.... Above all, let us shrink from no strife, moral or physical, within or without the nation, provided we are certain that the strife is justified, for it is only through strife, through hard and dangerous endeavor, that we shall ultimately win the goal of true national greatness.[3]

INTRODUCTION TO DOCUMENT 4

Although most newspapers supported government policy, there was plenty of dissent. Document 4 consists of five newspaper articles that appeared in the summer of 1899, shortly after Roosevelt's "Strenuous Life" speech, during the height of the controversy following President McKinley's decision to annex the Philippines. The first, an editorial from the *New York Evening Post*, directly challenged Roosevelt's ideas. The second piece is from the *New Orleans Times Democrat,* and it suggested that the war threatened to become more costly and difficult than its supporters had admitted.

The article from the *Baltimore Sun* contains an interview with an American naval commander newly returned from the Philippines who denied that the Filipinos were either "barbaric" or "uncivilized." "The True American," which appeared in the *Springfield Republican,* again challenged Roosevelt and condemned expansion as a violation of American democratic ideals. The last article is an anonymous letter from a black soldier to the editor of the *New York Age*—an African-American newspaper—that expressed anger at the racism of white American troops toward the Filipinos. Taken together, these pieces give a good sense of how controversial the question of empire had become.

4. PRESS OPPOSITION TO THE WAR (1899)

NEW YORK EVENING POST

. . . Governor Roosevelt's recent speech in Chicago . . . glorified war and fighting as the only remedies of a nation against what he is fond of calling on all occasions "ignoble peace." . . . This is the gospel of war for the sake of war, of fighting, not merely or necessarily for a just and righteous and inevitable cause, but for the effect upon your own virility. Whatever you do, you must fight. The worst thing that can happen to a man or a nation is to remain long in peace. That is to become "despicable," "ignoble," "slothful," an object of contempt to yourself and to the world. This is the view of the savage, the barbarian. . . .

The Roosevelt view of life is essentially a boy's view, and if it were to become the permanent basis of a national policy would make us the most turbulent people the world has ever seen. Our national life would become one perpetual Donnybrook fair, with "rows" with every power that got within range of us, for no other purpose than the development of our "virile strength," lest we become a nation of sloths.

Happily there is no danger of such a future for us. Our governor is not taken seriously by anybody except himself when he talks "war." . . . So long as he insists upon favoring war as the chief end of man, without which the human race can make no progress towards what Admiral Sampson so well calls the "true living which we all long for," the people of this country will never trust him in a station in which he can carry out his views. . . .[4]

NEW ORLEANS TIMES–DEMOCRAT

We are beginning to realize the fact—even the imperialists—that we have bought from Spain a very disagreeable guerilla war, in which there are no honors to win, but much loss, expense, and vexation of spirit. . . . As [the Philippines] is a land of swamps and mountains, an ideal country for guerilla warfare, with a malarial tropical climate disastrous to Americans, we can realize the bargain we bought from Spain. . . . It is time for us to count up the cost and see whether our Philippine bargain is worth what we are likely to pay for it before we get through, and then determine whether it would not be better to cease this war of McKinley's, which has accomplished so very little beyond showing the courage and fighting quality of our soldiers, and restore peace in the islands so as to allow their development, retaining such control over them that the United States would share in the prosperity and commerce that would come with peace and order.[5]

BALTIMORE SUN

Commander John D. Ford, fleet engineer of the Asiatic station, reached his home, No. 1522 West Lanvale street, on Saturday morning before noon, after an absence of a year and a half, most of which period he spent on board the cruiser "Baltimore," in the bay of Manila. . . .

"The Filipinos pictured in the sensational papers are not the men we are fighting. They are entirely distinct and separate. The fellows we deal with out there are not ignorant savages, fighting with bows and arrows, but an intelligent, liberty-loving people, full of courage and determination. The idea that the Filipino is an uncivilized being is a mistaken one. Originally the natives of those islands sprang from Japanese stock, and are identically the same race, with a change of language and customs. There was a time when the feudal system prevailed in Manila, but no vestige now remains, and the savagery of the people is found only in the very lowest class. . . .

"What they are fighting for now is absolute and entire liberty. They don't want us there or over them, and in the course of time might wear out our patience entirely. An excellent postal and telegraph system is in existence, which we wish very much we could get hold of. While they fight for entire freedom, all they ask is a chance for life, liberty, and the pursuit of happiness, and they care not whether it be a republic of their own or some form devised for them by the great United States of North America. I see nothing promising in the struggle now or any hope of speedy success on our part, unless many more troops are sent out. . . ."[6]

SPRINGFIELD [MASSACHUSETTS] REPUBLICAN

What is an American—a true American? It is to be first of all, we conceive, a friend of liberty and self-government at home and abroad. . . . There is not only open and brazen renunciation of the fundamental doctrines which make a republic, but there is the assertion, no longer thinly disguised, that our democracy is called of God to police the world—and that in order to do this we must doff the garments of peaceful republicanism, put on an old-world uniform, and, in the graphic language of Governor Roosevelt, "see that the outburst of savagery" (that we have stirred up by outraging the spirit of liberty) "is repressed once for all." It is a relentless programme, and one impossible of execution. Repression of that sort never represses—but we need not discuss that now.

Our firm belief and expectation is that the people of the United States will, soon or late, stand where they always have stood—with Lincoln and not with Roosevelt. The one is an American and the other represents Anglo-Americanism, and there is not room here for both. We shall stick to the new-world type. As it was in 1776, it must be now, else we shall recant and fall away from the simple yet prophetic and sufficient faith of Washington and Lincoln. Shall we exalt militarism more than struggling freedom, power more than principle, and hold physical dominion higher than the moral sway and helpfulness that has made liberty, as we have practised it with all our imperfections, the light of the world?[7]

NEW YORK AGE
LETTER TO THE EDITOR

I have mingled freely with the natives and have had talks with American colored men here in business and who have lived here for years, in order to learn of them the cause of their (Filipino) dissatisfaction and the reason for this insurrection, and I must confess they have a just grievance. All this never would have occurred if the army of occupation would have treated them as people. The Spaniards, even if their laws were hard, were polite and treated them with some consideration; but the Americans, as soon as they saw that the native troops were desirous of sharing in the glories as well as the hardships of the hard-won battles with the Americans, began to apply home treatment for colored peoples: curse them as damned niggers, steal [from] and ravish them, rob them on the street of their small change, take from the fruit vendors whatever suited their fancy, and kick the poor unfortunate if he complained, desecrate their church property, and after fighting began, looted everything in sight, burning, robbing the graves.

This may seem a little tall—but I have seen with my own eyes carcasses lying bare in the boiling sun, the results of raids on receptacles for the dead in search of diamonds. The [white] troops, thinking we would be proud to emulate their conduct, have made bold of telling their exploits to us. One fellow, member of the 13th Minnesota, told me how some fellows he knew had cut off a native woman's arm in order to get a fine inlaid bracelet. On upbraiding some fellows one morning, whom I met while out for a walk (I think they belong to a Nebraska or Minnesota regiment, and they were stationed on the Malabon road) for the conduct of the American troops toward the natives and especially as to raiding, etc., the reply was: "Do you think we could stay over here and fight these damn niggers without making it pay all it's worth? The government only pays us $13 per month: that's starvation wages. White men can't stand it." Meaning they could not live on such small pay. In saying this they never dreamed that Negro soldiers would never countenance such conduct. They talked with impunity of "niggers" to our soldiers, never once thinking that they were talking to home "niggers" and should they be brought to remember that at home this is the same vile epithet they hurl at us, they beg pardon and make some effeminate excuse about what the Filipino is called.

I want to say right here that if it were not for the sake of the 10,000,000 black people in the United States, God alone knows on which side of the subject I would be. And for the sake of the black men

Image 5.4 Louis Dalrymple, "School Begins"

This Louis Dalrymple cartoon captures the conflicts that came with the new territories acquired by the United States. How are different racial and ethnic groups depicted here? What does Uncle Sam represent?

Source: Puck, January 25, 1899. Courtesy Library of Congress.

who carry arms and pioneer for them as their representatives, ask them to not forget the present administration at the next election. Party be damned! We don't want these islands, not in the way we are to get them, and for Heaven's sake, put the party [Democratic] in power that pledged itself against this highway robbery. Expansion is too clean a name for it.

[Unsigned][8]

INTRODUCTION TO DOCUMENT 5

The public debate over American annexation of the Philippines proved so heated that a special congressional committee was appointed to investigate the conduct of the war. Although the Committee on the Philippines (chaired by Senator Henry Cabot Lodge) was established in January 1900, hearings did not begin until two years later. The following two interviews, part of the investigation, give a sense of the conduct of the war and of why it was so controversial. Robert P. Hughes was a brigadier general who commanded American troops in the Philippines at the turn of the century. Charles S. Riley had risen from private to first sergeant; he had served in the Philippines from October 1899 through March 1901.

5. PROCEEDINGS OF THE CONGRESSIONAL COMMITTEE ON THE PHILIPPINES (1902)

TESTIMONY OF ROBERT P. HUGHES

Sen. Rawlins: In burning towns, what would you do? Would the entire town be destroyed by fire or would only offending portions of the town be burned?

Gen. Hughes: I do not know that we ever had a case of burning what you would call a town in this country, but probably a barrio or a sitio; probably a half a dozen houses, native shacks, where the insurrectos would go in and be concealed, and if they caught a detachment passing they would kill some of them.

Sen. Rawlins: What did I understand you to say would be the consequences of that?

Gen. Hughes: They usually burned the village.

Sen. Rawlins: All of the houses in the village?

Gen. Hughes: Yes; every one of them.

Sen. Rawlins: What would become of the inhabitants?

Gen. Hughes: That was their lookout. . . . The destruction was as a punishment. . . .

Sen. Rawlins: The punishment in that case would fall, not upon the men, who could go elsewhere, but mainly upon the women and little children.

Gen. Hughes: The women and children are part of the family, and where you wish to inflict a punishment you can punish the man probably worse in that way than in any other.

Sen. Rawlins: But is that within the ordinary rules of civilized warfare? Of course you could exterminate the family, which would be still worse punishment.

Gen. Hughes: These people are not civilized.

Sen. Rawlins: But is that within the ordinary rules of civilized warfare?

GEN. HUGHES: No; I think it is not.

SEN. RAWLINS: You think it is not?

SEN. DIETRICH: In order to carry on civilized warfare both sides have to engage in such warfare. . . .

TESTIMONY OF CHARLES S. RILEY

Q. During your service there in the Philippine Islands did you witness what is generally known as the water cure?—A. I did.

Q. When and where?—A. On November 27, 1900, in the town of Igbaras, Iloilo Province, Panay Island. . . .

Q. You may state what you saw.—A. I saw the *presidente* standing in the—

Q. Whom do you mean by the presidente?—A. The head official of the town.

Q. The town of Igbaras?—A. Yes, sir.

Q. A Filipino?—A. Yes, sir.

Q. How old was he?—A. I should judge that he was a man of about forty or forty-five years.

Q. When you saw him, what was his condition?—A. He was stripped to the waist; he had nothing on but a pair of white trousers, and his hands were tied behind him. . . . He was then taken

THE HARVEST IN THE PHILIPPINES.

Image 5.5 Harvest in the Philippines

The war in the Philippines became a source of intense controversy soon after the end of the Spanish-American War. Rather than a schoolteacher, *Life's* cartoonist chose to depict Uncle Sam as a killer.

Source: Life, July 6, 1899. Courtesy University of Denver Penrose Library.

and placed under the tank, and the faucet was opened and a stream of water was forced down or allowed to run down his throat; his throat was held so he could not prevent swallowing the water, so that he had to allow the water to run into his stomach. . . .

Q. Was anything done besides forcing his mouth open and allowing the water to run down?—A. When he was filled with water it was forced out of him by pressing a foot on his stomach or else with their hands. . . .

Q. What had been his crime?—A. Information had been obtained from a native source as to his being an insurgent officer. After the treatment he admitted that he held the rank of captain in the insurgent army—an active captain. His police force, numbering twenty-five, were sworn insurgent soldiers. He was the *presidente* of the town and had been for a year, and he always showed himself to be friendly on the outside to the officers, and the men the same way.

SEN. BEVERIDGE: But in reality—

THE WITNESS: He was an insurgent officer and his men were insurgent soldiers. He acknowledged that, and his police acknowledged the same thing. When they took the oath as police they took the oath of an insurgent soldier.

THE CHAIRMAN: Were they supposed to be friendly to the United States?

THE WITNESS: They were; yes, sir.

Q. That was a pretense?—A. Yes, sir.

Q. And this was during the time of active warfare?—A. Yes, sir; during the entire time he held the place as the *presidente* in that town.

SEN. BURROWS: His offense was treachery to the American cause?—A. Yes, sir. . . .⁹

INTRODUCTION TO DOCUMENT 6

Woodrow Wilson, a distinguished political scientist, was a staunch advocate for an expanded role of the United States in the world. He penned this article for *The Atlantic* just months after the Philippine War ended, and a decade before he became president of the United States. Wilson outlined the importance of the war with Spain and pleaded with Americans to embrace their responsibilities abroad. How are his ideas similar or different from Roosevelt's?

6. "THE IDEALS OF AMERICA" (1902)

WOODROW WILSON

No war ever transformed us quite as the war with Spain transformed us. No previous years ever ran with so swift a change as the years since 1898. We have witnessed a new revolution. We have seen the transformation of America completed. That little group of states, which 125 years ago cast the sovereignty of Britain off, is now grown into a mighty power. That Little Confederation has now amassed an organized its energies. A confederacy is transformed into a nation. The battle of Trenton was not more significant than the battle of Manila. The nation that was one hundred and twenty-five years in the making has now stepped forth into the open arena of the world.

I ask you to stand with me at this new turning-point of our life, that we may look before and after, and judge ourselves alike in the light of that old battle fought here in the streets, and in the light of all the mighty processes of our history that have followed. We cannot too often give ourselves such challenge of self-examination. It will hearten, it will steady, it will moralize us to reassess our hopes, restate our ideals, and make manifest to ourselves again the principles and the purposes upon which we act. We are else without chart upon a novel voyage.

. . . We fought but the other day to give Cuba self-government. It is a point of conscience with us that the Philippines shall have it, too, when our work there is done and they are ready. But when will our work there be done, and how shall we know when they are ready? How, when our hand is withdrawn from her capitals and she plays her game of destiny apart and for herself, shall we be sure that Cuba has this blessing of liberty and self-government, for which battles are justly fought and revolutions righteously set afoot? If we be apostles of liberty and of self-government, surely we know what they are, in their essence and without disguise of form, and shall not be deceived in the principles of their application by mere differences between this race and that. . . .

Liberty is not itself government. In the wrong hands,—in hands unpracticed, undisciplined,—it is incompatible with government. Discipline must precede it,—if necessary, the discipline of being under masters. Then will self-control make it a thing of life and not a thing of tumult, a tonic, not an insurgent madness in the blood. Shall we doubt, then, what the conditions precedent to liberty and self-government are, and what their invariable support and accompaniment must be, in the countries whose administration we have taken over in trust, and particularly in those far Philippine Islands whose government is our chief anxiety? We cannot give them any quittance of

the debt ourselves have paid. They can have liberty no cheaper than we got it. They must first take the discipline of law, must first love order and instinctively yield to it. . . .

But we may set them upon the way with an advantage we did not have until our hard journey was more than half made. We can see to it that the law which teaches them obedience is just law and even-handed. . . . We can make order lovely by making it the friend of every man and not merely the shield of some. We can teach them by our fairness in administration that there may be a power in government which, though imperative and irresistible by those who would cross or thwart it, does not act for its own aggrandizement, but is the guarantee that all shall fare alike. That will infinitely shorten their painful tutelage. Our pride, our conscience will not suffer us to give them less.

And, if we are indeed bent upon service and not mastery, we shall give them more. We shall take them into our confidence and suffer them to teach us, as our critics. . . . The mere right to criticize and to have matters explained to them cools men's tempers and gives them understanding in affairs. This is what we seek among our new subjects: that they shall understand us, and after free conference shall trust us: that they shall perceive that we are not afraid of criticism, and that we are ready to explain and to take suggestions from all who are ready, when the conference is over, to obey.

. . . We have come to full maturity with this new century of our national existence and to full self-consciousness as a nation. And the day of our isolation is past. We shall learn much ourselves now that we stand closer to other nations and compare ourselves first with one and again with another. . . . It is by the widening of vision that nations, as men, grow and are made great. We need not fear the expanding scene. It was plain destiny that we should come to this, and if we have kept our ideals clear, unmarred, commanding through the great century and the moving scenes that made us a nation, we may keep them also through the century that shall see us a great power in the world.[10]

POSTSCRIPT

Mark Twain returned to the United States in October 1900, after nearly a decade overseas. He had supported American intervention in Cuba, for he believed our war against Spain to be the selfless act of a free people intent on helping a neighbor gain its liberty. Yet as the new century dawned he looked with growing horror on America's ongoing presence in Cuba and its ugly war in the Philippines. Twain became an outspoken anti-imperialist.

The cause elicited some of the most scathing words from his "pen warmed-up in hell," for Twain viewed imperial expansion, especially by America, as a betrayal of Christian and democratic ideals. On December 30, 1900, in the pages of the *New York Herald*, he greeted the new century with an attack on the role of churches and missionaries:

> I bring you the stately matron named Christendom, returning bedraggled, besmirched and dishonored from pirate raids in Kiao-Chow, Manchuria, South Africa and the Philippines, with her soul full of meanness, her pockets full of boodle, and her mouth full of pious hypocrisies. Give her soap and a towel, but hide the looking glass.

For the next several years, Twain wrote a series of articles, open letters, and reviews condemning American imperialism. He turned away from his original notion of the Spanish–American War as a good cause gone bad and came to see expansionist rhetoric as a cynical cover for avarice. Soon imperialist spokesmen accused Twain of treason, a charge that redoubled his activities. Patriotism, he argued, consisted of following one's own conscience; Filipinos resisting the American invasion were patriots, while American jingoists were traitors to their own ideals.

One of Twain's angriest attacks on American policy in the Philippines came in the article, "To the Person Sitting in Darkness" (*North American Review*, February 1901):

> . . . We have crushed a deceived and confiding people; we have turned against the weak and the friendless who trusted us; we have stamped out a just and intelligent and well-ordered republic; we have stabbed an ally in the back and slapped the face of a guest . . . we have robbed a trusting friend of his land and his liberty; we have invited our clean young men to shoulder a discredited musket and do bandit's work under a flag which bandits have been accustomed to fear, not to follow; we have debauched America's honor and blackened her face before the world. . . .

Perhaps Twain's most despairing antiwar statement was published posthumously. "I have told the whole truth," he declared, "and only dead men can tell the truth in this world. It can be published after I am dead." Twain wrote "The War-Prayer" in 1905, but it did not appear until six years after he died, in the November 1916 issue of *Harper's Monthly*, as millions of Europeans slaughtered each other in World War I. Twain describes a community preparing for war, with bands and parades swelling the patriotic fervor. On Sunday before the troops leave for the front, the church is filled, and the preacher offers a prayer asking the Lord to bless the soldiers' efforts with victory.

Just as the minister finishes his supplication, an aged stranger with long white hair and robes that reach to the floor ascends the pulpit. He motions the preacher aside and addresses the congregation. He bears a message from the Almighty. God has heard their words and will grant their wishes, the old man says, but they must know that along with their spoken prayer goes an unspoken supplication. ". . . O Lord, our God," the ancient one prays,

> help us to tear their soldiers to bloody shreds with our shells; help us to cover their smiling fields with the pale forms of their patriot dead; help us to drown the thunder of the guns with shrieks

of their wounded, writhing in pain; help us to lay waste their humble homes with a hurricane of fire; help us to wring the hearts of their unoffending widows with unavailing grief; help us to turn them out roofless with their little children to wander unfriended the wastes of their desolated land. . . . For our sakes who adore Thee, Lord, blast their hopes, blight their lives, protract their bitter pilgrimage, make heavy their steps, water their way with their tears, stain the white snow with the blood of their wounded feet! We ask it in the spirit of love, of Him Who is the Source of Love, . . . Amen.

[*After a Pause.*] Ye have prayed it; if ye still desire it, speak!—The messenger of the Most High waits.

It was believed afterwards that the man was a lunatic, because there was no sense in what he said.[11]

QUESTIONS

1. What ideas about racial groups do you find in Beveridge, Sumner, and Roosevelt? What was the relationship of those ideas to their views on overseas expansion?
2. Why did Roosevelt believe foreign territories would make America stronger?
3. How did ideas about "manhood" enter the debates on overseas expansion? What did the *New York Evening Post* editorial mean when they called Roosevelt's view of life "a boy's view"?
4. Describe Beveridge's belief about America's special mission to the world.
5. How did the various participants in this debate view the role of business, government, and the military in American foreign policy?
6. How do you reconcile Wilson's vision of American values with the report of military tactics used in the testimony to the Committee on the Philippines?

ADDITIONAL READING

On the ideological debate over war, see Stephen Kinzer, *The True Flag: Theodore Roosevelt, Mark Twain, and the Birth of American Empire* (2017). On America's emergence as a world power in the late nineteenth century, see Walter La Feber, *The New Empire: An Interpretation of American Expansion, 1860–1898* (1963), and Anders Stephanson, *Manifest Destiny* (1995). The role of racial beliefs in foreign policy is discussed in Rubin Weston, *Racism in U.S. Imperialism: The Influence of Racial Assumptions on American Foreign Policy, 1893–1946* (1972); Tunde Adeleke, *UnAfrican Americans* (1998); and especially Paul Kramer, *The Blood of Government* (2006). For the ideological bases of the new foreign policy, see Emily Rosenberg, *Spreading the American Dream* (1982). For an overview of the war and its aftermath, see David J. Silbey, *A War of Frontier and Empire* (2008). For those who opposed the expansionist late nineteenth-century foreign policy, see Robert Beisner, *Twelve Against Empire: The Anti-Imperialists, 1898–1900* (1975). For interpretations of American diplomatic history, see Walter La Feber, *The American Age: United States Policy at Home and Abroad Since 1750* (1989); Harvey Rosenfeld, *Diary of a Dirty Little War* (2000); and Ivan Musicant, *Empire by Default* (1998). For American relations with the Philippines, see Stanley Karnow, *In Our Image: America's Empire in the Philippines* (1989). For a geographer's perspective, see Neil Smith, *American Empire* (2003). For cultural historians' interpretations of empire, see Kristin L. Hoganson, *Fighting for American Manhood* (1998); Gail Bederman, *Manliness and Civilization* (1996); and Matthew Frye Jacobson, *Barbarian Virtues* (2000).

ENDNOTES

1. Albert J. Beveridge, *The Meaning of the Times and Other Speeches* (Indianapolis, IN: Bobbs Merrill, 1904), pp. 47–57.
2. William Graham Sumner, *War and Other Essays* (New Haven, CT: Yale University Press, 1911), pp. 297–334.
3. Theodore Roosevelt, *The Strenuous Life: Essays and Addresses* (New York: Century Company, 1900), pp. 1–10, 15–21.
4. The *Anti-Imperialist* v.1 n.3, July 4, 1889, pp. 44–45.
5. The *Anti-Imperialist*, v.1 n.3, July 4, 1889, pp. 69–70.
6. The *Anti-Imperialist*, v.1 n.3, July 4, 1889, pp. 71–72.
7. The *Anti-Imperialist*, v.1 n.4, August 20, 1899, pp. 27–28.
8. Letter from a colored soldier in Manila. First published in the New York Age, October 5, reprinted in *The Public* (Chicago), October 14, 1899, v.2 n.80, pp. 12–13.
9. *Hearings before the Committee on the Philippines of the United States Senate*, 57th Congress, 1st Session, Doc. No. 331. Washington: Government Printing Office, 1902), part 1, pp. 558–559, and part 2, pp. 1526–1527, 1536.
10. Woodrow Wilson, "The Ideals of America," *Atlantic Monthly* (December 1902).
11. Mark Twain, reprinted in *The Public* (Chicago), February 2, 1901, v.3 n.148, p. 687; Mark Twain, "To the Person Sitting in Darkness" (New York: Anti-Imperialist League of New York, 1901); Mark Twain, "The War Prayer," *Europe and Elsewhere* (New York: Harper and Brothers, 1923), pp. 394–398.

CHAPTER 6

MEATPACKING
AND MUCKRAKING

HISTORICAL CONTEXT

Chicago's growth during the nineteenth century was nothing short of amazing. It was a backwoods settlement in 1830, and in the 1840s, a provincial berg dwarfed by the likes of Cincinnati and St. Louis. With their commercial domination of the Ohio and Mississippi Rivers Valleys, the supremacy of those two cities over the American heartland seemed assured. But when Chicago established itself as the main western hub for railroad traffic, it began to grow at an astonishing rate, easily surpassing its midwestern rivals in just a few years. Over 100,000 Chicagoans in 1860 became a quarter million a decade later, a number that kept doubling every ten years until at the turn of the century, Chicago's population approached 2 million people. Here the goods flowed in—timber from the northwest, wheat and corn from prairie states, coal and iron ore from mines scattered across the middle west, and cattle from out on the plains. These raw materials were processed into lumber, meat, and steel, and then shipped back out, not just to the far corners of America but into the world aboard ships that sailed out of the Great Lakes to international ports. People were part of this flow of commodities. All American cities contained enormous numbers of immigrants but Chicago was at the high end of the trend. Roughly two-thirds of turn-of-the-century Chicago's citizens were either born overseas or had a parent who started life outside America. Then too, tens of thousands of rural and small-town migrants from neighboring states came pouring in. Along with enormous growth came horrifying social problems of poverty, illness, and social alienation. The "muckraking" journalist Lincoln Steffens described Chicago as "first in violence, deepest in dirt, lawless, unlovely, ill-smelling, irreverent, new; an overgrown gawk of a village, the 'tough' among cities, a spectacle for the nation."

Chicago was emblematic of the difficulties facing America in the new century. The Progressive Era, which lasted roughly from 1900 through World War I, was a set of responses to these problems. The Gilded Age had unleashed the incredible productive capacity of American business. With new technologies such as the telephone, massive infrastructure including tens of thousands of miles of railroad track, enormous amounts of capital invested in new corporations, factories on a scale never seen before, and a young and ambitious labor force, the national economy grew explosively. But rapid urbanization and industrialization had their costs. While enormous fortunes were built up (and displayed in such new play-grounds for the rich as Newport, Rhode Island), a disconcerting number of Americans went to bed hungry at night. Workers often put in ten- and twelve-hour days, six days a week, and many families barely made ends meet on the combined income of husband, wife, and children, all going out to work. Equally important, to the extent that government intervened in daily life, it was to assist the productive capacity of business—granting corporations limited liability, giving away public lands to encourage the development of new markets, and sending in troops to break strikes. Problems like garbage piling up in the streets, drinking water contaminated by sewage, and deadly streetcar crossings in every American town all contributed to a grudging reconsideration of the role of government in the lives of citizens.

Not everyone agreed on what reforms were needed, and historians have differed for decades on what to include or exclude within the category of "progressivism." But reformers generally believed that the sheer size of business created problems. America was more organized, centralized, and bureaucratic than ever before. For example, at the turn of the century, banker J.P. Morgan purchased Andrew Carnegie's steel plants and folded them into a new company called United States Steel, capitalized at an unheard of $1 billion. The old fears that massive agglomerations of wealth and power would crush economic opportunity, destroy workers' chance for a decent life, pollute democracy, and undermine the citizens' republic grew more intense than ever. Labor unions proliferated among the working class, and populist farmers organized against the incorporation of America. At the beginning of the twentieth century, the Progressive Era was a middle-class response to the situation. Crusading journalists, reform-minded women, college professors, preachers of the new "social gospel," liberal politicians, and even forward-thinking businessmen joined together in shifting coalitions to expose problems and seek solutions.

For many, the answer to growing corporate power was the countervailing force of government. To make democracy less vulnerable to corruption, cities reconfigured themselves, holding at-large elections for local offices, vesting power in "expert" managers, and assuring fair elections with the "Australian" (secret) ballot, all designed, it was said, to reduce the power of corrupt aldermen. States instituted the initiative, referendum, and recall to revitalize citizen participation in the political process. And in countless ways, the federal government weighed in, from the "trust-busting" of President Theodore Roosevelt (which broke up only a handful of businesses) to such regulatory legislation as the Federal Reserve Act of 1913 and the Clayton Antitrust Act of 1914 under Woodrow Wilson. Progressive reforms, however, were not always as progressive as their proponents claimed. At-large elections disenfranchised many neighborhoods, and state electoral reforms often became new tools for the powerful. Moreover, laws reigning in business frequently were written with the help of the very companies they were designed to regulate, and the results often reduced competition and encouraged bigness.

The progressives' style was as notable as their substance. As a middle-class movement led largely by well-educated people, progressives valued facts and figures, expert knowledge, and bureaucratic efficiency. The attorney Louis Brandeis, whom Woodrow Wilson appointed to the Supreme Court, pioneered the use of sociological knowledge in legal briefs. Precedent and case law were no longer enough to win the day, "scientifically" gathered data mattered too. The progressive style was fact-laden, logical, and systematic. Progressives placed great faith in the wisdom of those with the training and knowledge to address social problems in methodical ways. This emphasis on expertise gave a distinctly elitist cast to much of their thinking and writing, even as they professed reforms in the name of "the people" against special interests.

But parallel to the rhetoric of disinterested expertise was another language, often quite emotional, filled with moral and even religious fervor. One need only picture the Progressive (or Bull Moose) Party convention in Chicago in 1912. Having nominated former president Theodore Roosevelt to run as a third-party candidate for president, the delegates concluded their meetings by rising and singing in unison "Onward Christian Soldiers." One might even argue that the old revulsion against drinking, so common in many Protestant churches during the late nineteenth century, became the culmination of progressive reform when in 1920 Congress authorized prohibition through the Eighteenth Amendment to the Constitution.

In this chapter, we examine an example of this progressive reform impulse involving workers in the meatpacking industry. This was an entirely new form of production in the late nineteenth and early twentieth centuries, one which made it possible for, say, a cow grazing in Kansas to be eaten three or four days later by a family in New Jersey. This could not have occurred before the Civil War, yet it was commonplace by 1900. What happened? Technology was important—the railroad connected the Great Plains with the East, so that shipping goods over hundreds, even thousands of miles, now could be measured in hours. Also, refrigeration allowed freshly butchered beef and pork to be preserved. But equally important was the mental leap of thinking of meat as just one more product in the marketplace.

The key was keeping goods cheap through mass production and using every part of an animal—bone for buttons, gut for sporting goods, and hides for outerwear. If thousands of cattle—which required a lot of space to raise—could be brought together and slaughtered systematically, and every part of each animal made into a commodity with a market value, then costs would come down, manufacturers might ship dressed meat to distant places for less money than local butchers could produce it, and beef would be consumed by more and more new customers. Butchers—skilled tradesmen whose labor was expensive—could be replaced by countless unskilled workers who performed but one task over and over, such as cutting off a particular part of the cow as it came down the "disassembly line." These ideas did not occur all at once, but slowly a handful of Chicago entrepreneurs in competition with each other turned what had been a locally based business into a national industry. The result was the famous Packingtown on Chicago's South Side, roughly a mile-and-a-half square bordered by 39th and 51st Streets, and by Halsted and Western, filled with stockyards, slaughterhouses and meatpacking plants.

Packingtown stank. It was ugly, dangerous, and unhealthy. Entering Packingtown from the north, a visitor was greeted—or perhaps insulted—by two prominent landmarks. The main entrance to the Union Stockyards was an imposing stone and iron gate that dwarfed humans and served as a grim portent of the serious and difficult work inside. Snaking its way to the west of the stockyards was Bubbly Creek, a branch of the Chicago River named

Image 6.1 "In the Heart of the Great Union Stock Yards, Chicago" (*c.* 1909)

Cattle were driven to railroad depots on the Great Plains, then loaded onto cars bound for Chicago, where they were sorted and fattened in pens in enormous stockyards.

Source: Philadelphia? Kelley & Chadwick. Courtesy Library of Congress

for the carbolic acid gas that rose to the surface from the decaying wastes. The gasses of Bubbly Creek mixed with the odors of dying animals and decaying meat, and a series of uncovered dumps gave Packingtown its unforgettable smell.

Forty thousand people lived and worked in Packingtown. Most resided in poorly constructed frame houses that were often firetraps. Unlike better South Side neighborhoods, Packingtown's roads were largely unpaved and its sewage facilities were inadequate. The uncollected garbage, open sewers, and accumulated filth lowered health standards as well as human morale. Tuberculosis was the major scourge, but bronchitis, diphtheria, and other contagious diseases also claimed their victims. Children were especially vulnerable; one out of every three infants did not live to a second birthday.

The residents of Packingtown, mostly immigrants from central Europe and Scandinavia, tolerated these dreadful conditions for a chance to work in the packinghouses. The jobs they acquired were difficult and dangerous—very dangerous. And for risking lives and limbs, unskilled workers were paid between 15 and 18 cents per hour. Men and women were exposed to freezing temperatures, constant dampness, noxious chemicals, and razor-sharp tools. The pace of work, dictated by management, increased the chances of serious injury. Often the results read more like battlefield casualty reports than worker accidents. During the first six months of 1910, Swift and Company reported 3,500 injuries serious enough to require a physician's care. In 1917, Armour workers became ill or injured over 22,000 times.

A man named Upton Sinclair came to Packingtown in 1904. He did not come as a worker looking for a job but as a writer in pursuit of a subject. Workers had just lost a major strike, and Sinclair went to the stockyards to observe their lives. Though only in his twenties, he had already written a number of undistinguished but modestly popular novels. The literary marketplace rewarded sensational writing, and the ambitious young Sinclair had been successful with tales of love and blood and revenge. Even though writing dime novels earned him a fine living, it failed to satisfy his soul. Sinclair's early efforts at serious fiction were commercial and artistic failures. His characters, like the author himself, were consumed with the idea of individual genius, with romantic images of suffering and misunderstood individuals dedicated to their private visions. But then Upton Sinclair had what amounted to a religious conversion—he discovered socialism.

Various ideas for bringing the enormous new corporations under public control were advanced after 1900, but socialism was a radical but surprisingly popular solution. Socialists wanted to nationalize the means of production—factories, mills, and mines must be owned by the state; no more private profits for capitalists and low wages for workers. The socialists proposed to remake America through the electoral system, and they saw their cause as a patriotic calling. The Socialist Party never threatened to displace the Democrats or Republicans, but before World War I, dozens of socialists became legislators, mayors, and councilmen, while Eugene Debs of Terre Haute, Indiana, garnered 6 percent of the vote for president in 1912.

By 1904, Sinclair's faith in the socialist cause led him to write about the plight of American workers. New magazines like *McClure's* had published so-called muckraking journalists such as Ida Tarbell and Lincoln Steffens, who wrote exposés of civic and corporate

Image 6.2 "Chopping Meat, Sausage Department, Armour's Chicago" (1893) On Chicago's "disassembly lines," enormous businesses transformed cows and pigs into meat—killed, cut up, packed, and shipped out to the rest of the country.
Source: New York: Strohmeyer & Wyman. Courtesy Library of Congress.

corruption, but Sinclair was much more radical than they were, much more attuned to what he saw as class struggle. Also, he was a writer of fiction, not journalism. He went to Packingtown, studied the factories, the workers, and the "Back-of-the-Yards" neighborhoods, and imagined a story about an immigrant family who, he believed, represented much of what was wrong with American capitalism. He wrote rapidly and intensely. His novel, *The Jungle,* was first published in serial form in 1905, not in the mainstream press but in the *Appeal to Reason,* a popular socialist weekly based in Girard, Kansas.

The Jungle came out in book form in 1906 and was an instant success. Sinclair told the story of the Rudkus family, Lithuanian immigrants who came to America only to be used and discarded by the companies that owned Packingtown. The human and sanitary abuses Sinclair catalogued shocked Americans in 1906, and they continue to shock us today. Despite his attempts to preserve literary delicacy, some reviewers were scandalized by Sinclair's violations of good taste. A reviewer for *The Outlook* declared, "To disgust the reader by dragging him through every conceivable horror, physical and moral, and to depict with lurid excitement and with offensive minuteness the life in jail and brothel— all is to overstep the object." As you read about the meatpacking industry, think about how reformers framed their issues, how they sought support and what results they achieved. Would you characterize their movement as successful?

INTRODUCTION TO DOCUMENT 1

The publication of *The Jungle* and the wide readership it attracted gave ammunition to the politicians who were seeking reforms in the meatpacking industry. Jack London praised it as the "Uncle Tom's Cabin" of wage slavery. So effective was Sinclair's novel that even President Roosevelt entered the fight to demand change. The result of the ferment was the Meat Inspection Act of 1906. Far from a perfect piece of legislation, it represented a compromise between the meatpacking companies and the reformers. It helped to restore confidence in the industry, however it did little for the residents of Packingtown. As Sinclair later remarked, "I aimed at the public's heart, and by accident I hit it in the stomach." In the following scene, Sinclair's main character, Jurgis Rudkus, finds work after a long layoff due to injury.

1. FROM *THE JUNGLE* (1906)

UPTON SINCLAIR

. . . There was another interesting set of statistics that a person might have gathered in Packingtown— those of the various afflictions of the workers. . . . There were the men in the pickle-rooms, for instance, where old Antanas had gotten his death; scarce a one of these that had not some spot of horror on his person. Let a man so much as scrape his finger pushing a truck in the pickle-rooms, and he might have a sore that would put him out of the world; all the joints in his fingers might be eaten by the acid, one by one. Of the butchers and floorsmen, the beef-boners and trimmers, and all those who used knives, you could scarcely find a person who had the use of his thumb; time and time again the base of it had been slashed, till it was a mere lump of flesh against which the man pressed the knife to hold it. The hands of these men would be criss-crossed with cuts, until you could no longer pretend to count them or to trace them. They would have no nails,—they had worn them off pulling hides; their knuckles were swollen so that their fingers spread out like a fan. There were men who worked in the cooking-rooms, in the midst of steam and sickening odors, by artificial light; in these rooms the germs of tuberculosis might live for two years, but the supply was renewed every hour. There were the beef-luggers, who carried two-hundred-pound quarters into the refrigerator-cars; a fearful kind of work, that began at four o'clock in the morning, and that wore out the most powerful men in a few years. There were those who worked in the chilling-rooms, and whose special disease was rheumatism; the time-limit that a man could work in the chilling-rooms was said to be five years. There were the wool-pluckers, whose hands went to pieces even sooner than the hands of the pickle-men; for the pelts of the sheep had to be painted with acid to loosen the wool, and then the pluckers had to pull out this wool with their bare hands, till the acid had eaten their fingers off. There were those who made the tins for the canned-meat; and their hands, too, were a maze of cuts, and each cut represented a chance for blood-poisoning. Some worked at the stamping-machines, and it was very seldom that one could work long there at the pace that was set, and not give out and forget himself, and have a part of his hand chopped off. . . . As for the other men, who worked in tank-rooms full of steam, and in some of which there were open vats near the level of the floor, their peculiar trouble was that they fell into the vats; and when they were fished out, there was never enough of them left to be worth exhibiting,—sometimes they would be overlooked for days, till all but the bones of them had gone out to the world as Durham's Pure Leaf Lard! . . .

All this while that he was seeking for work, there was a dark shadow hanging over Jurgis; as if a savage beast were lurking somewhere in the pathway of his life, and he knew it, and yet could not help approaching the place. There were all stages of being out of work in Packingtown, and he faced in dread the prospect of reaching the lowest. There is a place that waits for the lowest man—the fertilizer-plant!

The men would talk about it in awe-stricken whispers. Not more than one in ten had ever really tried it; the other nine had contented themselves with hearsay evidence and a peep through the door. There were some things worse than even starving to death. They would ask Jurgis if he had worked there yet, and if he meant to; and Jurgis would debate the matter with himself. As poor as they were, and making all the sacrifices that they were, would he dare to refuse any sort of work that was offered to him, be it as horrible as ever it could? Would he dare to go home and eat bread that had been earned by Ona, weak and complaining as she was, knowing that he had been given a chance, and had not had the nerve to take it?—And yet he might argue that way with himself all day, and one glimpse into the fertilizer-works would send him away again shuddering. He was a man, and he would do his duty; he went and made application—but surely he was not also required to hope for success! . . .

The boss of the grinding room had come to know Jurgis by this time, and had marked him for a likely man; and so when he came to the door about two o'clock this breathless hot day, he felt a sudden spasm of pain shoot through him—the boss beckoned to him! In ten minutes more Jurgis had pulled off his coat and overshirt, and set his teeth together and gone to work. Here was one more difficulty for him to meet and conquer!

His labor took him about one minute to learn. Before him was one of the vents of the mill in which the fertilizer was being ground-rushing forth in a great brown river, with a spray of the finest dust flung forth in clouds. Jurgis was given a shovel, and along with half a dozen others it was his task to shovel this fertilizer into carts. That others were at work he knew by the sound, and by the fact that he sometimes collided with them; otherwise they might as well not have been there, for in the blinding dust-storm a man could not see six feet in front of his face. When he had filled one cart he had to grope around him until another came, and if there was none on hand he continued to grope till one arrived. In five minutes he was, of course, a mass of fertilizer from head to feet; they gave him a sponge to tie over his mouth, so that he could breathe, but the sponge did not prevent his lips and eyelids from caking up with it and his ears from filling solid. He looked like a brown ghost at twilight—from hair to shoes he became the color of the building and of everything in it, and for that matter a hundred yards outside it. The building had to be left open, and when the wind blew Durham and Company lost a great deal of fertilizer.

Working in his shirt-sleeves, and with the thermometer at over a hundred, the phosphates soaked in through every pore of Jurgis's skin, and in five minutes he had a headache, and in fifteen was almost dazed. The blood was pounding his brain like an engine's throbbing; there was a frightful pain in the top of his skull, and he could hardly control his hands. Still, with the memory of his four months' siege [of illness and unemployment] behind him, he fought on, in a frenzy of determination; and half an hour later he began to vomit—he vomited until it seemed as if his inwards must be torn to shreds. A man could get used to the fertilizer-mill, the boss had said, if he would only make up his mind to it; but Jurgis now began to see that it was a question of making up his stomach.

At the end of that day of horror, he could scarcely stand. He had to catch himself now and then, and lean against a building and get his bearings. Most of the men, when they came out, made straight for a saloon—they seemed to place fertilizer and rattle-snake poison in one class. But Jurgis was too ill to think of drinking—he could only make his way to the street and stagger on to a car. He had a sense of humor, and later on, when he became an old hand, he used to think it fun to board a street-car and see what happened. Now, however, he was too ill to notice it—how the people in the car began to gasp and sputter, to put their handkerchiefs to their noses, and transfix him with furious glances. Jurgis only knew that a man in front of him immediately got up and gave him a seat; and that half a minute later the two people on each side of him got up; and that in a full minute the crowded car was nearly empty—those passengers who could not get room on the platform having gotten out to walk.

Of course Jurgis had made his home a miniature fertilizer-mill a minute after entering. The stuff was half an inch deep in his skin—his whole system was full of it, and it would have taken a week not merely of scrubbing, but of vigorous exercise, to get it out of him. . . . He smelt so that he made all the food at the table taste, and set the whole family to vomiting; for himself it was three days before he could keep anything upon his stomach—he might wash his hands, and use a knife and fork, but were not his mouth and throat filled with the poison? . . .

With one member trimming beef in a cannery, and another working in a sausage factory, the family had a first-hand knowledge of the great majority of Packingtown swindles. For it was the custom, as they found, whenever meat was so spoiled that it could not be used for anything else, either to can it or else to chop it up into sausage. With what had been told them by Jonas, who had worked in the pickle-rooms, they could now study the whole of the spoiled-meat industry on the inside, and read a new and grim meaning into that old Packingtown jest—that they use everything of the pig except the squeal.

Jonas had told them how the meat that was taken out of pickle would often be found sour, and how they would rub it up with soda to take away the smell, and sell it to be eaten on free-lunch counters; also of all the miracles of chemistry which they performed, giving to any sort of meat, fresh or salted, whole or chopped, any color and any flavor and any odor they chose. In the pickling of hams they had an ingenious apparatus, by which they saved time and increased the capacity of the plant—a machine consisting of a hollow needle attached to a pump; by plunging this needle into the meat and working with his foot, a man could fill a ham with pickle in a few seconds. And yet, in spite of this, there would be hams found spoiled, some of them with an odor so bad that a man could hardly bear to be in the room with them. To pump into these the packers had a second and much stronger pickle which destroyed the odor—a process known to the workers as "giving them thirty per cent." Also, after the hams had been smoked, there would be found some that had gone to the bad. Formerly these had been sold as "Number Three Grade," but later on some ingenious person had hit upon a new device, and now they would extract the bone, about which the bad part generally lay, and insert in the hole a white-hot iron. After this invention there was no longer Number One, Two, and Three Grade—there was only Number One Grade. . . .

It was only when the whole ham was spoiled that it came into the department of Elzbieta. Cut up by the two-thousand-revolutions-a-minute flyers, and mixed with half a ton of other meat, no odor that ever was in a ham could make any difference. There was never the least attention paid to what was cut up for sausage; there would come all the way back from Europe old sausage that had been rejected, and that was mouldy and white—it would be dosed with borax and glycerine, and dumped into the hoppers, and made over again for home consumption. There would be meat that had tumbled out on the floor, in the dirt and sawdust, where the workers had tramped and spit uncounted billions of consumption germs. There would be meat stored in great piles in rooms; and the water from leaky roofs would drip over it, and thousands of rats would race about on it. It was too dark in these storage places to see well, but a man could run his hand over these piles of meat and sweep off handfuls of the dried dung of rats. These rats were nuisances, and the packers would put poisoned bread out for them; they would die, and then rats, bread and meat would go into the hoppers together. This is no fairy story and no joke; the meat would be shovelled into carts, and the man who did the shovelling would not trouble to lift out a rat even when he saw one— there were things that went into the sausage in comparison with which a poisoned rat was a tidbit. . . .[1]

INTRODUCTION TO DOCUMENT 2

Was *The Jungle* an accurate depiction of life in Packingtown? Historians have differed on this point. Certainly Sinclair got many details right, but his melodrama exaggerated the plight that any one family might endure. Before the *The Jungle* ends, Jurgis's home is repossessed, he goes to jail, Ona is sexually abused by her boss then dies, and Chicago effectively kills their children. Moreover, some have questioned how well Sinclair knew the packing industry; he spent only a few weeks in Packingtown, did not go into the factories very much, and gathered most of his information through interviews. Ralph Chaplin, also a writer and a political radical, was ambivalent, declaring in his autobiography *Wobbly*, "I thought it a very inaccurate picture of the stockyards district which I knew so well, but I waited for each installment eagerly and read it with great interest." Above all, Sinclair minimized the resources of workers to improve their own conditions. Antanas Kaztauskis's story was published in the magazine *The Independent* three months before Sinclair began his research for *The Jungle*. As you read, think about how this autobiography confirms or contradicts Sinclair's depiction of the lives of immigrant workers. Ask yourself about the role of unions, political organizations, taverns, churches, schools, and ethnic communities in daily life. How did working-class people adjust to their lives in America, what values and institutions did they cling to, and how did they reinterpret the American dream for themselves?

2. ANTANAS KAZTAUSKIS'S STORY (1904)

. . . In our house my room was in the basement. I lay down on the floor with three other men and the air was rotten. I did not go to sleep for a long time. I knew then that money was everything I needed. My money was almost gone and I thought that I would soon die unless I got a job, for this was not like home.

Here money was everything and a man without money must die.

The next morning my friends woke me up at five o'clock and said, "Now, if you want life, liberty and happiness," they laughed, "you must push for yourself. You must get a job. Come with us." And we went to the yards. Men and women were walking in by thousands as far as we could see. We went to the doors of one big slaughter house. There was a crowd of about 200 men waiting there for a job. They looked hungry and kept watching the door. At last a special policeman came out and began pointing to men, one by one. Each one jumped forward. Twenty-three were taken. Then they all went inside, and all the others turned their faces away and looked tired. I remember one boy sat down and cried, just next to me, on a pile of boards. Some policemen waved their clubs and we all walked on. I found some Lithuanians to talk with, who told me they had come every morning for three weeks. Soon we met other crowds coming away from other slaughter houses, and we all walked around and felt bad and tired and hungry.

That night I told my friends that I would not do this many days, but would go some place else. "Where?" they asked me, and I began to see then that I was in bad trouble, because I spoke no English. Then one man told me to give him $5 to give the special policeman. I did this and the next morning the policeman pointed me out, so I had a job. I have heard some big talk since then about my American freedom of contract, but I do not think I had much freedom in bargaining for this job with the Meat Trust. My job was in the cattle killing room. I pushed the blood along the gutter. . . . One Lithuanian, who worked with me, said, "They get all the blood out of those cattle and all the work out of us men." This was true, for we worked that first day from six in the morning till seven at night. The next day we worked from six in the morning till eight at night. The next day we had no work. So we had no good, regular hours. It was hot in the room that summer, and the hot blood made it worse.

I held this job six weeks and then I was turned off. I think some other man had paid for my job, or

perhaps I was too slow. The foreman in that room wanted quick men to make the work rush, because he was paid more if the work was done cheaper and quicker. I saw now that every man was helping himself, always trying to get all the money he could. At that time I believed that all men in Chicago were grafters when they had to be. They only wanted to push themselves.

. . . I kept walking around with many other Lithuanians who had no job. Our money was going and we could find nothing to do. At night we got homesick for our fine green mountains. We read all the news about home in our Lithuanian Chicago newspaper, *The Katalikas.* It is a good paper and gives all the news. In the same office we bought this song, which was written in Brooklyn by P. Brandukas. He, too, was homesick. It is sung all over Chicago now and you can hear it in the summer evenings through the open windows. In English it is something like this:

> Oh, Lithuania, so dear to me,
> Good-by to you, my Fatherland.
> Sorrowful in my heart I leave you,
> I know not who will stay to guard you. . . .

Those were bad days and nights. At last I had a chance to help myself. Summer was over and Election Day was coming. The Republican boss in our district, Jonidas, was a saloonkeeper. A friend took me there. Jonidas shook hands and treated me fine. He taught me to sign my name, and the next week I went with him to an office and signed some paper, and then I could vote. I voted as I was told, and then they got me back into the yards to work, because one big politician owns stock in one of those houses. Then I felt that I was getting in beside the game. I was in a combine like other sharp men. Even when work was slack I was all right, because they got me a job in the street cleaning department. I felt proud, and I went to the back room in Jonidas's saloon and got him to write a letter to Alexandria to tell her she must come soon and be my wife.

But this was just the trouble. All of us were telling our friends to come soon. Soon they came—even thousands. The employers in the yard liked this, because those sharp foremen are inventing new machines and the work is easier to learn, and so these slow Lithuanians and even green girls can learn to do it, and then the Americans and Germans and Irish are put out and the employer saves money, because the Lithuanians work cheaper. This was why the American labor unions began to organize us all just the same as they had organized the Bohemians and Poles before us.

Well, we were glad to be organized. We had learned that in Chicago every man must push himself always, and Jonidas had taught us how much better we could push ourselves by getting into a combine. Now, we saw that this union was the best combine for us, because it was the only combine that could say, "It is our business to raise your wages." . . . I joined the Cattle Butchers' Union. This union is honest and it has done me a great deal of good. It has raised my wages. The man who worked at my job before the union came was getting through the year an average of $9 a week. I am getting $11. In my first job I got $5 a week. The man who works there now gets $5.75.

It has given me more time to learn to read and speak and enjoy life like an American. I never work now from 6 A.M. to 9 P.M. and then be idle the next day. I work now from 7 A.M. to 5.30 P.M., and there are not so many idle days. The work is evened up.

With more time and more money I live much better and I am very happy. So is Alexandria. She came a year ago and has learned to speak English already. Some of the women go to the big store the day they get here, when they have not enough sense to pick out the clothes that look right, but Alexandria waited three weeks till she knew, and so now she looks the finest of any woman in the district. We have four nice rooms, which she keeps very clean, and she has flowers growing in boxes in the two front windows. We do not go much to church, because the church seems to be too slow. But we belong to a Lithuanian society that gives two picnics in summer and two big balls in winter, where we have a fine time. I go one night a week to the Lithuanian

Concertina Club. On Sundays we go on the trolley out into the country.

But we like to stay at home more now because we have a baby. When he grows up I will not send him to the Lithuanian Catholic school. They have only two bad rooms and two priests, who teach only in Lithuanian from prayer books. I will send him to the American school, which is very big and good. The teachers there are Americans and they belong to the Teachers' Labor Union, which has three thousand teachers and belongs to our Chicago Federation of Labor. I am sure that such teachers will give him a good chance. . . .

The union is doing another good thing. It is combining all the nationalities. The night I joined the Cattle Butchers' Union I was led into the room by a negro member. With me were Bohemians, Germans and Poles, and Mike Donnelly, the President, is an Irishman. He spoke to us in English and then three interpreters told us what he said. We swore to be loyal to our union above everything else except the country, the city and the State—to be faithful to each other—to protect the women workers—to do our best to understand the history of the labor movement, and to do all we could to help it on. Since then I have gone there every two weeks and I help the movement by being an interpreter for the other Lithuanians who come in. That is why I have learned to speak and write good English. The others do not need me long. They soon learn English, too, and when they have done that they are quickly becoming Americans.

But the best thing the union does is to make me feel more independent. I do not have to pay to get a job and I cannot be discharged unless I am no good. For almost the whole 30,000 men and women are organized now in some one of our unions and they all are directed by our central council. No man knows what it means to be sure of his job unless he has been fired like I was once without any reason being given. . . . You must get money to live well, and to get money you must combine. I cannot bargain alone with the Meat Trust. I tried it and it does not work. . . .[2]

INTRODUCTION TO DOCUMENTS 3 AND 4

The Jungle stirred up a storm of criticism. President Theodore Roosevelt obtained an advance copy of the book and appointed a committee to investigate the Chicago stockyards. At precisely the same time Sinclair pressed his case with Roosevelt. He sent the president a copy of *The Jungle,* and Roosevelt wrote to Sinclair directly, asking what the Department of Agriculture might do about the situation. In his response, Sinclair warned the president that the meatpacking companies were guilty not just of unhealthy practices but also bribery and corruption. Sinclair's letter is Document 3. Three months later, the committee appointed by Roosevelt completed its investigation of the meatpacking industry, and excerpts from that report are presented in Document 4. As Sinclair had anticipated, the committee found breaches of cleanliness in some plants but also many others that were quite hygienic. The passage reprinted here describes a plant that seemed to confirm many of *The Jungle's* accusations. Remember, however, that Sinclair wrote an indictment of capitalism—his point was that the power of the packinghouses and their desire for profit necessarily caused them to cut corners, cheat workers, and sell adulterated meat. The following report went to Congress and became evidence that helped pass Senator Albert Beveridge's bill to regulate the packing industry. Even in this most critical part of the investigators' report, note that they slight Sinclair's main concern, the working conditions of the employees in Packingtown.[3]

3. UPTON SINCLAIR TO PRESIDENT ROOSEVELT

MARCH 10, 1906

My dear President Roosevelt:

. . . I am glad to learn that the Department of Agriculture has taken up the matter of inspection, or lack of it, but I am exceedingly dubious as to what they will discover. I have seen so many people go out there and be put off with smooth pretences. A man has to be something of a detective, or else intimate with the working-men, as I have, before he can really see what is going on. And it is becoming a great deal more difficult since the publication of "The Jungle." I have received to-day a letter from an employe of Armour & Company, in response to my request to him to take Ray Stannard

Baker in hand and show him what he showed me a year and a half ago. He says: "He will have to be well disguised, for 'the lid is on' in Packingtown; he will find two detectives in places where before there was only one." You must understand that the thing which I have called the "condemned meat industry," is a matter of hundreds of thousands of dollars a month. I see in to-day's "Saturday Evening Post" that Mr. Armour declares in his articles . . . that "In Armour and Company's business not one atom of any condemned animal or carcass, finds its way, directly or indirectly, from any source, into any food product or food ingredient." Now, compare with that the following extract from a formal statement transmitted to Doubleday, Page & Company by Mr. Thomas H. McKee, attorney at law. . . who is a personal friend of Mr. Walter H. Page, and was sent out to Chicago by that firm to investigate the situation:

> With a special conductor, Mr. B. J. Mullaney, provided for me by Mr. Urion, attorney for Armour interests, I went through the Armour plant again. . . . I saw six hogs hung in line which had been condemned. A truck loaded with chopped up condemned hogs was in my presence (I followed it) placed in one of the tanks from which lard comes. I asked particularly about this and the inspector

together with Mr. Hull stated that lard and fertilizer would be the product from that tank. . . . Of the six condemned hogs referred to two were afflicted with cholers, their skin being red as blood and the legs scabbed; three were marked "tubercular," though they appeared normal to a layman, the sixth had an ulcer in its side which was apparent.

So much for Mr. McKee. For myself, I was escorted through Packingtown by a young lawyer who was brought up in the district, had worked as a boy in Armour's plant, and knew more or less ultimately every foreman, "spotter," and watchman about the

Image 6.3 "The Real Packingtown—If You Let the Packers Tell It" (1906)

Louis Glackens satirized the rosy descriptions of the meat packing industry made by the company owners. Upton Sinclair's lead character in *The Jungle*, Jurgis, is depicted at lower right as a well-heeled butcher, rather than a degraded factory worker. But perhaps most interesting are the vignettes that caricature the industry's claims that animals were well treated, quite at odds with the stark brutality depicted in *The Jungle* and the federal investigation of Packingtown.

Source: L. M. Glackens, in *Puck*, July 4, 1906

place. I saw with my own eyes hams, which had spoiled in pickle, being pumped full of chemicals to destroy the odor. I saw waste ends of smoked beef stored in barrels in a cellar, in a condition of filth which I could not describe in a letter. I saw rooms in which sausage meat was stored, with poisoned rats lying about, and the dung of rats covering them. . . .

Finally, I might add that I have a long affidavit from a man named Thomas F. Dolan, now at the head of the Boston & Maine News Bureau, who was for many years a superintendent in Armour's plant, and has letters to show that he was considered by Armour as the best man he ever employed. He makes oath to Armour's custom of taking condemned meat out of the bottoms of the tanks, into which they had been dropped with the idea of rendering them into fertilizer. It seems that the tanks are or were then built with a false bottom, which lets down on a hinge; and that when you stand at the top and see the meat dropped in, you are flooded by blinding clouds of steam which pour up from a pipe down in the tank. When this affidavit was published, Dolan was paid $5,000 by Armour to make another one contradicting himself. He took the $5,000 and went on to give away the whole story, which was published in the "Evening Journal," March 16, 1899. . . .

Baker knows intimately a man who is high in the counsels of Armour and Company, and was present at a conference in which Ogden Armour personally gave the decision to bribe Dolan.

. . . It would give me great pleasure to come down to Washington to see you at any time, but I would rather it was after you had read "The Jungle," because I have put a good deal of myself into that.

You ask—"Is there anything further, say in the Department of Agriculture, which you would suggest my doing?" I would suggest . . . that you find a man concerning whose intelligence and integrity you are absolutely sure; send him up here, or let me meet him in Washington, and tell him all that I saw, and how I saw it, and give him the names and addresses of the people who will enable him to see it. Then let him go to Packingtown as I did, as a working-man; live with the men, get a job in the yards, and use his eyes and ears; and see if he does not come out at the end of a few weeks feeling, as did the special correspondent of the London "Lancet," whom I met in Chicago, that the conditions in the packing-houses constitute a "menace to the health of the civilized world."

Thank you for your kind interest,
Very sincerely, Upton Sinclair.[4]

4. REPORT ON THE MEATPACKING INDUSTRY (1906)

The Senate and House of Representatives:
I transmit herewith the report of Mr. James Bronson Reynolds and Commissioner Charles P. Neill, the special committee whom I appointed to investigate into the conditions in the stock yards of Chicago and report thereon to me. . . . The conditions shown by even this short inspection to exist in the Chicago stock yards are revolting. It is imperatively necessary in the interest of health and of decency that they should be radically changed. Under the existing law it is wholly impossible to

secure satisfactory results. . . . I urge the immediate enactment into law of provisions which will enable the Department of Agriculture adequately to inspect the meat and meat food products entering into interstate commerce and to supervise the methods of preparing the same, and to prescribe the sanitary conditions under which the work shall be performed. . . .

Theodore Roosevelt
The White House, June 4, 1906

CONDITION OF THE YARDS

Before entering the buildings we noted the condition of the yards themselves as shown in the pavement, pens, viaducts, and platforms. The pavement is mostly of brick, the bricks laid with deep grooves between them, which inevitably fill with manure and refuse. Such pavement can not be properly cleaned and is slimy and malodorous when wet, yielding clouds of ill-smelling dust when dry. The pens are generally uncovered except those for sheep; these latter are paved and covered. The viaducts and platforms are of wood. Calves, sheep, and hogs that have died en route are thrown out upon the platforms where cars are unloaded. On a single platform on one occasion we counted fifteen dead hogs, on the next ten dead hogs. The only excuse given for delay in removal was that so often heard—the expense.

BUILDINGS

Ventilation—Systematic ventilation of the workrooms is not found in any of the establishments we visited. In a few instances electric fans mitigate the stifling air, but usually the workers toil without relief in a humid atmosphere heavy with the odors of rotten wood, decayed meats, stinking offal, and entrails.

   Equipment—The work tables upon which the meat is handled, the floor carts on which it is carried about, and the tubs and other receptacles into which it is thrown are generally of wood. In all the places visited but a single porcelain-lined receptacle was seen. Tables covered with sheet iron, iron carts, and iron tubs are being introduced into the better establishments, but no establishment visited has as yet abandoned the extensive use of wooden tables and wooden receptacles. These wooden receptacles are frequently found water soaked, only half cleansed, and with meat scraps and grease accumulations adhering to their sides, and collecting dirt. . . .

   Sanitary conveniences—Abominable as the above-named conditions are, the one that affects most directly and seriously the cleanliness of the food products is the frequent absence of any lavatory provisions in the privies. Washing sinks are either not furnished at all or are small and dirty. Neither are towels, soap, or toilet paper provided. Men and women return directly from these places to plunge their unwashed hands into the meat to be converted into such food products as sausages, dried beef, and other compounds. Some of the privies are situated at a long distance from the workrooms, and men relieve themselves on the killing floors or in a corner of the workrooms. Hence, in some cases the fumes of the urine swell the sum of nauseating odors arising from the dirty, blood-soaked, rotting, wooden floors—fruitful culture beds for the disease germs of men and animals. . . .

TREATMENT OF MEATS AND PREPARED FOOD PRODUCTS

A particularly glaring instance of uncleanliness was found in a room where the best grade of sausage was being prepared for export. It was made from carefully selected meats, and was being prepared to be eaten uncooked. In this case the employee carted the chopped-up meat across a room in a barrow, the handles of which were filthy with grease. The meat was then thrown out upon tables, and the employee climbed upon the table, handled the meat with his unwashed hands, knelt with his dirty apron and trousers in contact with the meat he was spreading out, and, after he had finished his operation, again took hold of the dirty handles of the wheelbarrow, went back for another load, and repeated this process indefinitely. Inquiry developed the fact that there was no water in this room at all, and the only method the man adopted for cleaning his hands was to rub them against his dirty apron or on his still filthier trousers.

   As an extreme example of the entire disregard on the part of employees of any notion of cleanliness in handling dressed meat, we saw a hog that had just been killed, cleaned, washed, and started on its way to the cooling room fall from the sliding rail to a dirty wooden floor and slide part way into a filthy men's privy. It was picked up by two employees, placed upon a truck, carried into the cooling room and hung up with other carcasses, no effort being made to clean it. . . .

   All of [the] canned products bear labels, of which the following is a sample: "The contents of this package have been inspected according to the act of Congress of March 3, 1891. QUALITY GUARANTEED."

The phraseology of these labels is wholly unwarranted. The Government inspectors pass only upon the healthfulness of the animal at the time of killing. They know nothing of the process through which the meat has passed since this inspection. They do not know what else may have been placed in the cans in addition to "inspected meat." As a matter of fact, they know nothing about the "contents" of the can upon which the packers place these labels—do not even know that it contains what it purports to contain. The legend "Quality guaranteed" immediately following the statement as to Government inspection is wholly unjustifiable. It deceives and is plainly designed to deceive the average purchaser, who naturally infers from the label that the Government guarantees the contents of the can to be what it purports to be. . . .

TREATMENT OF EMPLOYEES

The lack of consideration for the health and comfort of the laborers in the Chicago stock yards seem to be a direct consequence of the system of administration that prevails. The various departments are under the direct control of superintendents who claim to use full authority in dealing with the employees and who seem to ignore all considerations except those of the account book. Under this system proper care of the products and of the health and comfort of the employees is impossible, and the consumer suffers in consequence. The insanitary conditions in which the laborers work and the feverish pace which they are forced to maintain inevitably affect their health. Physicians state that tuberculosis is disproportionately prevalent in the stock yards, and the victims of this disease expectorate on the spongy wooden floors of the dark workrooms, from which falling scraps of meat are later shoveled up to be converted into food products.

Even the ordinary decencies of life are completely ignored. In practically all cases the doors of the toilet rooms open directly into the working rooms, the privies of men and women frequently adjoin, and the entrances are sometimes no more than a foot or two apart. In other cases there are no privies for women in the rooms in which they work, and to reach the nearest it is necessary to go up or down a couple of flights of stairs. In one noticeable instance the privy for the women working in several adjoining rooms was in a room in which men chiefly were employed, and every girl going to use this had to pass by the working places of dozens of male operatives and enter the privy, the door of which was not 6 feet from the working place of one of the men operatives. As previously noted, in the privies for men and women alike there are no partitions, but simply a long row of open seats. . . .

The neglect on the part of their employers to recognize or provide for the requirements of cleanliness and decency of the employees must have an influence that can not be exaggerated in lowering the morals and discouraging cleanliness on the part of the workers employed in the packing houses. The whole situation as we saw it in these huge establishments tends necessarily and inevitably to the moral degradation of thousands of workers, who are forced to spend their working hours under conditions that are entirely unnecessary and unpardonable, and which are a constant menace not only to their own health, but to the health of those who use the food products prepared by them. . . .[5]

INTRODUCTION TO DOCUMENTS 5 AND 6

The meatpacking industry had been very resistant to federal regulation, but *The Jungle* and subsequent publicity so stirred up the public that some sort of federal intervention was all but inevitable. Packinghouses quickly turned to damage control—the industry had to win back public confidence by seeming to be out front on reform. Even advertising shifted toward issues of cleanliness, as evident in Document 5. "The Massachusetts State Board of Health Endorses William Underwood

Company's Products," magazine ads in 1906 declared; "The report shows their ABSOLUTE PURITY and freedom from improper adulterants and preservatives. . . . [and] recommends the Wm. Underwood Co.'s CANNING PLANTS as MODELS to be copied by others in the same business." Document 6 is an open letter from Louis F. Swift, president of one of the largest packing houses in Chicago, that addressed these issues; the letter was reprinted in *The Outlook*, on June 23, 1906.

5. UNDERWOOD CANNED MEAT ADVERTISEMENT (1906)

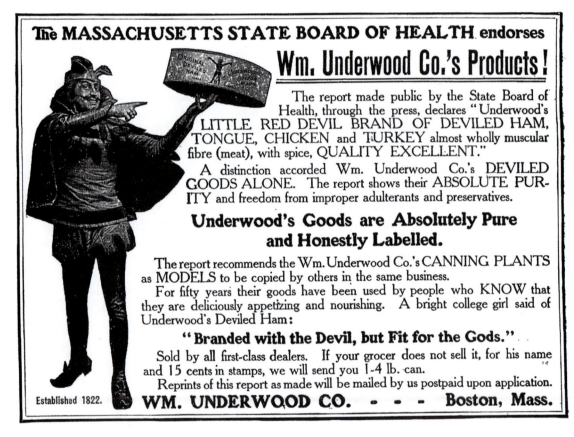

Image 6.4 Underwood canned meat advertisement (1906)

The Jungle prompted significant reforms in the meatpacking industry, reflected in the tone and content of advertisements thereafter. But note how Upton Sinclair's main concern, the welfare of the workers, saw little change.

Source: Country Life in America, October 1906. Courtesy Penrose Library, University of Denver.

6. LETTER FROM LOUIS F. SWIFT TO *THE OUTLOOK*

Swift & Company
Union Stock Yards.
Office of the President.
Chicago, June 14, 1906.

Government Supervision of the Meat Industry

No. 1. All cattle, sheep, and hogs purchased by Swift & Company are U.S. Government inspected, both before and after dressing. Those condemned in the ante-mortem inspection are refused and disposed of under local health authorities' supervision.

No. 2. The animals condemned by the Federal inspectors after dressing are destroyed under the inspector's supervision. Ante-mortem and post-mortem inspection is now furnished by the Government only when requested and not compulsory under present law. Swift & Company have always been strong advocates of thorough Government inspection both before and after slaughter, and we desire an extension of these regulations to cover all packing and slaughtering establishments, in order that uniform regulations may govern the entire industry; and to be compulsory.

No. 3. All processes in the preparation of meats to be under Federal inspection, which should require (*a*) that the meats are from healthy animals proper for food; (*b*) that the conditions under which the work is conducted are sanitary.

No. 4. The Government should pay the cost of inspection, thus affording the packer the same protection given the consumer. The packer does not produce any animals, and under Government inspection will not accept any showing traces of disease in the live examination. The packer now stands the loss of any animals condemned in the postmortem examination, and to add an inspection fee is unfair.

Swift & Company want to be fully understood when they say that the same *open-door policy* which has prevailed in their plants will continue, the public being welcome to inspect the conditions under which the work is conducted, Further, we desire the continuance of Government inspection for all of our own plants and its strict compulsory enforcement in all other plants, regulating both the inspection of dressed meats and all food products, and the conditions under which the work is performed. . . .

Louis F. Swift, President.

POSTSCRIPT

Louis Swift endorsed in almost every detail Senator Albert Beveridge's bill, which became the Meat Inspection Act of 1906. One reason that the large meat packers supported the bill can be found in a single sentence in Swift's letter:

> We desire the continuance of Government inspection for all of our own plants and its strict compulsory enforcement in all other plants, regulating both the inspection of dressed meats and all food products, and the conditions under which the work is performed.

Many independent butchers objected to the Meat Inspection Act because they simply would not be able to afford the equipment and labor to comply with its provisions. The large packers saw this as an opportunity to drive out small competitors and increase their markets. Moreover, the federal government acting as an impartial guarantor of cleanliness reassured the public at home and abroad, who returned to buying meat from the packing companies. In exchange for a bit of federal interference, the large packers now operated in a much more stable marketplace.

QUESTIONS

1. Do you think Upton Sinclair exaggerated the conditions in Packingtown? How does his account and letter to the president compare to the report in document 4? To Antanas Kaztauskis's story?
2. What did Upton Sinclair mean when he said that he aimed at the public's heart but hit it in the stomach? What accounts for the wide appeal of *The Jungle*?
3. What issues do these documents reveal about the role of government in protecting the health of citizens?
4. How did Sinclair think about the poor? About immigrants?
5. How would you characterize the relationship between business, workers and government in the Progressive Era based on these documents?

ADDITIONAL READING

The literature on the Progressive Era is extensive. Two classic works are Robert Wiebe, *The Search for Order* (1966), and Gabriel Kolko, *The Triumph of Conservatism* (1967). For a more recent synthesis of historians' thinking, see Steven J. Diner, *A Very Different Age* (1998); for politics in the era, see Michael McGerr, *A Fierce Discontent* (2005). For background on Chicago, see Dominic Pacyga, *Polish Immigrants and Industrial Chicago* (2003) and *Chicago: A Biography* (2011); and David L. Miller, *City of the Century* (1997). On the stockyards and Packingtown, see James R. Barrett, *Work and Community in the Jungle* (1988); Louise Caroll Wade, *Chicago's Pride* (1988); and Dominic Pacyga, *Slaughterhouse* (2015). *The Autobiography of Upton Sinclair* (1962) offers insight into the man, as do Kevin Mattson's *Upton Sinclair and the Other American Century* (2006) and Anthony Arthur's *Radical Innocent: Upton Sinclair* (2006). Related works include James Harvey Young, *Securing the Federal Food and Drug Act of 1906* (1989); Alan Dawley, *Struggles for Justice* (1991); and Elizabeth Sanders, *Roots of Reform* (1999).

ENDNOTES

1. Upton Sinclair, *The Jungle* (New York: Doubleday, 1906).
2. *The Independent*, v.57 (August 4, 1904), pp. 241–248.
3. President Roosevelt's letter to Sinclair located in the Theodore Roosevelt papers (microfilm), Division of Manuscripts, Library of Congress, Series 2, Reel 340, p. 103.
4. Letter from Upton Sinclair to President Theodore Roosevelt, March 10, 1906; Records of the Office of the Secretary of Agriculture, Record Group 16. National Archives and Records Administration.
5. Hearings before the Committee on Agriculture. . . on the So-Called "Beveridge Amendment" to the Agricultural Appropriation Bill. . .; 59th Congress, 1st Session. (Washington, D.C.: Government Printing Office, 1906).

CHAPTER 7

MOBILIZING FOR WAR

HISTORICAL CONTEXT

The 1914 outbreak of war in Europe presented several difficult problems to the United States government as it considered how to respond. The United States was not attacked, and millions of Americans—especially those with familial or emotional ties to Germany, Austria–Hungary, or Ireland—opposed the United States' entry into the war. For example, journalist H. L. Mencken openly defended Germany during the early years of the war. He ended letters to his German American friends with "May all Englishmen roast forever in hell! A pox upon the English!" or "The Kaiser must and shall win!" Mencken ended pro-German newspaper columns with "In Paris by Thanksgiving!" or "In Paris by Christmas!" Thousands of Americans opposed President Woodrow Wilson's decision in April 1917 to enter the conflict. Far from being a noble struggle—"a war to end all wars," as Wilson phrased it—writer Randolph Bourne predicted that the war would become an imperialistic land grab, while at home it would foster the suppression of civil liberties and the curtailment of free speech. War, Bourne wrote, "automatically sets in motion throughout society those irresistible forces of uniformity, for passionate cooperation with the Government in coercing into obedience the minority groups and individuals which lack the larger herd sense." Noting too the consolidation of power and resources, Bourne declared famously, "War is the health of the state."

Bourne defined patriotism as "merely the emotion that fills the herd when it imagines itself engaged in mass defense or massed attack." More than anything, he feared mob rule, and some of his fears were realized. Moved to frenzied anti-German prejudice, the "herd" cried for "100 percent Americanism." It demanded that hamburger and sauerkraut be renamed liberty sandwich and liberty cabbage, that German language and literature no longer be taught in public schools, that all things German be viewed with suspicion and disgust. Along with mindless hate came mindless violence. In Wyoming, a man who exclaimed "Hoch der Kaiser" on the day that Wilson delivered his war message was hanged, cut down while still alive, and forced to kneel and kiss the American flag. Near St. Louis, a mob attacked Robert Prager, a German American, bound him in an American flag, dragged him through the streets, and lynched him before a cheering crowd of 500 "patriots." For this crime, the leaders of the mob were tried and found not guilty. After the trial, one jury member remarked, "Well, I guess nobody can say we aren't loyal now." Such episodes would lead social critic Walter Lippmann to write in his influential essay *Public Opinion* (1922) that most American citizens are "mentally children or barbarians. . . . The stream of public opinion is stopped by them in little eddies of misunderstanding, where it is discolored with prejudices and farfetched analogy."

For Bourne, the great threat was the role that government might play in creating mass conformity. "It will be coercion from above that will do the trick rather than patriotism from below," he cautioned. True to his prediction, soon after America's entry into the war in 1917, the government officially began to shape the public's attitude toward the war effort and Germany. During the first month of the war, Wilson and his military leaders organized the Committee on Public Information (CPI) and placed George Creel, a Progressive supporter of Wilson and a muckraking journalist, at the head of the agency. At first, the CPI was no crude propaganda mill: in the early months, Creel saw his duty as providing information that enlightened Americans, not propaganda and censorship that altered or hid the truth. Like Wilson, Creel believed in the essential righteousness of the American cause, and he insisted that a mere recitation of "the facts"—the standard Progressive refrain—would be enough to convince anyone. As the war went on, however, the CPI promulgated vast amounts of propaganda. Its "Four Minute Men"—speakers who sang the praises of America's war effort in short talks given in public places—began to dwell more on German atrocities and less on American war aims. For the first time in America, movies became part of the home front effort, and soon upbeat films like *Pershing's Crusaders* and *Old Colored Fighters* gave way to hate productions such as *Prussian Cur* and *The Kaiser, the Beast of Berlin*.

The American war message was spread in a number of ways. The CPI distributed 75 million pamphlets, 6,000 press releases, and 14,000 drawings. Some 75,000 speakers stumped for their country. Certainly words—written or spoken—were important, but equally important were images, each one printed by the tens of thousands and emblazoned on posters across the country. Posters were employed, noted one authority on the subject, "to call for recruits . . . to request war loans, to make national policies acceptable, to spur industrial effort, to channel emotions such as courage or hate, to urge conservation of resources and inform the public of food and fuel substitutes." Posters announced personal appearances by celebrities, spread popular songs, and depicted flag ceremonies. Altogether, millions of posters were printed. For example, in the First Liberty Bond campaign to raise money for the war effort, two million posters appeared. This number increased to five million for the Second Liberty Bond campaign and nine million for the Third Liberty Bond campaign.

To understand the impact of these posters, one needs to imagine a time before computers, the Internet, the television, or even the mass use of radio. Although newspapers informed the literate public, posters supplied a primary means of mass communication, especially for selling products. Industries used posters to hawk their goods, newspapers and magazines used posters to entice readers, and circuses and motion picture theaters used posters to attract spectators. Posters were everywhere—on the fences of baseball parks, on the sides of public and private buildings, and on the wooden sandwich boards that men and boys wore to advertise some product or event. When the British passenger liner the *Lusitania* was sunk by a German U-boat on May 7, 1915, the United States exploded with anger. Newspapers mourned the 128 Americans lost in the tragedy, and Wilson threatened war. But perhaps the horror and meaning of the event was most fully portrayed in a poster released by the Boston Committee of Public Safety in June of 1915. The crude but powerful image drawn by Fred Spear shows a drowning woman clothed in a gossamer gown sinking to the bottom of the sea. In her arms she holds her baby. It is an almost surreal scene, both sensual and familial. "ENLIST" is the poster's simple message. Its impact was felt across the nation.

Spear's poster—like the millions that followed it—was "the weapon on the wall." Although it looked like art, in the fullest sense it was not art. Art seeks to extend the viewer's understanding of nature and life. War posters attempt to restrict the viewer's understanding. Peter Stanley, a historian of the subject, observed,

> A successful poster was one capable of only one interpretation. Most of the posters . . . did not seek a dialogue: they imposed, imparted, and impelled, but did not inquire. They sought to persuade the viewer, and then to have him or her act in ways regarded as useful by the sponsors of the posters.[1]

To do this, they dealt with slogans and basic, easily comprehensible visual images. To strike the proper response, however, those images had to be part of the viewer's cultural baggage, and they had to speak to the viewer's deepest needs, desires, or fears.

A number of important illustrators and artists turned their talents to poster making during the war. In mid-April 1917, Charles Dana Gibson, creator of the Gibson Girl and the editor of the original *Life* magazine, called upon artists to bring their creativity in the war effort. The result was the Division of Pictorial Publicity, which offered its services free of charge to the government. Such famous artists as James Montgomery Flagg, Howard Chandler Christy, and Joseph Pennell contributed to the output of the Division. Each artist brought to his work a distinctive style, and each labored to strike a particular chord in the viewer. James Montgomery Flagg appealed to simple, sentimental patriotism. In his most famous poster, a deadly serious Uncle Sam, modeled after the artist himself, points a finger at the viewer and announces, "I WANT YOU for the U.S. ARMY." Another poster, which pictures a sleeping woman dressed in the Stars and Stripes, reads, "WAKE UP, AMERICA! CIVILIZATION CALLS EVERY MAN WOMAN AND CHILD!" Howard Chandler Christy made earthier appeals. The Christy Girl exuded a wholesome sex appeal. In one Navy recruitment poster, a Christy Girl exclaims, "GEE! I WISH I WERE *A MAN . . . I'D* JOIN THE NAVY." In another, a more sultry Christy Girl says, "*I WANT YOU* FOR *THE NAVY.*" F. Strothman produced an effective Liberty Bond poster by portraying the Germans as Huns bent on destroying civilization. One of his posters shows a satanic, spike-helmeted German, his bayonet and hands dripping blood, staring at the viewer over the smoldering rubble of a destroyed city. "Beat Back the HUN with LIBERTY BONDS," reads the inscription.

INTRODUCTION TO DOCUMENT 1

George Creel began his working life as a journalist in Kansas City and Denver. But by the Progressive Era, he moved smoothly from crafting words as an investigative reporter to shaping sentences in the new field of advertising. He worked as a publicist for various causes, then as the United States entered World War I, he became the head of the government's effort to sell the war. Just a few years later, in 1920, Creel wrote a memoir of his work. *How We Advertised America* praised the arts of public relations. The book's subtitle gave away its author's theme: *The First Telling of the Amazing Story of the Committee on Public Information That Carried the Gospel of Americanism to Every Corner of the Globe.* Do you agree with Creel's claim that the war was as much a battle of ideas as of armies? Do you think that the CPI was a news bureau or a propaganda agency? What does Creel say?

1. *HOW WE ADVERTISED AMERICA* (1920)

GEORGE CREEL

. . . As Secretary Baker points out, the war was not fought in France alone. Back of the firing-line, back of armies and navies, back of the great supply-depots, another struggle waged with the same intensity and with almost equal significance attaching to its victories and defeats. It was the fight for the *minds* of men, for the "conquest of their convictions," and the battle-line ran through every home in every country.

It was in this recognition of Public Opinion as a major force that the Great War differed most essentially from all previous conflicts. The trial of strength was not only between massed bodies of armed men, but between opposed ideals, and moral verdicts took on all the value of military decisions. . . .

The Committee on Public Information was called into existence to make this fight for the "verdict of mankind," the voice created to plead the justice of America's cause before the jury of Public Opinion. . . . *In no degree was the Committee an agency of censorship, a machinery of concealment or repression. Its emphasis throughout was on the open and the positive. At no point did it seek or exercise authorities under those war laws that limited the freedom of speech and press.* In all things, from first to last, without halt or change, it was a plain publicity proposition, a vast enterprise in salesmanship, the world's greatest adventure in advertising.

Under the pressure of tremendous necessities an organization grew that not only reached deep into every American community, but that carried to every corner of the civilized globe the full message of America's idealism, unselfishness, and indomitable purpose. We fought prejudice, indifference, and disaffection at home and we fought ignorance and falsehood abroad. We strove for the maintenance of our own morale and the Allied morale by every process of stimulation; every possible expedient was employed to break through the barrage of lies that kept the people of the Central Powers in darkness and delusion; we sought the friendship and support of the neutral nations by continuous presentation of facts. We did not call it *propaganda*, for that word, in German hands, had come to be associated with deceit and corruption. Our effort was educational and informative throughout, for we had such confidence in our case as to feel that no other argument was needed than the simple, straightforward presentation of facts.

There was no part of the great war machinery that we did not touch, no medium of appeal that we did not employ. The printed word, the spoken word, the motion picture, the telegraph, the cable, the wireless, the poster, the sign-board—all these were used in our campaign to make our own people and all other peoples understand the causes that compelled America to take arms. All that was fine and ardent in the civilian population came at our call until more than one hundred and fifty thousand men and women were devoting highly specialized abilities to the work of the Committee, as faithful and devoted in their service as though they wore the khaki.

While America's summons was answered without question by the citizenship as a whole, it is to be remembered that during the three and a half years of our neutrality the land had been torn by a thousand divisive prejudices, stunned by the voices of anger and confusion, and muddled by the pull and haul of opposed interests. These were conditions that could not be permitted to endure. What we had to have was no mere surface unity, but a passionate belief in the justice of America's cause that should weld the people of the United States into one white-hot mass instinct with fraternity, devotion, courage, and deathless determination. The *war-will*, the will-to-win, of a democracy depends upon the degree to which each one of all the people of that democracy can concentrate and consecrate body and soul and spirit in the supreme effort of service and sacrifice. What had to be driven home was that all business was the nation's business, and every task a common task for a single purpose.

Starting with the initial conviction that the war was not the war of an administration, but the war of one hundred million people, and believing that public support was a matter of public understanding, we opened up the activities of government to the inspection of the citizenship. A voluntary censorship agreement safeguarded military information of obvious value to the enemy, but in all else the rights of the press were recognized and furthered. Trained men, at the center of effort in every one of the warmaking branches of government, reported on progress and achievement, and in no other belligerent nation was

there such absolute frankness with respect to every detail of the national war endeavor.

As swiftly as might be, there were put into pamphlet form America's reasons for entering the war, the meaning of America, the nature of our free institutions, our war aims, likewise analyses of the Prussian system, the purposes of the imperial German government, and full exposure of the enemy's misrepresentations, aggressions, and barbarities. Written by the country's foremost publicists, scholars, and historians, and distinguished for their conciseness, accuracy, and simplicity, these pamphlets blew as a great wind against the clouds of confusion and misrepresentation. . . .

The Four Minute Men, an organization that will live in history by reason of its originality and effectiveness, commanded the volunteer services of 75,000 speakers, operating in 5,200 communities, and making a total of 755,190 speeches, every one having the carry of shrapnel.

With the aid of a volunteer staff of several hundred translators, the Committee kept in direct touch with the foreign-language press, supplying selected articles designed to combat ignorance and disaffection. It organized and directed twenty-three societies and leagues designed to appeal to certain classes and particular foreign-language groups, each body carrying a specific message of unity and enthusiasm to its section of America's adopted peoples.

It planned war exhibits for the state fairs of the United States, also a great series of interallied war expositions that brought home to our millions the exact nature of the struggle that was being waged in France. In Chicago alone two million people attended in two weeks, and in nineteen cities the receipts aggregated $1,432,261.36.

The Committee mobilized the advertising forces of the country—press, periodical, car, and outdoor—for the patriotic campaign that gave millions of dollars worth of free space to the national service.

It assembled the artists of America on a volunteer basis for the production of posters, window-cards, and similar material of pictorial publicity for the use of various government departments and patriotic societies. A total of 1,438 drawings was used.

It issued an official daily newspaper, serving every department of government, with a circulation of one hundred thousand copies a day. For official use only, its value was such that private citizens ignored the supposedly prohibitive subscription price, subscribing to the amount of $77,622.58.

It organized a bureau of information for all persons who sought direction in volunteer war-work, in acquiring knowledge of any administrative activities, or in approaching business dealings with the government. In the ten months of its existence it gave answers to eighty-six thousand requests for specific information.

It gathered together the leading novelists, essayists, and publicists of the land, and these men and women, without payment, worked faithfully in the production of brilliant, comprehensive articles that went to the press as syndicate features.

One division paid particular attention to the rural press and the plate-matter service. Others looked after the specialized needs of the labor press, the religious press, and the periodical press. The Division of Women's War Work prepared and issued the information of peculiar interest to the women of the United States, also aiding in the task of organizing and directing.

Through the medium of the motion picture, America's war progress, as well as the meanings and purposes of democracy, were carried to every community in the United States and to every corner of the world. "Pershing's Crusaders," "America's Answer," and "Under Four Flags" were types of feature films by which we drove home America's resources and determinations, while other pictures, showing our social and industrial life, made our free institutions vivid to foreign peoples. . . .

Turning away from the United States to the world beyond our borders, a triple task confronted us. First, there were the peoples of the Allied nations that had to be fired by the magnitude of the American effort and the certainty of speedy and effective aid. . . . Second,

we had to carry the truth to the neutral nations, poisoned by German lies; and third, we had to get the ideals of America, the determination of America, and the invincibility of America into the Central Powers.

Unlike other countries, the United States had no subsidized press service with which to meet the emergency. As a matter of bitter fact, we had few direct news contacts of our own with the outside world, owing to a scheme of contracts that turned the foreign distribution of American news over to European agencies. The volume of information that went out from our shores was small, and, what was worse, it was concerned only with the violent and unusual in our national life. It was news of strikes and lynchings, riots, murder cases, graft prosecutions, sensational divorces, the bizarre extravagance of "sudden millionaires." Naturally enough, we were looked upon as a race of dollar-mad materialists, a land of cruel monopolists, our real rulers the corporations and our democracy a "fake."

Looking about for some way in which to remedy this evil situation, we saw the government wireless lying comparatively idle, and through the close and generous co-operation of the navy we worked out a news machinery that soon began to pour a steady stream of American information into international channels of communication. Opening an office in every capital of the world outside the Central Powers, a daily service went out from Tuckerton to the Eiffel Tower for use in France and then for relay to our representatives in Berne, Rome, Madrid, and Lisbon. . . . The Orient was served by telegraph from New York to San Diego, and by wireless leaps to Cavite and Shanghai. From Shanghai the news went to Tokio and Peking, and from Peking on to Vladivostok for Siberia. Australia, India, Egypt, and the Balkans were also reached, completing the world chain. . . .[2]

INTRODUCTION TO DOCUMENT 2

The creation of wartime publicity reached far down into American society. The National Committee of Patriotic Societies, based in Washington, D.C., sponsored a range of activities and published several pamphlets, including one called "Patriotic Posters." Much of the text was technical and aesthetic, advice that could apply to most graphic art for public display. But the war gave special meaning now to the work of artists. The authors criticized German poster art—"Masses of heavy opaque color cover up bad drawing, and crude, violent color schemes distract the eye from poor line, faulty composition, and even from absence of idea"—while praising French work as "alive with action" that "stimulates the civilian to do his part." Note how nativism blended seamlessly with America's sense of mission.

2. THE ARTIST'S CALL TO COLORS (1918)

NATIONAL COMMITTEE OF PATRIOTIC SOCIETIES

In 1917, when the call to arms was sounded from coast to coast, in place of Paul Revere to awaken the sleeping countryside there was chosen the poster—the *only* messenger which can go everywhere among us, and still remain everywhere with us. . . . The opportunity of the poster is knocking at the door of every studio in the land. The call is out for artists to rally to their colors and enlist their talents in the fight for their country.

Inspiration? When has there been greater? Because posters have largely been used in the past for strictly commercial purposes, many artists have failed to find sufficient interest in poster design to even inquire into its nature and possibilities. . . . Today there can be no hesitancy on the part of the artist to throw himself into the creation of posters with all the energy and enthusiasm he may once have reserved for great exhibition pictures. . . .

The hour is at hand when the art of this country can and must be emancipated from the influence of German technique. . . . German methods in commercial art have gained an alarming foothold in the schools, both public and private, throughout the country. And it requires no stretch of the imagination to see, in the promotion of German art by German agents, a part of the far reaching and insidious propaganda which was intended to popularize all things German until the time was ripe for material conquests. . . .

It is the duty of every art teacher, art director and art editor, as well as of the judges in every poster competition, to deny consideration to any submitted work which is clearly based on the German commercial art idea. . . . Only in this way can we open a path for the development of anything which can come to be called American art. Our artists must design American posters instead of copying German posters.[3]

INTRODUCTION TO DOCUMENT 3

The authors of "Patriotic Posters" made it clear that good work appealed to the emotions and motivated action; too much intellectual depth would leave viewers cold and unmoved. The following posters proved effective during World War I. They managed to create a world without complexity, a world that was two-dimensional. By stereotyping Germans, women, and their fellow Americans, the artists were able to pique emotions and bend reality. What appeals did they make? What fears were aroused? What values are embedded in these images?

Remember, war poster art is political in that it attempts to arouse a civic response. The challenge of such visual documents is the act of interpretation. Each poster can be "read." For example, Germans in American World War I posters are often portrayed as faceless or apelike, giving rise to the visual impression that they represent a subhuman enemy. As another example, the eyes of the central figure in the posters can also be read. What do the eyes say to each viewer? Do they seek to elevate or denigrate, challenge, or flirt with the viewer? Eyes that look up often increase the viewer's estimation of the subject and ennoble the cause that is being advanced. Eyes that look directly at the viewer are often meant to challenge. To read the posters intelligently, you have to examine the small as well as the large details and constantly ask yourself, "What response is this meant to arouse?" Finally, since the posters are reprinted here in black and white, try to imagine what colors were used in the originals, for color is also meaningful. Some colors, like primary red and black, are threatening and foreboding; others, like green, light blue, and silver, are uplifting.

3. THE POSTERS[4]

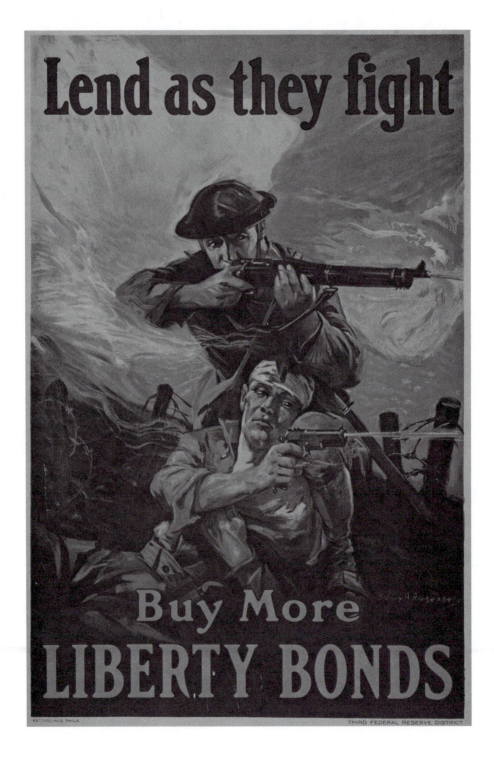

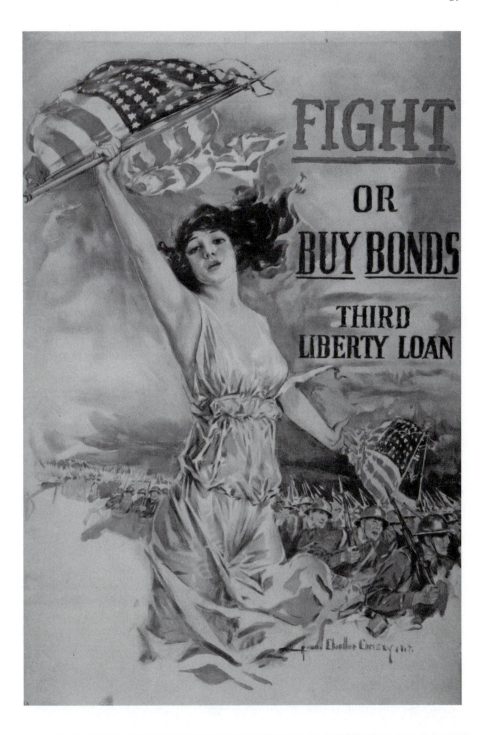

INTRODUCTION TO DOCUMENTS 4 AND 5

The Committee on Public Information developed tools of persuasion by using imagery, slogans, and ideas to convince Americans to support the war in whatever way that they could. But these were not the only instruments used to generate loyalty during war. Congress, as well as state and local governments, passed rules, ordinances, and statutes to curb dissent. Document 4 is an excerpt from the Espionage Act of June 1917, passed just two months after Congress declared war on Germany at the request of President Wilson. One year later, Congress passed the Sedition Act (Document 5), substantially expanding the range of offenses listed under the Espionage Act. What, according to the Sedition Act, was an acceptable form of dissent?

4. FROM THE ESPIONAGE ACT (JUNE 15, 1917)

Whoever, when the United States is at war, shall wilfully make or convey false reports or false statements with intent to interfere with the operation or success of the military or naval forces of the United States or to promote the success of its enemies and whoever when the United States is at war, shall wilfully cause or attempt to cause insubordination, disloyalty, mutiny, refusal of duty, in the military or naval forces of the United States, or shall wilfully obstruct the recruiting or enlistment service of the United States, to the injury of the service or of the United States, shall be punished by a fine of not more than $10,000 or imprisonment for not more than twenty years, or both.

5. FROM THE SEDITION ACT (MAY 16, 1918)

Whoever, when the United States is at war, shall wilfully make or convey false reports or false statements with intent to interfere with the operation or success of the military or naval forces of the United States, or to promote the success of its enemies, or shall wilfully make or convey false reports or false statements, or say or do anything except by way of bona fide and not disloyal advice to an investor or investors, with intent to obstruct the sale by the United States of bonds or other securities of the United States or the making of loans by or to the United States, and whoever when the United States is at war, shall wilfully cause or attempt to cause, or incite or attempt to incite, insubordination, disloyalty, mutiny, or refusal of duty, in the military or naval forces of the United States, or shall wilfully obstruct or attempt to obstruct the recruiting or enlistment services of the United States, and whoever, when the United States is at war, shall wilfully utter, print, write or publish any disloyal, profane, scurrilous, or abusive language about the form of government of the United States or the Constitution of the United States, or the military or naval forces of the United States, or the flag of the United States, or the uniform of the Army or Navy of the United States into contempt, scorn, contumely, or disrepute, or shall wilfully utter, print, write, or publish any language intended to incite, provoke, or encourage resistance to the United States, or to promote the cause of its enemies, or shall willfully display the flag of any foreign enemy, or shall willfully by utterance, writing, printing, publication, or language spoken, urge, incite, or advocate any curtailment of production in this country of any thing or things, product or products, necessary or essential to the prosecution of the war in which the United States may be engaged, with intent by such curtailment to cripple or hinder the United States in the prosecution of war, and whoever shall willfully advocate, teach, defend, or suggest the doing of any of the acts or things in this section enumerated, and whoever shall by word or act support or favor the cause of any country with which the United States is at war or by word or act oppose the cause of the United States therein, shall be punished by a fine of not more than $10,000 or the imprisonment for not more than twenty years, or both: Provided, That any employee or official of the United States Government who commits any disloyal act or utters any unpatriotic or disloyal language, or who, in an abusive and violent manner criticizes the Army or Navy or the flag of the United States shall be at once dismissed from the service. . . .

INTRODUCTION TO DOCUMENTS 6 AND 7

Once America entered the war, a campaign against all things German began. Many state and local governments acted to limit the influence of German culture. In Document 6 the California State Board of Education explained its decision to abolish instruction of the German language. In Document 7, the California Commissioner of Secondary Schools responded to a teacher who had urged that language instruction in German continue. The commissioner's reasoning demonstrates how quickly Germans came to be vilified once the United States declared war in April 1917.

6. FROM THE *BIENNIAL REPORT OF THE CALIFORNIA STATE BOARD OF EDUCATION* (1918)

Acting under the authority conferred upon us by law in the matter of the listing of high school textbooks and the approval of courses of study for the high schools, we have eliminated the study of German from the high schools of the state. This step has been taken as a war measure and we feel that we have been fully justified in the internment, at least for the duration of the war, of this "alien enemy" language. Investigation disclosed the fact that the high school texts in German were being used in an insidious manner for purposes of German propaganda. Whatever may be the occasion for the study of German in our public schools after the war is over, for literary or commercial reasons, it does not seem either logical or patriotic at the present time to continue instruction in a language that disseminates the ideals of autocracy, brutality and hatred.

We have revised the state series of music books and eliminated all German songs. The action was taken after a conference with the state council of defense and with the specific approval of that body.

A careful review has been made by a committee of the leading teachers of history in the state of the high school texts in history; and all that were found tainted with the propaganda of German "culture" have been stricken from the approved list of texts.

We are of the opinion that in this crisis in the history of the world when American has solemnly dedicated itself to the task of destroying the world menace of Prussian autocracy, the people of California are in no mood to permit the children in our schools to use any texts which in some form, subtle or avowed, are made the medium of excuses for German methods and glorification of German ideals.

LOYALTY OF TEACHERS

We desire to pay a tribute to the loyalty and patriotism of the teachers of California. They have responded to the requests for special instruction in patriotism and for appeals for co-operation in food conservation, Red Cross work, Thrift Stamp and Liberty Loan campaigns. Y.M.C.A. drives and other forms of war activity with a degree of cheerfulness and zeal that has been most gratifying. It is a remarkable fact that there has not been filed with the State Board of Education a single charge against a teacher, requesting the revocation of teaching credentials on the ground of disloyalty. We know of only two cases where normal school credentials have been revoked for this cause and there have come to our attention less than a dozen instances where teachers have been dismissed because of criticisms regarding their loyalty. When we remember that there are now over 18,000 teachers employed in the public schools of the state, this is a record of which California may well be proud.[5]

7. OPEN LETTER ON THE TEACHING OF THE GERMAN LANGUAGE

WILL C. WOOD, CALIFORNIA COMMISSIONER OF SECONDARY SCHOOLS

SACRAMENTO, CALIFORNIA, MAY 20, 1918

Dear Miss ____:

There is no doubt that the war lords of Germany have sought to use the study of German in American schools for the double purpose of retaining the loyalty of former citizens of Germany and fostering acceptance of German ideals by young Americans who study the language. Professor Voss, of the University of Wisconsin has said that the "beautiful and profitable task" of German-Americans is "to prepare the way in this country for the German spirit and the German conception of life." That he spoke for a considerable number of sympathizers is shown in a revelation of the activities of certain branches of the German-American Alliance recently investigated by Congress. That Alliance sought to promote the study of German for the express purpose of developing sympathy with the ideals of Germany—a sympathy that would excuse the Kaiser's mad forays against human civilization and especially that enlightened phase known as democracy. . . .

The teaching of German in America has been misused by German propagandists in a subtle but offensive manner. Textbooks have been filled with German propaganda and teachers have been told time without number that they must provide a "German atmosphere" for the teaching of German so that German ideals may thrive. German has been used as a weapon directed at the heart of American by German propagandists. Shall we assume that the Kaiser has ceased attempting to use it? . . .

The thing that remains after the language is forgotten, which is frequently very soon after ceasing the study, is an impression of the culture of a foreign nation, and certain linguistic ability. We can give linguistic training through the study of languages other than German. Only the culture argument remains to be disposed of. I admit that the literature of Germany before 1870 is worthy of study but I doubt whether in our study of German we can divorce German *culture* before 1870 from German *kultur* of recent date. Until that divorce is brought about, I do not believe that German can be taught safely in the public high schools.

. . . I note your intimation that some may consider the abolition of the teaching of German narrow-minded. The war has shown one thing conclusively—that democracy has been too trustful, too broad-minded in dealing with autocracy. Our broad-mindedness has been abused, our trust betrayed. It is true that we are not at war with the German language as such, but we are at war with Germany. And since Germany has used her language as she has used her submarines, to strike at the heart of America, we should intern the language for the period of the war.[6]

INTRODUCTION TO DOCUMENT 8

Randolph Bourne was right: the war enabled the Wilson administration, under powers granted by Congress, to unleash a wave of repression across America. The years from 1917 into the early 1920s witnessed powerful resistance to American participation in the war, all of which was met by intimidation, arrests, and deportations. Under the Espionage and Sedition Acts, U.S. attorneys brought charges against immigrants and radicals, people like Kate Richards O'Hare, Emma Goldman, and former Congressman Victor Berger of Milwaukee. Most famously targeted was Eugene V. Debs, leader of the railroad workers union and—by that point—a four-time Socialist Party candidate for president. Debs campaigned against the war. When three fellow socialists were arrested for speaking out, Debs told a crowd in Canton, Ohio that it had become, "extremely dangerous to exercise the Constitutional right of free speech in a country fighting to make democracy safe in the world." He went on, "They tell us that we live in a great free republic; that our institutions are democratic; that we are a free and self-governing people. This is too much, even for a joke." Federal agents arrested him under the Espionage and Sedition Acts for impeding conscription. Debs spoke to the federal court in Cleveland just before his sentence was pronounced.

8. EUGENE DEBS ADDRESSES THE COURT (1919)

Your Honor, years ago I recognized my kinship with all living beings, and I made up my mind that I was not one bit better than the meanest on earth. I said then, and I say now, that while there is a lower class, I am in it, and while there is a criminal element I am of it, and while there is a soul in prison, I am not free.

If the law under which I have been convicted is a good law, then there is no reason why sentence should not be pronounced upon me. I listened to all that was said in this court in support and justification of this prosecution, but my mind remains unchanged. I look upon the Espionage Law as a despotic enactment in flagrant conflict with democratic principles and with the spirit of free institutions.

Your Honor, I have stated in this court that I am opposed to form of our present Government; that

I am opposed to the social system in which we live; that I believed in the change of both—but by perfectly peaceable and orderly means.

Let me call your attention to the fact this morning that in this system five per cent of our people own and control two-thirds of our wealth; sixty-five per cent of the people, embracing the working class who produce all wealth, have but five per cent to show for it. . . .

I am thinking this morning of the men in the mills and factories; I am thinking of the men in the mines and on the railroads; I am thinking of the women who, for a paltry wage, are compelled to work out their lives; of the little children, who in this system, are robbed of their childhood, and in their early, tender years are seized in the remorseless grasp of Mammon, and forced into the industrial dungeons, there to feed the machines while they themselves are being starved body and soul. I see them dwarfed, diseased, stunted, their little lives broken, and their hopes blasted, because in this high noon of our twentieth century civilization money is still so much more important than human life. Gold is god and rules in the affairs of men. . . .

Your Honor, the five per cent of the people that I have made reference to constitute that element that absolutely rules our country. They privately own all our public necessities. They wear no crowns; they wield no scepters, they sit upon no thrones; and yet they are our economic masters and our political rulers. They control this Government and all of its institutions. They control the courts . . .

The five per cent of our people who own and control all of the sources of wealth, all of the nation's industries, all of the means of our common life, it is they who declare war. It is they who make peace. It is they who control our destiny. And so long as this

is true, we can make no just claim to being a democratic government, a self-governing people. . . .

This order of things cannot always endure. I have registered my protest against it. I recognize the feebleness of my effort, but, fortunately, I am not alone. There are multiplied thousands of others who, like myself, have come to realize that before we may truly enjoy the blessings of civilized life, we must reorganize society upon a mutual and cooperative basis; and to this end we have organized a great economic and political movement that spreads over the face of all the earth. . . .

Your Honor, I ask no mercy. I plead for no immunity. I realize that finally the right must prevail. I never so clearly comprehended as now the great struggle between the powers of greed on the one hand and upon the other the rising hosts of freedom.

I can see the dawn of a better day for humanity. The people are awakening. In due course they will come to their own.

When the mariner, sailing over tropic seas, looks for relief from his weary watch, he turns his eyes toward the southern cross, burning luridly above the tempest-vexed ocean. As the midnight approaches, the southern cross begins to bend, and the whirling worlds change their places, and with starry finger-points the Almighty marks the passage of time upon the dial of the universe, and though no bell may beat the glad tidings, the lookout knows that the midnight is passing and that relief and rest are close at hand.

Let the people everywhere take heart and hope everywhere, for the cross is bending, the midnight is passing, and joy cometh with the morning.

Your Honor, I thank you, and I thank all of this Court for their courtesy, for their kindness, which I shall remember always.

I am prepared to receive your sentence.[7]

POSTSCRIPT

The presiding judge sentenced Debs to ten years in prison and took away his right to vote. Debs appealed to the U.S. Supreme Court, which upheld the lower court in a unanimous decision, noting that in his speeches, Debs praised those who had obstructed the draft. Debs began serving his sentence in the federal penitentiary in Atlanta on April 13, 1919. While incarcerated, he ran for president a fifth time, in 1920, once again under the Socialist Party Banner. He garnered almost a million votes as "Prisoner #9653". President Warren Harding commuted Debs' sentence at the end of 1921 but refused to pardon him. Debs was given a hero's welcome when he returned to his hometown, Terre Haute, Indiana, but prison had broken his health. He died five years later.

QUESTIONS

1. How did George Creel describe America's effort at distributing wartime information?
2. To what core values did the posters appeal? How do they make those appeals? What stories do they tell? Which do you consider most effective?
3. What advantages do visual appeals have over written appeals?
4. Are posters like these propaganda? How do you feel about the use of propaganda in a democracy that privileges and prioritizes freedom?
5. Why do you think Congress passed the Espionage and Sedition Acts? Do you think it made the country safer?
6. Why do you think Eugene Debs was considered such a threat to the nation? What did he say about his opposition to the war?

ADDITIONAL READING

On the war's impact on domestic life, see David M. Kennedy, *Over Here: The First World War and American Society* (1980); Ronald Schaffer, *America in the Great War: The Rise of the War Welfare State* (1991); and Christopher Capozzola, *Uncle Sam Wants You: World War I and the Making of the Modern American Citizen* (2008). Opposition to the war is discussed in H. C. Peterson and Gilbert C. Fite, *Opponents of War, 1917–1918* (1957); William Preston Jr., *Aliens and Dissenters: Federal Suppression of Radicals, 1903–1933* (1953); and Frances R. Early, *A World Without War* (1997). Other works on the war include James Joll, *The Origins of the First World War* (1992); Thomas Knock, *To End All Wars: Woodrow Wilson and the Quest for a New World Order* (1992); Ellis Hawley, *The Great War and the Search for Modern Order* (1992); and Alan Dawley, *Changing the World: American Progressives in War and Revolution* (2003). On the history of advertising, see T. J. Jackson Lears, *Fables of Abundance* (1995); Roland Marchand, *Advertising the American Dream* (1986); and Stuart Ewen, *Captains of Consciousness* (1976). On posters and war advertising, see Joseph Darracott and Belinda Loftus, *First World War Posters* (1972); Philipp Fehl and Patricia Fenix, *World War I Propaganda Posters* (1969); Maurice Richards, *Posters of the First World War* (1969); and E. McNight Kauffer, *The Art of the Poster* (1924). Film is explored in Leslie DeBauche, *Reel Patriotism* (1997). On Eugene Debs, see Ray Ginger, *The Bending Cross: A Biography of Eugene Victor Debs* (1949); Nick Salvatore, *Eugene V. Debs, Citizen and Socialist* (1984); and Eugene V. Debs, *Writing of Eugene Debs* (2009).

ENDNOTES

1. Peter Stanley, *"What Did YOU Do in the War, Daddy?"* (New York: Oxford University Press, 1983), p. 7
2. George Creel, *How We Advertised America* (New York: Harper & Brothers, 1920).
3. Matlack Price, "The Opportunity of the Poster," *Arts & Decoration*, v.9 (1918), pp. 155–157.
4. All posters taken from the Library of Congress.
5. *Third Biennial Report of the State Board of Education, State of California, 1916–1918* (Sacramento: California State Printing Office, 1918), pp. 13–14.
6. Ibid., pp. 131–132.
7. David Karsner, ed., *Debs: His Authorized Life and Letters* (New York: Boni and Liveright, 1919), pp. 48–54.

CHAPTER 8

MARGARET SANGER AND THE BIRTH CONTROL MOVEMENT

HISTORICAL CONTEXT

As documented in chapter 6, Upton Sinclair aimed his arrows at the "meat trust," and his rhetoric attacking the greed of consolidated capital was very much in the Progressive tradition. But *The Jungle* found its moral center in the family, in the need to stop modern business from destroying families. The concern for home was central to Progressives, and the impetus for reform came especially from women, traditionally seen as defenders of the family. While the phrase "the personal *is* political" did not arise until half a century after the Progressive Era, it might well have described those years. Educated women such as Jane Addams, Florence Kelly, and Margaret Sanger—who all came of age in an era that still shunted women into the home and away from leadership roles in the public sphere—publicized women's and children's issues; raised public awareness of matters such as day care, playgrounds, and child labor; and turned the nation's attention to topics where public policy and home life met.

The use of contraceptive devices for family planning has become so common that it is difficult to imagine a time when it was shrouded in secrecy. Yet in 1914, when Margaret Sanger began to speak and write openly in behalf of birth control, she put herself in jeopardy of prosecution under the so-called Comstock Law of 1873, which prohibited mailing, importing, or selling materials of an "obscene, lewd, or lascivious" nature. Both she and her husband, William Sanger, were indicted under the law for distributing birth control information.

The irony is that family planning had been practiced in America for a century. (Indeed, ancient Greek and Roman doctors had prescribed a variety of contraceptive methods.) Couples limited their offspring by simply abstaining from sexual contact and by practicing *coitus interruptus*. Equally important, a variety of contraceptive devices, including forerunners of modern condoms, diaphragms, and douches, had been available since at least the early nineteenth century. Not only were such items discretely advertised in popular magazines, but retailers of contraceptive paraphernalia mailed printed circulars advertising their wares to couples whose wedding announcements appeared in the newspapers.

Image 8.1 Margaret Sanger, 1917

Margaret Sanger photographed the year she was convicted of violating the New York state law for opening a birth control clinic.

Source: New York: Bain News Service, 1917. Courtesy Library of Congress.

One bit of indirect evidence that the use of such devices was widespread is to be found in declining birthrates: In 1800, American families averaged slightly over 7 children; under 6 by 1825; 5.4 in 1850; 4.24 by 1880; and 3.54 in 1900. The overall fertility rate declined by half in a century, with most urban middle-class families having no more than two children.

The declining birthrate was not simply a matter of new technology changing peoples' lives. Couples' willingness to use contraceptive devices or to otherwise limit the size of their families had social, economic, and cultural origins. As Americans left the countryside for the city, and as the old artisan system of manufacture declined, large numbers of children usually became a hindrance rather than an aid to a family's economic well-being; in a modern urban setting, children entered a family more as mouths to feed than as hands to labor. A cash-based economy (in which people exchanged goods and labor for money) rather than a subsistence one (where work produced items for home consumption) made raising a child very costly and made the "return" on parents' "investment" in their children very slow. Class mattered too. Children still could be an asset in working class households, where they might enter the mills and mines at a young age, but white-collar and professional families, whose numbers were rising rapidly, focused on educating their children into the middle class, an expensive proposition in terms of time and money.

Other important social changes encouraged the use of birth control. The turn of the century witnessed a new emphasis on sexuality as an expression of passion, love, and intimacy. Contraception liberated these feelings from the fear of unwanted pregnancy. This was especially true for women, who had always borne the burden of child rearing. Birth control was part of a larger transformation of women's position in society. Important female voices were raised during the nineteenth and early twentieth century demanding new roles for women—roles apart from the home-centered ones of wife and mother, roles that placed women in the practical worlds of politics, business, and reform. Needless to say, the average of seven children per family in 1800, had it continued, would have made education and careers impossible for most women.

Even though contraception had been practiced for a century in America when Margaret Sanger began to champion the cause in the years just before and after World War I, her crusade generated great controversy. Part of the reason was that she was so open in her advocacy. The genteel Victorian code still held sway sufficiently that sex remained a subject most people preferred not to talk about in public. Even couples who practiced birth control—a criminal act, after all—were silent. Birth control advocates' open discussion of sex made them harbingers of the freer, less morally rigid styles of living and speaking that we associate with the 1920s.

But it was more than a matter of style alone. At the beginning of her crusade, Sanger allied herself with a variety of radical thinkers—feminists, socialists, and labor militants—and it was out of the creative, avant-garde ferment of New York City in the prewar era that she forged her ideas. Earlier feminists in the late nineteenth century often opposed the use of contraception, believing that birth control would make women more vulnerable to sexual aggression. In this way of thinking, abstinence and self-control became a form of sexual liberation because women rejected male desires.

So birth control was not merely a technique. Its distribution grew out of changing ideas about sex, the family, and the role of women. By the early twentieth century, birth control was linked to radical political ideologies, and Margaret Sanger believed it could contribute to the liberation of women, especially working-class women. She did not argue for the open distribution of contraceptive information and devices simply to expand the realm of personal freedom; she believed that limitation of family size was the key to freeing women from the physical dangers of serial childbearing and to giving them the opportunity to become active outside the home. Contraceptive devices and literature were illegal in most states for years after Sanger began her crusade. They remained a delicate subject until birth control pills became widely available in the 1960s; the Catholic Church prohibits their use today (feminists point out that the burden of contraception still falls on women). Nonetheless Sanger succeeded in opening the *public* debate that led to eventual legalization. Although she was forced to flee the country in 1914 for distributing literature about family limitation, she returned a few years later and founded the National Birth Control League, an organization supported by doctors, social workers, and other professionals from the mainstream of American life. In twenty years, with over 200 offices, it changed its name to Planned Parenthood.

There were ironies on the road to victory. Those who believed contraception to be against the laws of God and nature were marginalized and mostly dismissed as prudes or fanatics. But Sanger's morally earnest campaign to uplift the downtrodden through family planning moved onto a side rail of history, too. The birth control campaign succeeded when it became a movement by and for the middle class; family planning grew acceptable not because of some new passion for the plight of the poor but because it was indispensable to middle-class families balancing growing expenses, careers for both parents, sexual pleasure within marriage, the allures of consumer life, and the difficulties of raising children in urban or suburban nuclear families.

The debate over birth control takes us into a variety of important issues. These include the right of individuals to privacy versus the right of a community to regulate moral behavior, the ethnic make-up of the American people, the ability of women to control their own physical destinies by limiting family size, and the feeling of many people that opportunities for advancement were shrinking and that small families were one way to keep the American dream alive.

As you read these documents, ask yourself about the connections between personal and social issues. Was birth control merely a matter of individual choice, or was it about power, wealth, opportunity, and similar matters? How did gender, ethnicity, and social class figure in the debate?

INTRODUCTION TO DOCUMENT 1

Margaret Sanger burst on the scene in 1914 with the publication of the first issue of *The Woman Rebel*. The tabloid described itself as "A Monthly Paper of Militant Thought." Testimony to the editor's radical political commitments was the reprinting of the Preamble to the Charter of the Industrial Workers of the World:

> The working class and the employing class have nothing in common. . . . Between these two classes a struggle must go on until the workers of the world organize as a class, take possession of the earth and the machinery of production, and abolish the wage system. . . . It is the historic mission of the working class to do away with capitalism.

Making contraceptive devices available, then, was part of a much larger project of radical social change, embracing the liberation of women and of the working class. In the very first issue, Sanger explained herself in "Why the Woman Rebel?" Later on the same page, in an article entitled "The Prevention of Conception," Sanger made it clear that she would defy the laws against distributing birth control information.

1. FROM *THE WOMAN REBEL* (1914)

MARGARET SANGER

"WHY THE WOMAN REBEL?"

Because I believe that deep down in woman's nature lies slumbering the spirit of revolt.

Because I believe that woman is enslaved by the world machine, by sex conventions, by motherhood and its present necessary child-rearing, by wage

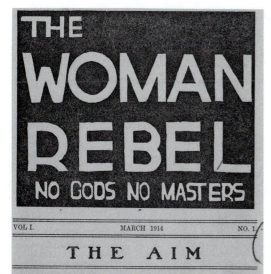

Image 8.2 From *The Woman Rebel* (1914)

The inaugural issue of Sanger's radical newspaper aimed squarely at the laws and conditions that subordinated women and often confined them to poverty. In 1914 Sanger was arrested for promoting contraceptives in the paper, a violation of the Comstock Law.

Source: National Archives and Records Administration.

slavery, by middle-class morality, by customs, laws and superstitions.

Because I believe that woman's freedom depends upon awakening that spirit of revolt within her against these things which enslave her.

Because I believe that these things which enslave woman must be fought openly, fearlessly, consciously.

Because I believe she must consciously disturb and destroy and be fearless in its accomplishment.

Because I believe in freedom, created through individual action.

Because I believe in the offspring of the immigrant, the great majority of whom make up the unorganized working class to-day. . . .

Because I believe that through the efforts of the industrial revolution will woman's freedom emerge.

Because I believe that not until wage slavery is abolished can either woman's or man's freedom be fully attained. . . .

"THE AIM"

This paper will not be the champion of any "ism."

All women are invited to contribute to its columns.

The majority of papers usually adjust themselves to the ideas of their readers but the WOMAN REBEL will obstinately refuse to be adjusted.

The aim of this paper will be to stimulate working women to think for themselves and to build up a conscious fighting character.

. . . It will be the aim of the WOMAN REBEL to advocate the prevention of contraception and to impart such knowledge in the columns of this paper.

Other subjects, including the slavery through motherhood; through things, the home, public opinion and so forth, will be dealt with.

It is also the aim of this paper to circulate among those women who work in prostitution; to voice their wrongs; to expose the police persecution which hovers over them and to give free expression to their thoughts, hopes and opinions.

And at all times the WOMAN REBEL will strenuously advocate economic emancipation.[1]

The second issue of *The Woman Rebel* announced that the United States postmaster banned the newspaper under section 211 of the U.S. Criminal Code, whose violation carried a maximum five-year prison sentence or a $5,000 fine. Copies of that issue and subsequent ones were confiscated. Anthony Comstock was the man responsible for the law and its enforcement. Comstock had a long career during the late nineteenth and early twentieth centuries as a crusader against vice. He founded the Society for the Suppression of Vice in 1873, which drew financial backing from some of America's wealthiest men, and he was appointed special agent of the U.S. Post Office Department. In an interview with Mary Alden Hopkins, who wrote a series of articles on the birth control controversy for *Harper's Weekly* in 1915, Comstock justified the laws against publicizing contraception.

2. ANTHONY COMSTOCK'S VIEWS ON BIRTH CONTROL (1915)

The three great crime-breeders of today are intemperance, gambling, and evil reading. The devil is sowing his seed for his future harvest. There is no foe so much to be dreaded as that which perverts the imagination, sears the conscience, hardens the heart, and damns the soul.

If you allow the devil to decorate the Chamber of Imagery in your heart with licentious and sensual things, you will find that he has practically thrown a noose about your neck and will forever after exert himself to draw you away from the "Lamb of God which taketh away sins of the world." You have practically put rope on memory's bell and placed the other end of the rope in the devil's hands, and, though you may will out your mind, the memory of some vile story or picture that you may have looked upon, be assured that even in your most solitary moments the devil will ring memory's bell and call up the hateful thing to turn your thoughts away from God and undermine all aspirations for holy things.

. . . My experience leads me to the conviction that once these matters enter through the eye and ear into the chamber of imagery in the heart of the child, nothing but the grace of God can ever erase or blot it out. . . .

When a man and woman marry they are responsible for their children. You can't reform a family in any of these superficial ways. You have to go deep down into their minds and souls. The prevention of conception would work the greatest demoralization. God has set certain natural barriers. If you turn loose the passions and break down the fear you bring worse disaster than the war. It would debase sacred things, break down the health of women and disseminate a greater curse than the plagues and diseases of Europe.[2]

Just before she was to be arrested for distributing contraceptive information, Sanger fled America for England, where she spent her time among European radicals, reformers, and family-planning professionals. But a few months later, her husband, William Sanger, was arrested by Anthony Comstock in New York City, then imprisoned for purveying lewd materials (he gave a copy of his wife's little book, *Family Limitation,* to one of Comstock's undercover agents). Margaret Sanger returned to New York, where she knew she would face trial. She was eventually acquitted, but in the meantime, she lectured, wrote essays, and opened the nation's first family-planning clinic.

Document 3 comes from the introduction to a book Sanger edited called *The Case for Birth Control* (1917). In this brief essay, she summarized much of the argument she had been promulgating since returning to the United States. While her commitment to poor and working women is still evident here, her style had changed considerably since *The Woman Rebel.* Sanger was in the midst of concentrating all of her efforts on birth control, distancing herself from the radical positions she had staked out earlier. Perhaps she thought this was the practical way to achieve her most important goal. Or maybe the experience of exile had tempered her ardor. Certainly, Sanger now spent more time among wealthy women who helped finance both her trial defense and the birth control movement. Note how the tone of this essay differs from that of *The Woman Rebel*—radical passion gives way to fact-laden analysis in the name of practical reform, very much the progressive style.

Image 8.3 The Sanger Clinic, New York City, 1916
Sanger opened this birth control clinic in Brooklyn—the first of its kind in the United States—on October 16, 1916. Ten days later it was shut down.
Source: Courtesy Library of Congress.

3. FROM *THE CASE FOR BIRTH CONTROL (1917)*

MARGARET SANGER

Before I attempt to refute the arguments against birth control, I should like to tell you something of the conditions I met with as a trained nurse and of the experience that convinced me of its necessity and led me to jeopardize my liberty in order to place this information in the hands of the women who need it.

My first clear impression of life was that large families and poverty went hand in hand. I was born and brought up in a glass factory town in the western part of New York State. I was one of eleven children—so I had some personal experience of the struggles and hardships a large family endures.

When I was seventeen years old my mother died from overwork and the strain of too frequent child bearing. I was left to care for the younger children and share the burdens of all. When I was old enough I entered a hospital to take up the profession of nursing.

In the hospital I found that seventy-five percent of the diseases of men and women are the result of ignorance of their sex functions. I found that every department of life was open to investigation and discussion except that shaded valley of sex. . . .

So great was the ignorance of the women and girls I met concerning their own bodies that I decided to specialize in woman's diseases and took up gynecological and obstetrical nursing.

A few years of this work brought me to a shocking discovery—that knowledge of the methods of controlling birth was accessible to the women of wealth while the working women were deliberately kept in ignorance of this knowledge!

I found that the women of the working class were as anxious to obtain this knowledge as their sisters of wealth, but that they were told that there are laws on the statute books against imparting it to them. And the medical profession was most religious in obeying these laws when the patient was a poor woman.

For the laws against imparting this knowledge force these women into the hands of the filthiest midwives and the quack abortionists—unless they bear unwanted children—with the consequence that the deaths from abortions are almost wholly among the working-class women.

No other country in the world has so large a number of abortions nor so large a number of deaths of women resulting therefrom as the United States of America. Our law makers close their virtuous eyes. A most conservative estimate is that there are 250,000 abortions performed in this country every year.

How often have I stood at the bedside of a woman in childbirth and seen the tears flowing in gladness and heard the sigh of "Thank God" when told that her child was born dead! What can man know of the fear and dread of unwanted pregnancy? What can man know of the agony of carrying beneath one's heart a little life which tells the mother every instant that it cannot survive? Even were it born alive the chances are that it would perish within a year.

Do you know that three hundred thousand babies under one year of age die in the United States every year from poverty and neglect, while six hundred thousand parents remain in ignorance of how to prevent three hundred thousand more babies from coming into the world the next year to die of poverty and neglect?

I found from records concerning women of the underworld that eighty-five percent of them come from parents averaging nine living children. And that fifty percent of these are mentally defective.

We know, too, that among mentally defective parents the birth rate is four times as great as that of the normal parent. Is this not cause for alarm? Is it not time for our physicians, social workers and scientists to face this array of facts and stop quibbling about woman's morality? I say this because it is these same people who raise objection to birth control on the ground that it *may* cause women to be immoral.

Solicitude for woman's morals has ever been the cloak Authority has worn in its age-long conspiracy to keep woman in bondage. . . .

Is woman's health not to be considered? Is she to remain a producing machine? Is she to have time to think, to study, to care for herself? Man cannot travel to his goal alone. And until woman has knowledge to control birth she cannot get the time to think and develop. Until she has the time to think, neither the suffrage question nor the social question nor the labor question will interest her, and she will remain the drudge that she is and her husband the slave that he is just as long as they continue to supply the market with cheap labor. . . .

Am I to be classed as immoral because I advocate small families for the working class while Mr. [Theodore] Roosevelt can go up and down the length of the land shouting and urging these women to have large families and is neither arrested nor molested but considered by all society as highly moral? . . .[3]

INTRODUCTION TO DOCUMENT 4

As a Jesuit priest, Michael P. Dowling articulated a position familiar to the Catholic Church and its followers. Document 4 is excerpted from his pamphlet *Race-Suicide* (1915), which couched arguments against birth control in the language of duty, self-sacrifice, religious obligation, and family values. Whereas Sanger argued for the right of women and the poor to make individual decisions about contraception, Dowling appealed to the good of the community, which he asserted took precedence over personal needs or desires. Note that the phrase "race-suicide" in this era was highly charged but not clearly defined. Usually it did not imply the entire human race but "civilized" people and, by implication, the white race. For Dowling, "race-suicide" was more specifically a religious failure to spread the faith with large Christian families.

4. FROM *RACE-SUICIDE* (1915)

MICHAEL P. DOWLING

. . . At three different epochs in human history, the Creator made known His will. Just as to the first man, He said: "Increase and multiply," so a thousand years later to the second father of humanity, to Noe [Noah], and to his sons, He spoke a pregnant word, and it bore the same burden, "Increase and multiply and fill the earth"; for so we read in Genesis. Still another thousand years rolled on and the same blessing was repeated, for the word of the Lord came to Abraham: "Fear not; I am thy protector and thy reward exceeding great." The patriarch answered: "What wilt Thou give me; behold, I have no child." Then God brought him forth out of the tent, saying: "Look up to the heavens and number the stars, if thou canst; so shall thy seed be." The reward of Abraham's faith is paternity.

And after that, from Abraham to the last of the prophets, text on text and example after example, confirm the doctrine that children are the blessing of marriage, no matter what the new gospel of selfishness may proclaim. In the Old Testament curse alternates with blessing: "He who is blessed shall be a father, the cursed shall stand alone." If it is said to the just, "Thy wife shall be like a fruitful vine," to the wicked man and the sinner comes the sentence: "In a single generation his name will be blotted out.". . .

God said: "Increase and multiply"; man says: "Let us fear to increase and multiply; the earth might become too narrow; the fewer there are to share the good things of life the more there will be for each. . . ."

. . . Malthus, in his book entitled "Principles of Population As It Affects the Future Improvement of Society," gave the impetus to the movement. He held that the population of the earth increases more rapidly than the means of subsistence, because population advances almost in a geometrical proportion, as two, four, eight, sixteen, while the fertility of the land increases approximately only in an arithmetical proportion, as one, two, three, four, five and so on. Hence, the continually increasing population must eventually exceed the capacity of the earth to supply food. . . .

But the facts are against the theory that the earth is inadequate to support the growth of population. The United States, even with the wasteful methods of farming now in vogue, could feed hundreds of millions. Under different conditions even little Ireland would be capable of supporting three times its present population. Brazil, Peru, Mexico have room for teeming millions within their borders. Portions of the dark continent of Africa were once densely peopled; so was Asia Minor; and they might become garden spots of the earth once more. There is still plenty of elbow room on the globe. . . .

God makes no mistakes, and for every soul He creates and infuses into a mortal body, He furnishes what is needful for its well-being. History may be reviewed in vain for an instance of any considerable country wherein poverty and want can be fairly traced to the increase of the number of mouths beyond the power of the accompanying hands to fill them. In most cases they can, more properly, be attributed to unjust laws, misgovernment, destructive warfare, decadent commerce, a disregard of the Divine law, vice and crime. . . .

Can it be possible that wealth is the natural enemy of infancy and childhood? And is the instinct of reproduction weaker in the privileged classes, the spirit of self-denial more pronounced? Is it not rather that large families are looked upon with disdain as a plebeian institution, entailing too much sacrifice, debarring the mother from many pleasures she is unwilling to forgo? Is it not because every new birth requires the expense account to be overhauled, several chapters of travel to be blotted out, transfers to be made to the side of the nurse and the governess, balls and parties and receptions to be given up? . . .

We must get back to Christian principles and mold Christian lives, till the humblest sees that life is not all for pleasure, self-ease and enjoyment, that duty and conscience must play a great part and march in the vanguard of true progress.[4]

INTRODUCTION TO DOCUMENT 5

In its series of articles by Mary Alden Hopkins on contraception in 1915, *Harper's Weekly* published the thoughts of several doctors. While we cannot assume that the following statements represented the opinions of the entire medical profession, they do give a sense of the arguments offered by physicians. The only doctor who spoke unequivocally in favor of contraception to *Harper's* (the first interview here) was Dutch, not American, and a woman, not a man.

5. PHYSICIANS' STATEMENTS ABOUT BIRTH CONTROL (1915)

DR. ALETTA JACOBS

Very often the mothers in this hospital did not want the babies that were born to them. They were actually glad when the babies were born dead. No, they were not bad women—just ordinary, every-day women. Sometimes it was because they already had enough babies, sometimes because the previous baby was still so little, sometimes because they were so very poor, sometimes for other reasons. But whether the reason was a good one or a bad one, the fact remained that the baby was not desired. Now it seemed to me that a baby should not be a punishment. If a woman does not want a child it is better both for her and for the child that she should not have one.

Moreover, I noticed that many of the sickly children born in the hospital were children that had been born against their mothers' wishes. The mothers' state of mind during pregnancy had affected the baby. Besides this there were many children with very bad heredity—mental sickness and physical sickness in the parents, which would very probably appear in the offspring. These children should never have been born.

Sometimes a mother would say to me. "No wonder the baby is puny and sick. Why, when this child was conceived my husband was as drunk as could be." For reasons like these I decided that mothers should be taught how to prevent conception.

Children should be born not oftener than once in three years. For the first year the mother should devote herself to caring for the child. The second year she should have to get back her vitality and strength. The third year she may again become pregnant.[5]

DR. HOWARD A. KELLY

Let me enunciate these fundamental principles which must control my judgment:

1. That the medical profession must continually deal with the moral aspects of a case, and today our great loss is the unwillingness of some doctors to have anything to do with morals, because they have had no moral training and have done no moral thinking. . . .

2. That in times of great decadence we are not to try to accommodate ourselves to decadent conditions by temporizing expedients, but by the highest moral remedies and by righteousness—*at whatever cost.* Practically I find that the people who came to me having used various mechanical means of preventing conception, have lost something in their married life which ought to have been more precious to them than life itself. All meddling with the sexual relation to secure facultative sterility degrades the wife to the level of a prostitute.

Therefore there is no right or decent way of controlling births but by total abstinence. . . .[6]

DR. JOHN W. WILLIAMS

I make it a rule to refuse to discuss the question with perfectly healthy, normal persons. On the other hand, if I find that a wife is steadily losing ground as the result of rapidly recurring pregnancies, I send for the husband and say that in my opinion as a medical man it is highly advisable that his wife should not have another child for a specified length of time. In that event I advise him as to the most efficacious method of preventing conception; as I consider it more intelligent to prevent a breakdown than to treat it after it has occurred.

I give the same advice after certain serious obstetrical complications, and in women who are suffering from tuberculosis, certain forms of heart disease and other serious chronic disease, in which I know by experience that another pregnancy will subject the patient to serious danger. In such cases I consider it more conservative to give such advice than to be obliged to perform a therapeutic abortion after pregnancy has occurred.

Finally, in the presence of certain chronic diseases, which to my mind will always complicate the occurrence of pregnancy, and in which therapeutic abortion is necessary to relieve immediate danger to the patient's life, I hold that it is justifiable to render the patient sterile by operative means. . . .

In other words, I do not believe that the physician is justified in giving advice as to the prevention of conception solely for the convenience of his patients, but should limit it entirely to those cases which present a definite medical indication for the temporary or permanent avoidance of pregnancy. To my mind any other course practically places the physician in the same class as the professional abortionist.[7]

DR. R.C. BRANNON

I beg to take issue with you, in regard to your propaganda for the control of births, as being subversive to religion, morals, and health of both men and women. This, when you come to sift the matter down to its final analysis, is what is shortening the lives of the human race, making weaklings in mind and body the children of strong men, and wrecking the nerves and bodies of women who ought to be the proud and happy mothers of a dozen healthy children.

The prevention of large families has caused an increase in insanity, tuberculosis, Bright's disease, diabetes and cancer, and I am willing to submit the proposition to the judgment of three of the greatest gynecologists in the United States. I have stepped in the breach and used my influence to curtail the bad practice of limiting the size of the family, as my experience as a physician of twenty years' practise has proven to my mind that it is the most hurtful, and wicked sin that was ever indulged in since the world was created. It is a swift and sure road to the grave.

Man was put here to multiply and replenish the earth. How terrible has been the punishment of many a rich man I have known—perhaps poor and struggling in early life, who decided he would escape the responsibility of rearing a large family, with the result when a little past life's prime his wife died of a cancer, and what enjoyment did either of them derive from his fortune of more than a half million dollars; filthy lucre begotten by miserly habits, that rightly should have been expended unselfishly in bringing up a large family that would have blessed the earth.[8]

INTRODUCTION TO DOCUMENT 6

By the end of the decade, Sanger's arguments had fully taken on the Progressive Era style—fact laden, scientific, and analytical. The following debate occurred in New York City in 1920. Note that there is no apparent fear of arrest here; the issue of birth control had become part of open public discourse. Sanger shared the stage with Winter Russell, a prominent New York City attorney.

6. DEBATE BETWEEN MARGARET SANGER AND WINTER RUSSELL (1920)

WINTER RUSSELL

. . . I am a member of the bar of the State of New York. I trust that I have due regard and respect for the statutes, the constitution, and the laws of this great city, state and nation. But I hold them as the veriest trash when they come up against the laws of Nature. The laws of Nature cannot be revised. They cannot be repealed. There is no power in this whole universe that can change these laws, and you have to deal with that.

That means you can't get pleasure without paying for it. Nature is inexorable in bringing about her retribution. It does not need any balance book. You can never embezzle. You can't cheat. You can't get away from it. . . .

You must pay at last for your own debt. Those are the laws. Now we recognize it in physics. Energy cannot be annihilated. Birth control says "yes." You shall pay the price. You can annihilate that energy and drink from the cup of pleasure, but you don't take the responsibility—the duty and the care. . . . It is along the lines of the people who are alchemists, who think they can turn the base metals into gold. It is an age-long dream. It is a belief that has been held from the beginning of time. That thing cannot be done. That is the law of life—of God—that you have to pay. . . .

MARGARET SANGER

. . . The only weapon that women have and the most uncivilized weapon that they have to use if they will not submit to having children every year or every year and a half, the weapon they use is abortion. We know how detrimental abortion is to the physical side as well as to the psychic side of the woman's life, and yet there are in this nation, because of these generalities and opinions that are here before us, that are stopping the tide of progress, we have more than one million women with abortions performed on them each year. . . . We speak of the rights of the unborn. I say that it is time to speak of those who are already born. . . .

We find in the South that where children come according to Nature, every year and one-half, that as soon as they are able, they are shuffled and hustled on in to take the place and compete with their father in the factories. That is the place that society has for the children of the poor. . . . In some of the factories of Lowell and Fall River, Mass., it was found that of the children who work and toil there, under ten years of age, that 85% of them come from families of eight—their mothers have given birth to eight children—and we find in the South very much the same thing, excepting a higher percentage of 90 to 93% of the children there.

That is not the only thing. We have a condition not only as these that I have related, but we have a condition again that is more disastrous to the race than child labor or infant mortality, and that is the transmission of venereal disease to the race that is to come. . . . We know, too, that out of this terrible scourge of venereal disease that we have 90% of the insanity in this country, due to syphilis. Anyone who is dealing with fundamentals would know that these people should use means to protect themselves against having children. They should absolutely in due regard to themselves, to their children and to the race, not allow a child to be born while that disease is running riot in the system, and then we have that terrible consequence which is insanity. . . .

We have here 400,000 feeble-minded people in the United States, that any authority on this subject would say to you, "Not one of them should have been born." They never should have been born and sometimes these parents are perfectly normal, and yet this taint has gone through the blood and has left this perfectly normal, physical person, who arrives at the adult age with all its physical functions, and yet it has the mentality of a child eight years of age. The feeble-minded man or woman is of no use to itself or society, and it would be better if we were living in a real civilization that they should not have been born. Only 40,000 of this 400,000 are entered in institutions, and the others are living among us, producing and reproducing their progeny and providing abundant material and opportunity for the continuance of charities and other institutions for ages and generations more to come.

We found also in one institution—a so-called reformatory where they take the girls of the underworld—prostitutes—in Geneva, Ill., they find that 50% of these girls coming into the underworld—the prostitutes—was of this cause, that she belonged to the feeble-minded, and again we find that 89% of these came from large families. . . .

Also our child labor—we make laws in Washington against child labor, hoping we will wipe that out of existence. For fifty years they have been trying to wipe child labor off the books in the United States, but they have not succeeded and they will never succeed until they establish birth control clinics in those districts where these women are, where they put in birth control clinics, like they have in Holland—in every industrial section in the United States where women can come to trained nurses and physicians and get from them scientific information whereby they may control birth. . . .

Now, Mr. Russell has said some things that are very interesting to me, He tells us that we cannot have pleasure without pain. It is a man who is speaking. (*Laughter and applause.*) It is very peculiar that Nature only works on the one side of the human family when it comes to that law. She applies all the pain to the woman. It is absurd—a perfectly absurd argument in the face of rational intelligence (*applause*) to talk about marriage being for one purpose. . . .

WINTER RUSSELL

May I say at the outset that I did not say we could not have pleasure without pain. I said we could not have pleasure without paying for it and the man has to pay. (*Laughter.*) . . . Mrs. Sanger sees poverty, she sees misery and she sees unwanted children. To be sure, there are many thousands of these homes where, sad to say, the children are unwanted, but they have made this devout prayer to God, I believe, for children, and they have gotten them. They have gotten what I believe to be the greatest wealth and treasure of the Kingdom of Heaven that there is on the face of the earth, and when they get that, they have to pay for it. They have to pay and take the responsibility. . . .

I am going to give you a picture of the block on which I was born and brought up, that I have watched

for 30 years. Thirty years ago I began to watch the block. There were 17 families, 34 people at the start; 34 people who were successful, they believe, in this little town of 3,500 people. It had a fine high school, a State Normal School—one of the foremost in the State. It had a Boys' School known nationally, if not internationally, and they were 34 people in 17 homes. . . .

Out of . . . 17 families, 9 are extinct. Nine are dead and gone. They have passed away. Is that race suicide? Out of the 8 who remain, out of the 34 people, out of these 8 families, there are 26 grandchildren. My father's family produced 12 of the 26. Out of 33 of the families, there are 14 grandchildren if you except

Image 8.4 American Birth Control League, *Birth Control Review* (1923)

Founded in 1921, the American Birth Control League promoted the right of women to control their own fertility.

Source: Sophia Smith Collection, Smith College.

mine. I think I am an exception. There is race suicide. Don't tell me that that is one exceptional block. I can duplicate that block on every street in that town except one blessed community, Little Canada. They were not Americans. They were vulgar. They were poor. They want big families, but from these poor families in Little Canada, there have come the French Canadians. From them come doctors, lawyers, and teachers, and they are inheriting the town. There is race suicide.

I can duplicate that block in practically every American city in this country. I can duplicate that block in every apartment house on the west side. . . . America is dying today—the America that we know.

MARGARET SANGER

. . . I am speaking for the millions of women who are crushed with over child-bearing, whose lives are broken and who have become drudges in the family today. I am speaking for the mothers and the individual here and there does not concern me in the least. They may be an exception, but I know there are millions and millions of women who are married, who are just as self-controlled as anyone Mr. Russell can show us, who are living in a terror of pregnancy, and they have men who are just as good to them. Men are not all beasts. . . .

Birth control will free the mother from the trap of pregnancy. It will save the child from that procession of coffins, as well as from the toil of mill and factory.

Birth control will make parenthood a voluntary function instead of an accident as it is today. When motherhood and childhood is free, we then can go hand in hand with man, to remake the world, for the glorification as well as the emancipation of the human race. (*Applause.*) . . .[9]

INTRODUCTION TO DOCUMENT 7

In 1922, Sanger published *The Pivot of Civilization.* Here she elaborated on some of the arguments from her debate with Winter Russell, especially the idea that "overfecundity" of the "degenerate classes" was responsible for poverty and crime. Words like "feeble-minded" "moron," and "imbecile" had the imprimatur of science in the early twentieth century, though their meanings were far from clear. Sanger also used phrases like "human waste," "human weeds," the "unfit," and "dead weight" to describe the poor and the disabled; she argued that charity only encouraged over-breeding; she advocated that the state administer IQ tests to identify "degenerates" and prevent them from breeding uncontrollably. While eugenicists in the 1920s called for stopping particular populations from reproducing, especially immigrants, African Americans, and the poor, Sanger was less clear about precisely whom the feeble-minded were.

7. FROM *THE PIVOT OF CIVILIZATION* (1922)

MARGARET SANGER

. . . There is but one practical and feasible program in handling the great problem of the feeble-minded. That is, as the best authorities are agreed, to prevent the birth of those who would transmit imbecility to their descendants. Feeble-mindedness as investigations and statistics from every country indicate is invariably associated with an abnormally high rate of fertility. Modern conditions of civilization, as we are continually being reminded, furnish the most favorable breeding-ground for the mental defective, the moron, the imbecile. . . .

Modern studies indicate that insanity, epilepsy, criminality, prostitution, pauperism, and mental defect, are all organically bound up together and that the least intelligent and the thoroughly degenerate classes in every community are the most prolific. Feeble-mindedness in one generation becomes pauperism or insanity in the next. There is every indication that feeble-mindedness in its protean forms is on the increase, that it has leaped the barriers, and that there is truly, as some of the scientific eugenists have pointed out, a feeble-minded peril to future generations—unless the feeble-minded are prevented from reproducing their kind. To meet this emergency is the immediate and peremptory duty of every State and of all communities. . . .

Here is a case showing the astonishing ability to "increase and multiply," organically bound up with delinquency and defect of various types:

The parents of a feeble-minded girl, twenty years of age, who was committed to the Kansas State Industrial Farm on a vagrancy charge, lived in a thickly populated Negro district which was reported by the police to be headquarters for the criminal element of the surrounding state. . . . The mother married at fourteen, and her first child was born at fifteen. In rapid succession she gave birth to sixteen live-born children and had one miscarriage. The first child, a girl, married but separated from her husband. . . . The fourth, fifth and sixth, all girls, died in infancy or early childhood. The seventh, a girl, remarried after the death of her husband, from whom she had been separated. The eighth, a boy, who early in life began to exhibit criminal tendencies, was in prison for highway robbery and burglary. The ninth, a girl, normal mentally, was in quarantine at the Kansas State Industrial Farm at the time this study was made; she had lived with a man as his common-law wife, and had also been arrested several times for soliciting. The tenth, a boy, was involved in several delinquencies when young and was sent to the detention house but did not remain there long. The eleventh, a boy . . . at the age of seventeen was sentenced to the penitentiary for twenty years on a charge of first-degree robbery; after serving a portion of his time he was paroled, and later was shot and killed in a fight. The twelfth, a boy, was at fifteen years of age implicated in a murder and sent to the industrial school, but escaped from there on a bicycle which

he had stolen; at eighteen he was shot and killed by a woman. The thirteenth child, feeble-minded, is the girl of the study. The fourteenth, a boy, was considered by the police to be the best member of the family; his mother reported him to be much slower mentally than his sister just mentioned; he had been arrested several times. Once he was held in the detention home and once sent to the State Industrial school; at other times, he was placed on probation. The fifteenth, a girl sixteen years old, has for a long time had a bad reputation. Subsequent to the commitment of her sister to the Kansas State Industrial Farm, she was arrested on a charge of vagrancy, found to be syphilitic, and quarantined in a state other than Kansas. At the time of her arrest, she stated that prostitution was her occupation. . . . [quoted from the U.S. Public Health Service: Psychiatric Studies of Delinquents. Reprint no. 598, pp. 64–65.]

We do not object to feeble-mindedness simply because it leads to immorality and criminality. . . . We object because both are burdens and dangers to the intelligence of the community. As a matter of fact, there is sufficient evidence to lead us to believe that the so-called "borderline cases" are a greater menace than the out-and-out "defective delinquents" who can be supervised, controlled and prevented from procreating their kind. The advent of the Binet-Simon and similar psychological tests indicates that the mental defective who is glib and plausible, bright looking and attractive, but with a mental vision of seven, eight or nine years, may not merely lower the whole level of intelligence in a school or in a society, but may be encouraged by church and state to increase and multiply until he dominates and gives the prevailing "color"—culturally speaking—to an entire community.

The advocate of Birth Control realizes as well as all intelligent thinkers the dangers of interfering with personal liberty. Our whole philosophy is, in fact, based upon the fundamental assumption that man is a self-conscious, self-governing creature, that he should not be treated as a domestic animal; that he must be left free, at least within certain wide limits, to follow his own wishes in the matter of mating and in procreation of children. Nor do we believe that the community could or should send to the lethal chamber the defective progeny resulting from irresponsible and unintelligent breeding.

But modern society, which has respected the personal liberty of the individual only in regard to the unrestricted and irresponsible bringing into the world of filth and poverty an overcrowding procession of infants fore-doomed to death or hereditable disease, is now confronted with the problem of protecting itself and its future generations against the inevitable consequences of this long-practised policy of *laisser-faire*.

The emergency problem of segregation and sterilization must be faced immediately. Every feeble-minded girl or woman of the hereditary type, especially of the moron class, should be segregated during the reproductive period. Otherwise, she is almost certain to bear imbecile children, who in turn are just as certain to breed other defectives. The male defectives are no less dangerous. Segregation carried out for one or two generations would give us only partial control of the problem. Moreover, when we realize that each feeble-minded person is a potential source of an endless progeny of defect, we prefer the policy of immediate sterilization, of making sure that parenthood is absolutely prohibited to the feeble-minded. . . .

This degeneration has already begun. Eugenists demonstrate that two-thirds of our manhood of military age are physically too unfit to shoulder a rifle; that the feeble-minded and syphilitic, the irresponsible and the defective breed unhindered; that

women are driven into factories and shops on day-shift and night-shift; that children, frail carriers of the torch of life, are put to work at an early age; that society at large is breeding an ever increasing army of under-sized, stunted and dehumanized slaves; that the vicious circle of mental and physical defect delinquency and beggary is encouraged, by the unseeing and unthinking sentimentality of our age, to populate asylum, hospital and prison. . . .

The great principle of Birth Control offers the means whereby the individual may adapt himself to and even control the forces of environment and heredity. Entirely apart from its Malthusian aspect or that of the population question, Birth Control must be recognized, as the Neo-Malthusians pointed out long ago, not "merely as the key of the social position," and the only possible and practical method of human generation, but the very pivot of civilization. Birth Control which has been criticized as negative and destructive, is really the greatest and most truly eugenic method, and its adoption as part of the program of Eugenics would immediately give a concrete and realistic power to that science. As a matter of fact, Birth Control has been accepted by the most clear thinking and far seeing of the Eugenists themselves as the most constructive and necessary of the means to racial health. . . .[10]

POSTSCRIPT

Laws against transmitting contraceptive information and devices were gradually repealed, overturned, or ignored. But the general acceptance of birth control was accompanied by a shift away from its radical beginnings. Slowly, the movement became professionalized. Clinics proliferated, run by middle-class professionals, including doctors, nurses, social workers, and public health administrators. With bureaucratization and professionalization from the 1920s onward came a distinctly elitist shift in direction. When the early opponents of contraception spoke their fears of "race-suicide," they usually meant that "inferior" peoples—immigrants, the poor, and blacks—would out-reproduce old-stock, respectable white people. The solution, many now suggested, was eugenics, the "science" of human engineering. Legalized contraceptives could limit the "breeding" of "racially inferior" peoples. Looking back, Sanger wrote in her *Autobiography*, "The eugenists wanted to shift the birth-control emphasis from less children for the poor to more children for the rich. We went back of that and sought first to stop the multiplication of the unfit."[11] Sanger had become less concerned with empowering the poor to resist their oppression, more with stopping them from producing so many "unfit" babies. She never adopted the nativist and xenophobic assumptions of many eugenicists, and she never threw her lot with the racists. Yet Sanger's fascination with social engineering—with the "scientific" improvement of the race—in an era rising ethnic hatred worldwide was, to say the least, disturbing. By the 1930s, the American eugenics movement was of keen interest to the German political party known as the Nazis, led by Adolph Hitler.

QUESTIONS

1. How and why did the birth control movement change over time?
2. Do you see similarities between the effort to advance birth control and the reforms of the meatpacking industry, as presented in the prior chapter? Would you deem birth control a "progressive" measure as advocated by Sanger in the 1910s and 1920s?
3. Did Michael Dowling and Winter Russell use the same arguments to oppose Sanger's position? Do you see distinctions between their positions and values?
4. Note that Sanger, Comstock, Russell, and Dowling all argue that their position will best protect the public. Given this shared emphasis, how did they come to such differing conclusions about public policy?
5. Summarize Sanger's position in *The Pivot of Civilization*. How had her arguments changed by 1922?
6. How does the birth control debate resonate with contemporary discussions on abortion?

ADDITIONAL READING

For the birth control movement, the best general history of sex and ideology is Estelle Friedman and John D'Emilio, *Intimate Matters* (1988). The literature on birth control is extensive; see Ellen Chesler, *Woman of Valor: Margaret Sanger and the Birth Control Movement in America* (1992); Jean H. Baker, *Margaret Sanger: A Life of Passion* (2012); Jonathan Eig, *The Birth of the Pill: How Four Crusaders Reinvented Sex and Launched a Revolution* (2014); David M. Kennedy, *Birth Control in America* (1970); Andrea Tone, *Devices and Desires* (2001); and Linda Gordon, *The Moral Property of Women* (2007). Related works include Elaine Tyler May, *Great Expectations: Marriage and Divorce in Post Victorian America* (1980); Janet Farrell Brodie, *Contraception and Abortion in Nineteenth Century America* (1994); and Mary Odem, *Delinquent Daughters* (1996). On the larger context of motherhood, see Linda Gordon, *Pitied But Not Entitled: Single Mothers and the History of Welfare* (1994). On the advent of feminism in this era see Nancy F. Cott, *The Grounding of Modern Feminism* (1987), and Rosalind Rosenberg, *Beyond Separate Spheres: Intellectual Roots of Modern Feminism* (1982).

ENDNOTES

1. *The Woman Rebel*, v.1 n.1 (March 1914), page 1. Records of the Post Office, Record Group 28, National Archives.
2. *Harper's Weekly* v.60, May 22, 1915, pp. 489–490.
3. Margaret Sanger, *The Case for Birth Control* (New York, 1917), pp. 5–7, 8–11.
4. Michael P. Dowling, *Race-Suicide* (New York, 1915), pp. 1–13.
5. Mary Alden Hopkins, "What Doctors Say of Birth Control," *Harper's Weekly*, v.61, October 16, 1915, p. 380.
6. Ibid.
7. Ibid.
8. Ibid., pp. 380–382.
9. *Debate between Margaret Sanger and Winter Russell* (New York: The Fine Arts Guild, 1920).
10. Margaret Sanger, *The Pivot of Civilization* (New York, 1922), pp. 80–86, 91, 100–102, 175, 189.
11. Margaret Sanger, *An Autobiography* (New York: Norton, 1938), pp. 374–375.

CHAPTER 9

SCIENCE, RELIGION, AND THE SCOPES TRIAL

HISTORICAL CONTEXT

The 1920 census revealed that for the first time, America was an urban nation. More than half of the country's 105 million people now lived in towns of at least 2,500. This was emblematic of deeper changes. By the 1920s, America had experienced decades of urbanization, industrialization, and immigration. Corporate wealth was highly concentrated. Business and government bureaucracies were larger than ever, and so too was America's working class. Much of the population was richer, more highly educated, and had ever-increasing access to consumer culture—cars, movies, radios, home appliances, ready-to-wear clothes, and so on. Stereotypes of "the Jazz Age" are overdrawn, but the old Victorian ways of the late nineteenth century—thrift, probity, modesty, sobriety, hard work—while far from gone, now coexisted uneasily with a greater emphasis on individual self-expression and pleasure. The change did not come at once, but by the end of World War I, in the prosperous 1920s, the hallmarks of modernity were everywhere.

The 1920s also saw a reaction against modernity. The rolling back of immigration reached its height in mid-decade, political radicals were hounded into silence, and prohibition attempted to stop not just drinking but the perceived moral laxity that went with it. A second Ku Klux Klan arose, as much midwestern as southern this time. Its avowed goal was to reassert an older racial and ethnic hierarchy, targeting not only African Americans but also Jews and Catholics. The decade, in a word, witnessed a deep clash of cultures.

Economic dynamism reigned in the cities. In rural America, however, there was no pronounced prosperity. Low prices for rural commodities stretched the financial resources of millions of farmers and took their toll on the small towns that depended on them. Electrical lines had yet to reach much of rural America, which remained as isolated as it had been in the nineteenth century. But the divisions between city and country life were more than just economic or technological. While many urban Americans reconciled their religious beliefs with scientific advancements in biology and geology, rural Americans often held to a strict fundamentalist interpretation of the Bible. They insisted that humankind and the world itself were much younger than such scientists as Charles Darwin claimed. To be sure, fundamentalism was not restricted just to rural America, but cultural and religious conservatism combined with economic stasis made the urban–rural division seem very wide.

Adherence to "that old-time religion" in small, rural Dayton, Tennessee, led to the decade's greatest showdown between the values of rural and urban America. Dayton lived in the shadow of urban prosperity. To its southwest, Chattanooga served as the hub of the region, attracting northern investment capital and surplus population. Dayton—the "other Dayton," people called it, not the bigger one in Ohio—enjoyed only modest, fitful growth and prosperity. To be sure, some residents saw hopeful signs of a better future. Most of its major streets were paved, a few automobiles navigated those streets, trains and buses made regular stops, the tax rate was one of the lowest in the state, and Dayton was the county seat for a large farming community. However, with all this, the town's business section was small, and its prospects for the future were not great. To most outsiders, Dayton seemed—and largely was—a quiet, sleepy southern town.

In 1925, it was not just Dayton that seemed backward; the entire state of Tennessee appeared behind the times to liberal-thinking, religiously progressive Americans. In that year, John Washington Butler, a respected 49-year-old farmer who had been elected to the Tennessee legislature the previous year, introduced a bill to make it illegal to teach the theory of evolution in the state's public schools. Butler's crusade was fired by passionate intensity, and those who opposed the bill were paralyzed by a lack of conviction. The faculty of the University of Tennessee maintained a deafening public silence, although in private many opposed the bill. The officials of the state's Department of Education were similarly mute, and the leaders of the Tennessee Academy of Science joined the silent chorus. As for the legislators themselves, they sat back and hoped that the entire embar-

rassment would go away. But it wouldn't, and it was less risky politically to vote yes than no. The governor signed the bill on March 21, 1925.

The passage of the antievolution law did not end the public debate over the issue. In fact, it did just the opposite. In Dayton, George Rappelyea, a native of New York who was the manager of the Cumberland Coal and Iron Company of Dayton, expressed the opinion that the law was bunk. Down at Robinson's Drug Store, several natives of Dayton disagreed. Both sides discussed the merits of the case, but getting nowhere, they called in an outside opinion. Rappelyea summoned John Scopes, the local biology teacher, from the tennis courts and asked his

Image 9.1 William Jennings Bryan and J. W. Butler, 1925
Butler was the Tennessee state legislator who introduced the antievolution bill in 1925; Bryan testified against teaching evolution.
Source: Courtesy of Tennessee State Library and Archives.

opinion of the law. Scopes remarked that it would be impossible to teach biology without breaking the new law and that he had already broken the antievolution law in the classroom. The discussion—the heat it generated and the passions it inflamed—gave Rappelyea an idea. Why not have a test case for the law in Dayton? Scopes could teach a class on evolution, the police could arrest him for breaking the Butler law, and a trial could be staged in Dayton. It would put the town on the map and be good for local business at the same time. The trial will be "a big sensation," Rappelyea said. "Why not bring a lot of doctors and preachers here? Let's get H. G. Wells and a lot of big fellows." At first, Scopes declined the offer. The thought of having an arrest and conviction on his record did not sit well with him. But eventually, he relented. "It was just a drugstore discussion that got past control," he later remarked.

H. G. Wells did not travel to Dayton, but a lot of other "big fellows" did. William Jennings Bryan quickly offered his services to the Christian defenders of the Butler law. Bryan

was nearing the end of a long, industrious, and distinguished, if a bit disappointing, career. In 1896, he had exploded on the national scene with his "Cross of Gold" speech at the Democratic Presidential Convention in Chicago, in which he advocated inflating America's money supply with "free silver" to help workers and farmers get out from under crushing indebtedness. Bryan sought the nomination for the presidency as the "Great Commoner," the candidate of the aggrieved in an era of capitalist rapacity, the man who could bring the angry third-party Populists back to the Democratic Party. A great orator and a passionate believer, Bryan threw his heart and soul into the campaign, but he lost the election. Only 36 years of age in 1896, he was young enough to try again. In 1900, he was nominated by the Democratic Party to run once more for the presidency, and again he lost. In 1908, the Democrats again chose Bryan to carry their standard, and for the third time he lost. After the 1908 election, he became increasingly involved in social crusades. In 1909, he announced his conversion to the prohibitionist cause and joined the fight

Image 9.2 John Scopes and George Rappelyea, Dayton, Tennessee, June 1925

Scopes (left) was encouraged by Rappelyea to test Tennessee's newly passed antievolution law in the classroom. This photograph was taken one month before the trial began in Dayton, Tennessee.

Source: Photographed by Watson Davis. Courtesy Smithsonian Institution, Record Unit 7091: Science Service, Records, 1902–1965. Image SIA 2008-1122.

to make America dry. For a brief time before World War I, he served as Woodrow Wilson's Secretary of State. When President Wilson wrote a statement harshly rebuking the Germans over the sinking of the Lusitania in 1915, Bryan resigned from the cabinet and thereafter campaigned against American involvement in the war. He brought that same intensity to all of his beliefs.

After the Great War ended, Bryan became an antievolutionist. With the same passion with which he had once embraced free silver, he lashed out against the Darwin's theories. People must shun liberal modernism and return to the teachings of the Bible: "You believe in the ages of rocks: I believe in the Rock of Ages," he told his opponents. Consistent with this view, in 1924 Bryan drafted the text of an antievolution bill passed by the Florida legislature, which made it illegal "to teach as true Darwinism or any other hypothesis that links man in blood relationship to any other form of life." Thus, when the call came from Dayton to stand witness for his beliefs, Bryan hurried to Tennessee to defend the Butler law.

Clarence Seward Darrow ventured to Dayton to defend Scopes and the Darwinian view of evolution. Like Bryan, Darrow was a product of small-town America. He had been born and reared in Kinsman, Ohio, the son of a preacher who had undergone a crisis of faith from which he emerged an agnostic. Clarence Darrow was clearly his father's son. He was skeptical of philosophical and religious absolutes, and he placed more faith in scientific rationalism than the untested teachings of the would-be guardians of public and private morality. Although he loved rural America—and held dear the independent rural ideal—he made his reputation in Chicago and became most closely identified with urban society. Yet Darrow presented a mass of contradictions: He started his career as a lawyer for railroad corporations but became the country's leading attorney for workers, leftists and radicals; he passionately defended the rights of blacks but scoffed at equal rights for women; and he lived well and spent lavishly but harbored a belief in socialism. One thing he was certain of though: the state should defend, not restrict, a person's right of self-expression, and free speech was the foremost example of self-expression. It was this principle that drew Darrow from Chicago to Dayton. Scopes had the right to teach the theory of evolution even if the Tennessee legislature said he could not.

Joining Darrow and Bryan in Dayton were journalists, preachers, and an odd assortment of curious spectators. There was the white-haired, wild-eyed T. T. Martin, field secretary for the Anti-Evolution League, who urged all who would listen to "Drive Hell out of the High Schools." There was a party of Seventh Day Adventists who drove around Dayton in an automobile that proudly displayed a sign proclaiming, "Get Right with God." There were the many mountaineers who came into Dayton to see what all the commotion was about. One of them allegedly explained his position and that of many of Butler's defenders: "Well, brother, my way's the safest; just believe what the Bible says and quit trying to figure out something different."

Of all the reporters who traveled to Dayton, H. L. Mencken was the most famous and notorious. He was the consummate skeptic. A newspaperman from Baltimore, he was opposed to all that was smug and overconfident in the American character. He attacked "puritanism," decried the country's worship of business, and lambasted conventional morality and religion. For Mencken, Bryan represented the worst side of the American character. Bryan's confident refusal to subject any of his beliefs to questioning and his willingness to use the power of government to make other people live by his rules repelled Mencken. In the Scopes trial, Mencken saw repressive Bryanism writ large. On the day the trial began, Mencken wrote:

> The trial of the infidel Scopes . . . will greatly resemble, I suspect, the trial of a prohibition agent accused of mayhem in Union Hill, New Jersey. That is to say, it will be conducted with the most austere regard for the highest principles of jurisprudence. Judge and jury will go to extreme lengths to assure the prisoner the last and least of his rights. He will be protected in his person and feelings by the full military and naval power of the State of Tennessee. No one will be permitted to pull his nose, to pray publicly for his condemnation or even to make a face at him. But all the same he will be bumped off inevitably when the time comes, and to the applause of all right-thinking men.[1]

The Scopes trial dominated the news. Indeed, in the still, intense summer heat of Dayton, Bryan and Darrow defended two different worldviews, one rooted in nostalgic memory of America's rural past and the other based on the tenets of scientific modernism. For Americans in 1925, the Scopes trial symbolized their country in transition. When Darrow and Bryan engaged in their famous confrontation, two worlds collided.

INTRODUCTION TO DOCUMENTS 1, 2, AND 3

Document 1 is an excerpt from George William Hunter's *A Civic Biology*, the 1914 textbook that John Scopes used to teach evolution. Note the racial and class assumptions in this science text and its praise for eugenics as a technique of social engineering. What cultural and social values did supposedly impartial "science" advocate?

In Document 2, one of the leading southern critics of evolution outlines his concerns. J. W. Porter led the fight to ban evolution in Kentucky schools, citing flawed texts such as Hunter's *A Civic Biology* as his evidence. Porter was particularly concerned by the growing circulation of these texts in southern high schools and universities. Such concern led directly to the passage of the Butler Act in Tennessee, which is Document 3. Note that "normal" schools were those that trained future teachers. Why did Porter and Butler so ardently oppose students reading texts such as Hunter's? What did Porter mean when he wrote that "the theory of evolution denies man's moral responsibility?"

1. FROM *A CIVIC BIOLOGY* (1914)

GEORGE WILLIAM HUNTER

The Doctrine of Evolution.—We have now learned that animal forms may be arranged so as to begin with very simple one-celled forms and culminate with a group which contains man himself. This arrangement is called the *evolutionary series.* Evolution means change, and these groups are believed by scientists to represent stages in complexity of development of life on the earth. Geology teaches that millions of years ago, life upon the earth was very simple, and that gradually more and more complex forms of life appeared, as the rocks formed latest in time show the most highly developed forms of animal life. The great English scientist, Charles Darwin, from this and other evidence, explained the theory of evolution. This is the belief that simple forms of life on the earth slowly and gradually gave rise to those more complex and that thus ultimately the most complex forms came into existence. . . .

Evolution of Man.—Undoubtedly there once lived upon the earth races of men who were much lower in their mental organization than the present inhabitants. If we follow the early history of man upon the earth, we find that at first he must have been little better than one of the lower animals. He was a nomad, wandering from place to place, feeding upon whatever living things he could kill with his hands. Gradually he must have learned to use weapons, and thus kill his prey, first using rough stone implements for this purpose. As man became more civilized, implements of bronze and of iron were used. About this time the subjugation and domestication of animals began to take place. Man then began to cultivate the fields, and to have a fixed place of abode other than a cave. The beginnings of civilization were long ago, but even to-day the earth is not entirely civilized.

The Races of Man.—At the present time there exist upon the earth five races or varieties of man, each very different from the other in instincts, social customs, and, to an extent, in structure. These are the Ethiopian or negro type, originating in Africa; the Malay or brown race, from the islands of the Pacific; the American Indian; the Mongolian or yellow race, including the natives of China, Japan, and the Eskimos; and finally, the highest type of all, the Caucasians, represented by the civilized white inhabitants of Europe and America. . . .

Improvement of Man.—If the stock of domesticated animals can be improved, it is not unfair to ask if the health and vigor of the future generations of men and women on the earth might not be improved by applying to them the laws of selection. This improvement of the future race has a number of factors in which we as individuals may play a part. . . .

Eugenics.—When people marry there are certain things that the individual as well as the race should demand. The most important of these is freedom from germ diseases which might be handed down to the offspring. Tuberculosis, syphilis, that

dread disease which cripples and kills hundreds of thousands of innocent children, epilepsy, and feeble-mindedness are handicaps which it is not only unfair but criminal to hand down to posterity. The science of being well born is called *eugenics*.

The Jukes.—Studies have been made on a number of different families in this country, in which mental and moral defects were present in one or both of the original parents. The "Jukes" family is a notorious example. The first mother is known as "Margaret, the mother of criminals." In seventy-five years the progeny of the original generation has cost the state of New York over a million and a quarter of dollars, besides giving over to the care of prisons and asylums considerably over a hundred feeble-minded, alcoholic, immoral, or criminal persons. Another case recently studied is the "Kallikak" family. This family has been traced back to the War of the Revolution, when a young soldier named Martin Kallikak seduced a feeble-minded girl. She had a feeble-minded son from whom there have been to the present time 480 descendants. Of these 33 were sexually immoral, 24 confirmed drunkards, 3 epileptics, and 143 *feeble-minded*. The man who started this terrible line of immorality and feeble-mindedness later married a normal Quaker girl. From this couple a line of 496 descendants have come, with *no* cases of feeble-mindedness. The evidence and the moral speak for themselves!

Parasitism and Its Cost of Society.—Hundreds of families such as those described above exist to-day, spreading disease, immorality, and crime to all parts of this country. The cost to society of such families is very severe. Just as certain animals or plants become parasitic on other plants or animals, these families have become parasitic on society. They not only do harm to others by corrupting, stealing, or spreading disease, but they are actually protected and cared for by the state out of public money. Largely for them the poorhouse and the asylum exist. They take from society, but they give nothing in return. They are true parasites.

The Remedy.—If such people were lower animals, we would probably kill them off to prevent them from spreading. Humanity will not allow this, but we do have the remedy of separating the sexes in asylums or other places and in various ways preventing intermarriage and the possibilities of perpetuating such a low and degenerate race. Remedies of this sort have been tried successfully in Europe and are now meeting with success in this country.

Blood Tells.—Eugenics show us, on the other hand, in a study of the families in which are brilliant men and women, the fact that the descendants have received the *good* inheritance from their ancestors. The following, taken from Davenport's *Heredity in Relation to Eugenics*, illustrates how one family has been famous in American History.

In 1667 Elizabeth Tuttle,

> of strong will, and of extreme intellectual vigor, married Richard Edwards of Hartford, Conn., a man of high repute and great erudition. From their one son descended another son, Jonathan Edwards, a noted divine, and president of Princeton College. Of the descendants of Jonathan Edwards much has been written; a brief catalogue must suffice: Jonathan Edwards, Jr., president of Union College; Timothy Dwight, president of Yale; Sereno Edwards Dwight, president of Hamilton College; Theodore Dwight Woolsey, for twenty-five years president of Yale College; Sarah, wife of Tapping Reeve, founder of Litchfield Law School, herself no mean lawyer; Daniel Tyler, a general in the Civil War and founder of the iron industries of North Alabama; Timothy Dwight, second, president of Yale University from 1886 to 1898; Theodore William Dwight, founder and for thirty-three years warden of Columbia Law School; Henrietta Frances, wife of Eli Whitney, inventor of the cotton gin, who, burning the midnight oil by the side of her ingenious husband, helped him to his enduring fame; Merrill Edwards Gates, president of Amherst College; Catherine Maria Sedgwick of graceful pen; Charles Sedgwick Minot, authority on biology and embryology in the

Harvard Medical School; Edith Kermit Carow, wife of Theodore Roosevelt; and Winston Churchill, the author of *Coniston* and other well-known novels.

> Of the daughters of Elizabeth Tuttle distinguished descendants also came: Robert Treat Paine, signer of the Declaration of Independence; Chief Justice of the United States Morrison R. Waite; Ulysses S. Grant and Grover Cleveland, presidents of the United States. These and many other prominent men and women can trace the characters which enabled them to occupy the positions of culture and learning they held back to Elizabeth Tuttle.

Euthenics.—Euthenics, the betterment of the environment, is another important factor in the production of a stronger race. The strongest physical characteristics may be ruined if the surroundings are unwholesome and unsanitary. The slums of a city are "at once symptom, effect, and cause of evil." A city which allows foul tenements, narrow streets, and crowded slums to exist will spend too much for police protection, for charity, and for hospitals.

Every improvement in surroundings means improvement of the chances of survival of the race. In the spring of 1913 the health department and street-cleaning department of the city of New York cooperated to bring about a "clean up" of all filth, dirt, and rubbish from the houses, streets, and vacant lots in that city. During the summer of 1913 the health department reported a smaller percentage of deaths of babies than ever before. We must draw our own conclusions. Clean streets and houses, clean milk and pure water, sanitary housing, and careful medical inspection all do their part in maintaining a low rate of illness and death, thus reacting upon the health of the citizens of the future. . . .[2]

2. EVOLUTION—A MENACE (1922)

J. W. PORTER

The recent general uprising against the teaching of evolution in our schools has brought forth the charge that Christians are attempting to force the Bible as a textbook upon State schools. There

are those who are no doubt sincere in this contention; while others are evidently making this charge to divert attention from the real issue. Those who are protesting, and will continue to protest against the teaching of evolution in our schools, have not asked that the Bible be made a textbook in these institutions. They do not believe in a combination of Church and State. On the other hand, they are vigorously opposed to a combination of Infidelity and State. Since the Bible is not taught in these schools, those of us who believe the Bible to be the very word of God feel that we have all the more right to request that instruction in these institutions should not be contrary to and subversive of the teaching of the Bible. If Bible teaching is eliminated, we must insist that it shall not be discredited, derided and denied. We have not contended that Christ shall become a part of the curriculum, but we do earnestly contend that He shall not be crucified on the cross of a false philosophy, called evolution.

The excuse is offered for the teachers of evolution, that they only present the Darwinian hypothesis as a theory. The only objection to this statement is that it is not true. . . . this theory is taught as a fact. These textbooks in many instances were suggested and endorsed by those who teach them. The doctrine of these textbooks is taught and commended in the classroom. . . . Why should not the teacher present the Bible account of Creation? Is this account ruled out as false and impossible? In none of these textbooks is the history of Creation, as it appears in the Bible, either suggested or referred to as possible. When mentioned in the classroom, which is seldom, it is discredited.

Is it asking too much that the authors of our textbooks accord as much respect to the Bible as they do to the books of Charles Darwin? Apparently, there can be but one reason for ignoring the Scriptural record of Creation. This reason is, that those who teach evolution utterly reject the account of Creation contained in the book of Genesis. . . .

The real test of any philosophy—and evolution is at most a philosophy which attempts to explain the development of the world—is to carefully note the effects or fruits of it. Let us therefore glance at some of the fruits of this unproved and unprovable theory of evolution.

1. The theory of evolution denies man's moral responsibility. . . .
2. The theory of evolution denies the Gospel remedy for sin. . . . In its scheme, there is no place for one to die for another, but to the contrary, the stronger kills the weaker in order that the stronger may survive. . . .
3. It destroys belief in the Bible and thus takes away from the people the greatest civilizing force known to the world. . . .
4. It is wrecking the faith of many students in all our state institutions and not a few in denominational schools. . . .
5. It undermines all the fundamentals of Christianity. It denies the supernatural in the scheme and process of life. It finds no place for a miracle, or a miracle-working God. . . .
6. It robs man of his spiritual nature and makes him a developed beast. . . .
7. It exalts the law of the jungle. . . . Evolution knows neither God nor mercy, but only "variation" and brute strength.
8. Evolution logically and inevitably leads to war.[3]

3. THE BUTLER ACT (1925)

HOUSE BILL NO. 185: Butler

An Act prohibiting the teaching of the Evolution Theory in all the Universities, Normals and all other public schools of Tennessee, which are supported in whole or in part by the public school funds of the State, and to provide penalties for the violations thereof.

SECTION 1. BE IT ENACTED BY THE GENERAL ASSEMBLY OF THE STATE OF TENNESSEE, That it shall be unlawful for any teacher in any of the Universities, normal and all other public schools of the State which are supported in whole or in part by the public school funds of the state, to teach any theory that denies the story of the Divine Creation of man as taught in the Bible, and to teach instead that man has descended from a lower order of animals.

SECTION 2. BE IT FURTHER ENACTED, That any teacher found guilty of the violation of this Act, shall be guilty of a misdemeanor and upon conviction, shall be fined not less than One Hundred ($100.00) Dollars nor more than Five Hundred ($500.00) Dollars for each offense. . . .

Passed March 13, 1925.[4]

INTRODUCTION TO DOCUMENT 4

Clarence Darrow's cross-examination of William Jennings Bryan in the case of *Tennessee v. John Thomas Scopes* has been edited to highlight the conflict between the two men. Most of the normal legal objections and rulings have been removed. Because of the extreme heat and fears that the building could not withstand the number of spectators, the day-long examination was moved outdoors. Consider how both men articulated and defended their views.

Image 9.3 Final day of the Scopes Trial, July 20, 1925

Clarence Darrow, standing at right, questions William Jennings Bryan at the trial. John Scopes is in the foreground, with his back to the camera, second from left (with hand held to his face).

Source: Photographed by Watson Davis. Courtesy Smithsonian Institution, Record Unit 7091: Science Service, Records, 1902-1965. Image SIA 2007-0124.

4. DARROW VERSUS BRYAN (1925)

DARROW: You have given considerable study to the Bible, haven't you, Mr. Bryan?

BRYAN: Yes, sir, I have.

D: Do you claim that everything in the Bible should be literally interpreted?

B: I believe everything in the Bible should be accepted as it is given there; some of the Bible is given illustratively. For instance: "Ye are the salt of the earth." I would not insist that man was actually salt, or that he had flesh of salt, but it is used in the sense of salt as saving God's people.

D: You believe the story of the flood to be a literal interpretation?

B: Yes, sir.

D: How long ago was the flood, Mr. Bryan?

B: Let me see Usher's calculation about it?

D: Surely. (*He hands a Bible to the witness*)

B: It is given here as 2348 years B.C.

D: Well, 2348 years B.C. You believe that all the living things that were not contained in the ark were destroyed?

B: I think the fish may have lived.

D: Outside of the fish?

B: I cannot say.

D: You cannot say?

B: No, except that just as it is, I have no proof to the contrary.

D: I am asking you whether you believe?

B: I do.

D: That all living things outside of the fish were destroyed?

B: What I say about the fish is merely a matter of humor.

D: I understand. . . .

B: I accept that, as the Bible gives it, and I have never found any reason for denying, disputing, or rejecting it. . . .

D: Don't you know there are any number of civilizations that are traced back to more than 5000 years?

B: I know we have people who trace things back according to the number of ciphers they have. But I am not satisfied they are accurate.

D: You are not satisfied there is any civilization that can be traced back 5000 years?

B: I would not want to say there is because I have no evidence of it that is satisfactory.

D: Would you say there is not?

B: Well, so far as I know, but when the scientists differ, from 24,000,000 to 306,000,000 in their opinion, as to how long ago life came here, I want them nearer, to come nearer together before they demand of me to give up my belief in the Bible. . . .

D: Let me make this definite. You believe that every civilization on the earth and every living thing, except possibly fishes, that came out of the ark were wiped out by the flood?

B: At that time.

D: At that time. And then, whatever human beings, including all the tribes, that inhabited the world, and have inhabited the world, and who run their pedigree straight back, and all the animals, have come onto the earth since the flood?

B: Yes.

D: Within 4200 years. Do you know a scientific man on the face of the earth that believes any such thing?

B: I cannot say, but I know some scientific men who dispute entirely the antiquity of man as testified to by other scientific men.

D: Oh, that does not answer the question. Do you know of a single scientific man on the face of the earth that believes any such thing as you stated, about the antiquity of man?

B: I don't think I have ever asked one the direct question.

D: Quite important, isn't it?

B: Well, I don't know as it is.

D: It might not be?

B: If I had nothing else to do except speculate on what our remote ancestors were and what our remote descendants may be—but I have been more interested in Christians living right now, to make it much more important than speculation on either the past or the future.

D: You have never had any interest in the age of the various races and people and civilization and animals that exist upon the earth today? Is that right?

B: I have never felt a great deal of interest in the effort that has been made to dispute the Bible by the speculations of men, or the investigations of men. . . .

D: . . . Now, I ask you if you know if it was interesting enough, or important enough for you to try to find out about how old these ancient civilizations were?

B: No; I have not made a study of it.

D: Don't you know that the ancient civilizations of China are 6000 or 7000 years old, at the very least?

B: No; they would not run back beyond the creation, according to the Bible, 6000 years.

D: You don't know how old they are, is that right?

B: I don't know how old they are, but probably you do. I think you would give the preference to anybody who opposed the Bible, and I give the preference to the Bible.

D: I see. Well, you are welcome to your opinion. Have you any idea how old the Egyptian civilization is?

B: No.

D: Do you know of any record in the world, outside of the story of the Bible, which conforms to any statement that it is 4200 years ago or thereabouts that all life was wiped off the face of the earth?

B: I think they have found records. . . .

D: Mr. Bryan, don't you know that there are many old religions that describe the flood?

B: No, I don't know.

D: You know there are others besides the Jewish?

B: I don't know whether there are records of any other religion which refer to this flood.

D: Don't you ever examine religion so far as to know that?

B: Outside of the Bible?

D: Yes.

B: No; I have not examined to know that, generally.

D: You have never examined any other religions?

B: Yes, sir.

D: Have you ever read anything about the origins of religions?

B: Not a great deal.

D: You have never examined any other religion?

B: Yes, sir.

D: And you don't know whether any other religion ever gave a similar account of the destruction of the earth by the flood?

B: The Christian religion has satisfied me, and I have never felt it necessary to look up some competing religions. . . .

D: Did you ever read a book on primitive man? Like Tyler's *Primitive Culture,* or Boas, or any of the great authorities?

B: I don't think I ever read the ones you have mentioned.

D: Have you read any?

B: Well, I have read a little from time to time. But I didn't pursue it, because I didn't know I was to be called as a witness.

D: You have never in all your life made any attempt to find out about the other peoples of the earth—how old their civilizations are—how long they had existed on earth, have you?

B: No, sir; I have been so well satisfied with the Christian religion that I have spent no time trying to find arguments against it. . . . [Your] purpose is to cast ridicule on everybody who believes in the Bible, and I am perfectly willing that the world shall know that these gentlemen have no other purpose than ridiculing every Christian who believes in the

D: We have the purpose of preventing bigots and ignoramuses from controlling the education of the United States and you know it, and that is all. . . .

B: I am not trying to get anything into the record. I am simply trying to protect the Word of God against the greatest atheist or agnostic in the United States. (*Prolonged applause*) I want the papers to know I am not afraid to get on the stand in front of him and let him do his worst. I want the world to know. (*Prolonged applause*)

D: Does the statement, "The morning and the evening were the first day," and "The morning and the evening were the second day," mean anything to you?

B: I do not think it necessarily means a twenty-four-hour day.

D: You do not?

B: No.

D: What do you consider it to be?

B: I have not attempted to explain it. If you will take the second chapter—let me have the book. (*Examines the Bible*) The fourth verse of the second chapter says: "These are the generations of the heavens and of the earth, when they were created in the day that the Lord God made the earth and the heavens." The word "day" there in the very next chapter is used to describe a period. I do not see that there is any necessity for construing the words, "the evening and the morning," as meaning necessarily a twenty-four-hour day, "in the day when the Lord made the heaven and the earth."

D: Then, when the Bible said, for instance, "and God called the firmament heaven. And the evening and the morning were the second day," that does not necessarily mean twenty-four hours? . . .

B: No. But I think it would be just as easy for the kind of God we believe in to make the earth in six days as in six years or in 6,000,000 years or in 600,000,000 years. I do not think it important whether we believe one or the other.

D: Do you think those were literal days?

B: My impression is they were periods, but I would not attempt to argue as against anybody who wanted to believe in literal days.

D: Have you any idea of the length of the periods?

B: No; I don't.

D: Do you think the sun was made on the fourth day?

B: Yes.

D: And they had evening and morning without the sun?

B: I am simply saying it is a period.

D: They had evening and morning for four periods without the sun, do you think?

B: I believe in creation as there told, and if I am not able to explain it I will accept it. Then you can explain it to suit yourself.

D: Mr. Bryan, what I want to know is, do you believe the sun was made on the fourth day?

B: I believe just as it says there.

D: Do you believe the sun was made on the fourth day?

B: Read it.

D: I am very sorry; you have read it so many times you would know, but I will read it again:

And God said, let there be lights in the firmament of the heaven, to divide the day from the night; and let them be for signs, and for seasons, and for days, and years. And let them be for lights in the firmament of the heaven, to give light upon the earth; and it was so. And God made two great lights; the greater light to rule the day, and the lesser light to rule the night; He made the stars also. And God set them in the firmament of the heaven, to give light upon the earth, and to rule over the day and over the night, and to divide the light from the darkness; and God saw that it was good. And the evening and the morning were the fourth day.

Do you believe, whether it was a literal day or a period, the sun and the moon were not made until the fourth day?

B: I believe they were made in the order in which they were given there. . . .

D: Cannot you answer my question?

B: I have answered it. I believe that it was made on the fourth day, in the fourth day.

D: And they had the evening and the morning before that time for three days or three periods. All right, that settles it. Now, if you call those periods, they may have been a very long time. . . .

B: Your Honor, I think I can shorten this testimony. The only purpose Mr. Darrow has is to slur at the Bible, but I will answer his question. I will answer it all at once, and I have no objection in the world, I want the world to know that this man, who does not believe in a God, is trying to use a court in Tennessee—

D: I object to that.

B: (*Continuing*)—to slur at it, and while it will require time. I am willing to take it.

D: I object to your statement. I am examining you on your fool ideas that no intelligent Christian on earth believes.

THE Court: Court is adjourned until tomorrow morning.[5]

Image 9.4 People in line for the funeral service of William Jennings Bryan, Washington, D.C. (1925)

Bryan's death, just days after the end of the Scopes trial, prompted reflections on what seemed to be a growing divide between urban and rural America.

Source: Courtesy Library of Congress.

INTRODUCTION TO DOCUMENTS 5 AND 6

Five days after the end of the Scopes trial, Bryan suffered a cerebral hemorrhage and died. Several memorials and commentaries on his life immediately followed, reflections not just on the man but the larger significance of the Scopes trial. H. L. Mencken published his "In Memoriam: W. J. B.," in the Baltimore *Evening Sun* on July 27, 1925, the day after Bryan's death. Mencken rewrote the piece for the October 1925 issue of the *American Mercury*, which is the version reprinted as Document 5. Mencken's words capture the suspicion of urban for rural America and also the divisions of class, education, faith, and region. What accounts for Mencken's hostility? In Document 6, Reverend Joseph Sizoo eulogizes Bryan in starkly different terms. How do you account for such widely divergent assessments of the man and his work? Do Mencken and Sizoo share any common understandings of Bryan as an individual?

5. "IN MEMORIAM: W. J. B." (1925)

H. L. MENCKEN

There was something peculiarly fitting in the fact that [Bryan's] last days were spent in a one-horse Tennessee village, beating off the flies and gnats, and that death found him there. The man felt at home in such simple and Christian scenes. He liked people who sweated freely, and were not debauched by the refinements of the toilet. Making his progress up and down the Main street of little Dayton, surrounded by gaping primates from the upland valleys of the Cumberland Range, his coat laid aside, his bare arms and hairy chest shining damply, his bald head sprinkled with dust—so accoutred and on display, he was obviously happy. He liked getting up early in the morning, to the tune of cocks crowing on the dunghill. He liked the heavy, greasy victuals of the farmhouse kitchen. He liked country lawyers, country pastors, all country people. He liked country sounds and country smells.

I believe that this liking was sincere—perhaps the only sincere thing in the man. His nose showed no uneasiness when a hillman in faded overalls and hickory shirt accosted him on the street, and besought him for light upon some mystery of Holy Writ. The simian gabble of the cross-roads was not gabble to him, but wisdom of an occult and superior sort. In the presence of city folks he was palpably uneasy. Their clothes, I suspect, annoyed him, and he was suspicious of their too delicate manners. He knew all the while that they were laughing at him—if not at his baroque theology, then at least at his alpaca pantaloons. But the yokels never laughed at him. To them he was not the huntsman but the prophet, and toward the end, as he gradually forsook mundane politics for more ghostly concerns, they began to elevate him in their hierarchy. When he died he was the peer of Abraham. His old enemy, [Woodrow] Wilson, aspiring to the same white and shining robe, came down with a thump. But Bryan made the grade. His place in Tennessee hagiography is secure. If the village barber saved any of his hair, then it is curing gall-stones down there today.

But what label will he bear in more urbane regions? One, I fear, of a far less flattering kind. Bryan lived too long, and descended too deeply into the mud, to be taken seriously hereafter by fully literate men, even of the kind who write schoolbooks. There was a scattering of sweet words in his funeral notices, but it was no more than a response to conventional sentimentality. The best verdict the most romantic editorial writer could dredge up, save in the humorless South, was to the general effect that his imbecilities were excused by his earnestness—that under his clowning, as under that of the juggler of Notre Dame, there was the zeal of a steadfast soul. . . .

This talk of sincerity, I confess, fatigues me. If the fellow was sincere, then so was P. T. Barnum. The word is disgraced and degraded by such uses. He was, in fact, a charlatan, a mountebank, a zany without sense or dignity. His career brought him into contact with the first men of his time; he preferred the company of rustic ignoramuses. It was hard to believe, watching him at Dayton, that he had traveled, that he had been received in civilized societies, that he had been a high officer of state. He seemed only a poor clod like those around him, deluded by a childish theology, full of an almost pathological hatred of all learning, all human dignity, all beauty, all fine and noble things. He was a peasant come home to the barnyard. Imagine a gentleman, and you have imagined everything that he was not. What animated him from end to end of his grotesque career was simply ambition—the ambition of a common man to get his hand upon the collar of his superiors, or, failing that, to get his thumb into their eyes. He was born with a roaring voice, and it had the trick of inflaming half-wits. His whole career was devoted to raising those half-wits against their betters, that he himself might shine.

His last battle will be grossly misunderstood if it is thought of as a mere exercise in fanaticism—that is, if Bryan the Fundamentalist Pope is mistaken for one of the bucolic Fundamentalists. There was much more in it than that, as everyone knows who saw him on the field. What moved him, at bottom, was simply hatred of the city men who had laughed at him so long, and brought him at last to so tatterdemalion an estate. He lusted for revenge upon them. He yearned to lead the anthropoid rabble against them, to punish them for their execution upon him by attacking the very vitals of their civilization. He went far beyond the bounds of any merely religious frenzy, however inordinate. When he began denouncing the notion that man is a mammal even some of the hinds at Dayton were agape. And when, brought upon Clarence Darrow's cruel hook, he writhed and tossed in a very fury of malignancy, bawling against the veriest elements of sense and decency like a man frantic—when he came to that tragic climax of his striving there were snickers among the hinds as well as hosannas.

Upon that hook, in truth, Bryan committed suicide, as a legend as well as in the body. . . .

Thus he fought his last fight, thirsting savagely for blood. All sense departed from him. He bit right and left, like a dog with rabies. He descended to demagogy so dreadful that his very associates at the trial table blushed. His one yearning was to keep his yokels heated up—to lead his forlorn mob of imbeciles against the foe. That foe, alas, refused to be alarmed. It insisted upon seeing the whole battle as a comedy. Even Darrow, who knew better, occasionally yielded to the prevailing spirit. One day he lured poor Bryan into the folly I have mentioned: his astounding argument against the notion that man is a mammal. I am glad I heard it, for otherwise I'd never believe it. There stood the man who had been thrice a candidate for the Presidency of the Republic—there he stood in the glare of the world, uttering stuff that a boy of eight would laugh at. The artful Darrow led him on: he repeated it, ranted for it, bellowed it in his cracked voice. So he was prepared for the final slaughter. He came into life a hero, a Galahad, in bright and shining armor. He was passing out a poor mountebank.[6]

6. A EULOGY FOR BRYAN (1925)

REVEREND DR. JOSEPH R. SIZOO

Some years ago—it seems only like yesterday—Mr. Bryan delivered a lecture to a group of some 500 students in a mid-Western college. His theme was "The Value of an Ideal." He spoke with that amazing clarity which so characterized all his addresses, not only of the place of an ideal in life, but also of the various ideals which men may hold, and then that highest of all ideals—Christian service.

How profoundly he moved that group of young men Mr. Bryan never knew. There was one student in that audience for whom it changed the whole program of his life. . . .

I was that student. The stirring plea marked the beginning of a whole new attitude to life and I bring my testimony to the memory of a man who never knew how greatly he had changed that life. . . .

. . . There was a threefold splendor about this nobleman which will ever challenge those who have lived in his day and who are to carry on in the days to come.

One: He had a capacity for noble living. He was a man with an upturned face and an upward life. His life was an open book beyond all reproach. His character was unsullied to the very end.

You can turn the searching light of a critical publicity on any page of his past through all manner of personal and political fortunes of later life and not one page is smutted or soiled or stained. There was no shadow of self-seeking or gain in him. There was no skeleton in the closet. . . .

Two: He had a deep capacity for love. He was a great friend and never played fast and lose with friendship. . . . Political opposition never lost him personal friendships. His love was genuine with rich and poor alike; it knew no order, breed or birth. Differing from men who held contrary convictions, he still held them within the grasp of lifelong affections.

. . . He never lost sight of humanity. His heart beat and his pulse throbbed for the needs of his fellow-men. He kept many a weary vigil on the hilltop of the world, wondering what might be done to help, never resting till the crown of thorns had been lifted and the golden crown of happiness and peace put in its place. . . .

Three: He had a rich capacity for faith. . . .

How often he said that happiness will be restored, prosperity will beat again with its angel wings and peace will come with its eternal abiding, when men come back to the simple, elemental forces of life like honesty, reverence and faith in God. . . .

In a day full of intellectual bewilderment when many Christians are growing uncertain of their convictions, when multitudes have misgivings less the things they have believed may prove false; in a day when many become obsessed with despair like that of a man who has played his last card and lost, Mr. Bryan grew more sure and his faith more profound.

. . . God bless and hallow the heritage and memory of William Jennings Bryan.[7]

INTRODUCTION TO DOCUMENT 7

British journalist Samuel Ratcliffe toured the United States during the early twentieth century and avidly followed the Scopes trial. Just after Bryan's death, he wrote a keen reflection on the meaning of the trial and predicted that the religious divisions on display in Dayton would bedevil Americans for decades to come. Does Ratcliffe's assessment resonate with your understanding of American life and culture today? How does he understand the conflict between fundamentalist Christianity and modern life?

7. AMERICA AND FUNDAMENTALISM (1925)

S. K. RATCLIFFE

Large numbers of English people have been amused and startled by the recent affair in Tennessee. They have likewise been greatly puzzled by it; and perhaps no recent event in America stands more in need of explanation, in all its bearings, than the verdict of "Guilty" in the Dayton trial and the fine imposed upon the high-school teacher, John T. Scopes, for violating the Anti-Evolution Law of the State of Tennessee.

[In] 1922, I described what appeared to be at that time the more salient characteristics of the reaction that was affecting the American churches and colleges after the war. The movement against enlightenment had gathered great force. An organized attack was being made upon liberal professors and ministers. In colleges subject to denominational influences religious tests were being applied. Modernist preachers were having to fight for the retention of their pulpits. There was a violent recrudescence of millennial belief, and . . . the movement called Fundamentalism adopted its aggressive policy. . . .

It would be accurate to say, however, that so recently as four years ago the fear of Evolution that is now so much in evidence was not a governing part of the Fundamentalist consciousness. At all events, it had not then obtained possession of the old-fashioned religious public, as, under the leadership of W. J. Bryan, it was soon to do. The first indication of the coming struggle that received widespread notice in the Press was the introduction into the Kentucky Legislature of a Bill designed to forbid the teaching of evolutionary doctrine in public schools and colleges. The defeat of this measure by one vote was treated as a political joke or an isolated curiosity. But those who knew the educational conditions of the Southern States were aware that the attempt in Kentucky was the first manoeuvre in a campaign that would probably develop into a grave spiritual civil war involving the entire country.

The late W. J. Bryan was, from the beginning, the unchallenged leader of the lay forces of Fundamentalism. No man in America knew so well as he the formidable strength of the country's religious conservatism. His extraordinary experience as a politician-evangelist had made him aware of the field of conquest awaiting him in the South and West. His party was rapidly organized, and it had large financial reserves to draw upon. . . . Mr. Bryan, good Democrat that he was, calculated that by making an attack, State by State, upon the modernists and evolutionists he might hope to achieve, as the crowning work of his life, a triumphant affirmation in the laws of the United States of the doctrines which were to him the fundamentals equally of Christianity and Americanism.

Thus, for the Fundamentalists, the passage of the Tennessee Anti-Evolution Law, early in the present year, was an important initial victory.

. . . Dayton is not an isolated incident. It is a symptom. W. J. Bryan was not an accident or a freak. He was a representative Westerner, and a portent. Behind him and the agitation to which he devoted his marvelous energy and eloquence during his last years there lies a complicated social condition, the phenomena of which are certainly deserving of study.

Mr. Frank R. Kent, an able journalist on the staff of the *Baltimore Sun*, in an article written just after the trial, asks us to believe that the real drama in Dayton was not in the court. It was in the townsfolk,

who are typical of a great multitude of American citizens. . . . In [this area] there are almost no Catholics, Episcopalians, or Jews. There are Methodists, Baptists, Presbyterians, and half-a-dozen other denominations; and Mr. Kent makes the surprising statement that of the 2,000 people in Dayton not more than fifty are without some touch with one or other of the nine evangelical churches, and that this proportion prevails in the towns throughout Tennessee, the neighboring States, and kindred regions further west. Take religion away from such places, and the desolation and distress would be pitiable to contemplate, while to think of convincing these people, even the relatively educated section of church members, of the soundness of Evolution as opposed to their view of Bible truth, would be fantastic.

. . . There has been in the United States, since the beginning of the century, vast expansion of colleges, State universities, and technical institutes. . . . The number of college graduates is constantly and rapidly increasing [and] . . . the great majority of the youths and girls who obtain the coveted advantage of a college education come from the small town or rural community where social life is centred in the churches. They step into the stimulating atmosphere of a large institution, where the students are allowed the most complete freedom, and where, in the absence of the classical humanities, the main interest is concentrated in the departments of history, economics, and science. . . . The resulting situation is not difficult to imagine. The student goes from his home in Iowa or Nebraska to the State university, or to one of the vast conglomerate universities of Chicago, or some other centre. He makes the immediate discovery that the small body of religious and patriotic doctrine which is the whole of orthodoxy in his hometown has no place in the new world he has entered. . . .

. . . [W]e cannot wonder that many parents, who may have no sympathy whatever with the Fundamentalists, should be resentful in the knowledge that their sons and daughters are studying in institutions which, necessarily secular by American law and custom, are open to the charge of permitting and encouraging a multiple assault upon traditional faiths. . . .

However these things may be, we may perceive the gathering evidence of a conflict that cannot fail to be painful. . . . America is on the eve of a final encounter between its vast inertia of "plain Bible religion" and the spirit of the modern world. If the Fundamentalists elect to pursue the course marked out for them by Bryan the main result will be a mass of wreckage, amid which the inevitable church schisms will be relatively unimportant.[8]

POSTSCRIPT

After nine minutes of deliberation, the jury found John Scopes guilty of violating the Butler law, and the court fined him $100. The verdict was later reversed on a technicality. The Butler Act was repealed by the Tennessee Legislature forty years later in 1967. But that wasn't the end of it. In 2005, Bryan College, an evangelical institution in Dayton founded just after the Scopes Trial, built a statue of William Jennings Bryan in front of the Rhea County courthouse. Twelve years later, a statue of Clarence Darrow appeared, erected by the local historical society. Many in Dayton, including some Christians, supported the Darrow statue, arguing that it represented part of the town's history. Others disagreed. One local leader described it as an "ongoing attempt by secularists in America to blur or remove symbols reminding us of our Judeo-Christian heritage," and a Dayton woman displayed a sign in her store reading, "Darrow ACLU's Favorite Communist." The conflict between science and religion has never gone away, and today a third of Americans tell pollsters that they do not believe in evolution.[9]

QUESTIONS

1. Did the content of the book *A Civic Biology* surprise you? Why was J. W. Porter so disturbed by texts such as these? Why did he reject evolution?
2. Do you see connections between the ideas put forth in Hunter's *A Civic Biology* and Margaret Sanger's writings in chapter 8?
3. Which tensions do you think were most prominent in the Scopes trial—country versus city, science versus religion, or educated elite versus the uneducated poor? Do any of those issues persist today?
4. Have there been other times in American history when religious fundamentalism became especially prominent? In what ways does fundamentalism represent a social as well as a religious movement? In your view, are Ratcliffe's observations still relevant?
5. What was at stake for men like Darrow and Bryan in the trial?
6. What social and class tensions boil beneath Mencken's obituary of Bryan?

ADDITIONAL READING

Ray Ginger, *Six Days or Forever* (1958), tells the story of the *Scopes* trial in all its detail and with all its color. Also see Edward J. Larson, *Summer for the Gods: The Scopes Trial and America's Continuing Debate over Science and Religion* (1997), and Ronald L. Numbers, *Darwinism Comes to America* (1998). For the religious issues involved, see Norman F. Furniss, *The Fundamentalist Controversy, 1918–1933* (1958), and Charles Alan Israel, *Before Scopes: Evangelism, Education and Evolution in Tennessee, 1870–1925* (2004). Bryan's last years are covered in Lawrence Levine, *Defender of the Faith* (1965). For an excellent biography of Bryan, see Michael Kazin, *A Godly Hero* (2006). Clarence Darrow told his own story in *The Story of My Life* (1932). For Mencken, see William Manchester, *Disturber of the Peace* (1952), and Fred Hobson, *Mencken: A Life* (1995). Other important works on the 1920s and their legacy include Lynn Dumenil, *The Modern Temper* (1995); Nancy MacClean, *Behind the Mask of*

Chivalry (1995); Roland Marchand, *Advertising the American Dream* (1985); Desmond King, *Making Americans* (2000); and David Goldberg, *Discontented America* (1999). For a long view of evolution, see Edward J. Larson, *Evolution: The Remarkable History of a Scientific Theory* (2004).

ENDNOTES

1. *Baltimore Evening Sun*, July 10, 1925.
2. George William Hunter, *A Civic Biology* (Cincinnati, OH: American Book Company, 1914).
3. J. W. Porter, *Evolution—A Menace* (Nashville: Sunday School Board, Southern Baptist Convention, 1922), pp. 21–22, 82–84.
4. *Public Acts of the State of Tennessee Passed by the Sixty-Fourth General Assembly* (1925).
5. *The World's Most Famous Court Trial: Tennessee Evolution Case* (Cincinnati, OH: National Book Company, 1925).
6. Alaistair Cooke, comp., *The Vintage Mencken* (New York: Random House, 1955), pp. 161–167. Copyright 1926 by Alfred A. Knopf, Inc., and renewed 1954 by H. L. Mencken. Reprinted from *A Mencken Chrestomathy* by H. L. Mencken by permission of Alfred A. Knopf., Inc.
7. *New York Times*, August 1, 1925, p. 2.
8. S. K. Ratcliffe, "America and Fundamentalism," *The Contemporary Review*, July 1, 1925, p. 128.
9. Richard Fausset, "At Site of Scopes Trial, Darrow Statue Belatedly Joins Bryan's," *New York Times*, July 15, 2017, p A9

CHAPTER 10

THE GREAT DEPRESSION

HISTORICAL CONTEXT

Great literature, we like to believe, is timeless, so Shakespeare's works will endure forever. No doubt he gave voice to emotional truths that touch very diverse people. But interpretations of the meanings of Shakespeare's plays have varied widely over the years, and these interpretations have been shaped by events taking place in the interpreters' own times. Shakespeare himself was enmeshed in the social, religious, and political issues of Elizabethan England, and his plays are full of direct and indirect references to those issues. Or, to give an example from American literary history, Herman Melville's *Moby Dick* (1851) was mostly ignored during the nineteenth century; it became acknowledged as great literature only in the 1920s, long after the author's death. Melville's work tended to be very skeptical of human perfectibility and social progress, and such skepticism resonated more for the intellectuals of the early twentieth century than for those in the nineteenth century.

Artists and writers always are influenced by the context of their times, and how their works are received depends on the historically shaped beliefs of those who behold them. This was especially true during the 1930s. Of course, the descent into economic depression that began with the stock market crash of October 1929 was felt most directly in material life. The previous decade had brought prosperity for middle- and upper-class Americans. True, the 1920s were hard times for farmers and the urban poor, but a larger number of people than ever before had more income and could afford more consumer goods than at any time in U.S. history. With the Great Depression, however, came massive cuts in wages and employment. Per capita disposable income dropped about one-third, while the unemployment rate reached 25 percent in the early 1930s. Although working-class people were hit hardest, for they had the fewest resources to fall back on, the downward spiral of the economy tugged at almost everyone. To put it simply, most families still had the necessities of life and even some luxuries, but most had less than before. More important, the number of families slipping into poverty grew dramatically.

Beyond the shrinkage of material resources, Americans' confidence was shaken. No one seemed to know when, how, or if the crisis would end. Franklin Roosevelt's New Deal helped some, but politicians and economists had no permanent solutions. The depression made people question the most fundamental tenets of the American creed: that our economy and society ensured a brighter future for all, that equality of opportunity was the American way, that hard work would be rewarded, and that the American dream of prosperity was still attainable. How could they believe such things when the leaders and heroes of the 1920s—businessmen, financiers, and great captains of wealth—seemed as confused as everyone else, when breadlines grew ever longer and when unemployment and poverty wore the familiar faces of family and friends? (Ironically, the very phrase "The American Dream" was coined in 1931.)

Much of the art and literature of the era reflected these changed perceptions. It was not as if the writers and artists of the twenties had been celebrants of American culture. On the contrary, the carnage of World War I, the meanness of the Versailles treaty, and the postwar era's gaudy materialism—these all alienated many talented people, creating a "lost generation" of American writers. Several exiled themselves to Paris (Ernest Hemingway and F. Scott Fitzgerald among them), but even those who stayed in the United States wrote with a bitterness born of betrayal. John Dos Passos captured his generation's loathing of the money grubbing, the spiritual emptiness, and the unseemly hedonism that often came masked by pious espousals of democratic ideals. Most writers would have agreed with H. L. Mencken that the more a man declared his own honesty, patriotism, or piety, the more likely he was a scoundrel or a thief. Above all, the literature of the 1920s stressed the individual's need to make a separate peace with the world; each person must suffer his or her pain alone and must find his or her own joy or community, but all must know that God, society, or money could not save them.

Ironically, literature written during the Great Depression contained less of this cynicism. In the midst of the crisis, writers and artists no longer felt so peripheral to their culture. The worship of business that characterized America in the 1920s marginalized all who felt that the life of the mind—scholarship, artistic creation, the humanities—counted for more than dollars. As the Great Depression continued, Americans' belief that millionaires were heroes worthy of emulation grew shaky. For some intellectuals, there was a strange exhilaration in others' loss of faith in the American dream. If the competitive economy had atomized people, the depression could bring them together as each other's keepers, and there is no doubt that the rediscovery of community—of workers, regions, racial or ethnic groups—was an important theme of the writing of the decade.

Moreover, the crisis called for new *ideas*, intellectuals' specialty. On the most functional level, this meant the channeling of university people like economists and sociologists into the government. But even novelists and painters became tied to the Roosevelt administration. The New Deal appropriated funds for agencies like the Federal Writers' Project (in which the government underwrote the creation of plays, oral histories, and travel guides), the Works Progress Administration (which hired unemployed artists to paint murals on federal buildings), and the Farm Security Administration (in which unemployed photographers—including such great camera artists as Dorothea Lange, Walker Evans, and Ansel Adams—documented the lives of homeless families, unemployed workers, and southern tenant farmers). So a relatively small amount of government aid and, more important, a sense of being socially useful made the Great Depression a period of tremendous energy and excitement in the arts.

This notion of being socially useful took highly political forms. For some, the crisis intensified a hatred of modernity, including cities, factories, and all that was progressive. This tendency was exemplified by the Southern Agrarians, a group of fiction writers, poets, and historians who self-consciously rejected the booming growth and power of the twentieth century to extol the virtues of small-scale life on the land, more particularly in the rural South. The agrarians were fundamentally conservative and nostalgic, and certainly they were blind to the poverty and racism of the southern past. Still, theirs was a powerful critique of the aggrandizing, money-worshiping, and progress-loving elements of American culture.

More commonly, artists and writers turned to the left. Many believed that capitalism, with its enormous concentrations of private wealth and power, made a few people rich while it impoverished the masses, and the Great Depression certainly seemed to offer evidence. Their political and economic solutions varied widely, from New Deal reforms through socialism, communism, and anarchism. What united them all, however, was their commitment to depicting common folk struggling against the system that exploited them. Much of the 1920s' elitism and irony were gone, for the new literature sought to be a tool of empowerment. Rather than maintaining a detached and critical distance from America, intellectuals now strove to make the arts and humanities instruments of change by depicting ordinary people in their daily struggles, sometimes being overwhelmed and sometimes winning symbolic or real triumphs.

Poverty, exploitation, and disease—the arts revealed life in all its grimness. Indeed, the primary task of creative expression, many would have argued, was to expose human misery and to unmask the evil system that caused it. However, it was at this historical moment of crisis that glimmers of hope also appeared in literature, hope arising from a renewed faith that masses of men and women could be makers of their own destinies, that they might seize as their birthright America's unfulfilled democratic promise.

Such an environment was not congenial to "art for art's sake," the belief that creativity was pure mental work that soared above the "real world." The new view was that artists and intellectuals must never again become mere aesthetes, escaping from daily life to challenge themselves only by creating beautiful, if empty, works. They had an obligation to engage the issues confronting people. One can see this shift in the styles of artistic expression: a renewed emphasis on realism and naturalism in fiction, less stress on abstraction in painting, and, above all, a shift to the documentary style, a mode of expression that appeared to deny the presence of the artist altogether. Documentary style pretends to be artless: The camera just records what is going on; the writer merely reports what he or she sees. The documentary style—seemingly objective, dispassionate, and factually accurate—became very common in fiction and nonfiction and in film and photography, for it appeared to reveal human suffering in the most clear and unmediated way, and by so doing, it sounded an unmistakable call for reform.

INTRODUCTION TO DOCUMENT 1

President Franklin Roosevelt, his wife Eleanor, and other government leaders received thousands of letters, some asking for assistance, others applauding the New Deal, and still others condemning it. Document 1 gives a sense of the range of opinions expressed by citizens, including racist and nativist attacks on the poor, warnings that the New Deal smacked of communism and declarations that, if something more was not done soon, revolution was inevitable. Above all, there were pleas for help from the poor themselves.

1. AMERICANS WRITE TO THEIR LEADERS

ELKADER IOWA
SEPTEMBER 11 1934
MR. FRANKLIN ROOSEVELT

Dear President Roosevelt
I am in a terrible perdicament So I thought of you to send my plea of trouble to you because I drempt the other night that I Should write to you thinking that may = be I could get Some help from you as long as no one els will help me out I am an old woman Seventy two years old and an invalid that is the worst of it I can't get around at all. I bin Sitting in a chair for years already if I am not in bed I can't walk alone atall So that makes it pretty hard fore me to be put out of my home the one I worked so hard for over forty-Six years, So please help me Some way or I will half to Sine my last bit away if I could only raise thirteen Hundred Dollars than I could Stay in my home Oh. So please help me Mr. Roosevelt and answer right away or els it will be to late if I ever get onto my feet I Sure will try and pay you back. I helped So many out but it Seems now that I am in the grattes trouble no = body will help me So please Mr. Roosevelt help me
Sincerly Mrs. A. M. U.[1]

FEBRUARY 1936
MR. AND MRS. ROOSEVELT
WASH. D.C.

Dear Mr. President:
I'm a boy of 12 years. I want to tell you about my family My father hasn't worked for 5 months He went plenty times to relief, he filled out application. They won't give us anything. I don't know why. Please you do something. We haven't paid 4 months rent, Everyday the landlord rings the door bell, we don't open the door for him. We are afraid that will be put out, been put out before, and don't want to happen again. We haven't paid the gas bill, and the electric bill, haven't paid grocery bill for 3 months. My brother goes to Lane Tech. High School. he's eighteen years old, hasn't gone to school for 2 weeks because he got no carfare. I have a sister she's twenty years, she can't find work. My father he staying home. All the time he's crying because he can't find work. I told him why are you crying daddy, and daddy said why shouldn't I cry when there is nothing in the house. I feel sorry for him. That night I couldn't sleep. The next morning I wrote this letter to you, in my room. Were American citizens and were born in Chicago, Ill. and I don't know why they don't help us Please answer right away because we need it. will starve Thank you. God bless you.

Anonymous
Chicago, Ill.[2]

FAYETTEVILLE, W.VA.
NOVEMBER 4, 1936
WASHINGTON, D.C.

My dear Mrs. Roosevelt:—

I am wondering whether or not a letter to you from a wholly unbiased and unprejudiced person will be a little helpful to you and your husband. I know (and you know!) that you have strenuous days ahead. I feel possibly that the viewpoint of certain representative village people here represent current opinion throughout the country and that a few of the remarks I heard in an Editor's office this morning may give you an idea of what is in people's minds—now that the election is over. It is a saner viewpoint than yesterday! not a thing can be done about matters except to discuss them!

I voted the straight Democratic ticket as usual. The Editor in whose office I spent a few moments this morning is a Republican. . . .

THE EDITOR: —"—We hope sincerely that things will turn out all right, but, my heavens, this orgy of spending!"

REPUBLICAN: —"—Now that he's had such a landslide he'll go crazy with spending and giving. He'll think, 'why need I bother about what this person or that thinks!'"

DEMOCRAT: —"—He's done a lot that's constructive. My only regret is the slaughtering of livestock and ploughing under of wheat. But he couldn't foresee the drought." . . .

The above may give you an idea of the trend of thought. Personally I have found that the more you give the lower classes the more they want. Never satisfied. In my charitable work I become discouraged and it makes me know what your husband is up against. The people (some) are so simple-minded. They think the President is going to keep on giving. My gardener (White) and my maid (col.) voted democratic this election, not from coercion on my part but because "Roosevelt will take care of us."

Some of us (conservative democrats) regret the prevalence of certain graft in minor county officials, Relief offices, Welfare, etc. but I know it's all too far away for you to control . . .
I am very sincerely yours,
NGS (Mrs. RJS).[3]

NEW YORK, N.Y.
OCTOBER 1939
MR. HARRY HOPKINS
WASHINGTON, D.C.

Dear Mr. Hopkins:

. . . I have found out after careful investigation that we are feeding many foreigners who send out their wives to work and who have money in the bank. While the men drink wine and play cards in saloons and cafes. I have spoken to one Italian whom I met. And I ask him what he was doing for a living. He said me drinka da dago red wine and play cards and send the wife out to work. Isn't a very good thing for us to support them. No wonder the taxpayers are grumbling about taxes. Most of them are a race of black hands murders boot leggers bomb throwers. While most of the sheeney jews as they are called are a race of dishonest people who get rich by swindling, faking and cheating the poor people. Besides the jews are responsible by ruining others in business by the great amount of chisling done. And selling even below the cost prices, in order to get all the others business. The foreigners and jews spend as little as they can to help this country. And, they live as cheap as they can. And, work as cheap as they can, and save all the money they can. And when they have enough they go back to their country. Why don't we deport them under the section of the United States Immigration Laws which relates to paupers and those who become a public charge. The Communist Party is composed mostly by foreigners and jews. The jews are the leaders of the movement and urge the downfall of this government. . . .
A Taxpayer[4]

HORNELL, NEW YORK
MARCH 7, 1934
U.S. SENATOR ROBERT F. WAGNER
SENATE BUILDING,
WASHINGTON, D.C.

My Dear Senator:

It seems very apparent to me that the Administration at Washington is accelerating its pace towards socialism and communism. Nearly every public statement from Washington is against stimulation of business which would in the end create employment.

Everyone is sympathetic to the cause of creating more jobs and better wages for labor; but, a program continually promoting labor troubles, higher wages, shorter hours, and less profits for business, would seem to me to be leading us fast to a condition where the Government must more and more expand it's relief activities, and will lead in the end to disaster to all classes. . . .

I am not addicted to annoying public office holders with correspondence but if there are any private rights left in this country, then I would appreciate an early reply to this letter, so that I may take such action as is still possible to protect myself and family. *With kindest personal regards,*

Yours truly,
W. L. C. [male][5]

NASHVILLE, TENNESSEE
AUGUST 15, 1936
MRS. FRANKLIN D. ROOSEVELT

Dear Lady,

Will you please warn the people of whats going to happen in America if these property owners dont quit making industrial slaves out of their laborers and working them on starvation wages, paying them a wage whereby they cannot obtain the desires of life, or else installing machinery and laying the common laborer off of his job to starve to death.

We dont want a revolution in this country where innocent men, women, and children will be shot down without mercy like they are doing in spain and also like they did in Russia. We want peace on earth good will toward men. You know mrs. Roosevelt with the majority of us poor people we desire good things as well as the higher classes of society. For instance we desire a nice home to live in with sanitary surroundings. we desire a nice refrigadaire, electric stove, fan, nice furniture, radio, a nice car with money to take a vacation, but one cannot have these desires of life at a wage of 8.00 10.00 or $12.00 per week, and if we could, we could not accumalate no money and would have to go on being industrial slaves and our children would fall under the same yoke of bondage that we and our fore parents were under. And never be considered no more than an ordinary slaves. . . .

After all, it is natural with any human being to want to obtain the desires of life with the least physical exertion possible. But the great majority of the men that wear the overalls and are forced by the task master or property holder to exert their bodies strenuously every day do not get even proper and sufficient food to maintain their bodies while at work. . . .

This alone will bring on a revolution if it is not remedi[e]d. There would not be so many crimes committed if every man and boy were out from under bondage of hard labor and were getting the desires of life. We have plenty young John Dillingers, pretty boy Floyds, Jessie James roaming all over our land today wanting jobs, desiring to marry and settle down and live a comfortable life and cannot get hold of enough money to buy a marriage license. And the next thing we know they strike back at the ones that are responsible for their being in that condition. Mrs. Roosevelt this nation is hanging over a giant powder keg just waiting for someone to light a match. . . .

. . . I am thirty four years old married and have one daughter. I have a eighth grade education, I got a job last week as labourer on the new courthouse here, although I am a painter by trade, and just because I am a little crippled on my right side the contractor would not work me, he said the insurance company would not allow him to.

And so I cannot see a very bright prospect in life. Although my wife slaves in a cotton mill but I want a job so as I can get her out of it, for I am afraid she has contracted tuberculosis. hoping an answer, I remain

Yours, Sincerely, [Mr.] DBP[6]

INTRODUCTION TO DOCUMENTS 2, 3, AND 4

The Roosevelt administration established several programs to address the poverty of the Great Depression. Among these was the Resettlement Administration in 1935, designed to move poor families to entirely new areas, often in government-planned communities. Though the program was short-lived and somewhat unpopular in Congress, it involved a significant investment in documentary photography. Ben Shahn, Arthur Rothstein, and Dorothea Lange were just three of the many artists who were hired to photograph rural poverty as part of the Resettlement Administration. They produced thousands of pictures, some of which have become iconic representations of both the trials but also the persistence of the American people in the Great Depression.

It is easy to assume that the following photographs were neutral representations, devoid of argument and message and simply candid images of American life. But ask yourself how the photographers captured their subjects, how they framed the context, and what emotion or impression they hoped to leave in their viewers.

The first two photographs were taken in early 1936 by Dorothea Lange, who was spending a month photographing migrant farm laborers in California for the Resettlement Administration. Lange recalled being "drawn by a magnet" to Florence Thompson and her children at this camp in Nipomo. Thompson told Lange that she was thirty-two and had been living on vegetables from the surrounding fields and birds that her children were able to kill. She asked no questions of Lange but did not object to her photograph being taken. The picture on the left was published in contemporary San Francisco news outlets and immediately struck a chord. Why do you suppose it spoke so powerfully to Americans, and why has it continued to draw us in? Given that Dorothea Lange took many pictures of Florence Thompson, what explains the power of the photograph at left, which became an American icon of hard times, as opposed to the one at right?

Ben Shahn was another photographer for the Resettlement Administration, who spent months traveling through the American South. Here he photographed a young girl in the cotton fields in 1935, taking pains to label the photograph with the following information: "Schools for colored children do not open until January 1st so as not to interfere with cotton picking."

Arthur Rothstein was only twenty years old—a college senior—when he was hired by the Resettlement Administration as its first photographer, assigned to capture rural and small-town America. His photograph of a demonstration by unemployed workers in the spring of 1936 captures the political moment of the mid-1930s, when many turned toward more radical solutions. As Rothstein wrote of his work, the goal was "to move people to action." In your view does Rothstein's photograph send a political message?

2. DESTITUTE PEAPICKERS IN CALIFORNIA (FEBRUARY 1936)

DOROTHEA LANGE

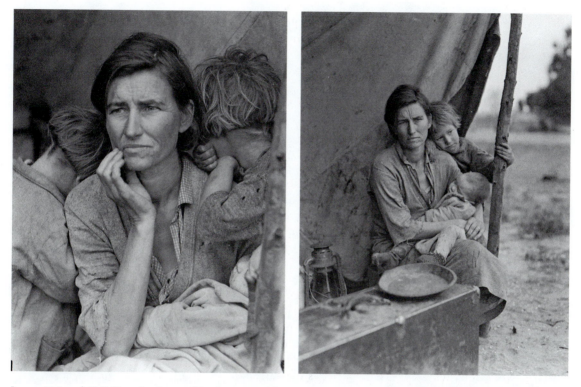

Image 10.1 and 10.2 Dorothea Lange, "Destitute pea pickers in California; a 32 Year Old Mother of Seven Children"

Source: Courtesy Library of Congress, Prints and Photographs Division LC-USF34-9058-C.

3. YOUNG COTTON PICKER, PULASKI COUNTY, ARKANSAS (OCTOBER 1935)

BEN SHAHN

Image 10.3 Ben Shahn, "Young Cotton Picker, Pulaski County, Arkansas"
Source: Courtesy Library of Congress, Prints and Photographs Division FSA/OWI LC-USF33-006218-M5.

4. DEMONSTRATION OF THE UNEMPLOYED. COLUMBUS, KANSAS (MAY 1936)

ARTHUR ROTHSTEIN

Image 10.4 Arthur Rothstein, "Demonstration of the Unemployed. Columbus, Kansas," May 1936
Source: Courtesy Library of Congress, Prints and Photographs Division LC-USF34-005162-E.

INTRODUCTION TO DOCUMENT 5

The federal government's funding of documentary photography in the Farm Security Administration extended to other areas of American life. The Works Progress Administration, perhaps best known for constructing highways, bridges, dams, and post offices across the nation, many of which still stand today, also housed the Federal Writers' Project, designed to employ artists by paying them to document folkways and histories of Americans at all stations in life. Several who would later become renowned authors—including Richard Wright, Saul Bellow, and John Cheever—began their careers employed by the Federal Writers' Project. One such individual was Ralph Ellison, who was paid to interview African Americans in Harlem in the late 1930s. Ellison acknowledged that his work with the Federal Writers' Project broadened his understanding of black life, which in turn shaped his midcentury masterpiece, *Invisible Man.* His interviews in Harlem also helped him develop an ear for vernacular speech. This "documentary" approach, though far from neutral, reflected the Depression-era engagement with the nation's myriad local cultures, an attempt to capture the diversity of experience that made up a larger American identity.

5. "A POOR WHITE IS A BRING DOWN"

RALPH ELLISON, INTERVIEW WITH AN AFRICAN-AMERICAN MUSICIAN, HARLEM, JUNE 15, 1939

I was sitting up on the bandstand drumming, trying to make myself some eat-up change. Wasn't such a crowd in the place that night, just a bunch a them beer-drinkers. I was looking down at em dancing and wishing that things would liven up. Then a man came up and give me four dollars just to sing one number. Well, I was singing for that man. I was really laying it Jack, just alike Marian Anderson. What the hell you talking about; I'd sing all night after that cat done give me four bucks.... But this is what brings you down. One a these bums come up to the stand and says to the banjo player: "If you monkeys don't play some music, Im gonna throw you outta de jernt."

Man, I quit singing and looked at that sonofabitch. Then I got mad. I said. "Where the goddam hell you come from, you gonna throw somebody outa *this* band? How you get so bad? Why you poor Brooklyn motherfriger, I'll wreck this goddam place with you."

... You see he thought cause we was black he could talk like he wanted to. In a night club and drinking beer! I fixed him. I bet he wont try that no more.

Man a poor white is a bring-down. He aint got nothing. He caint get nothing. And he thinks cause hes white hes got to impress you cause you black.

Then some of em comes up and try to be your friend. Like the other night; I'm up on the stand drumming and singing, trying to make myself some change. I was worried. I got a big old boy, dam near big as me, and every time I look up hes got to have something. Well the other night I hadnt made a dam thing. And I was sitting there drumming when one of those bums what hangs around the place— one a these slaphappy jitterbugs, comes up to me and says: "You stink!"

Now you know that made me mad before I even knowed what he was talking about. A white cat coming up to me and talking about I stink! I said 'What you talking about? What you mean I stink? He said: "You aint a good fellow like the other cats. You

wont take me up to Harlem and show me around." I said: "Hell yes, mammydodger, I stink! If that's what you mean Im gon always stink. You'll never catch me carrying a bunch of you poor sonsabitches up there. What the hell you gonna do when you get up there? You aint got nothing. Hell, you por as I am. I dont see you coming down to Harlem to carry me up to show me the Bronx. You darn right I stink.' Man, he just looks at me now and says: "Jack, you sho a funny cat."

Can you beat that? He oughta know I aint got no use for him. DAM!

Another one comes up to me—another one of those beer drinking bums— and says: "I want to go up to your house sometime."

I said: "Fo what! Now you tell me fo what!" I said: "What-in-the-world do you want to come up to *my* place for? You aint got nothing and I sho aint got nothing. Whats a poor colored cat and a poor white cat gonna do together? You aint got nothing cause you too dumb to get it. And I aint got nothing cause I'm black. I guess you got your little ol skin, that's the reason? Im supposed to feel good cause you walk in my house and sit in my chairs? Hell, that skin aint no more good to you than mine is to me. You caint marry one a Du Ponts daughters, and I know dam well I caint. So what the hell you gon do up to my place?"

Aw man, I have to get these white cats told. They think you supposed to feel good cause they friendly to you. Boy I don't fool with em. They just the reason I caint get ahead now. They try to get all a mans money. That's just the reason I found me a place up the street here. Got two rooms in a private house with a private bath. These others cats go down to Ludwig Baumans and give him all their money so they can meet you on the street and say 'Oh you *must* come up to my apartment sometimes. Oh yes, yes, I have some lovely furniture. You just must come up sometime; you know man, they just want to show off. But me I done got wise. Im getting my stuff outa junk shops, second hand stores, anywhere. I aint giving these Jews my money. . . .

See this bag? I got me a head a cabbage and two ears a corn. Im going up here and get me a side a bacon. When I get home, gonna cook the cabbage and bacon, gonna make me some corn fritters and set back in my twenty-five-dollars-a-month room and eat my fritters and cabbage and tell the Jews to forgit it! Jack I'm just sitting back waiting, cause soon things is gonna narrow down to the fine point. Hitlers gonna reach in a few months and grab and then thingsll start. All the white folksll be killing off one another. And I hope they do a good job! Then there wont be nobody left but Sam. Then we'll be fighting it out amongs ourselves. That'll be a funky fight. Aw hell yes! When Negroes start running things I think I'll have to get off the earth before its too late![7]

INTRODUCTION TO DOCUMENT 6

Tom Kromer grew up in West Virginia, where his father had been a coal miner and then a glass-blower. Kromer was a talented student, and he enrolled at Marshall College, but the death of his father and his own lack of funds caused him to drop out before finishing a degree. The Great Depression soon followed, and Kromer was left a vagrant. For a few years, he rode freight trains across the country. Finally, he was able to join the Civilian Conservation Corps, which afforded him the time and money to write his autobiographical *Waiting for Nothing* (1935). The author Lincoln Steffens assisted Kromer in having the manuscript published by Alfred A. Knopf Company. Perhaps more than any other Depression-era book, this one gave a sense, not only of hopeless wandering but also of the terror of being homeless. Kromer left nothing out: the alcoholism, the cruelty of the police and the middle class, the violence of "stiffs" against each other, and the ever-pressing need for "three hots and a flop"—food and shelter.

6. FROM *WAITING FOR NOTHING*

TOM KROMER

I crouch here in this doorway of the blind baggage. For five hours I have huddled here in the freezing cold. My feet dangle down beneath the car. The wind whistles underneath and swings them back and forth. The wheels sing over the rails. Up in front of me the engine roars through the blackness, that is blacker than the night. The smoke and the fire belch into the sky and scatter into scorching sparks that burn my back and neck. I do not feel the wind that swings my legs. They are frozen. I have no feeling in them. I slink far back in this door and put my hands over my face. Great God, but I am miserable. I cannot stand this much longer. I was a fool for nailing the blind baggage of this passenger. I was a fool, and now I am freezing to death.

I think. How am I ever going to get off this drag if it ever does stop? I can't walk. My feet, that are frozen, will not hold me up. I sit here and think, and I doze. I awake with a jerk.

"You damn fool," I say, "you can't go to sleep here. You will fall under those wheels that sing beneath you. Those wheels would make quick work of you, all right. Those wheels would make mincemeat of you. You would not be cold any more."

I begin to sing. I sing loud. I yell at the top of my voice, because of the roar of the wheels and the sound of the wind underneath me. I don't want to fall under those wheels. I am only a stiff, and I know that a stiff is better off dead, but I don't want to fall under those wheels. I can feel myself getting dopey. I try to sing louder. I try to hear my voice over the sound of the wind and the cars, but I cannot. I cannot keep awake. I can see that I cannot keep awake. I am falling asleep. I wonder if this is the way a guy freezes to death. I am not so cold now. I am almost warm. The wind roars just as loud as before. It must be just as cold as it was before. But I am not cold. I am warm. Great Christ, I must not let myself freeze to death. I swing my arms. I reach my head far out over the side of the car. The wind tears at my face, but I keep it there until the tears run down my cheeks. Oh, Christ, won't this drag never stop?

I feel the buckle of this drag beneath me. I feel it jerk and throw me forward. I hear the whine of air for brakes. I grab the sides of this car with all my might. My frozen fingers slip, then hold. I am not scared. I am not afraid. I just grab the sides of the car and hold. I feel this train slacken speed. I see the scattered lights of a town. Only a few lights, but I see that this drag is going to stop. I begin to laugh. I laugh like a crazy man when I see that this drag is going to stop.

I hang on with all my might. There will be a jerk when this drag stops. I do not want to go under those wheels. We pull to a stop in front of this jerk-water station. There will be no bulls [police] in this place. The thing to do is to get off this drag before it starts again. It will not stay here long. How am I going to reach the ground? My legs are numb. They are frozen. They will not hold me up. I rub them fast and hard. I feel them sting and burn as the blood begins to run. I try to move them. I can move them. I can see them move. But I feel nothing when they move. I pull myself to my feet. I am standing. I can

see that I am standing, but I cannot feel the car beneath my feet. I reach out over the side of the car and grab the ladder. I climb down. I hold with one hand and guide my legs with the other, but I climb down. I stop at this last step. It is a long way to the ground for my frozen feet. I jump. I fall face-down in the cinders at the side of the track. This drag whistles the high ball. She pulls out. I lie here in the cinders with my bleeding face and watch the coaches go by. I lie here in the cinders with my frozen legs that have no feeling in them. I shiver as I think of that blind baggage with the roar of the wheels and the sound of the wind underneath. I push my fists into the ground and get to my feet. I grimace at the pain that shoots through my legs, but I grit my teeth and walk.

What I want right now is a cup of coffee. A cup of good hot coffee will always warm a guy up. I am too cold to want to eat. I make it to the main stem of this town. There are lights in the few stores that are still open. I pass a restaurant. There is a sign in the window. It says: "Try our ten-cent hamburgers." I wonder if they would let a frozen stiff try their ten-cent hamburgers. I walk in. There are two customers eating. I walk up to this bird behind the counter. He backs away. He glances at his cash register. He has a scared look on his face. I look in the mirror that lines the wall. I do not blame this guy for being scared. What I see scares me, too. My face is as black as the ace of spades. It is smeared with blood from the cuts of the cinders as they scraped my face. I hit those cinders hard.

"Buddy," I say, "I am broke. Could you spare me a cup of coffee?"

"I can't spare you nothin'," he says. "Beat it before I throw you out."

Imagine this bastard. I am half starved and half froze, and he turns me down for a lousy cup of coffee. I am too cold to even cuss him out. I want to cuss him out, but I am too cold. I walk down the street and hit these other two restaurants. They turn me down flat. I can't get me anything to warm me up. But there is one thing I will have to get, and that is a flop. In weather like this a stiff has got to have a flop.

"Where is the town bull?" I say to this guy on the corner.

"You will find him in the garage," he says. "He will be shootin' the bull by the stove in the garage."

I walk over to this garage and find this hick cop by the stove in the office.

"Chief," I say, "I want to get locked up in the can. I am on the fritz with no place to flop."

"The jail ain't no hotel," he says. "I can't lock you up. I can't louse the jail up by locking you up."

Well, if this is not a hell of a note! A stiff can't even break into a lousy can. They call this a free country, and a stiff can't even break into jail to get away from the cold and the wind.

"Can I warm up a little by your fire?" I say. "I am froze."

"Get this straight," this bull says; "we have no use for lousy stiffs in this town. The best thing you can do is to hit the highway away from here."

"What is a stiff supposed to do, shoot himself?" I say.

"If I catch you in this town tomorrow, it will be a good thing if you do shoot yourself," he says.

I go out to the street and walk. I walk fast. I do not feel like walking fast, but I have to to keep from freezing to death. That's how cold I am. I pass a pecan grove. Over away from the road I can see a shack with a light in it. I knock on the door. An old man comes to the door with a lantern in his hand.

"Hello," I say. "Have you got somewhere a guy could flop for the night around here? I am freezing to death, with no place to flop."

He puts his hand on the top of my head.

"Son, do you believe in Christ?" he says.

"Sure," I say, "I believe in Christ. Have you got some place I could flop around here?"

"The last days are upon us," he says. "The sound of the trumpet is soon upon us. Repent or you burn in everlasting flame."

This guy is as batty as a loon. I can see that.

"Have you got some place I could flop outside?" I say. "An old shed or something?"

Outside will not be too far away from this guy. He is ready for the booby-hatch.

"The lamb that is lost is the care of the Lord," he says.

He leads the way to this building where they store the pecans. It is a big place. The floor is covered with piles of these pecans. He takes a shovel and digs a hole down in one of these piles, he puts two burlap sacks in the bottom of it.

"Son," he says, "lay down in this hole and rest."

I get in.

He covers me up with pecans, and piles sacks on top of me. My face is all that is sticking out of the hole. He puts a sack over my face.

"Rest that you may better fight the battles of the Lord," he says.

He takes his lantern and goes back to his shack.

It is pitch-dark in here now. I lie under these pecans and think. Here I am lying down in a hole. Here I am covered up with pecans. Before I went on the fritz, I was lying nights in a feather bed. I thought I was hard up then. I had a decent front. I had my three hots and a flop. Can you imagine a guy thinking he is hard up when he has his three hots and a flop? That was two years ago, but two years are ten years when you are on the fritz. I look ten years older now. I looked like a young punk then. I was a young punk. I had some color in my cheeks. I have hit the skids since then. This is as low down as a guy can get, being down in a hole with pecans on top of him for covers. If a guy had any guts, he wouldn't put up with this. I think. Why should one guy have a million dollars, and I am down in a hole with pecans on top of me for covers? Maybe that guy has brains. Maybe he works hard. I don't know. What is that to me if he is there and I am here? Religion, they say in the missions. Religion and morals. What are religion and morals to me, if I am down in a hole with pecans on top of me? Who is there to say that this world belongs to certain guys? What right has one guy to say: This much of the world is mine; you can't sleep here?

I lie here in the darkness and think. It is too cold to sleep. On the blind baggage of the drag I could not keep my eyes open. Now I cannot close them. I listen to these rats that rustle across the floor. I pull this sack off my face and strain my eyes through the blackness. I am afraid of rats. Once in a jungle [hobo camp] I awoke with two on my face. Since then I dream of rats that are as big as cats, who sit on my face and gnaw at my nose and eyes. I cannot see them. It is too dark. I cannot lie here and wait with my heart thumping against my ribs like this. I cannot lie here and listen to them patter across the floor, and me not able to see them. I pull myself out of these pecans and get to my feet. I tiptoe out to the road. I do not want to wake this crazy old codger who dug the hole for me. I do not want to hurt his feelings, and besides, he might go off his nut.

I walk. I lower my head far down to keep the whistling wind from cutting my face like a knife. I listen to the creak of the trees as the wind tears through them. I keep to the left of the road. I cannot hear the sounds of the cars as they come up behind me. You can hear nothing for the roar of the wind. From time to time I turn my head to stare through the night for signs of a headlight. When I see one, I stop in my tracks and hold out my hand for a ride. They do not stop when they see me raise my hand. They step on the gas and go faster. They do not care to pick up a worn-out stiff with blisters on his feet. It is night. They are afraid. They are afraid of being knocked in the head. I do not blame them for being afraid. You cannot tell what a stiff might do when he is as cold and fagged as I am. A stiff is not himself when he is as cold as I am.

I reach the town and skirt it. I am afraid of rats, and this town bull has a face like a rat. I reach the yards and crawl into one of these cars that line the tracks. I shove the doors almost shut. I do not shut it tight. If they start moving these cars during the night, I want to be ready for a quick get-away. I take this newspaper out of my pocket and spread it on the floor. I take off my shoes and use them for a pillow. I lie down, I am all in. I am asleep in a minute.

I do not know how long I am asleep. I awake with a jerk. Something has awakened me. All at once I am wide-eyed and staring. There is a feeling of queerness in the top of my head. I know that feeling. I get that feeling when there is something wrong. I had that feeling once when a drag I was on went over the ditch. That feeling was in the top of my head just

before a guy I was talking to on the street dropped dead. My breath comes in short gasps. There is a crawling feeling all over me. A tingle starts at my feet and runs to my hair. I feel a chill in the roots of my hair. I know what that is. My hair is standing up. I raise up on my elbow. The rustle I make as I move on the paper sounds like thunder in the quietness of the car. A ray of light comes through the opening in the door. It is not strong enough to reach to the other end of the car, but I know that there is nothing there. It is in back of me. Whatever it is that is in this car is in back of me. . . .

Then, through the dark, comes this squeal. It is a wild squeal. A squeal like something is mad and crazy. It is like something that has lost its mind. I feel it bound through the air and land on my back. It knocks me down to the floor. These sharp claws bite into the nape of my neck. The long fingers grip my throat so that my breath comes in sobs. I am strangling. I grab at these claws. I feel a man's wrist. A strong wrist. A wrist that is all covered with hair like an animal's. I am down on my belly on the floor of the car. These fingers like hot iron press tighter and tighter. I feel these knees that bore into the small of my back. My neck wrenches backward. So far back I wait to hear it snap. Dizzier I get, and dizzier. Like in a dream I know that these claws that bite into my neck are trying to kill me, to choke me to death. I struggle blindly in the darkness.

I throw myself to my back. I feel the claws loosen their grip. I feel them slide off my neck and tear the flesh off in strips. I feel the burn on my throat and the moistness that I know is blood. I stumble to my feet as he sprawls on the floor. I am facing him now in the dark. He scrambles to his feet. He is only a shapeless mass in front of me. It is a shapeless mass that wants to kill me, to choke me till there is no life in me. I see it hurl itself through the air. I brace myself against the side of the car and kick out with my foot with all my might. I feel it hit, hard. I hear a grunt, a squeally grunt that a pig might give. My foot is buried in his belly. He thuds to the floor. He rolls over and over, but he is up again in a second. There is a flash in his hand. Through the ray of light that comes through the door I see this flash. My spine creeps. I know what that flash is. It is a knife. I cannot let him get at me with the knife. I cannot let him rip me open with the knife. He is going to murder me with the knife. I have to get out of here. Great Christ, I have to get out of here. I leap towards the door and reach it. I claw at it and try to pry it open. It is caught. The splinters bury themselves in my finger-nails. I do not notice the pain. I am too afraid to notice the pain of a splinter in my nails. Again behind me I hear that scream.

I swing around. The knife flashes through the air above my head. I grab at the hairy wrist that holds the knife. The razor-sharp edge slashes my arms. I know it slashes my arms because of the scorched feeling and the wet that spurts against my face. I struggle with the wrist that holds the knife and the arm that clubs at my head. I am getting weak. The loss of blood has made me weak. I cannot hold the arm that clutches the knife. I glue my eyes to this flash that quivers and shakes over my head as we strain in the ray that comes through the door from the moonlight. Nearer it comes and nearer. I twist the wrist with all my strength. I twist till I hear the snap of it through our panting and

scuffling. I hear this scream again as the arm goes limp and the knife clatters to the box-car floor. I start to dive for the knife on the floor and feel this fist that smashes to my face. I sprawl to the other end of the car. I grope in the dark and try to get up. I cannot. I am too weak to get to my feet. I lie here and tremble on the floor.

Through the ray of light that comes from the door I see this guy stand and stare at the floor. The gleam of the knife is there. He does not pick it up. He is not looking at the knife. It is this pool of blood from my slashed-up arm he is staring at. He stares like a guy in a trance at this blood. He flops to his knees and splashes his hands in the blood and screams. He splashes his hands in the pool of blood and smears it all over his face. I can see him quiver and shake and hear his jabber as he smears the blood. I lie here and wait for the flash of the knife, but it does not come. He leaps to his feet and jumps towards the door of the car. He jabbers and babbles as he shoves against it. He slides it open and leaps to the tracks. I can hear his screams as he crashes through the thickets.

I lie in the darkness with my bloody arm and shiver and sob in my breath.[8]

INTRODUCTION TO DOCUMENTS 7 AND 8

In the following two pieces, Meridel Le Sueur offers us chilling accounts of how women were affected by the Depression. "Women on the Breadlines" (1932) captures some of the same wandering, hopeless quality of Kromer's novel. As Le Sueur points out, however, many vagrant women would rather starve alone than face the shame of asking for help. "Women on the Breadlines" appeared in *New Masses*, the cultural organ of the Communist Party of America. The editors appended a note criticizing the article for its despairing tone. In Document 8, "I Was Marching," which appeared in *New Masses* two years later, Le Sueur took a much more affirmative position. The immediate subject was the 1934 Minneapolis Teamsters strike. Here Le Sueur described the terrors of the strike, not merely the fearful confrontation with police but also the deeper terror of a middle-class person, raised to value individual achievement, losing herself in collective action. But as Le Sueur argues here, individualism was now a dead end, and joint resistance a source of change and hope.

7. WOMEN ON THE BREADLINES (1932)

MERIDEL LE SUEUR

I am sitting in the city free employment bureau. It's the woman's section. We have been sitting here now for four hours. We sit here every day, waiting for a job. There are no jobs. Most of us have had no breakfast. Some have had scant rations for over a year. Hunger makes a human being lapse into a state of lethargy, especially city hunger. Is there any place else in the world where a human being is supposed to go hungry amidst plenty without an outcry, without protest, where only the boldest steal or kill for bread, and the timid crawl the streets, hunger like the beak of a terrible bird at the vitals?

We sit looking at the floor. No one dares think of the coming winter. There are only a few more days of summer. Everyone is anxious to get work to lay up something for that long siege of bitter cold. But there is no work. Sitting in the room we all know it. That is why we don't talk much. We look at the floor dreading to see that knowledge in each other's eyes. There is a kind of humiliation in it. We look away from each other. We look at the floor. It's too terrible to see this animal terror in each other's eyes.

So we sit hour after hour, day after day, waiting for a job to come in. There are many women for a single job. A thin sharp woman sits inside the wire cage looking at the book. For four hours we have watched her looking at the book. She has a hard little eye. In the small bare room there are half a dozen women sitting on the benches waiting. Many come and go. Our faces are all familiar to each other, for we wait here every day.

This is a domestic employment bureau. Most of the women who come here are middle aged, some have families, some raised their families and are now alone, some have men who are out of work. Hard times and the man leaves to hunt for work. He doesn't find it. He drifts on. The woman probably doesn't hear from him for a long time. She expects it. She isn't surprised. She struggles alone to feed the many mouths. Sometimes she gets help from the charities. If she's clever she can get herself a good living from the charities, if she's naturally a lick spittle, naturally a little docile and cunning. If she's proud then she starves silently, leaving her children to find work, coming home after a day's searching to wrestle with her house, her children.

Some such story is written on the faces of all these women. There are young girls too, fresh from the country. Some are made brazen too soon by the city. There is a great exodus of girls from the farms into the city now. Thousands of farms have been vacated completely in Minnesota. The girls are trying to get work. The prettier ones can get jobs in the stores when there are any, or waiting on table but these jobs are only for the attractive and the adroit, the others, the real peasants, have a more difficult time. . . .

It's one of the great mysteries of the city where women go when they are out of work and hungry. There are not many women in the bread line. There are no flop houses for women as there are for men, where a bed can be had for a quarter or less. You don't see women lying on the floor at the mission in the free flops. They obviously don't sleep in the jungle or under newspapers in the park. There is no law I suppose against their being in these places but the fact is they rarely are.

Yet there must be as many women out of jobs in cities and suffering extreme poverty as there are men. What happens to them? Where do they go? Try to get into the Y.W.C.A. without any money or looking down at heel. Charities take care of very few and only those that are called "deserving." The lone girl is under suspicion by the virgin women who dispense charity.

I've lived in cities for many months broke, without help, too timid to get in bread lines. I've known many women to live like this until they simply faint on the street from privations, without saying a word to anyone. A woman will shut herself up in a room until it is taken away from her, and eat a cracker a day and be as quiet as a mouse so there are no social statistics concerning her.

I don't know why it is, but a woman will do this unless she has dependents, will go for weeks, verging on starvation, crawling in some hole, going through the streets ashamed, sitting in libraries, parks, going for days without speaking to a living soul like some exiled beast, keeping the runs mended in her stockings, shut up in terror in her own misery, until she becomes too super sensitive and timid to even ask for a job. . . .

We are in a jungle and know it. We are beaten, entrapped. There is no way out. Even if there were a job, even if that thin acrid woman came and gave everyone in the room a job for a few days, a few hours, at thirty cents an hour, this would all be repeated tomorrow, the next day and the next. . . .

So we sit in this room like cattle, waiting for a non existent job, willing to work to the farthest atom of energy, unable to work, unable to get food and lodging, unable to bear children; here we must sit in this shame looking at the floor, worse than beasts at a slaughter. . . .

It's not the suffering, not birth, death, love that the young reject, but the suffering of endless labour without dream, eating the spare bread in bitterness, a slave without the security of a slave.

Editorial Note: This presentation of the plight of the unemployed woman, able as it is, and informative, is defeatist in attitude, lacking in revolutionary spirit and direction which characterize the usual contribution to *New Masses*. We feel it our duty to add, that there is a place for the unemployed woman, as well as man, in the ranks of the unemployed councils and in all branches of the organized revolutionary movement. Fight for your class, read *The Working Woman*, join the Communist Party.[9]

8. I WAS MARCHING (1934)

MERIDEL LE SUEUR

I have never been in a strike before. It is like looking at something that is happening for the first time and there are no thoughts and no words yet accrued to it. If you come from the middle class, words are likely to mean more than an event. You are likely to think about a thing, and the happening will be the size of a pin point and the words around the happening very large, distorting it queerly. It's a case of "Remembrance of things past." When you are in the event, you are likely to have a distinctly individualistic attitude, to be only partly there, and to care more for the happening afterwards than when it is happening. That is why it is hard for a person like myself and others to be in a strike.

Besides, in American life, you hear things happening in a far and muffled way. One thing is said and another happens. Our merchant society has been built upon a huge hypocrisy, a cut-throat competition which sets one man against another and at the same time an ideology mouthing such words as "Humanity," "Truth," the "Golden Rule," and such.

Now in a crisis the word falls away and the skeleton of that action shows in terrific movement.

For two days I heard of the strike. I went by their headquarters, I walked by on the opposite side of the street and saw the dark old building that had been a garage and lean, dark young faces leaning from the upstairs windows. I had to go down there often. I looked in. I saw the huge black interior and live coals of living men moving restlessly and orderly, their eyes gleaming from their sweaty faces.

I saw cars leaving filled with grimy men, pickets going to the line, engines roaring out. I stayed close to the door, watching. I didn't go in. I was afraid they would put me out. After all, I could remain a spectator. A man wearing a polo hat kept going around with a large camera taking pictures.

I am putting down exactly how I felt, because I believe others of my class feel the same as I did. I believe it stands for an important psychic change that must take place in all. I saw many artists, writers, professionals, even business men and women standing across the street, too, and I saw in their faces the same longings, the same fears.

The truth is I was afraid. Not of the physical danger at all, but an awful fright of mixing, of losing myself, of being unknown and lost. I felt inferior. I felt no one would know me there, that all I had been trained to excel in would go unnoticed. I can't describe what I felt, but perhaps it will come near it to say that I felt I excelled in competing with others and I knew instantly that these people were *NOT* competing at all, that they were acting in a strange, powerful trance of movement *together*. And I was filled with longing to act with them and with fear that I could not. I felt I was born out of every kind of life, thrown up alone, looking at other lonely people, a condition I had been in the habit of defending with various attitudes of cynicism, preciosity, defiance and hatred. . . .

The next day, with sweat breaking out on my body, I walked past the three guards at the door. They said, "Let the women in. We need women." And I knew it was no joke. . . .

I found the kitchen organized like a factory. Nobody asks my name. I am given a large butcher's apron. I realize I have never before worked anonymously. At first I feel strange and then I feel good. The forewoman sets me to washing tin cups. There are not enough cups. We have to wash fast and rinse them and set them up quickly for buttermilk and coffee as the line thickens and the men wait. . . .

Then I am changed and put to pouring coffee. At first I look at the men's faces and then I don't look any more. It seems I am pouring coffee for the same tense, dirty sweating face, the same body, the same blue shirt and overalls. Hours go by, the heat is terrific. I am not tired. I am not hot. I am pouring coffee. I am swung into the most intense and natural organization I have ever felt. I know everything that is going on. These things become of great matter to me.

Eyes looking, hands raising a thousand cups, throats burning, eyes bloodshot from lack of sleep, the body dilated to catch every sound over the whole city. Buttermilk? Coffee?

"Is your man here?" the woman cutting sandwiches asks me.

"No," I say, then I lie for some reason, peering around as if looking eagerly for someone, "I don't see him now."

But I was pouring coffee for living men. . . .

That night at eight o'clock a mass-meeting was called of all labor. It was to be in a parking lot two blocks from headquarters. All the women gather at the front of the building with collection cans, ready to march to the meeting. I have not been home. It never occurs to me to leave. The twilight is eerie and the men are saying that the chief of police is going to attack the meeting and raid headquarters. The smell of blood hangs in the hot, still air. Rumors strike at the taut nerves. The dusk looks ghastly with what might be in the next half hour.

"If you have any children," a woman said to me, "you better not go." I looked at the desperate women's faces, the broken feet, the torn and hanging pelvis, the worn and lovely bodies of women who persist under such desperate labors. I shivered, though it was 96 and the sun had been down a good hour. . . .

I am one of them, yet I don't feel myself at all. It is curious. I feel most alive and yet for the first time in my life I do not feel myself as separate. I realize then that all my previous feelings have been based on feeling myself separate and distinct from others and now I sense sharply faces, bodies, closeness and my own fear is not my own alone, nor my hope. . . .

THE NEXT DAY

Two men died from that day's shooting. Men lined up to give one of them a blood transfusion, but he died. Black Friday men called the murderous day. Night and day workers held their children up to see the body of Ness who died. Tuesday, the day of the funeral, one thousand more militia were massed downtown.

It was still over ninety in the shade. I went to the funeral parlors and thousands of men and women were massed there waiting in the terrific sun. One block of women and children were standing two hours waiting. I went over and stood near them. I didn't know whether I could march. I didn't like marching in parades. Besides, I felt they might not want me.

I stood aside not knowing if I would march. I couldn't see how they would ever organize it anyway. No one seemed to be doing much.

At three-forty some command went down the ranks. I said foolishly at the last minute, "I don't belong to the auxiliary—could I march?" Three women drew me in. "We want all to march," they said gently. "Come with us."

The giant mass uncoiled like a serpent and straightened out ahead and to my amazement on a lift of road I could see six blocks of massed men, four abreast, with bare heads, moving straight on and as they moved, uncoiled the mass behind and pulled it after them, I felt myself walking, accelerating my speed with the others as the line stretched, pulled taut, then held its rhythm.

Not a cop was in sight. The cortege moved through the stop-and-go signs, it seemed to lift of its own dramatic rhythm, coming from the intention of every person there. We were moving spontaneously in a movement, natural, hardy and miraculous.

We passed through six blocks of tenements, through a sea of grim faces and there was not a sound.

There was the curious shuffle of thousands of feet, without drum or bugle, in ominous silence, a march not heavy as the military, but very light, exactly with the heart beat.

I was marching with a million hands, movements, faces and my own movement was repeating again and again, making a new movement from the many gestures, the walking, falling back, the open mouth crying, the nostrils stretched apart, the raised hand, the blow falling, and the outstretched hand drawing me in.

I felt my legs straighten. I felt my feet join in that strange shuffle of thousands of bodies moving with direction, of thousands of feet and my own breath with the gigantic breath. As if an electric charge had passed through me, my hair stood on end. I was marching.[10]

INTRODUCTION TO DOCUMENTS 9 AND 10

From the shocking images of American poverty in the documentary photographs to the attempts to capture regional and racial dialects in the oral histories and working-class fiction, there was a pervasive aim of broadening access to culture in the 1930s. Perhaps the most memorable of these efforts was the stirring performance of contralto Marian Anderson at the Lincoln Memorial in April 1939.

Anderson had begun to sing as a child at the Union Baptist Church in Philadelphia and continued to impress audiences with her virtuosity in the choir. Though local conservatories refused to admit her as a student because of her race, she gained substantial support after winning a 1925 competition to sing with the New York Philharmonic Symphony Orchestra and went on to perform across Europe. She returned to the United States in 1935 with a triumphant appearance at Carnegie Hall, then gave a concert at the Roosevelt White House, and for the next few years toured across North America.

Yet despite her box office power, she was subject to the same segregation laws that other African Americans experienced. In 1939, Howard University hoped to arrange a concert for her at Washington D.C.'s Constitutional Hall, which was owned by the Daughters of the American Revolution (DAR), a civic organization. A few years earlier, the DAR had adopted a rule barring African Americans from performing at the hall after some members protested against blacks and whites being seated in proximity to one another.

The DAR denied that they had turned down Anderson because of her race—there was a mere booking conflict, they said. Others in the organization argued that keeping Anderson out of Constitution Hall was a simply a matter of obeying the law, that their rule against black performers aligned with the segregation policies in the District of Columbia, which dated back to the Woodrow Wilson administration. Ending segregation, the DAR argued, was not their problem but something to be solved by the District as a whole. Eleanor Roosevelt, in response, resigned her membership in the DAR. Her explanation to the organization's president, Mrs. Henry M. Robert, is Document 9. The next day, Roosevelt addressed her decision in her syndicated column, "My Day," giving the country a sense of her reasoning.

Image 10.5 Robert S. Scurlock, photograph of Marian Anderson performing in front of the Lincoln Memorial

Some of the 75,000 of all races who converged between the Lincoln Memorial and the Washington Monument on Easter Sunday to hear Marian Anderson. Thousands more tuned in to listen over the radio.

Source: Scurlock Records, Archives Center, National Museum of American History, Smithsonian Institution.

9. ELEANOR ROOSEVELT TO HENRY M. ROBERT

FEBRUARY 26, 1939

My dear Mrs. Robert:

I am afraid that I have never been a very useful member of the Daughters of the American Revolution, so I know it will make very little difference to you whether I resign, or whether I continue to be a member of your organization.

However, I am in complete disagreement with the attitude taken in refusing Constitution Hall to a great artist. You have set an example which seems to me unfortunate, and I feel obliged to send in to you my resignation. You had an opportunity to lead in an enlightened way and it seems to me that your organization has failed.

I realize that many people will not agree with me, but feeling as I do this seems to me the only proper procedure to follow.

Very sincerely yours,
[Eleanor Roosevelt][11]

10. "MY DAY" (FEBRUARY 27, 1939)

ELEANOR ROOSEVELT

. . . I have been debating in my mind for some time, a question which I have had to debate with myself once or twice before in my life. Usually I have decided differently from the way in which I am deciding now. The question is, if you belong to an organization and disapprove of an action which is typical of a policy, should you resign or is it better to work for a changed point of view within the organization? In the past, when I was able to work actively in any organization to which I belonged, I have usually stayed until I had at least made a fight and had been defeated.

. . . Even then, I have, as a rule, accepted my defeat and decided I was wrong or, perhaps, a little too far ahead of the thinking for the majority at that time. I have often found that the thing in which I was interested was done some years later. But in this case, I belong to an organization in which I can do no active work. They have taken an action which has been widely talked of in the press. To remain as a member implies approval of that action, and therefore I am resigning.[12]

INTRODUCTION TO DOCUMENT 11

Eleanor Roosevelt's decision attracted considerable attention and more than a few accusations that she was using this as a political opportunity. But the larger problem was the system of segregation in the District, which also prevented Anderson from singing at a local high school when she had been barred from Constitution Hall. In light of this situation, Roosevelt worked with Interior Secretary Harold Ickes to arrange for Anderson to sing in the open air on the steps of the Lincoln Memorial. Anderson's agent, Sol Hurok, lauded the plan to hold the concert in front of the memorial as a clear message to those who had snubbed the singer because of her race.

Eleanor Roosevelt's intervention helped her husband's ongoing efforts to court black voters away from their historic loyalty to the Republican Party and into the fold of the Democratic New Deal coalition. The administration must have delighted at the letter (Document 11), written by a resident of Harlem to Interior Secretary Ickes, who introduced Anderson at the Lincoln Memorial to the 75,000 listening on the mall and the hundreds of thousands more across the country who thrilled at her performance over the radio.

11. LOUISE JEFFERSON TO HAROLD ICKES (1939)

My dear Mr. Ickes,
It is safe to say that eight million Negroes listened to the glorious voice of Miss Marion [sic] Anderson on Sunday last: listened with gratitude for her offering but with deeper gratitude to you for making it possible.

The occasion was the most significant and distinctive that has yet occurred to promote better race relations and to sponsor Negro achievement.

Please accept my thanks and congratulations for affording this honor and privilege.
Most Respectfully,
Louise E. Jefferson[13]

POSTSCRIPT

Marian Anderson's performance was just one of many moments of hope in the midst of the Great Depression. Another such moment came when the rising black star of the prize ring, Joe Louis, defeated Max Baer in September 1935. Times were hard on Chicago's South Side before the crash, and they were harder now. Richard Wright, author of the era's great novel of African American life, *Native Son*, described black Chicago's joy at Louis's victory. Folks streamed out of taverns, pool halls, and rooming houses where they had listened to the fight. "Lawd, they'd never seen or heard the like of it before. They shook the hands of strangers. They clapped one another on the back. It was like a revival." Two hours later, down on 47th Street, 25,000 people formed a snake line and wove in and out of traffic. "*Something* had happened alright," Wright wrote, "and it had happened so confoundingly sudden that the whites in the neighborhood were dumb with fear. They felt—you could see it in their faces—that *something* had ripped loose, exploded. Something which they had long feared and thought was dead." The quiet, dignified Louis's triumph was so much more than a mere victory in the ring.

> Four centuries of oppression, of frustrated hopes, of black bitterness, felt even in the bones of the bewildered young, were rising to the surface. Yes, unconsciously they had imputed to the brawny image of Joe Louis all the balked dreams of revenge, all the secretly visualized moments of retaliation, AND HE HAD WON! Good Gawd Almighty!

It was a symbolic victory, of course, and the feelings couldn't last forever. But for now, Wright wrote, Louis's conquest was,

> the concentrated essence of black triumph over white. From the symbol of Joe's strength, they took strength, and in that moment all fear, all obstacles were wiped out, drowned. They stepped out of the mire of hesitation and irresolution and were free! Invincible! A merciless victor over a fallen foe! Yes, they had felt all that—for a moment.[14] . . .

QUESTIONS

1. Why did people write to President and Mrs. Roosevelt? What did they ask for, and what opinions did they express about the Depression's origins and solutions?
2. In what sense were Depression-era writings and photographs hopeful or despairing? What vision did they offer of collective or individual action?
3. How did the Great Depression alter people's daily lives? Do you see evidence that it affected women differently? African-Americans?
4. Why did Tom Kromer blur the line between fiction and autobiography?
5. Do the photographs inspire emotional responses in you? Fear? Sadness? Pride?
6. Why do you think Marian Anderson's concert—and the story behind it—made national news?

ADDITIONAL READING

Important accounts of the Great Depression include David Kennedy, *Freedom from Fear* (1999); Alan Brinkley, *The End of Reform* (1995); Ronald Edsforth, *The New Deal* (2000); and Alonzo

Hamby, *For the Survival of Democracy: Franklin Roosevelt and the World Crisis of the 1930s* (2007). For an account of the Roosevelt administration, see William E. Leuchtenburg's *The FDR Years: On Roosevelt and His Legacy* (1995). The flavor of the times is captured in the oral history by Studs Terkel, *Hard Times* (1970), and Ann Banks, *First Person America* (1981). Some aspects of culture in the decade are covered in Anthony Lee, *Painting on the Left* (1999); Michael Denning, *The Cultural Front* (1996); and Lewis Erenberg, *Swingin' the Dream* (1998). On the west, see Timothy Egan, *The Worst Hard Time: the Untold Story of the Those Who Survived the Great American Dust Bowl* (2006), and James Gregory, *American Exodus: The Dust Bowl Migration and California Okie Subculture* (1989). On workers' response to the crisis, see Lizabeth Cohen, *Making a New Deal* (1991). On the Depression and race, see Patricia Sullivan, *Days of Hope: Race and Democracy in the New Deal Era* (1996). On the most famous outlaw of the era, see Elliott J. Gorn, *Dillinger's Wild Ride* (2009). For Joe Louis in the 1930s, see Randy Roberts, *Joe Louis: Hard Times Man* (2010). On the Federal Writers' Project, see Federal Writers' Project, *These Are Our Lives* (1967), and Jerrold Hirsch, *Portrait of America: A Cultural History of the Federal Writers' Project* (2003); on photography, see William Stott, *Documentary Expression and Thirties America* (1973). Finally, for more on Americans' relationship with Franklin Roosevelt, see Lawrence and Cornelia Levine, *The People and the President* (2002).

ENDNOTES

1. Federal Emergency Relief Administration Central Files, Box 4, National Archives, found in Robert S. McElvaine, *Down and Out in the Great Depression* (Chapel Hill: University of North Carolina Press, 1983), letter 59.
2. Federal Emergency Relief Administration: New General Subject Files, 1935–1936" files, Box #4, "Anonymous Letters," found in McElvaine, *Down and Out*, letter 75.
3. Eleanor Roosevelt Papers, Franklin Delano Roosevelt Library, Hyde Park, Box 2727.
4. McElvaine, *Down and Out* letter 107.
5. Robert F. Wagner Papers, Drawer 1-A-3, Georgetown University Library, found in McElvaine, *Down and Out*, letter 108.
6. Eleanor Roosevelt Papers, FDR Library, Box 2725, found in McElvaine, Down and Out, letter 141.
7. Ellison, Ralph. [City Street]. New York City, New York, 1939. Folklore Project, Life Histories, 1936–1939, U.S. Work Projects Administration, Federal Writers Project, Library of Congress.
8. Tom Kromer, *Waiting for Nothing and Other Writings*, edited by Arthur D. Casciato and James L. W. West (Athens: University of Georgia Press, 1986), pp. 94–103.
9. Meridel Le Sueur, "Women on the Breadlines," originally published in the *New Masses* (January 1932), from *Harvest: Collected Stories*. Reprinted with the permission of The Permissions Company, Inc., on behalf of West End Press, Albuquerque, New Mexico.
10. Meridel Le Sueur, "I Was Marching," *New Masses* (September 18, 1934), pp. 16–18, courtesy of International Publishers, Inc.
11. File copy of letter from Eleanor Roosevelt to the President-General of the Daughters of the American Revolution, February 26, 1939, National Archives.
12. Eleanor Roosevelt, "My Day," February 27, 1939.
13. Letter from Louise E. Jefferson to Secretary Harold Ickes, Office of the Secretary of the Interior, Record Group 48, National Archives.
14. Richard Wright, "Joe Louis Uncovers Dynamite," *New Masses* (October 8, 1935).

CHAPTER 11

THE GOOD WAR

HISTORICAL CONTEXT

The sheer size of American efforts in World War II was staggering. More than 16 million men and women served in the armed forces; some 320,000 were killed and another 800,000 wounded (though, keep in mind, an estimated 60 million people died throughout the world). American women and minorities served in unprecedented numbers, facilitating the total mobilization of economic resources. From an unemployment high of around 25 percent in 1933, the war virtually eliminated joblessness less than a decade later. Rural Americans, including whites, blacks and Mexicans poured into the cities to work in the war-related industries. The media, especially radio and the movies, brought current events home as never before, and the government's Office of War Information saw to it that the nation's fighting spirit remained high.

At the beginning of 1941, almost a year before we entered the conflict, the United States was a nervous island of peace in a world torn by war. In Europe, the Nazis were on the march. During the previous year, the blitzkrieg assaults of Adolf Hitler's German armies overran Denmark, Norway, Belgium, Holland, and France. Nazi planes rained death and destruction over large sections of southern England, bombing London repeatedly. In Eastern Europe, Joseph Stalin's Soviet forces attacked Finland, and in the Mediterranean, Benito Mussolini's Italian troops assaulted Greece. Finally, Japan—which had already invaded Manchuria and China—signed an ominous alliance with Germany and Italy, proclaimed "a new order in Eastern Asia," and promptly invaded French Indochina.

Through all this fighting the United States kept its distance, maintaining fragile neutrality. But for President Franklin D. Roosevelt neutrality in action did not imply neutrality in thought. He wanted peace but not peace at any price. After winning reelection in November 1940 for an unprecedented third term, he began to move more boldly in foreign affairs, expressing opinions and requesting legislation that edged the United States toward more active involvement. On the night of January 6, 1941, in his annual message to Congress, Roosevelt spelled out the dangers facing America, but in the end, he articulated the core values of a new international order:

> The first is freedom of speech and expression—everywhere in the world. The second is freedom of every person to worship God in his own way—everywhere in the world. The third is

freedom from want—which, translated into world terms, means economic understanding that secures to every nation a healthy peacetime life for its inhabitants—everywhere in the world. The fourth is freedom from fear—which, translated into world terms, means a worldwide reduction of armaments to such a point and in such a fashion that no nation will be in a position to commit an act of physical aggression against any neighbor—anywhere in the world.

In straightforward language, Roosevelt's "Four Freedoms" proposed a moral order. His were not merely fighting words but fighting ideals. After the United States entered the war in December 1941, Roosevelt's advisers knew that they needed more still; they needed images—powerful, emotional symbols—to visualize the American war effort. To do this, his administration turned to Norman Rockwell, the country's preeminent illustrator and best-loved artist. Since the second decade of the century, Rockwell's *Saturday Evening Post* covers had brilliantly captured mythical small-town, middle-class America. A boy in a baseball cap, a red-headed girl in pigtails, Santa Claus getting ready for Christmas, and a barbershop quartet singing in harmony—these were some of Rockwell's favorite subjects.

Rockwell's assignment was to turn Roosevelt's words into images. He did so brilliantly. The four paintings—*Freedom of Speech, Freedom of Worship, Freedom from Want,* and *Freedom from Fear*—ran as covers for *The Saturday Evening Post* from February 20, 1943, to March 13, 1943. They were then reproduced and distributed across the nation as posters, reminders to millions of Americans of the cause for which their soldiers were fighting and dying (see Document 2).

The images Rockwell created were dramatic and compelling, each of them instantly familiar. In *Freedom of Speech* a humbly dressed young man, a worker, stands alone in a town meeting to express his views while other, older men lift their eyes in attention, if not agreement. *Freedom of Worship* portrays the diversity of America, presenting men and women, blacks and whites, and Catholics, Protestants, and Jews worshipping together. Across the picture in gold letters are the words: "Each according to the dictates of his own conscience." *Freedom from Want* presents a big, loving family gathered round the table for Thanksgiving dinner. *Freedom from Fear* shows a mother and father tucking their two young children safely into bed for the night. The tension in the painting is provided by the folded newspaper held by father; the half visible headline reads "BOMBINGS KI . . . HORROR HIT. . . ."

In essence, Rockwell painted America exactly how most Americans wanted to see themselves. We provided food for the hungry, safety for the defenseless, freedom for the persecuted, and respect for each person's opinions. All this, of course, silently contrasted with America's wartime enemies, and the unspoken message was that the freedoms Roosevelt and Rockwell exulted were under siege by Germany, Italy and Japan.

The contrasts between "us" and "them," the defenders and the aggressors, freedom extenders and freedom deniers, eventually gave rise to the notion of World War II as the "Good War." It is difficult to describe any war as "good," but certainly World War II was, from an American perspective, a just war. The United States was attacked. More, it was a war fought against tyrants who ruthlessly committed war crimes ranging from cruel treatment of prisoners to the Holocaust. For decades, right up to our own day, histories, novels, comic books, movies, and television shows have presented the "Good War" of Roosevelt and Rockwell.

Are the books and films and television shows wrong? Were Roosevelt's words and Rockwell's images false? No, Americans and their Allies who fought against Nazi Germany and imperial Japan confronted governments capable of great evil, governments without respect for human lives or civil liberties, and governments determined to extend their influence and racist ideologies at the expense of other countries. Still, the Four Freedoms sometimes confused American ideals with reality. Freedom of worship was a hard won right, yet as Martin Luther King Jr. observed years later, noon on Sunday was the most segregated hour of the week. American agriculture produced amazing bounty, yet the Farm Security Administration photographs in Chapter 10 documented terrible hunger. As the Roosevelt administration well understood, if we intended to broadcast to the world our noble intentions, we had best get our own house in order.

African Americans, of course, were keenly aware that racism was not unusual in the United States. Throughout the late 1930s and early 1940s, as Germany marched into battle in Europe and ultimately declared war on the United States, African-American journalists and political leaders pointed out that Klansmen and anti-Semites in America supported "Hitlerism" at home. One African-American journalist commented, "The only difference between the Japanese murdering defenseless Chinese and the lynching of Negroes by their fellow Americans is one of degree." He hoped that the racist barbarities of the Germans and the Japanese would make Americans "stop and think" about racial injustices committed in the United States.

Even after the Japanese bombed Pearl Harbor and the United States entered the fray, African Americans stressed that the war against racist ideology had a home front. Jim Crow military bases in the South, discrimination in defense plants, and segregation inside the U.S. Army and Navy all pointed to the fact that the War offered little refuge from racism. African-American journalists called for a "double victory" (VV) campaign that would defeat fascism abroad and racism at home. How was it, they asked, that black and white soldiers could die fighting together in Europe and Asia but not eat together in a restaurant in Washington, D.C.? As African-American poet Langston Hughes wrote: "You tell me that Hitler/Is a mighty bad man/I guess he took lessons/From the ku klux klan."

Japanese Americans contended with other difficulties. Although German Americans and Italian Americans generally were treated like any other citizens during the war, the government sent nearly the entire population of Japanese Americans—more than 100,000 people, most of them United States citizens—to ten internment camps located in six western states. The camps were little more than prisons, set in barren wastelands, but the detainees had committed no crimes nor had there been any substantial threats of disloyalty. Overcrowded wooden barracks, barbed wire, armed guards, dusty windswept conditions, bad food, and substandard medical care greeted the innocent victims of prejudice. Although many Japanese Americans questioned the legality of internment, the Supreme Court in *Korematsu v. United States* (1944) upheld the government's action.

Other American minorities also suffered during the Good War. Mexican Americans in western states faced hostility and discrimination. During the Great Depression, the government deported tens of thousands of Mexicans and Mexican Americans—again, largely U.S. citizens—to Mexico in a program of "repatriation." Less than a decade later, confronted by wartime labor shortages, the government's Bracero (work hands) Program welcomed immigrants from Mexico. This led to ethnic and cultural clashes in the Southwest. Many Anglos viewed Latino youths as low-level war profiteers, stereotyping them as long-haired, zoot-suited, knife-carrying criminals. The ethnic tensions simmered in Los Angeles, boiling over into bloodshed in the June 1943 "Zoot Suit riots." Although American servicemen provoked most of the violence, the riots were blamed on Latino men.

Despite the discrimination they faced at home, African Americans, Mexican Americans, and Japanese Americans fought for their country. They reinterpreted the struggle as an opportunity to prove their devotion to American freedom. The World War II era might not have been as unblemished as the movies depicted, but Americans overwhelmingly supported the *ideal* of the Four Freedoms. They recognized the threat posed by Japan and Germany, and in the long run, fighting racism overseas sometimes spilled over to fighting it at home.

The following documents examines sources of unity and division in the United States prompted by the war. We concentrate first upon the debate over the Lend Lease Bill, the president's proposed aid to England in early 1941, nearly a year before the United States was at war with Germany or Japan. This was, by extension, a debate over our possible involvement in the war itself, a challenge to America's neutrality, isolation, and deep skepticism about European wars. The Lend Lease debate was the occasion for Roosevelt's Four Freedoms speech. Once the Japanese attacked Pearl Harbor, a year later, the United States entered the war. But the surprise attack tapped deep anxieties and racial fears on the west coast, leading to the evacuation of Japanese Americans from their homes. In fighting against fascism and racism, America was fighting for political freedom and racial tolerance—at least that is what wartime publicity said. If the realities of American society often fell short of our ideals, that tension helped shape postwar American politics.

INTRODUCTION TO DOCUMENTS 1 AND 2

The first two documents articulate the values that the Roosevelt administration believed were essential to American society. Delivered on January 6, 1941, almost a full year before the United States entered the war, FDR's Four Freedoms speech attempted both to prepare Americans for the looming conflict and to express the country's core beliefs. Norman Rockwell gave visual expression to Roosevelt's Four Freedoms, and his paintings were seen all over America when the *Saturday Evening Post* published them as cover art early in 1943. Reading Roosevelt's words and examining Rockwell's paintings in the context of World War II leads to a series of questions. For example, were FDR's Four Freedoms simply a ruse to prepare Americans for war? In Rockwell's paintings, where did truth end and propaganda begin? Does propaganda sometimes contain its own truths? Is the word *ideology* is a better word than propaganda, meaning a set of ideals that describe the way people believe their world actually *is* or at least *should be*? What was the emotional appeal of the Four Freedoms?

1. ANNUAL MESSAGE TO CONGRESS, JANUARY 6, 1941

FRANKLIN D. ROOSEVELT

Mr. President, Mr. Speaker, Members of the Seventy-Seventh Congress:

I address you, the Members of the Seventy-seventh Congress, at a moment unprecedented in the history of the Union. I use the word "unprecedented," because at no previous time has American security been as seriously threatened from without as it is today. . . .

Every realist knows that the democratic way of life is at this moment being directly assailed in every part of the world—assailed either by arms, or by secret spreading of poisonous propaganda by those who seek to destroy unity and promote discord in nations that are still at peace.

During sixteen long months this assault has blotted out the whole pattern of democratic life in an appalling number of independent nations, great and small. The assailants are still on the march, threatening other nations, great and small.

Therefore, as your President, performing my constitutional duty to "give to the Congress information of the state of the Union," I find it, unhappily, necessary to report that the future and the safety of our country and of our democracy are overwhelmingly involved in events far beyond our borders. . . .

The need of the moment is that our actions and our policy should be devoted primarily—almost exclusively—to meeting this foreign peril. For all our domestic problems are now a part of the great emergency. . . . We are committed to the proposition that principles of morality and considerations for our own security will never permit us to acquiesce in a peace dictated by aggressors and sponsored by appeasers. We know that enduring peace cannot be bought at the cost of other people's freedom. . . .

Therefore, the immediate need is a swift and driving increase in our armament production. . . . Let us say to the democracies: "We Americans are vitally concerned in your defense of freedom. We are putting forth our energies, our resources and our organizing powers to give you the strength to regain and maintain a free world. We shall send you, in ever-increasing numbers, ships, planes, tanks, guns. This is our purpose and our pledge."

In fulfillment of this purpose we will not be intimidated by the threats of dictators that they will regard as a breach of international law or as an act of war our aid to the democracies which dare to resist their aggression. Such aid is not an act of war, even if a dictator should unilaterally proclaim it so to be. . . .

We must all prepare to make the sacrifices that the emergency—almost as serious as war itself—demands. Whatever stands in the way of speed and efficiency in defense preparations must give way to the national need.

A free nation has the right to expect full cooperation from all groups. A free nation has the right to look to the leaders of business, of labor, and of agriculture to take the lead in stimulating effort, not among other groups but within their own groups.

The best way of dealing with the few slackers or trouble makers in our midst is, first, to shame them by patriotic example, and, if that fails, to use the sovereignty of Government to save Government.

As men do not live by bread alone, they do not fight by armaments alone. . . . There is nothing mysterious about the foundations of a healthy and strong democracy. The basic things expected by our people of their political and economic systems are simple. They are:

Equality of opportunity for youth and for others.
Jobs for those who can work.
Security for those who need it.
The ending of special privilege for the few.
The preservation of civil liberties for all.
The enjoyment of the fruits of scientific progress in a wider and constantly rising standard of living.

These are the simple, basic things that must never be lost sight of in the turmoil and unbelievable complexity of our modern world. The inner and abiding strength of our economic and political systems is dependent upon the degree to which they fulfill these expectations.

Many subjects connected with our social economy call for immediate improvement.

As examples:

We should bring more citizens under the coverage of old-age pensions and unemployment insurance.
We should widen the opportunities for adequate medical care.
We should plan a better system by which persons deserving or needing gainful employment may obtain it.

I have called for personal sacrifice. I am assured of the willingness of almost all Americans to respond to that call. . . .

In the future days, which we seek to make secure, we look forward to a world founded upon four essential human freedoms.

The first is freedom of speech and expression—everywhere in the world.

The second is freedom of every person to worship God in his own way—everywhere in the world.

The third is freedom from want—which, translated into world terms, means economic understandings which will secure to every nation a healthy peacetime life for its inhabitants—everywhere in the world.

The fourth is freedom from fear—which, translated into world terms, means a world-wide reduction of armaments to such a point and in such a thorough fashion that no nation will be in a position to commit an act of physical aggression against any neighbor—anywhere in the world.

That is no vision of a distant millennium. It is a definite basis for a kind of world attainable in our own time and generation. That kind of world is the very antithesis of the so-called new order of tyranny which the dictators seek to create with the crash of a bomb.

To that new order we oppose the greater conception—the moral order. A good society is able to face schemes of world domination and foreign revolutions alike without fear.

Since the beginning of our American history, we have been engaged in change—in a perpetual peaceful revolution—a revolution which goes on steadily, quietly adjusting itself to changing conditions—without the concentration camp or the quick-lime in the ditch. The world order which we seek is the cooperation of free countries, working together in a friendly, civilized society.

This nation has placed its destiny in the hands and heads and hearts of its millions of free men and women; and its faith in freedom under the guidance of God. Freedom means the supremacy of human rights everywhere. Our support goes to those who struggle to gain those rights or keep them. Our strength is our unity of purpose. To that high concept there can be no end save victory.[1]

2. THE FOUR FREEDOMS (1943)

NORMAN ROCKWELL

Image 11.1: Rockwell's Four Freedoms (1943)

Norman Rockwell painted his version of Roosevelt's Four Freedoms—freedom of speech, of worship, from want, and from fear—as cover art for the *Saturday Evening Post* early in 1943, when the outcome of the war was far from certain. What messages were conveyed by these images? How would you describe the emotional tone of each?

Charles Lindbergh became an American hero in 1927, the first lone man to cross the Atlantic—from Long Island to Paris—in his airplane the "Spirit of St Louis." After the kidnapping and murder of their first child and the killer's protracted trial, Lindberg and his wife left the United States for Europe. While there they attended the Summer Olympic games of 1936 in Berlin, as the guests of the Germans. Lindbergh was deeply impressed with German military power. Some wondered whether he had become sympathetic to the Nazis, especially after he returned to the United States in 1939 and made comments that echoed a rising chorus of anti-Semitism. In 1941 he testified before Congress against the Lend Lease bill, arguing that it was the first step in drawing America into the war. His statement was widely reprinted in the press, and it resonated with many Americans who, disillusioned by the carnage of a world war that had ended just twenty years earlier, held isolationist views.

Three days after Lindbergh testified, British Prime Minister Sir Winston Churchill took to the airwaves to communicate the state of the war effort to his countrymen. London was under siege by German bombers and rockets, and Churchill used the opportunity to buoy Britons' spirits. He extolled the progress of the British military against powerful German forces, but only with American aid, Churchill said, could Britain defeat the Nazis.

Churchill and Lindbergh represented polarized sides of a nationwide debate over the Lend Lease bill, a debate that dominated the news in the winter of 1940–1941. America had moved decisively toward neutrality in the 1930s, but now, many argued, aid to Britain was the best way to keep us out of the war. Of course, this was not just about pragmatism, as Lindbergh seemed to argue. As you read, ask how Lindbergh and Churchill each presented his case and framed what was at stake for America and the world. Both claimed the road to peace, yet their recommendations could not be more at odds with one another.

3. CHARLES LINDBERGH, TESTIMONY REGARDING LEND LEASE (1941)

Mr. Chairman, and gentlemen, in the hope that it will save time and add to clarity, I have attempted to outline briefly my reasons for opposition to this bill. In general, I have two. I oppose it, first, because I believe it is a step away from the system of government in which most of us in this country believe. Secondly, I oppose it because I think it represents a policy which will weaken rather than strengthen our Nation.

The first point is simply my opinion as an American citizen. . . .

. . . I have never taken the stand that it makes no difference to us who wins this war in Europe. It does make a difference to us, a great difference. But I do not believe that it is either possible or desirable for us in America to control the outcome of European wars. When I am asked which side I would like to have win, it would be very easy for me to say "the English." But, gentlemen, an English victory, if it were possible at all, would necessitate years of war and an invasion of the Continent of Europe. I believe this would create prostration, famine, and disease in Europe—and probably in America—such as the world has never experienced before. This is why I say that I prefer a negotiated peace to a complete victory by either side.

This bill is obviously the most recent step in a policy which attempts to obtain security for America by controlling internal conditions in Europe. The policy of depleting our own forces to aid England is based upon the assumption that England will win this war. Personally, I do not believe that England is in a position to win the war. If she does not win, or unless our aid is used in negotiating a better peace than could otherwise be obtained, we will be responsible for futilely prolonging the war and adding to the bloodshed and devastation in Europe, particularly among the democracies. In that case, the only advantage we can gain by our action lies in whatever additional time we obtain to prepare ourselves for defense. But instead of consolidating our own defensive position in America, we are sending a large portion of our armament production abroad.

. . . England cannot obtain an air strength equal to Germany's without great assistance from the United States; and my personal opinion is that, regardless of how much assistance we send, it will not be possible for American and British aviation concentrated in the small area of the British Isles, to equal the strength of German aviation, with unlimited bases throughout the Continent of Europe. . . .

With this picture of Europe in mind, I now return to my statement that, from the standpoint of aviation, the attempt to gain supremacy of the air in Europe weakens our security in America. . . . What we are doing in following our present policy, is giving up an ideal defensive position in America for a very precarious offensive position in Europe. I would be opposed to our entering the internal wars of Europe under any circumstances. But it is an established fact today, that our army and our air force are but poorly equipped on modern standards, and even our Navy is in urgent need of new equipment. If we deplete our forces still further, as this bill indicates we may, and if England should lose this war, then, gentlemen, I think we may be in danger of invasion, although I do not believe we are today. If we are ever invaded in America, the responsibility will lie upon those who send our arms abroad.

I advocate building strength in America because I believe we can be successful in this hemisphere. I oppose placing our security in an English victory because I believe that such a victory is extremely doubtful.

I am opposed to this bill because I believe it endorses a policy that will lead to failure in war, and to conditions in our own country as bad or as worse than those we now desire to overthrow in Nazi Germany.

I do not believe that the danger to America lies in an invasion from abroad. I believe it lies here at home in our own midst, and that it is exemplified by the terms of this bill—the placing of our security in the success of foreign armies, and the removal of power from the Representatives of the people of our own land.[2]

4. PRIME MINISTER WINSTON CHURCHILL, SPEECH ON FEBRUARY 9, 1941

. . . A mighty tide of sympathy, of good will and of effective aid, has begun to flow across the Atlantic in support of the world cause which is at stake. Distinguished Americans have come over to see things here

at the front, and to find out how the United States can help us best and soonest. . . .

We may be sure that the war is soon going to enter upon a phase of greater violence. Hitler's confederate,

Mussolini, has reeled back in Albania, but the Nazis—having absorbed Hungary and driven Rumania into a frightful internal convulsion—are now already upon the Black Sea. A considerable Nazi German army and air force is being built up in Rumania, and its forward tentacles have already penetrated Bulgaria. . . .

Much will certainly happen as American aid becomes effective, as our air power grows, as we become a well-armed nation, and as our armies in the East increase in strength. But nothing is more certain than that, if the countries of southeastern Europe allow themselves to be pulled to pieces one by one, they will share the fate of Denmark, Holland and Belgium. And none can tell how long it will be before the hour of their deliverance strikes. . . .

But after all, the fate of this war is going to be settled by what happens on the oceans, in the air, and—above all—in this Island. It seems now to be certain that the Government and the people of the United States intend to supply us with all that is necessary for victory. In the last war the United States sent two million men across the Atlantic. . . . This is not a war of vast armies . . . but we do need most urgently an immense and continuous supply of war materials and technical apparatus of all kinds. We need them here and we need to bring them here.

Image 11.2: Lend Lease aid to Britain (1942)

With the Allied "V" for victory, the Ocean Gallant cargo carrier built for Britain through the Lend Lease bill is towed to sea in New England.

Source: Courtesy Library of Congress.

We shall need a great mass of shipping in 1942, far more than we can build ourselves, if we are to maintain and augment our war effort in the West and in the East. . . .

The other day, President Roosevelt gave his opponent in the late Presidential Election a letter of introduction to me, and in it he wrote out a verse, in his own handwriting, from Longfellow, which he said "applies to you people as it does to us." Here is the verse:

> . . . Sail on, O Ship of State!
> Sail on, O Union, strong and great!
> Humanity with all its fears,

> With all the hopes of future years,
> Is hanging breathless on thy fate!

What is the answer that I shall give, in your name, to this great man, the thrice-chosen head of a nation of a hundred and thirty millions? Here is the answer which I will give to President Roosevelt: Put your confidence in us. Give us your faith and your blessing, and, under Providence, all will be well.

We shall not fail or falter; we shall not weaken or tire. Neither the sudden shock of battle, nor the long-drawn trails of vigilance and exertion will wear us down. Give us the tools, and we will finish the job.

INTRODUCTION TO DOCUMENT 5

When the United States entered the war after the attack on Pearl Harbor on December 7, 1941 the ideological stakes were clear. As presented to the public over the next four years, this was not simply a battle of great powers for military supremacy. America joined her allies in a death struggle, democracy versus autocracy, freedom versus slavery, universal equality versus blood-and-soil nationalism. Above all, our opponents embraced murderous faith in master-race ideologies that led to the Holocaust in Europe and the subjugation of non-Japanese people in Asia.

There was no U.S. equivalent to the Nazi extermination of Jews, Gypsies, gays, and others or the Japanese "Rape of Nanjing." But America's struggles with race did not disappear in wartime. The U.S. military remained rigidly segregated throughout the conflict. African-American journalists, activists, and even soldiers highlighted the hypocrisy of a Jim Crow army fighting for democracy. The black press exposed, for example, lynchings and beatings at Fort Bragg in North Carolina and Fort Benning in Georgia—much of the worst violence committed by military police. African-American soldiers were proud to participate in the war effort, but they were impatient that their efforts were usually limited to support roles, that their officers were mostly white southerners (whom the Army said "understood Negroes"), and that black troops were given very limited opportunities to rise in the ranks. Moreover, black soldiers were court martialed in disproportionate numbers and faced jail time and even executions far out of proportion to their numbers.

In 1944, a young black second lieutenant named Jack R. Robinson from Los Angeles was tried for insubordination at Camp Hood, Texas. Robinson was asked to move to the back of a bus per southern custom of deference and segregation, even though the Army disapproved of the practice. He refused, was arrested by military police, and was tried by court martial. The following testimonies differ about what happened on that day in July. Where do they agree and disagree, and what was at stake? What do you think happened?

5. THE COURT MARTIAL OF JACK R. ROBINSON, UNITED STATES ARMY (JULY 1944)

STATEMENT OF SECOND LIEUTENANT JACK R. ROBINSON, 0-103158 COMPANY B, 761ST TANK BATTALION, CAMP HOOD, TEXAS

. . . I got on the Camp Hood bus. I entered at the front of the bus and moved toward the rear and saw a colored girl sitting in a seat at the middle of the bus. I sat down beside the girl. . . . I sat down there and we rode approximately five or six blocks on the bus and the bus driver turns around and tells me to move to the rear which I did not do. He tells me that if I don't move to the rear he will make trouble for me when we get to the bus station, and I told him that was up to him. When we got to the bus station a lady got off the bus before I got off, and she tells me that she is going to prefer charges against me. That was a white lady. And I said that's all right, too, I don't care if she prefers charges against me. The bus driver asked me for my identification card. I refused to give it to him. He then went to the Dispatcher and told him something. What he told them I don't know. He then comes back and tells the people that this nigger is making trouble. I told the bus driver to stop fucking with me, so he gets the rest of the men around there and starts blowing his top and someone calls the MP's. . . . The only time I made any statement was when this fellow called me a nigger. I didn't have any loud nor boisterous conversation. That's the only profane language I used if you call it profane . . . I want to tell you right now sir, this private you got out there, he made a statement. The Private over in that room I told him that if he, a private, ever called me that name (a nigger) again I would break him [in two.] (The private referred to was later called to the MP Orderly Room and identified as being Pfc Ben W Mucklerath, 37061068, Company D, 149th Tng Bn, 90th Regt IRTC, Camp Hood, Texas).

STATEMENT OF PRIVATE FIRST CLASS BEN W. MUCKLERATH, 37061068, COMPANY D, 149TH TNG BN, 90TH REGT, IRTC, CAMP HOOD, TEXAS

I saw a white lady step off the bus and start into the Bus Station. A colored Lt. also got off the bus and was directing obscene language at her, he said "You better quit fuckin' with me." That's all I heard him say at the time. He said this in the presence of a large number of ladies and children, and it was plainly heard by those present. . . . When the white lady had first stepped off the bus and started toward the Bus Station, Lt. Robinson was approximately three paces behind her, following her, and he turned around and went back to the bus driver, and at that time I went into the Bus Station to call the MP's, but I heard him using some very obscene and vulgar language; I distinctly heard him say, "son-of-a-bitch," and some other words which I could not hear plainly. He was talking in a course, rough and harsh tone of voice and could be plainly heard by all the women and children and soldiers present. His conduct, generally, was very unbecoming to an officer and a gentleman. . . . I had not at any time called the Lt. a "nigger," and had not at any time spoken to nor said anything to the Lt.

STATEMENT OF MRS. ELIZABETH POITEVINT, CIVILIAN EMPLOYEE, PX #10, CAMP HOOD, TEXAS

On the 6th of July 1944, at approximately 10:00 p.m. I left PX #10 where I work and got the bus at Bus Stop #23, to go to the Central Bus Station. When we got on the bus a colored girl was there and got on the bus and sat down about middleways of the bus I was sitting about five seats back on the other side of the bus. A colored Second Lieutenant got on the bus there and sat down beside the colored girl. We were going up Battalion Avenue and stopped at another Bus Stop and some white women, most of them with their babies, got on the bus. The driver came back to the colored Lt. and said, "Lieutenant, will you move to the back of the bus so these people can sit down?" The colored Lt. said, "I certainly will not. I paid my fare and I don't intend to move out of this seat," and he said, "I'm going to sit right here, and driver, you go right back up to the front of this bus and sit down and drive this bus to wherever you're going, because I don't intend to move." . . . When we got to the Central Bus Station we all got off, and the driver asked the Lieutenant for his identification card, and the Lt. said, "I haven't done anything and I'm not going to show you my identification card, I'm going to get on another bus and go on." The driver said, "I want your identification card to turn you in," then I said to the driver, "If you want any witnesses as to what he has done to you, you can call on me, because I've heard everything he has said." Then the Lt. turned to me and said, "Listen here you dammed old woman, you have nothing to say about what's going on. I didn't want to get into this, they drafted me into this, and my money is just as good as a white man's." And I told him, I said, "Well, listen buddy, you ought to know where you should sit on a bus." I started on to the Bus Station and I asked the bus driver if he was going to report, and I told him that if he didn't report the colored Lieutenant that I was going to report him to the MP's, I had to wait on them during the day, but I didn't have to sit with them on the bus. . . .

STATEMENT OF MR. MILTON N. RENEGAR, BUS DRIVER, SOUTHWESTERN BUS COMPANY

I did not say anything to the colored Lt when he first sat down, until I got around to Bus Stop #18, and then I asked him, I said "Lt., if you don't mind, I have several ladies to pick up at this Stop and will have a load of them before I get back to the Central Bus Station, and would like for you to move back to the rear of the bus if you don't mind." When I asked him to move back to the rear he just sat there, and I asked him to move back there the second time. When I asked him the second time he

started cursing and the first thing he said was, "I'm not going to move a God dammed bit." I told him that I had a load of ladies to pick up and that I was sure they wouldn't want to ride mixed up like that, and told him I'd rather he would either move back to the rear or get off the bus, one of the two. He kept on cursing and saying that he wasn't going to get back, and I told him that he could either get back or he'd be sorry of it when I got to the Bus Station, or words to that effect. He kept saying something about it after I started up the bus, but I could not understand what he was saying. He continued to sit there with the colored girl and the girl did not say anything. . . . Everybody on the bus was mad about it. I had asked the Lt. in a nice way to move and he had refused. One of the ladies who was riding said, "I don't mind waiting on them all day, but when I get on the bus at night to go home, I'm not about to ride all mixed up with them. . . ."

STATEMENT OF MRS. VIRGINIA JONES

I was with Lt. Jack R. Robinson of the night of 6 July 1944. We left the colored officers club and caught a bus in front of the officers club. I got on the bus first and sat down, and Lt. Robinson got on and came and sat beside me. I sat in the fourth seat from the rear of the bus, which I have always considered the rear of the bus. The bus driver looked back at us, and then asked Lt. Robinson to move. Lt. Robinson told the bus driver to go on and drive the bus. The bus driver told Lt. Robinson to move again, and Lt. Robinson said, "I'm not moving." The bus driver stopped the bus, came back and balled his fist and said, "Will you move to the back?" Lt. Robinson said, "I'm not moving," so the bus driver stood there and glared a minute and said, "Well, just sit there until we get down to the bus station."

We got to the bus station and Lt. Robinson and I were the last two to leave the bus. The bus driver detained Lt. Robinson and demanded to see his pass. Lt. Robinson said, "My pass?," and the bus driver said, "Yes, I want to see your pass." Lt Robinson asked him what did he mean wanted to see his pass, and we then got off the bus. A woman walked up to Lt. Robinson and shook her finger in his face and said, "I'm going to report you because you had a right to move when he asked you to. . . ."

Then Lt. Robinson and I walked over to the Temple Bus Stop and we stood there for a few minutes and the MP's arrived. . . . He walked over to the MP's and just about that time this same woman walked up and started to accuse him of something. . . . The only thing Lt. Robinson said to this lady was "Go away and leave me alone,' and she walked away immediately. I did not hear him say anything vile nor vulgar at any time, nor did he raise his voice."[3]

INTRODUCTION TO DOCUMENTS 6 AND 7

Before the trial began, Robinson contacted Truman Gibson, an aide to Secretary of War Henry Stimson who was sympathetic to civil rights. Robinson suspected the reason the bus driver asked him to move back was because the woman he sat next to was very fair skinned—she looked white. He asked Gibson about contacting the NAACP or African-American newspapers, and though Robinson did not want to cause trouble for the Army, he strongly believed that he had been unfairly treated. Had Robinson not been a star college athlete in 1944, and had he not contacted Gibson, one has to wonder how his case would have turned out. A few years later, he became known to the public as Jackie Robinson, the man who integrated Major League Baseball.

In the United States, people of Japanese ancestry faced racial discrimination of a different sort. Asians had been coming to the West Coast in substantial numbers since after the Civil War, though the Chinese were banned by the Exclusion Act of 1882. Western agriculture demanded labor, and Japanese immigrants filled in some of the gap left by the excluded Chinese. Anti-Asian racism forced a slowdown in Japanese emigration with the 1907 "Gentleman's Agreement" between Japan and the United States, and it virtually ceased under Immigration Act of 1924. Anti-miscegenation laws assured that Japanese-American children would not marry native-born Americans. Thus, when Imperial Japan attacked the United States at Pearl Harbor in late 1941, few Japanese nationals had come to America in thirty years, so that two-thirds of West Coast Japanese were native English speakers and American citizens by birth.

Yet the surprise attack on the American fleet in Hawaii raised questions about their loyalty. Within weeks of American entry into the war, General John DeWitt—commanding general of the Western Defense Command—convinced President Roosevelt that Japanese Americans posed a dire threat to the security of the West Coast. In response, on February 19, 1942, Roosevelt authorized the War Department to evacuate almost 112,000 people of Japanese ancestry from the West Coast, mostly Americans, but now removed to internment camps in the interior west. The order was based upon the notion that persons of Japanese ancestry presented a clear and present threat to American security as potential saboteurs of the American war effort.

In his letter to General DeWitt, who was in charge of effecting the evacuation, Secretary of War Stimson asked him to

> not disturb, for the time being at least, Italian aliens and person of Italian lineage except where they are, in your judgment, undesirable or constitute a definite danger to the performance of your mission to defend the West Coast. I ask that you take this action in respect to Italians for the reason that I consider such persons to be potentially less dangerous, as a whole, than those of other enemy nationalities. Because of the size of the Italian

population and the number of troops and facilities which would have to be employed to deal with them, their inclusion in the general plan would greatly overtax our strength.[4]

Document 6 is a local evacuation order from Oakland, California, authored by General Dewitt, which informs Japanese Americans how to proceed. Document 7 is DeWitt's assessment of the entire operation one year later, after the most intense phase of panic regarding Japanese Americans had passed. In it, he argues why such a dramatic action was necessary.

6. EVACUATION ORDER

DEVELOPMENT AND EXECUTION OF EVACUATION PLAN 99

WESTERN DEFENSE COMMAND AND FOURTH ARMY WARTIME CIVIL CONTROL ADMINISTRATION

Presidio of San Francisco, California

INSTRUCTIONS
TO ALL PERSONS OF
JAPANESE
ANCESTRY
LIVING IN THE FOLLOWING AREA:

All of that portion of the County of Alameda, State of California, within that boundary beginning at the point at which the southerly limits of the City of Berkeley meet San Francisco Bay; thence easterly and following the southerly limits of said city to College Avenue; thence southerly on College Avenue to Broadway; thence southerly on Broadway to the southerly limits of the City of Oakland; thence following the limits of said city westerly and northerly, and following the shoreline of San Francisco Bay to the point of beginning.

Pursuant to the provisions of Civilian Exclusion Order No. 27, this Headquarters, dated April 30, 1942, all persons of Japanese ancestry, both alien and non-alien, will be evacuated from the above area by 12 o'clock noon, P.W.T., Thursday May 7, 1942.

No Japanese person living in the above area will be permitted to change residence after 12 o'clock noon, P.W.T., Thursday, April 30, 1942, without obtaining special permission from the representative of the Commanding General, Northern California Sector, at the Civil Control Station located at:

> 530 Eighteenth Street,
> Oakland, California.

Such permits will only be granted for the purpose of uniting members of a family, or in cases of grave emergency.

The Civil Control Station is equipped to assist the Japanese population affected by this evacuation in the following ways:

1. Give advice and instructions on the evacuation.
2. Provide services with respect to the management, leasing, sale, storage or other disposition of most kinds of property, such as real estate, business and professional equipment, household goods, boats, automobiles and livestock.
3. Provide temporary residence elsewhere for all Japanese in family groups.
4. Transport persons and a limited amount of clothing and equipment to their new residence.

100 JAPANESE EVACUATION FROM THE WEST COAST

THE FOLLOWING INSTRUCTIONS MUST BE OBSERVED:

1. A responsible member of each family, preferably the head of the family, or the person in whose name most of the property is held, and each individual living alone, will report to the Civil Control Station to receive further instructions. This must be done between 8:00 A. M. and 5:00 P. M. on Friday, May 1, 1942, or between 8:00 A. M. and 5:00 P. M. on Saturday, May 2, 1942.

2. Evacuees must carry with them on departure for the Assembly Center, the following property:
   (a) Bedding and linens (no mattress) for each member of the family;
   (b) Toilet articles for each member of the family;
   (c) Extra clothing for each member of the family;
   (d) Sufficient knives, forks, spoons, plates, bowls and cups for each member of the family;
   (e) Essential personal effects for each member of the family.

All items carried will be securely packaged, tied and plainly marked with the name of the owner and numbered in accordance with instructions obtained at the Civil Control Station. The size and number of packages is limited to that which can be carried by the individual or family group.

3. No pets of any kind will be permitted.

4. No personal items and no household goods will be shipped to the Assembly Center.

5. The United States Government through its agencies will provide for the storage at the sole risk of the owner of the more substantial household items, such as iceboxes, washing machines, pianos and other heavy furniture. Cooking utensils and other small items will be accepted for storage if crated, packed and plainly marked with the name and address of the owner. Only one name and address will be used by a given family.

6. Each family, and individual living alone will be furnished transportation to the Assembly Center or will be authorized to travel by private automobile in a supervised group. All instructions pertaining to the movement will be obtained at the Civil Control Station.

Go to the Civil Control Station between the hours of 8:00 A. M. and 5:00 P. M., Friday, May 1, 1942, or between the hours of 8:00 A. M. and 5:00 P. M., Saturday, May 2, 1942, to receive further instructions.

> J. L. DEWITT
> Lieutenant General, U. S. Army
> Commanding

April 30, 1942

See Civilian Exclusion Order No. 27.

Image 11.3: Evacuation Instructions, 1942

Source: Final Report. Japanese Evacuation from the West Coast 1942 (Washington, DC: Government Printing Office, 1943).

7. GENERAL DEWITT, FINAL REPORT ON THE EVACUATION OF JAPANESE (1943)

Headquarters Western Defense Command
and Fourth Army
Office of the Commanding General
Presidio of San Francisco, California
June 5, 1943

To: Chief of Staff, United States Army, War Department, Washington, D.C.

. . . The evacuation was impelled by military necessity. The security of the Pacific Coast continues to require the exclusion of Japanese from the area now prohibited to them and will so continue as long as that military necessity exists. The surprise attack at Pearl Harbor by the enemy crippled a major portion of the Pacific Fleet and exposed the West Coast to an attack which could not have been substantially impeded by defensive fleet operations. More than 115,000 persons of Japanese ancestry resided along the coast and were significantly concentrated near many highly sensitive installations essential to the war effort. Intelligence services records reflected the existence of hundreds of Japanese organizations in California, Washington, Oregon and Arizona which, prior to December 7, 1941, were actively engaged in advancing Japanese war aims. These records also disclosed that thousands of American-born Japanese had gone to Japan to receive their education and indoctrination there and had become rabidly pro-Japanese and then had returned to the United States. Emperor worshipping ceremonies were commonly held and millions of dollars had flowed into the Japanese imperial war chest from the contributions freely made by Japanese here. The continued presence of a large, unassimilated, tightly knit racial group, bound to an enemy nation by strong ties of race, culture, custom and religion along a frontier vulnerable to attack constituted a menace which had to be dealt with. Their loyalties were unknown and time was of the essence. The evident aspirations of the enemy emboldened by his recent successes made it worse than folly to have left any stone unturned in the building up of our defenses. It is better to have had this protection and not to have needed it than to have needed it and not to have had it—as we have learned to our sorrow.

. . . On February 14, 1942, I recommended to the War Department that the military security of the Pacific Coast required the establishment of broad civil control, anti-sabotage and counter-espionage measures, including the evacuation therefrom of all persons of Japanese ancestry. In recognition of this situation, the President issued Executive Order 9055 on February 19, 1942, authorizing the accomplishment of these and any other necessary security measures.

J. L. DeWitt, Lieutenant General,
U.S. Army, Commanding.[5]

INTRODUCTION TO DOCUMENTS 8, 9, AND 10

In 1943 noted photographer Ansel Adams traveled to the Manzanar Internment Camp in the high desert east of California's Sierra Nevada Mountains. These are just three of his views of the camp, where Japanese-Americans made now made their homes in an arid corner of the state.

8. BASEBALL GAME AT MANZANAR RELOCATION CENTER, CALIFORNIA (1943)

ANSEL ADAMS

Image 11.4: Ansel Adams, Baseball game at Manzanar Relocation Center, California

Baseball was a particularly favorite pastime at several of the Japanese American internment camps, with regular league schedules and organized teams.

Source: Courtesy Manzanar War Relocation Center Photographs. Library of Congress.

9. CATHOLIC CHURCH, MANZANAR RELOCATION CENTER, CALIFORNIA (1943)

ANSEL ADAMS

Image 11.5: Catholic Church, Manzanar (1943)

Japanese Americans quickly tried to establish some sense of normalcy in the internment camps, including freedom of worship. Here barracks were transformed into a Catholic Church.

Source: Courtesy Manzanar War Relocation Center Photographs, Library of Congress.

10. ROY TAKENO READING PAPER, MANZANAR RELOCATION CENTER, CALIFORNIA (1943)

ANSEL ADAMS

Image 11.6: Roy Takeno Reading Paper (1943)

These photographs highlight the way Japanese Americans internees sought to create dignity and stability even when their rights had been suspended. Note that Adams highlights freedom of press and religion in his images.

Source: Courtesy Manzanar War Relocation Center Photographs, Library of Congress.

INTRODUCTION TO DOCUMENTS 11 AND 12

The order interning Japanese Americans was immediately challenged in the courts. Document 11 is the Supreme Court's majority opinion in *Hirabayashi v. United States* (1943), the first case that tested the constitutionality of the order. In this case, an American citizen of Japanese ancestry refused to register for evacuation. He also deliberately violated a curfew that ordered Japanese and Japanese Americans to stay within their homes after 8:00 PM every night. The legal question, then, centered on the president's Executive Order 9066 and Congress's ratification of that order mandating the internment camps. Document 11 is from the majority opinion, written by Chief Justice Harlan Stone. Associate Justice Frank Murphy concurred with the majority, but in Document 12 he expressed his fear that the decision set a dangerous precedent. In these two opinions, how did the court justify the federal evacuation order? Given that Justice Murphy found some elements of the order so troubling, why did he concur with the majority in upholding its constitutionality? By the next year, incidentally, Justice Murphy dissented in the *Korematsu* decision, another court case in which the majority upheld the constitutionality of Executive Order 9066.

11. OPINION OF THE COURT
HIRABAYASHI V. UNITED STATES (1943)

CHIEF JUSTICE HARLAN STONE

. . . The war power of the national government is "the power to wage war successfully." . . . It extends to every matter and activity so related to war as substantially to affect its conduct and progress. The power is not restricted to the winning of victories in the field and the repulse of enemy forces. It embraces every phase of the national defense, including the protection of war materials and the members of the armed forces from injury and from the dangers which attend the rise, prosecution and progress of war. . . . Since the Constitution commits to the Executive and to Congress the exercise of the war power in all the vicissitudes and conditions of warfare, it has necessarily given them wide scope for the exercise of judgment and discretion in determining the nature and extent of the threatened injury or danger and in the selection of the means for resisting it. . . . Where, as they did here, the conditions call for the exercise of

judgment and discretion and for the choice of means by those branches of the Government on which the Constitution has placed the responsibility of warmaking, it is not for any court to sit in review of the wisdom of their action or substitute its judgment for theirs.

The actions taken must be appraised in the light of the conditions with which the President and Congress were confronted in the early months of 1942, many of which, since disclosed, were then peculiarly within the knowledge of the military authorities. On December 7, 1941, the Japanese air forces had attacked the United States Naval Base at Pearl Harbor without warning, at the very hour when Japanese diplomatic representatives were conducting negotiations with our State Department ostensibly for the peaceful settlement of differences between the two countries. Simultaneously or nearly so, the Japanese attacked Malaysia, Hong

Kong, the Philippines, and Wake and Midway Islands. On the following day their army invaded Thailand. Shortly afterwards they sank two British battleships. On December 13th, Guam was taken. On December 24th and 25th they captured Wake Island and occupied Hong Kong. On January 2, 1942, Manila fell, and on February 10th Singapore, Britain's great naval base in the East, was taken. On February 27th the battle of the Java Sea resulted in a disastrous naval defeat to the United Nations. By the 9th of March Japanese forces had established control over the Netherlands East Indies; Rangoon and Burma were occupied; Bataan and Corregidor were under attack.

Although the results of the attack on Pearl Harbor were not fully disclosed until much later, it was known that the damage was extensive, and that the Japanese by their successes had gained a naval superiority over our forces in the Pacific which might enable them to seize Pearl Harbor, our largest naval base and the last stronghold of defense lying between Japan and the west coast. That reasonably prudent men charged with the responsibility of our national defense had ample ground for concluding that they must face the danger of invasion, take measures against it, and in making the choice of measures consider our internal situation, cannot be doubted. . . .

In the critical days of March 1942, the danger to our war production by sabotage and espionage in this area seems obvious. . . . At a time of threatened Japanese attack upon this country, the nature of our inhabitants' attachments to the Japanese enemy was consequently a matter of grave concern. Of the 126,000 persons of Japanese descent in the United States, citizens and non-citizens, approximately 112,000 resided in California, Oregon and Washington at the time of the adoption of the military regulations. Of these approximately two-thirds are citizens because [they were] born in the United States. Not only did the great majority of such persons reside within the Pacific Coast states but they were concentrated in or near three of the large cities, Seattle, Portland and Los Angeles, all in Military Area No. 1.

There is support for the view that social, economic and political conditions which have prevailed since the close of the last century, when the Japanese began to come to this country in substantial numbers, have intensified their solidarity and have in large measure prevented their assimilation as an integral part of the white population. In addition, large numbers of children of Japanese parentage are sent to Japanese language schools outside the regular hours of public schools in the locality. Some of these schools are generally believed to be sources of Japanese nationalistic propaganda, cultivating allegiance to Japan. Considerable numbers, estimated to be approximately 10,000, of American-born children of Japanese parentage have been sent to Japan for all or a part of their education.

Congress and the Executive, including the military commander, could have attributed special significance, in its bearing on the loyalties of persons of Japanese descent, to the maintenance by Japan of its system of dual citizenship. Children born in the United States of Japanese alien parents, and especially those children born before December 1, 1924, are under many circumstances deemed, by Japanese law, to be citizens of Japan. No official census of those whom Japan regards as having thus retained Japanese citizenship is available, but there is ground for the belief that the number is large. . . .

As a result of all these conditions affecting the life of the Japanese, both aliens and citizens, in the Pacific Coast areas, there has been relatively little social intercourse between them and the white population. The restrictions, both practical and legal, affecting the privileges and opportunities afforded to persons of Japanese extraction residing in the United States, have been sources of irritation and may well have tended to increase their isolation, and in many instances their attachments to Japan and its institutions.

Viewing these data in all their aspects, Congress and the Executive could reasonably have concluded that these conditions have encouraged the continued attachment of members of this group to Japan and Japanese institutions. These are only some of the many considerations which those charged with the responsibility for the national defense could take into account in determining the nature and extent of the danger of espionage and sabotage, in the event of invasion or air raid attack. The extent of that danger could be definitely known only after the event and after it was too late to meet it. Whatever views we may entertain regarding the loyalty to this country of the citizens of Japanese ancestry, we cannot reject as unfounded the judgment of the military authorities and of Congress that there were disloyal members of that population, whose number and strength could not be precisely and quickly ascertained. We cannot say that the war-making branches of the Government did not have ground for believing that in a critical hour such persons could not readily be isolated and separately dealt with, and constituted a menace to the national defense and safety, which demanded that prompt and adequate measures be taken to guard against it.

Appellant does not deny that, given the danger, a curfew was an appropriate measure against sabotage. It is an obvious protection against the perpetration of sabotage most readily committed during the hours of darkness. If it was an appropriate exercise of the war power its validity is not impaired because it has restricted the citizen's liberty. Like every military control of the population of a dangerous zone in war time, it necessarily involves some infringement of individual liberty, just as does the police establishment of fire lines during a fire, or the confinement of people to their houses during an air raid alarm—neither of which could be thought to be an infringement of constitutional right. Like them, the validity of the restraints of the curfew order depends on all the conditions which obtain at the time the curfew is imposed and which support the order imposing it.

But appellant insists that the exercise of the power is inappropriate and unconstitutional because it discriminates against citizens of Japanese ancestry, in violation of the Fifth Amendment. The Fifth Amendment contains no equal protection clause and it restrains only such discriminatory legislation by Congress as amounts to a denial of due process. . . .

Distinctions between citizens solely because of their ancestry are by their very nature odious to a free people whose institutions are founded upon the doctrine of equality. For that reason, legislative classification or discrimination based on race alone has often been held to be a denial of equal protection. . . . We may assume that these considerations would be controlling here were it not for the fact that the danger of espionage and sabotage, in time of war and of threatened invasion, calls upon the military authorities to scrutinize every relevant fact bearing on the loyalty of populations in the danger areas. Because racial discriminations are in most circumstances irrelevant and therefore prohibited, it by no means follows that, in dealing with the perils of war, Congress and the Executive are wholly precluded from taking into account those facts and circumstances which are relevant to measures for our national defense and for the successful prosecution of the war, and which may in fact place citizens of one ancestry in a different category from others.[6]

12. CONCURRING OPINION, *HIRABAYASHI V. UNITED STATES* (1943)

JUSTICE FRANK MURPHY

It is not to be doubted that the action taken by the military commander in pursuance of the authority upon him was taken in complete good faith and in the firm conviction that it was required by considerations of public safety and military security. Neither is it doubted that the Congress and the Executive, working together, may generally employ such measures as are necessary and appropriate to provide for the common defense and to wage war "with all the force necessary to make it effective. This includes authority to exercise measures of control over persons and property which would not in all cases be permissible in normal times.

It does not follow, however, that the broad guaranties of the Bill of Rights and other provisions of the Constitution protecting essential liberties are suspended by the mere existence of a state of war. It has been frequently stated and recognized by this Court that the war power, like the other great substantive powers of government, is subject to the limitations of the Constitution. We give great deference to the judgment of the Congress and of the military authorities as to what is necessary in the effective prosecution of the war, but we can never forget that there are constitutional boundaries which it is our duty to uphold. It would not be supposed, for instance, that public elections could be suspended or that the prerogatives of the courts could be set aside, or that persons not charged with offenses against the law of war could be deprived of due process of law and the benefits of trial by jury, in the absence of a valid declaration of martial law.

Distinctions based on color and ancestry are utterly inconsistent with our traditions and ideals. They are at variance with the principles for which we are now waging war. We cannot close our eyes to the fact that, for centuries, the Old World has been torn by racial and religious conflicts and has suffered the worst kind of anguish because of inequality of treatment for different groups. There was one law for one and a different law for another. Nothing is written more firmly into our law than the compact of the Plymouth voyagers to have just and equal laws. To say that any group cannot be assimilated is to admit that the great American experiment has failed, that our way of life has failed when confronted with the normal attachment of certain groups to the land of their forefathers. . . .

Today is the first time, so far as I am aware, that we have sustained a substantial restriction of the personal liberty of citizens of the United States based upon the accident of race or ancestry. Under the curfew order here challenged, no less than 70,000 American citizens have been placed under a special ban and deprived of their liberty because of their particular racial inheritance. In this sense, it bears a melancholy resemblance to the treatment accorded to members of the Jewish race in Germany and in other parts of Europe. The result is the creation in this country of two classes of citizens for the purposes of a critical and perilous hour—to sanction discrimination between groups of United States citizens on the basis of ancestry. In my opinion, this goes to the very brink of constitutional power.

. . . In view, however, of the critical military situation which prevailed on the Pacific Coast area in the spring of 1942 and the urgent necessity of taking prompt and effective action to secure defense installations and military operations against the risk of sabotage and espionage, the military authorities should not be required to conform to standards of regulatory action appropriate to normal times. . . . Accordingly, I think that the military arm, confronted with the peril of imminent enemy attack and acting under the authority conferred by the Congress, made and allowable judgment at the time the curfew restriction was imposed. Whether such a restriction is valid today is another matter.[7]

INTRODUCTION TO DOCUMENT 13

By early 1943, there were already Japanese Americans serving in the military, but they had been limited to noncombat areas after the attack on Pearl Harbor. This was true of the 100th Infantry Battalion, which was primarily made up of members of the Hawaii Army National Guard. These men were determined to demonstrate their loyalty to the nation in the wake of Pearl Harbor. Their bravery persuaded the U.S. Army to recruit more Japanese Americans, most of whom were taken from the internment camps. On January 22, 1943, the War Department activated a battalion of Japanese-American citizens with President Roosevelt's full support, arguing that "Americanism is a matter of the mind and heart; Americanism is not, and never was, a matter of race or ancestry." The result was the 442nd Combat

Team, which, combined with the 100th Infantry Battalion, grew to 18,000 soldiers and became the most decorated unit in U.S. military history. Their bravery fighting through Italy, France, and Germany in 1944 and 1945 became legendary, and is evidenced in Document 13, a letter of commendation from Chief of Staff of the U.S. Army Dwight Eisenhower at the end of the war.

13. "THE FINEST TRADITIONS OF THE ARMED FORCES" (1946)

DWIGHT D. EISENHOWER

10 APRIL 1946

The 442d Regimental Combat Team . . . is cited for outstanding accomplishment for the period 5 to 14 April 1945 in the vicinity of Serravezza, Carrara, and Fosdinovo, Italy. When the 92d Infantry Division with the 442d Regimental Combat Team attached was ordered to open the Fifth Army offensive by executing a diversionary attack on the Ligurian Coast of Italy, the combat team was ordered to make the main effort of the attack. It was done by executing a daring and skillful flanking attack on the positions which formed the western anchor of the formidable Gothic Line. In 4 days, the attack destroyed positions which had withstood the efforts of friendly troops for 5 months. This was accomplished in the face of skilled enemy forces nearly equal in strength to the attacking forces and who had at least 5 months in which to improve their position. The 442d Regimental Combat Team drove forward, despite heavy casualties. Allowing the enemy no time for rest or reorganization, the combat team liberated the city of Carrara, seized the heights beyond, and opened the way for further advances on the way to the key road center and port of Le Spezia and to Genoa. It accomplished the mission of creating a diversion along the Ligurian Coast, which served as a feint for the subsequent breakthrough of the Fifth Army forces into Bologna and the Po Valley. The successful accomplishment of this mission turned a diversionary action into a full scale and victorious offensive, which played an important part in the final destruction of the German armies in Italy. The gallantry and esprit de corps displayed by the officers and men of the 44sd Regimental Combat Team in bitter action against a formidable enemy exemplify the finest traditions of the armed forces of the United States.

By order of the Secretary of War:
Dwight D. Eisenhower[8]

POSTSCRIPT

The military service of the 442nd Combat Team is rightly celebrated not just in the United States but also in France, where Japanese-American soldiers are still remembered for liberating Bruyeres on their way toward Germany. Daniel Inouye, a soldier in the 442nd, went on to become one of the longest serving U.S. senators in American history until his death in 2012. Such bravery and honorable service contrasted sharply with the shame of internment. Assessing the evacuation in 1943, Secretary of War Henry Stimson commended Japanese Americans for their response to the order, acknowledging that it was "unfortunate . . . to require the same treatment for all persons of Japanese ancestry, regardless of their individual loyalty to the United States. But in emergencies, where the safety of the Nation is involved, consideration of the rights of individuals must be subordinated to the common security."

In 1988 President Ronald Reagan signed the Civil Liberties Act into law, providing a presidential apology and payment of $20,000 to those Japanese Americans who were interned as a result of Executive Order 9066. In 2011, Acting Solicitor General Neal Katyal informed the public of an important finding: government lawyers defending Executive Order 9066 at the time of the *Hirabayashi* and *Korematsu* court challenges had withheld evidence from the Office of Naval Intelligence that only a small number of Japanese Americans posed a potential security threat, and many of these individuals were already known to the government. Such information would have undermined the government's case that it was impossible to separate loyal from disloyal Japanese Americans.

QUESTIONS

1. How would you describe Norman Rockwell's paintings of Roosevelt's Four Freedoms? Why do you think they resonated with Americans during the war?
2. What were Lindbergh's objections to American aid to Britain? Would you describe him as an isolationist?
3. Why do we often think of World War II as the "Good War" and those who fought it as the "Greatest Generation"?
4. How did citizens reconcile the idealism of the Four Freedoms with tensions on the home front, such as Executive Order 9066 and its effects?
5. What were the arguments for and against Japanese internment? Were they persuasive?
6. What do the *Hirabayashi v. United States* opinions reveal about the home front in World War II?

ADDITIONAL READING

For the war as the fundamental experience of the generation, see Studs Terkel's oral history, *The Good War* (1984), and Tom Brokaw, *The Greatest Generation* (1996). On the global conflict, see John Keegan, *The Second World War* (2005). On Franklin Roosevelt's leadership during the war, see James MacGregor Burns, *Roosevelt: The Soldier of Freedom* (1970), and Robert Dallek, *Franklin D. Roosevelt and American Foreign Policy, 1932–1945* (1979). The home front and the battlefront are covered in David M. Kennedy, *Freedom from Fear: The American People in Depression and War, 1929–1945* (1999). Laura Claridge, *Norman Rockwell: A Life* (2001) presents a good case for viewing Rockwell as an important and original American artist. Stuart Murray and James McCabe, *Norman Rockwell's Four Freedoms: Images That Inspire a Nation* (1993) provides important background for the paintings. On Japanese internment, see Peter Irons, *Justice at War: The Story of the Japanese Internment Cases* (1983); Dorothea Lange, Linda Gordon, and Gary Okihiro, *Impounded: Dorothea Lange and the Censored Images of Japanese American Internment* (2006); and Lawson Fusao Inada, *Only What We Could Carry: The Japanese American Internment Experience* (2000). The service of Japanese Americans is covered in Orville C. Shirey, *Americans: The Story of the 442d Combat Team* (1946). African Americans during the war are examined in Neil Wynn, *The Afro-American and the Second World War* (1976), and Phillip McGuire, *Taps for a Jim Crow Army: Letters from Black Soldiers in World War II* (1993). On Jackie Robinson's life and contributions, see Jules Tygiel, *Baseball's Great Experiment: Jackie Robinson and His Legacy* (1983), and Arnold Rampersad, *Jackie Robinson: A Biography* (1997). Mexican Americans during the war, especially in Los Angeles, are studied in Mauricio Mazon, *The Zoot-Suit Riots* (1988); Eduardo Obregon Pagan, *Murder at the Sleepy Lagoon: Zoot Suits, Race, and Riot in Wartime L.A.* (2006); and Elizabeth Escobedo, *From Coveralls to Zoot Suits: The Lives of Mexican American Women on the World War II Home Front* (2013).

ENDNOTES

1. *Congressional Record,* 1941, v.87, part 1.
2. Hearings Before the Committee on Foreign Relations. United States Senate. Seventy-Seventh Congress (Washington, D.C.: Government Printing Office, 1941), pp. 490–492.
3. Testimony from Box 16, Folder 19, Jackie Robinson Collection, NAACP Collection, Library of Congress.
4. *Final Report. Japanese Evacuation from the West Coast 1942* (Washington, D.C.: Government Printing Office, 1943), pp. 25–26.
5. Ibid., pp. vii–viii.
6. *Hirabayashi v. United States,* 320 U.S. 81 (1943).
7. Ibid.
8. War Department General Orders 34, 10 April 1946, as amended by War Department General Orders 106, 20 September 1946. U.S. Army Center of Military History.

CHAPTER 12

BATTLING COMMUNISM AT HOME

HISTORICAL CONTEXT

What is it exactly that we do as historians? We search through the primary sources of the past—letters, diaries, newspapers, government documents, business records, and so forth—looking for patterns and trends, trying to give order to a chaotic jumble of events and thoughts. And then we construct stories. We do not write fiction, but neither do we tell the whole truth, for the absolute truth, the capital "T" truth, is unknowable and perhaps even an illusion itself. In an attempt to understand and organize the past, we use broad generalities to denote the temper or preoccupations of an era.

Look at the organization of the earlier chapters of this book. There are separate sections on the eras of Reconstruction, the Progressive Era, World War I, the 1920s, the Great Depression, and World War II. The implication is that, during the Progressive Era, for example, notions of progress and the improvement of life consumed America. But we know that not all people were involved in progressive crusades—perhaps only the smallest minority was—and that for some people, such as African Americans and many immigrants, the very idea of the Progressive Era was a cruel irony. Nevertheless, textbooks and lectures on America in the early twentieth century usually stress progressivism as the grand organizing principle in part because prominent people during that era sought fundamental changes and governments at all levels responded with major new legislation. "Progressivism" captures these changes but if we focus on them alone, we miss much that was going on during these years, including some very unprogressive trends.

The Cold War forms a similar organizing principle for the period after World War II. On one level, the rivalry between the United States and the Soviet Union—or between West and East or capitalism and communism—was quite real. The foreign policies of both countries emphasized some form of expanded spheres of influence, whether economic or military or both, and the two world powers generally opposed each other on crucial issues. How and why this rivalry developed is still debated by historians. After all, the two countries had been allies between 1941 and 1945 in the war against Nazi Germany. How had allies become opponents within months of the end of World War II without an overtly hostile act by either side?

The answer is complex. The rivalry began with the October 1917 revolution in Russia. Although U.S. officials had favored the liberal revolution earlier that year, a revolution that had overthrown Czar Nicholas and installed a moderate republican government, they did not support the October revolutionaries led by Vladimir Ilyich Lenin, a communist who opposed Russia's participation in World War I. Lenin and his Bolshevik supporters ended Russia's experiment with democracy and republicanism, pulled their country out of the war, and established the Soviet Union. American leaders reacted by briefly sending an invading army to overthrow the Bolsheviks. The U.S. government also supported a propaganda campaign that placed the Soviet Union in the worst possible light, emphasizing the murderousness of the new regime, the hypocrisy of the leaders, and the failure of their ideas.

During the 1920s, the U.S. government tried to ignore the USSR as much as possible. Occasionally a popular novelist would criticize the Soviets, or a left-leaning idealist would praise Lenin and the Russians, but there was little intellectual or financial commerce between the countries. That changed in November of 1933, sixteen years after the establishment of the communist state, when the Franklin Roosevelt administration officially recognized and established diplomatic relations with the Soviet Union. Mired in the Great Depression, Roosevelt in part hoped that the recognition of the USSR would open new markets for American products, especially since the Russian economy seemed to be outperforming the West. The dream of the great Russian market proved largely chimerical. George F. Kennan, America's preeminent authority on the Soviet Union, was skeptical of the relationship from the beginning. He wrote in his memoirs thirty years after Roosevelt renewed diplomatic ties, "Never—neither then nor at any later date—did I consider the Soviet Union a fit ally or associate, actual or potential, for this country."[1]

Some Americans, however, began to regard the Soviet Union in a new light during the 1930s. Faced with economic hardships at home and the growing threat of Nazi Germany in Europe, many Americans, especially those on the political left, believed that the Soviet Union offered the best solution for both problems. Communism appeared more humane than capitalism during the Depression, and collective security seemed more effective than isolationism. Yet other Americans, probably most, continued to view the Soviets as an enemy that would subvert Christianity, democracy, and capitalism, all that they believed was decent in the world. They pointed to two events as keys to Soviet behavior. The first was a series of purges conducted by Soviet premier Joseph Stalin. From his first years in office in the mid-1920s, Stalin had demonstrated a deep sense of suspicion, even paranoia; he distrusted his own military leaders and feared betrayal by government officials. His solution was the ruthless elimination of all suspected enemies. The full extent of Stalin's terror has only emerged in recent years, but it has long been clear that millions died. The purges made Americans question Stalin's methods and the morality of his regime. The questioning turned to outright hatred after the announcement of the German–Russian Nonaggression Pact in late August 1939. After opposing the Nazis throughout most of the 1930s, Stalin cynically ignored his own expressed beliefs and entered into an agreement with Hitler. Making matters worse, in early September the Soviet Union joined Germany in invading and dividing Poland. For most Americans, the purges and the Nonaggression Pact stripped the Soviet Union of its thin veneer of idealism and showed it to be a ruthless, cynical totalitarian state.

But morality is often an inconvenient basis for foreign policy, and in 1941, America's official position with the Soviet Union abruptly reversed. First, Hitler violated the Nonaggression Pact and invaded the Soviet Union. Then—after the Japanese attacked American forces at Pearl Harbor—Germany declared war on the United States. Suddenly the United States and the Soviet Union were allies, partners in an odd marriage of convenience in which neither country really liked or trusted the other. But until Germany and Japan were defeated, it was a marriage in which there could be no divorce.

During World War II, American opinion makers gave Joseph Stalin and the Soviet Union a facelift. Reporters dubbed Stalin "Uncle Joe" and portrayed him as a kindly, if stern, father figure, the sort of patriarch who always had the best interests of the family in mind. In the movie *Mission to Moscow,* Hollywood characterized him as a thoughtful, pipe-smoking, and farsighted political leader concerned above all with collective security and the well-being of his people. Other World War II films—*Three Russian Girls, Song of Russia, Boys from Stalingrad, The North Star,* and *Days of Glory*—presented similar views of Stalin. "War has put Hollywood's traditional conception of the Moscovites through the wringer," noted a 1942 *Variety* columnist, "and they have come out shaved, washed, sober, good to their families, Rotarians, brother Elks, and 33rd Degree Masons." In short, popular culture reinforced official political culture. This was no coincidence, of course; Hollywood was closely monitored and advised by the Office of War Information.

After the end of the war, relations between the United States and the Soviet Union chilled rapidly. Disputes over the fates of Poland and Eastern Europe, the partition of Germany, control over atomic weapons, and other issues divided the two countries, leading to a war of rhetoric and a mood of suspicion. In February 1946, Stalin warned Soviet citizens that there could never be a lasting peace with the capitalistic West, suggesting that economic sacrifices, and even war, lay ahead. Supreme Court Justice William O. Douglas called the speech "the declaration of World War III." And so it went—tough talk on one side resulted in equally strident language on the other, difficult issues assumed insurmountable proportions, and the gulf between the two world superpowers widened.

The result was the Cold War, the central fact of American foreign policy between the end of World War II in 1945 and the fall of the communist government in the Soviet Union in 1991. Through a series of flash points ranging from Greece, Turkey, and Berlin to Korea, Vietnam, and Cuba, the two sides jockeyed for advantage in a deadly, global game of chess. Without actually ever going to war against each other, they were never fully at peace. To each, the other was an implacable enemy bent on world domination. Moreover, each side viewed the other as an ideological enemy—one was the exponent of capitalism, liberal democracy, and religious liberty, and the other of communism, social equality, and freedom from religious dogma.

The Cold War dominated and defined American life. It became the organizing principle of our popular culture, which boiled down to a series of "us" against "them" confrontations. Hollywood parlayed the theme into successful movies, from such "B" films as *I Was a Communist for the FBI, My Son John,* and *Big Jim McLain* to acclaimed works like *Fail Safe, On the Beach,* and *Dr. Strangelove.* From John Wayne's westerns to James Bond's action adventures, the Cold War helped to define the plots. Popular writers and television produc-ers also capitalized on the Cold War. John Le Carre, William F. Buckley Jr., and Tom Clancy wrote bestsellers that revolved around the Cold War, and television shows such as *The Man from U.N.C.L.E.* and *I Spy* used the Cold War to sell consumer products. Even in interna-tional sporting events, the Cold War gave winning and losing monumental importance.

The following documents helped define and portray the Soviet Union for the American people in the earliest years of the Cold War. As you read them consider the authorship and the underlying agenda. How did they contribute to the construction of a Cold War mental-ity? How did they reinforce or call into question the dominant Cold War paradigm? How did they give shape and meaning to the lives of millions of Americans?

INTRODUCTION TO DOCUMENT 1

On March 12, 1947, President Harry Truman addressed a joint session of Congress in an attempt to win approval for a defense aid package for Greece and Turkey, whose governments were em-battled against armed dissidents. One Republican Senator told Truman that he would have to "scare the hell out of the American people" to get Congress to appropriate the money. Consider how Truman tried to achieve that end. How did he characterize the Cold War between East and West, communism and capitalism? How did his language enflame the nature of the struggle? The President's ideas articulated here came to be called the "Truman Doctrine." It asserted America's willingness to send armed forces wherever "communist subversion" threatened. Compare the values articulated here by Truman with those of President Roosevelt—his predecessor—in January 1941 (Chapter 11, Document 1). Note that while the earlier speech focused on the threat of fascism, Truman emphasized the threat of communism with equal intensity.

1. THE TRUMAN DOCTRINE (MARCH 12, 1947)

PRESIDENT HARRY TRUMAN

The gravity of the situation which confronts the world today necessitates my appearance before a joint session of the Congress. The foreign policy and the national security of this country are involved.

One aspect of the present situation, which I wish to present to you at this time for your consideration and decision, concerns Greece and Turkey.

The United States has received from the Greek Government an urgent appeal for financial and eco-nomic assistance. . . .

The very existence of the Greek state is today threatened by the terrorist activities of several thou-sand armed men, led by communists, who defy the

Government's authority at a number of points, particularly along the northern boundaries. . . .

Greece must have assistance if it is to become a self-supporting and self-respecting democracy. The United States must supply this assistance. We have already extended to Greece certain types of relief and economic aid but these are inadequate. There is no other country to which democratic Greece can turn. No other nation is willing and able to provide the necessary support for a democratic Greek Government.

The British Government, which has been helping Greece, can give no further financial or economic aid after March 31. Great Britain finds itself under the necessity of reducing or liquidating its commitments in several parts of the world, including Greece. . . .

Greece's neighbor, Turkey, also deserves our attention. The future of Turkey as an independent and economically sound state is clearly no less important to the freedom-loving peoples of the world than the future of Greece. . . .

As in the case of Greece, if Turkey is to have the assistance it needs, the United States must supply it. We are the only country able to provide that help.

I am fully aware of the broad implications involved if the United States extends assistance to Greece and Turkey, and I shall discuss these implications with you at this time.

One of the primary objectives of the foreign policy of the United States is the creation of conditions in which we and other nations will be able to work out a way of life free from coercion. This was a fundamental issue in the war with Germany and Japan. Our victory was won over countries which sought to impose their will, and their way of life, upon other nations.

To ensure the peaceful development of nations, free from coercion, the United States has taken a leading part in establishing the United Nations. The United Nations is designed to make possible lasting freedom and independence for all its members. We shall not realize our objectives, however, unless we are willing to help free peoples to maintain their free institutions and their national integrity against aggressive movements that seek to impose on them totalitarian regimes. This is no more than a frank recognition that totalitarian regimes imposed on free peoples, by direct or indirect aggression, undermine the foundations of international peace and hence the security of the United States.

The peoples of a number of countries of the world have recently had totalitarian regimes forced upon them against their will. The Government of the United States has made frequent protests against coercion and intimidation, in violation of the Yalta Agreement, in Poland, Rumania and Bulgaria. I must also state that in a number of other countries there have been similar developments.

At the present moment in world history nearly every nation must choose between alternative ways of life. The choice is too often not a free one.

One way of life is based upon the will of the majority, and is distinguished by free institutions, representative government, free elections, guarantees of individual liberty, freedom of speech and religion, and freedom from political oppression.

The second way of life is based upon the will of the minority forcibly imposed upon the majority. It relies upon terror and oppression, a controlled press and radio, fixed elections, and the suppression of personal freedoms.

I believe that it must be the policy of the United States to support free peoples who are resisting attempted subjugation by armed minorities or by outside pressures.

I believe that we must assist free peoples to work out their own destinies in their own way. . . .

The seeds of totalitarian regimes are nurtured by misery and want. They spread and grow in the evil soil of poverty and strife. They reach their full growth when the hope of a people for a better life has died. We must keep that hope alive. The free peoples of the world look to us for support in maintaining their freedoms.

If we falter in our leadership, we may endanger the peace of the world—and we shall surely endanger the welfare of this nation.

Great responsibilities have been placed upon us by the swift movement of events. I am confident that the Congress will face these responsibilities squarely.

The onset of the Cold War began even before the end of World War II, both inside and outside Washington, D.C. In 1944 conservative members of the film industry—concerned about the influence of communism in Hollywood—formed the Motion Picture Alliance for the Preservation of American Ideals (MPA). The MPA actively fought what it considered subversive and anti-American messages in screenwriting and film production. Members of the Alliance argued that Hollywood, with the federal government's assistance, dwelled on the dangers of fascism to the exclusion of the communist menace. They worried by the end of World War II that that Hollywood's producers and executives were naïve at best about the threat of communist propaganda. The MPA issued a series of explicit recommendations to shape the content of the American film in 1947. A portion of this "Screen Guide for Americans" is reproduced in Document 2, in which the MPA warns that communists regularly insinuated into movies messages that might easily go unnoticed but that powerfully influenced audiences.

Among the authors of the "Screen Guide" was Ayn Rand, a Russian émigré who as a screenwriter, novelist, and nonfiction writer became a tireless advocate for the free enterprise system against what she saw as the omnipresent threat of collectivism, particularly communism. The "Screen Guide" became a tool in the subsequent House Committee on Un-American Activities (HUAC) investigations of Hollywood, as well as the FBI's work in policing the film industry. As you read the guide, ask yourself what assumptions it makes about American film makers and movie goers, about propaganda, and art. Why do the authors worry so much about the vulnerability of America to communist subversion?

2. THE SCREEN GUIDE FOR AMERICANS (1947)

THE MOTION PICTURE ALLIANCE FOR THE PRESERVATION OF AMERICAN IDEALS

The influence of Communists in Hollywood is due, not to their own power, but to the unthinking carelessness of those who profess to oppose them. Red propaganda has been put over in some films produced by innocent men, often by loyal Americans who deplore the spread of Communism throughout the world and wonder why it is spreading.

If you wish to protect your pictures from being used for Communistic purposes, the first thing to do is to drop the delusion that political propaganda consists only of political slogans.

Politics is not a separate field in itself. Political ideas do not come out of thin air. They are the result of the **moral premises** which men have accepted.

Whatever people believe to be the good, right and proper human actions—**that** will determine their political opinions. . . .

The purpose of the Communists in Hollywood is **not** the production of political movies openly advocating Communism. Their purpose is to **corrupt our moral premises by corrupting non-political movies**—by introducing small, casual bits of propaganda into innocent stores—thus making people absorb the basic premises of Collectivism **by indirection and implication.**

We present below a list of the more common devices used to turn non-political pictures into carriers of political propaganda. It is a guide list for all those who do not wish to help advance the cause of Communism.

1. DON'T TAKE POLITICS LIGHTLY
2. DON'T SMEAR THE FREE ENTERPRISE SYSTEM

... **Don't** attack individual rights, individual freedom, private action, private initiative, and private property. These things are essential parts of the Free Enterprise System, without which it cannot exist.

Don't preach the superiority of public ownership as such over private ownership. **Don't** preach or imply that all publicly-owned projects are noble, humanitarian undertakings by grace of the mere fact that they are publicly-owned—while preaching, at the same time, that private property or the defense of private property rights is the expression of some sort of vicious greed, of anti-social selfishness or evil.

3. DON'T SMEAR INDUSTRIALISTS

... all too often industrialists, bankers, and businessmen are presented on the screen as villains, crooks, chiselers or exploiters. ... A constant stream of such pictures becomes pernicious political propaganda: It creates hatred for all businessmen in the mind of the audience, and makes people receptive to the cause of Communism. ...

4. DON'T SMEAR WEALTH
5. DON'T SMEAR THE PROFIT MOTIVE
6. DON'T SMEAR SUCCESS
7. DON'T GLORIFY FAILURE
8. DON'T GLORIFY DEPRAVITY
9. DON'T DEIFY "THE COMMON MAN"

"The common man" is one of the worst slogans of Communism—and too many of us have fallen for it, without thinking.

... Communism preaches the reign of mediocrity, the destruction of all individuality and all personal distinction, the turning of men into "masses", which means an undivided, undifferentiated, impersonal, average, **common** herd. ...

America is the land of the **uncommon man.** It is the land where man is free to develop his genius—and to get its just rewards. ... It is **not** the land where one glories or its taught to glory in one's mediocrity.

10. DON'T GLORIFY THE COLLECTIVE

This point requires your careful and thoughtful attention.

There is a great difference between free co-operation and forced collectivism. It is the difference between the United States and Soviet Russia. But the Communists are very skillful at hiding the difference and selling you the second under the guise of the first. You might miss it. The audience won't.

Co-operation is the free association of men who work together by voluntary agreement, each deriving from it his own personal benefit.

Collectivism is the forced herding together of men into a group, with the individual having no choice about it, no personal motive, no personal reward, and subordinating himself blindly to the will of others. ...

11. DON'T SMEAR AN INDEPENDENT MAN ...
12. DON'T USE CURRENT EVENTS CARELESSLY. ...

Of all current questions, be most careful about your attitude toward Soviet Russia. ... Look out for remarks that praise Russia directly or indirectly. ...

Don't suggest to the audience that the Russian people are free, secure and happy, that life in Russia is just about the same as in any other country—while actually the Russian people live in constant terror under a bloody, monstrous dictatorship ...

13. DON'T SMEAR AMERICAN POLITICAL INSTITUTIONS

Now a word of warning about the question of free speech. The principle of free speech requires that we do not use **police force** to forbid the Communists the expression of their ideas—which means that we do not **pass laws** forbidding them to speak. But the principle of free speech **does not** require that we furnish the Communists with the means to preach their ideas, and **does not** imply that we owe them jobs and support to advocate our own destruction at our own expense. The Constitutional guaranty of free speech reads "Congress shall pass no laws—" It does not require employers to be suckers.

... Let the Communists preach what they wish (so long as it remains mere talking) at the expense of those and in the employ of those who share their ideas. Let them create their own motion picture studios, if they can. But let us put an end to their use of our pictures, our studios and our money for the purpose of preaching our expropriation, enslavement and destruction. Freedom of speech does not imply that it is our duty to provide a knife for the murderer who wants to cut our throat.[2]

INTRODUCTION TO DOCUMENTS 3 AND 4

The House Committee on Un-American Activities actively investigated Hollywood. Filmmakers and actors, singers, writers, and university teachers, all came before the Committee. Many of those who cooperated—giving testimony that implicated colleagues for radical activities, often with little evidence—believed they were defending America against an insidious communist enemy. Individuals who refused to testify—and some of these served prison time for contempt of Congress—believed they were defending the rights of citizens against a rogue government. Charges that the former were rats spilling their guts for careerist gain or cowardice while the latter were dupes of the communists poisoned life among intellectuals for decades.

Several so-called friendly witnesses came before the HUAC's "Hearings Regarding the Communist Infiltration of the Motion Picture Industry." Their goals in cooperating with the investigations were complex but many hoped to demonstrate that Hollywood was aligned with American values. One such friendly witness was Jack Warner, one of the heads of Warner Brothers Studios, whose testimony is excerpted as Document 3. As you read his statement and the exchange with the Committee, notice that Warner comes under considerable criticism from the Chief Investigator Robert Stripling, for his company's production of *Mission to Moscow*, a 1942 film that had sympathetically portrayed the Soviet Union at the time that it was allied with the United States to defeat Nazi Germany.

Unlike Warner, other members of the Hollywood film industry were deemed "unfriendly" and were subpoenaed by HUAC to answer questions about their political beliefs. Some of these producers, directors, and screenwriters became known as the "Hollywood Ten." They refused to answer HUAC's questions and were jailed for contempt of Congress. On the day after Jack Warner's testimony, a group of writers, actors, and producers who called themselves the "Committee on the First Amendment" took out an ad in the *Hollywood Reporter* to state their opposition to what they considered a clear violation of civil liberties by HUAC. Their statement is reproduced as Document 4. Note that all parties involved in this conflict—MPA, friendly witnesses, HUAC, and opponents of the investigation—consider themselves defenders of American values and freedoms.

3. TESTIMONY OF JACK WARNER TO THE HOUSE COMMITTEE ON UN-AMERICAN ACTIVITIES

OCTOBER 20, 1947

It is a privilege to appear again before this committee to help as much as I can in facilitating its work.

I am happy to speak openly and honestly in an inquiry which has for its purpose the reaffirmation of American ideals and democratic processes. . . . Our American way of life is under attack from without and from within our national borders. I believe it is the duty of each loyal American to resist those attacks and defeat them.

Freedom is a precious thing. It requires careful nurturing, protection, and encouragement. It has flourished under the guaranties of our American Constitution and Bill of rights to make this country the ideal of all men who honestly wish to call their souls their own.

. . . Ideological termites have burrowed into many American industries, organizations, and societies. Wherever they may be, I say let us dig them out and get rid of them. My brothers and I will be happy to subscribe generously to a pest-removal fund. We are willing to establish such a fund to ship to Russia the people who don't like our American system of government and prefer the communistic system to ours.

. . . If there are Communists in our industry, or any other industry, organization, or society who seek to undermine our free institutions, let's find out about it and know who they are. Let the record be spread clear, for all to read and judge. The public is entitled to know the facts.

. . . Many charges, including the fantasy of "White House pressure" have been leveled at our wartime production Mission to Moscow. . . . That picture was made when our country was fighting for its existence, with Russia as one of our allies. It was made to fulfill the same wartime purpose for which we made such other pictures . . . If making Mission to Moscow in 1942 was a subversive activity, then the American Liberty ships which carried food and guns to Russian allies and the American naval vessels which convoyed them were likewise engaged in subversive activities. The picture was made only to help a desperate war effort and not for posterity.

The Warner Bros. interest in the preservation of the American way of life is no new thing with our company. Ever since we began making motion pictures we have fostered American ideals and done whatever we could to protect them.

. . . We can't fight dictatorships by borrowing dictatorial methods. Nor can we defend freedom by curtailing liberties, but we can attack with a free press and a free screen.

Subversive germs breed in dark corners. Let's get light into those corners. That, I believe, is the purpose of this hearing and I am happy to have had the opportunity to testify. . . .

ROBERT Stripling, HUAC's Chief Investigator: Well, is it your opinion now, Mr. Warner, that *Mission to Moscow* was a factually correct picture, and you made it as such?

W. I can't remember.

S. Would you consider it a propaganda picture?

W. In what sense?

S. In the sense that it portrayed Russia and communism in an entirely different light from what it actually was?

W. I am on record about 40 times or more that I have never been in Russia. I don't know what Russia was like in 1937 or 1944 or 1947, so how can I tell you if it was right or wrong?

S. Don't you think you were on dangerous ground to produce as a factually correct picture one which portrayed Russia—

W. No; we were not on dangerous ground in 1942, when we produced it. There was a war on. The world was at stake.

S. In other words—

W. We made the film to aid in the war effort, which I believe I have already stated.

S. Whether it was true or not?

W. As far as I was concerned, I considered it true to the extent as written in Mr. Davies' book.

S. Well, do you suppose that your picture influenced the people, who saw it in this country, the millions of people who saw it in this country?

W. In my opinion, I can't see how it would influence anyone. We were in a war and when you are in a fight you don't ask who the fellow is who is helping you.

S. Well, due to the present conditions in the international situation, don't you think it was rather dangerous to write about such a disillusionment as was sought in that picture?

W. I can't understand why you ask me that question, as to the present conditions. How did I, you, or anyone else know in 1942 what the conditions were going to be in 1947? I stated in my testimony our reason for making the picture, which was to aid the war effort. . . .[3]

4. ADVERTISEMENT FROM THE *HOLLYWOOD REPORTER* (OCTOBER 21, 1947)

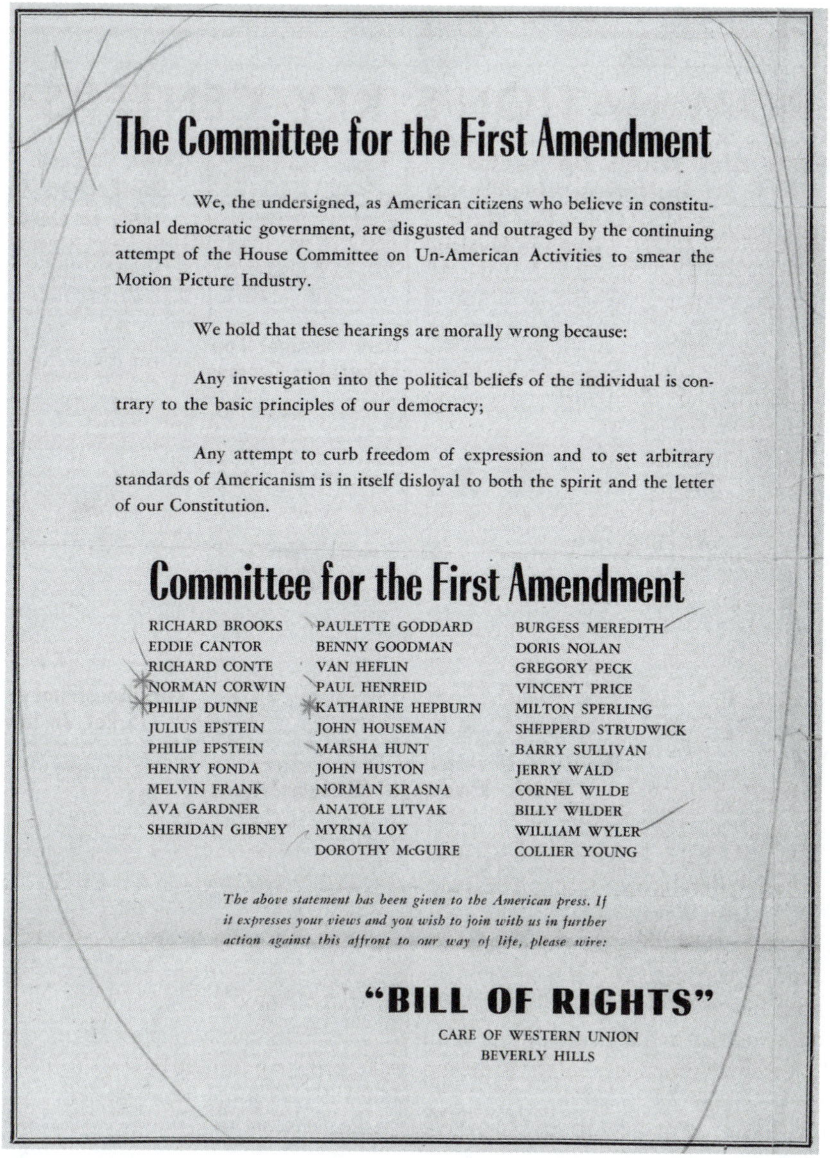

The Committee for the First Amendment

We, the undersigned, as American citizens who believe in constitutional democratic government, are disgusted and outraged by the continuing attempt of the House Committee on Un-American Activities to smear the Motion Picture Industry.

We hold that these hearings are morally wrong because:

Any investigation into the political beliefs of the individual is contrary to the basic principles of our democracy;

Any attempt to curb freedom of expression and to set arbitrary standards of Americanism is in itself disloyal to both the spirit and the letter of our Constitution.

Committee for the First Amendment

RICHARD BROOKS	PAULETTE GODDARD	BURGESS MEREDITH
EDDIE CANTOR	BENNY GOODMAN	DORIS NOLAN
RICHARD CONTE	VAN HEFLIN	GREGORY PECK
NORMAN CORWIN	PAUL HENREID	VINCENT PRICE
PHILIP DUNNE	KATHARINE HEPBURN	MILTON SPERLING
JULIUS EPSTEIN	JOHN HOUSEMAN	SHEPPERD STRUDWICK
PHILIP EPSTEIN	MARSHA HUNT	BARRY SULLIVAN
HENRY FONDA	JOHN HUSTON	JERRY WALD
MELVIN FRANK	NORMAN KRASNA	CORNEL WILDE
AVA GARDNER	ANATOLE LITVAK	BILLY WILDER
SHERIDAN GIBNEY	MYRNA LOY	WILLIAM WYLER
	DOROTHY McGUIRE	COLLIER YOUNG

The above statement has been given to the American press. If it expresses your views and you wish to join with us in further action against this affront to our way of life, please wire:

"BILL OF RIGHTS"

CARE OF WESTERN UNION
BEVERLY HILLS

Image 12.1: Statement of the Committee of the First Amendment.

In response to the HUAC investigations of supposed communists in Hollywood, a group of actors and writers responded with this statement. On what grounds did HUAC believe these investigations were constitutional and necessary?

Source: Records of the House of Representatives, Record Group 233, National Archives Identifier 25466014.

INTRODUCTION TO DOCUMENTS 5 AND 6

The perceived threat of communism extended to all areas of American life, including the nation's universities. Perhaps the earliest and most significant episode occurred at the University of Washington in 1948, beginning just after the investigations of subversion in Hollywood. In Seattle, newly elected Republican State Representative Albert Canwell introduced a bill to investigate communist activities in Washington State. He became chair of his state's Committee on Un-American Activities. The committee quickly focused on radical activity at the University of Washington, and after the hearings were completed the university dismissed three professors for their admitted membership in the Communist Party of the United States. Document 5 is the statement of the University's president, Raymond Allen, who forcefully concurred with Canwell that Communist Party membership was grounds for firing professors. In Document 6, Herbert Phillips—one of the fired professors—responds that such actions violated the university's own grounds for dismissal.

The University of Washington hearings and dismissals were important for being the first of their kind, setting the precedent for loyalty investigations that rippled across American colleges and universities in the late 1940s and 1950s. With heightened scrutiny of any political activity deemed radical, many professors avoided such subjects in their classrooms to protect their jobs. As you read, ask yourself how both Allen and Philipps can claim to be defending democracy. Does Allen substantiate his claim that communists are intellectually unfree? Why does he see communist ideology and the pursuit of truth at odds?

5. COMMUNISTS SHOULD NOT TEACH IN AMERICAN COLLEGES (1948)

PRESIDENT RAYMOND B. ALLEN

A member of the Communist Party should not be permitted to teach in an American college because he is not a free man. If the purpose of education is to seek out and to teach the truth wherever it may lead, as Jefferson taught, then the first duty and obligation of the teacher is that he be a free man. Any restraint upon the teacher's freedom is an obstacle to his performance of his highest scholarly functions. But the teacher's freedom consists of something more than an absence of restraints placed upon him by the institution that employs him. It demands as well an absence of restraints placed upon him by his political affiliations, by dogmas that stand in the way of a free search for truth, or by rigid adherence to a "party line" that sacrifices dignity, honor and integrity to the accomplishment of political ends. Men, and especially the teacher and the scholar, must be free to think and discover and believe, else there will be no new thought, no discovery, and no progress. But these freedoms are barren if their fruits are to be hidden away and denied. Men must be free, of course, but they must also be free, and willing, to stand up and profess what they believe so that all may hear.

It is obvious that the Communist Party does not allow its members this freedom. As a member of the Party, a man cannot be free; he is a slave to immutable dogma and to a clandestine organization which masquerades as a political party. He has abdicated control over his intellectual life.

The issue between communism and education is the effect that Communist Party membership has upon the freedom of the teacher and upon the morale and professional standards of the profession. It is not an issue of civil liberties. No man has a constitutional right to belong to any profession merely because his political affiliations are legal or illegal.

... the Communist Party, U.S.A., with its concealed aims and objectives, with its secret and clandestine methods and techniques, with its consistent failure to put its full face forward in the Jeffersonian tradition, reflects upon the integrity of the institution that employs its members and upon a whole educational system that has failed, with rare exceptions, to take the Communist issue seriously.

... Communism is the antithesis of the living, hopeful, positive democracy we as a people have chosen to live by and to live for. Communism is a doctrine of fear, of little faith, of the submergence of the human spirit to the vicious ends of a materialistic tyranny. Free education and its quest for truth cannot gain, indeed must surely lose, if it is entrusted to the keeping of the robot prophets of such a creed.[4]

6. RESPONSE BY HERBERT J. PHILLIPS, ON THE DISMISSAL OF COMMUNIST PROFESSORS AT THE UNIVERSITY OF WASHINGTON (1948)

The central issue involved in the Washington dismissals, and the issue that justifies the professors concerned in bringing the matter before the American academic world as sharply as possible, is the issue of whether or not political opinions or affiliations should henceforth constitute a condition for employment in institutions of instruction. The University of Washington operated under a tenure code that explicitly omitted political grounds in specifying a definitive list of causes for dismissal. These causes were:

1. Incompetence
2. Immorality or dishonesty
3. Neglect of duty
4. Physical or mental incapacity
5. Conviction of a felony involving moral turpitude

In the trial before a faculty Tenure Committee which was also provided for by our excellent Tenure Code, the University Administration deliberately refused to attempt to prove that Mr. Butterworth and myself, who are both admitted present members of the Communist Party, were either of us individually guilty of any of the causes in the Code. The University counsel repeatedly asserted that it was their intention to establish that membership in the Communist Party, in and of itself, constituted grounds for dismissal. They argued that such membership per se entailed guilt of at least three of the causes in the Code—to wit, incompetence, immorality or dishonesty, and neglect of duty. Not only were none of these faults proven against Mr. Butterworth and myself, but in our defense we produced positive evidence which was apparently convincing in the minds of eight of the eleven man committee that we actually were competent, had moral integrity and were conscientious in the performance of our duties....

Image 12.2: Protesting the Canwell Committee investigations at the University of Washington, 1948
Source: Courtesy Museum of History and Industry, Seattle.

I believe that the Washington dismissals constitute a grave danger to academic freedom and to our American system of free education. It is true that the American public is not friendly to communism and probably has difficulty being enthusiastic about the defense of the academic freedom and civil rights of Communists. Mr. Butterworth and I believe that this unfriendliness is based upon misconceptions deliberately cultivated by our major sources of information. I personally believe that it is to the credit of the American people that they are unfriendly toward an organization of the type they think the Communist Party to be. I am in a position to know that their beliefs about our party are false. It will be part of my struggle for reinstatement to help clear up some of these misconceptions. . . . Wherever antidemocratic forces have triumphed, they have begun the attack upon democratic institutions by attacking the Communists. It is thus the duty of all friends of democracy, whether Communist or non-Communist, to help refute the basic lies about communism. . . .[5]

INTRODUCTION TO DOCUMENTS 7, 8, AND 9

The investigations into subversion in Hollywood and in universities matched an equally vigorous search for communist influence in government, including President Truman's 1947 search for disloyal civil servants. Then, on February 9, 1950, Senator Joseph McCarthy of Wisconsin upped the ante at a Lincoln birthday speech in Wheeling, West Virginia. After briefly extolling the virtues of the sixteenth American president, McCarthy quickly turned to his real theme, the subversion of the American government by traitors from within. McCarthy declared that he held in his hand a list of fifty-seven traitors undermining America from their positions in the American State Department. McCarthy repeated this claim of enemies working deep within the government, but he never revealed any names. The bombshell speech in Wheeling was inserted into the *Congressional Record*, and is Document 7. Two days after he delivered this speech, Senator McCarthy sent a telegram to President Truman challenging him to act more vigorously against the internal communist threat. For the next few years, McCarthy and his accusations were constantly in the news. Document 8 is McCarthy's telegram to President Truman, and Document 9 is Truman's equally forceful reply, which was never sent.

7. SPEECH IN WHEELING, WEST VIRGINIA, FEBRUARY 9, 1950

SENATOR JOSEPH MCCARTHY

. . . Five years after a world war has been won, men's hearts should anticipate a long peace, and men's minds should be free from the heavy weight that comes with war. But this is not such a period—for this is not a period of peace. This is a time of the "cold war." This is a time when all the world is split into two vast, increasingly hostile armed camps—a time of a great armaments race.

The great difference between our western Christian world and the atheistic Communist world is not political, ladies and gentlemen, it is moral. There are other differences, of course, but those could be reconciled. For instance, the Marxian idea of confiscating the land and factories and running the entire economy as a single enterprise is momentous. Likewise, Lenin's invention of the one-party police state as a way to make Marx's idea work is hardly less momentous.

Stalin's resolute putting across of these two ideas, of course, did much to divide the world. With only those differences, however, the East and the West could most certainly still live in peace.

The real, basic difference, however, lies in the religion of immoralism—invented by Marx, preached feverishly by Lenin, and carried to unimaginable extremes by Stalin. This religion of immoralism, if the Red half of the world wins—and well it may—this religion of immoralism will more deeply wound and damage mankind than any conceivable economic or political system. . . .

Ladies and gentlemen, can there by anyone here tonight who is so blind as to say that the war is not on? Can there be anyone who fails to realize that the Communist world has said, "The time is now"—that this is the time for the show-down between the democratic Christian world and the Communist atheistic world?

Unless we face this fact, we shall pay the price that must be paid by those who wait too long.

Six years ago, at the time of the first conference to map out peace—Dumbarton Oaks—there was within the Soviet orbit 180,000,000 people. Lined up on the antitotalitarian side there were in the world at that time roughly 1,625,000,000 people. Today, only 6 years later, there are 800,000,000 people under the absolute domination of Soviet Russia—an increase of over 400 percent. On our side, the figure has shrunk to around 500,000,000. In other words, in less than 6 years the odds have changed from 9 to 1 in our favor to 8 to 5 against us. This indicates the swiftness of the tempo of Communist victories and American defeats in the cold war. As one of our outstanding historical figures once said, "When a great democracy is destroyed, it will not be because of enemies from without, but rather because of enemies from within."

The truth of this statement is becoming terrifyingly clear as we see this country each day losing on every front.

At war's end we were physically the strongest nation on earth and, at least potentially, the most powerful intellectually and morally. Ours could have been the honor of being a beacon in the desert of destruction, a shining living proof that civilization was not yet ready to destroy itself. Unfortunately, we have failed miserably and tragically to arise to the opportunity.

The reason why we find ourselves in a position of impotency is not because our only powerful potential enemy has sent men to invade our shores, but rather because of the traitorous actions of those who have been treated so well by this Nation. It has not been the less fortunate or members of minority groups who have been selling this Nation out, but rather those who have had all the benefits that the wealthiest nation on earth has had to offer—the finest homes, the finest college education, and the finest jobs in Government we can give.

This is glaringly true in the State Department. There the bright young men who are born with silver spoons in their mouths are the ones who have been worst. . . . In my opinion the State Department, which is one of the most important government departments, is thoroughly infested with Communists.

I have in my hand 57 cases of individuals who would appear to be either card carrying members or certainly loyal to the Communist Party, but who nevertheless are still helping to shape our foreign policy.

One thing to remember in discussing the Communists in our Government is that we are not dealing with spies who get 30 pieces of silver to steal the blueprints of a new weapon. We are dealing with a far more sinister type of activity because it permits the enemy to guide and shape our policy. . . .

As you hear this story of high treason, I know that you are saying to yourself, "Well, why doesn't the Congress do something about it?" Actually, ladies and gentlemen, one of the important reasons for the graft, the corruption, the dishonesty, the disloyalty, the treason in high Government positions—one of the most important reasons why this continues is a lack of moral uprising on the part of the 140,000,000 American people. In the light of history, however, this is not hard to explain.

It is the result of an emotional hang-over and a temporary moral lapse which follows every war. It is the apathy to evil which people who have been subjected to the tremendous evils of war feel. As the people of the world see mass murder, the destruction of defenseless and innocent people, and all of the crime and lack of morals which go with war, they become numb and apathetic. It has always been thus after war.

However, the morals of our people have not been destroyed. They still exist. This cloak of numbness and apathy has only needed a spark to rekindle them. Happily, this spark has finally been supplied.

As you know, very recently the Secretary of State proclaimed his loyalty to a man guilty of what has always been considered as the most abominable of all crimes—of being a traitor to the people who gave him a position of great trust. The Secretary of State in attempting to justify his continued devotion to the man who sold out the Christian world to the atheistic world, referred to Christ's Sermon on the Mount as a justification and reason therefor, and the reaction of the American people to this would have made the heart of Abraham Lincoln happy.

When this pompous diplomat in striped pants, with a phony British accent, proclaimed to the American people that Christ on the Mount endorsed communism, high treason, and betrayal of a sacred trust, the blasphemy was so great that it awakened the dormant indignation of the American people.

He has lighted the spark which is resulting in a moral uprising and will end only when the whole sorry mess of twisted, warped thinkers are swept from the national scene so that we may have a new birth of national honesty and decency in Government.[6]

8. TELEGRAM FROM SENATOR MCCARTHY TO PRESIDENT TRUMAN, FEBRUARY 11, 1950

Reno Nev Feb 11, 1950
The President
The White House

In a Lincoln Day Speech at Wheeling Thursday night I stated that the State Department harbors a nest of communists and communist sympathizers who are helping to shape our foreign policy. I further stated that I have in my possession the names of 57 communists who are in the State Department at present. A State Department spokesman . . . denied this and claimed that there is not a single communist in the department. You can convince yourself of the falsity of the State Department claim very easily. You will recall that you personally appointed a board to screen State Department employees for the purpose of weeding out fellow travelers. Your board did a pains-taking job, and named hundreds which it listed as "dangerous to the security of the nation," because of communistic connections.

While the records are not available to me, I know absolutely that of one group of approximately 300 certified to the secretary for discharge, he actually discharged only approximately 80. I understand that this was done after lengthy consultation with Alger Hiss. I would suggest therefore, Mr. President, that you simply pick up your phone and ask Mr. Acheson how many of those whom your board had labeled as dangerous, he failed to discharge. The day the House Un-American Activities Committee exposed Alger Hiss as an important link in an international communist spy ring, you signed an order forbidding the State Departments, giving the Congress any information in regard to the disloyalty or the communistic connections of anyone in that department, despite this State Department blackout, we have been able to compile a list of 57 communists in the State Department. This list is available to you, but you can get a much longer list by ordering Secretary Acheson to give you a list of these whom your own board listed as being disloyal, and who are still working in the State Department. I believe the following is the minimum which can be expected of you in this case

(1) that you demand that Acheson give you and the proper Congressional Committee the names and a complete report on all of those who were placed in the Department by Alger Hiss, and all of those still working in the State Department who were listed by your Board as bad security risks because of the communistic connections.

(2) that under no circumstances could a Congressional Committee obtain any information or help from the Executive Department in exposing communists.

Failure on your part will label the Democratic Party of being the bed-fellow of intern-national communism. Certainly this label is not deserved by the hundreds of thousands of loyal American Democrats throughout the nation, and by the sizable number of able loyal Democrats in both the Senate and the House.

Joe McCarthy US S[enator] Wis[consin][7]

9. UNSENT DRAFTED TELEGRAM FROM PRESIDENT TRUMAN TO SENATOR MCCARTHY (FEBRUARY 1950)

My dear Senator:

I read your telegram of February eleventh from Reno, Nevada with a great deal of interest and this is the first time in my experience, and I was ten years in the Senate, that I ever heard of a Senator trying to discredit his own Government before the world. You know that isn't done by honest public officials. Your telegram is not only not true and an insolent approach to a situation that should have been worked out between man and man but it shows conclusively that you are not even fit to have a hand in the operation of the Government of the United States.

I am very sure that the people of Wisconsin are extremely sorry that they are represented by a person who has as little sense of responsibility as you have. Sincerely yours, HST.[8]

INTRODUCTION TO DOCUMENT 10

Joseph McCarthy made the fear of internal subversion palpable, but many Americans, especially those in the arts, responded with strong words of their own. In this document, the poet Thomas McGrath explains to HUAC in 1953 why he refused to cooperate with them. McGrath was born in 1916 to a poor family of Irish farmers in Sheldon, North Dakota. He eventually attended the University of North Dakota, won a Rhodes scholarship, served in World War II, did graduate work at Louisiana State University, and finally landed a position at Los Angeles State University in 1950. His refusal to testify three years later cost him his job. When he gave his explanation, McGrath was not well known, but by the end of his life, many critics considered him a great poet in the tradition of Walt Whitman. Why did McGrath refuse to "name names"? Do you agree or disagree with his decision?

10. STATEMENT TO THE HOUSE COMMITTEE ON UN-AMERICAN ACTIVITIES (1953)

THOMAS MCGRATH

After a dead serious consideration of the effects of this committee's work and of my relation to it, I find that for the following reasons I must refuse to cooperate with this body.

In the first place, as a teacher, my first responsibility is to my students. To cooperate with this committee would be to set for them an example of accommodation to forces which can only have, as their end effect, the destruction of education itself. Such accommodation on my part would ruin my value as a teacher, and I am proud to say that a great majority of my students—and I believe this is true of students generally—do not want me to accommodate myself to this committee. In a certain sense, I have no

Image 12.3: Thomas O'Halloran photograph of Des Moines, Iowa (1959)

A crowd in Des Moines gathers to catch a glimpse of Soviet Premier Nikita Kruschev, who toured the United States in 1959 and spent time learning about agriculture while in Iowa.

Source: Courtesy Library of Congress.

choice in the matter—the students would not want me back in the classroom if I were to take any course of action other than the one I am pursuing.

Secondly, as a teacher, I have a responsibility to the profession itself. We teachers have no professional oath of the sort that doctors take, but there is a kind of unwritten oath which we follow to teach as honestly, fairly and fully as we can. The effect of the committee is destructive of such an ideal, destructive of academic freedom. As Mr. Justice Douglas has said: "This system of spying and surveillance with its accompanying reports and trials cannot go hand in hand with academic freedom. It produces standardized thought, not the pursuit of truth." A teacher who will tack and turn with every shift of the political wind cannot be a good teacher. . . .

Thirdly, as a poet I must refuse to cooperate with the committee on what I can only call esthetic grounds. The view of life which we receive through the great works of art is a privileged one—it is a view of life according to probability or necessity, not subject to the chance and accident of our real world and therefore in a sense truer than the life we see lived all around us. I believe that one of the things required of us is to try to give life an esthetic ground, to give it some of the pattern and beauty of art. I have tried as best I can to do this with my own life, and while I do not claim any very great success, it would be anticlimactic, destructive of the pattern of my life, if I were to cooperate with the committee.

These, then are reasons for refusing to cooperate, but I am aware that none of them is acceptable to the committee. When I was notified to appear here, my first instinct was simply to refuse to answer committee questions out of personal principle and on the grounds of the rights of man and let it go at that. On further consideration, however, I have come to feel that such a stand would be mere self-indulgence and that it would weaken the fight which other witnesses have made to protect the rights guaranteed under our Constitution. Therefore I further refuse to answer the committee on the grounds of the fourth amendment. I regard this committee as usurpers of illegal powers and my enforced appearance here as in the nature of unreasonable search and seizure.

I further refuse on the grounds of the first amendment, which in guaranteeing free speech also guarantees my right to be silent. Although the first amendment expressly forbids any abridgement of this and other freedoms, the committee is illegally engaged in the establishment of a religion of fear. I cannot cooperate with it in this unconstitutional activity. Lastly, it is my duty to refuse to answer this committee, claiming my rights under the fifth amendment as a whole and in all its parts, and understanding that the fifth amendment was inserted in the Constitution to bulwark the first amendment against the activities of committees such as this one, that no one may be forced to bear witness against himself.

INTRODUCTION TO DOCUMENT 11

Joseph McCarthy became inordinately powerful in the early 1950s, with nearly half the country supporting his crude but effective crusade in the Senate. Newly elected President Eisenhower in fact authorized the FBI to extend its efforts to disrupt the work of the Communist Party in the United States. The president also refused to grant clemency to Ethel and Julius Rosenberg, who had been convicted of spying for the Soviet Union. Yet Eisenhower was also disgusted by McCarthy's anti-communist tactics, though he never publicly denounced the latter. When Senator McCarthy began to investigate the U.S. army, the president pushed back by refusing to turn over documents. Eventually these hearings exposed McCarthy's tactics to the public, and soon thereafter the Senate censured him for "conduct unbecoming" a senator. The year before this censure,

Eisenhower spoke to the graduating class at Dartmouth in 1953, pivoting from a straightforward commencement address to a pointed critique of the increasing intolerance of the anti-communist crusade. The president's speech is excerpted as Document 11.

11. COMMENCEMENT ADDRESS, DARTMOUTH COLLEGE, JUNE 14, 1953

PRESIDENT DWIGHT D. EISENHOWER

You must have courage to look at all about you with honest eyes—above all, yourself. And we go back to our standards. Have you actually measured up? If you have, it is that courage to look at yourself and say, well, I failed miserably there, I hurt someone's feelings needlessly, I lost my temper—which you must never do except deliberately. You did not measure up to your own standards.

Now, if you have the courage to look at yourself, soon you begin to achieve a code or a pattern that is closer to your own standards. By the same token, look at all that is dear to you: your own family. Of course, your children are going to be the greatest, the most extraordinary that ever lived. But, also, look at them as they are, occasionally.

Look at your country. Here is a country of which we are proud, as you are proud of Dartmouth and all about you, and the families to which you belong. But this country is a long way from perfection—a long way. We have the disgrace of racial discrimination, or we have prejudice against people because of their religion. We have crime on the docks. We have not had the courage to uproot these things, although we know they are wrong. And we with our standards, the standards given us at places like Dartmouth, we know they are wrong.

Now, that courage is not going to be satisfied—your sense of satisfaction is not going to be satisfied, if you haven't the courage to look at these things and do your best to help correct them, because that is the contribution you shall make to this beloved country in your time. Each of us, as he passes along, should strive to add something.

It is not enough merely to say I love America, and to salute the flag and take off your hat as it goes by, and to help sing the Star Spangled Banner. Wonderful! We love to do them, and our hearts swell with pride, because those who went before you worked to give to us today, standing here, this pride.

And this is a pride in an institution that we think has brought great happiness, and we know has brought great contentment and freedom of soul to many people. But it is not yet done. You must add to it.

Don't join the book burners. Don't think you are going to conceal faults by concealing evidence that they ever existed. Don't be afraid to go in your library and read every book, as long as that document does not offend our own ideas of decency. That should be the only censorship.

How will we defeat communism unless we know what it is, and what it teaches, and why does it have such an appeal for men, why are so many people swearing allegiance to it? It is almost a religion, albeit one of the nether regions.

And we have got to fight it with something better, not try to conceal the thinking of our own people. They are part of America. And even if they think ideas that are contrary to ours, their right to say them, their right to record them, and their right to have them at places where they are accessible to others is unquestioned, or it isn't America.[9]

QUESTIONS

1. Why did anticommunism become such a divisive issue in American life?
2. How did Senator McCarthy become so powerful?
3. Why do you think so much attention was paid to alleged communist activities in Hollywood, in the arts, and on college campuses?
4. Tom McGrath, Herbert Phillips, and Raymond Allen all invoke "freedom," but what does each mean by using the term?
5. How do you explain that both those opposed to and in favor of the HUAC investigations believed they were fighting to protect American freedom?
6. Do you think the Cold War was more about foreign or domestic policy?

ADDITIONAL READING

The origin of the Cold War has been one of the most hotly debated topics in American history. An outstanding overview of the era is provided in Walter LaFeber, *America, Russia, and the Cold War* (1985). Daniel Yergin, *Shattered Peace* (1982) recounts the early years of the Cold War. Gar Alperovitz, *Atomic Diplomacy* (1985) suggests that the Cold War began even before the end of World War II; also see John L. Gaddis, *Strategies of Containment* (1982). Many of the leading American actors of the period have written memoirs. Among the best are Dean Acheson, *Present at Creation: My Years in the State Department* (1969), and George F. Kennan, *Memoirs, 1925–1950* (1967). For more general works, see James T. Patterson, *Grand Expectations: The United States, 1945–1974* (1996), and Melvin Leffler, *A Preponderance of Power: National Security, The Truman Administration, and the Cold War* (1992). The impact of the Cold War on domestic politics and culture has also been considered in depth. David M. Oshinsky, *A Conspiracy So Immense: The World of Joseph McCarthy* (1983) shows how the Cold War worked its way into politics. Stephen J. Whitfield, *The Culture of the Cold War* (1996) traces the impact of the Cold War on American life. Larry Ceplair and Steven Englund, *The Inquisition in Hollywood: Politics of the Film Industry, 1930–1960* (1983) is a detailed study of the relationship between Washington and Hollywood. See also John Sbardellati, *J. Edgar Hoover Goes to the Movies: The FBI and the Origins of Hollywood's Cold War* (2012), and Lary May, *The Big Tomorrow: Hollywood and the Politics of the American Way* (2000). For a broad synthesis of the era, see John Lewis Gaddis, *The Cold War* (2005). Other books on culture and the Cold War include K. A. Cuordileone, *Manhood and American Political Culture in the Cold War* (2004); Thomas Patrick Doherty, *Cold War, Cool Medium* (2005); and Mary L. Dudziak, *Cold War Civil Rights* (2002).

ENDNOTES

1. George F. Kennan, *Memoirs 1925-1950* (Boston: Little, Brown, 1967), p. 57.
2. "Screen Guide for Americans," issued by the Motion Picture Alliance for the Preservation of American Values (Beverly Hills, CA, 1947).
3. *Hearings Regarding the Communist Infiltration of the Motion Picture Industry*, 80th Congress, First Session (Washington, D.C.: Government Printing Office, 1947), pp. 7–45. This exchange has been edited for length.
4. Raymond B. Allen, in *The American Scholar*, v.18 n.3 (Summer 1949), 326–328.
5. Herbert Phillips, in *The American Scholar*, v.18 n.3 (Summer 1949), 330–331.
6. *Congressional Record*, 81st Congress, 2d Session, pp. 1954–1957.
7. Truman Administration Secretary's Files, Identifier 201514, National Archives.
8. President's Truman's Secretary's Files, identifier 201514, National Archives.
9. Gerhard Peters and John T. Wooley, The American Presidency Project.

CHAPTER 13

THE FREEDOM STRUGGLE: STATES' RIGHTS VERSUS FEDERAL INTERVENTION

HISTORICAL CONTEXT

In 1954, the U.S. Supreme Court decided unanimously in the landmark case *Brown v. the Board of Education of Topeka, Kansas,* that the segregationist doctrine of "separate but equal" public schools for blacks and whites inherently violated constitutional guarantees because segregated black schools were underfunded and inferior. The decision implicitly questioned the entire southern Jim Crow legal system that formally kept blacks and whites apart in schools, hotels, trains, public swimming pools, restrooms, and a variety of other locations.

It takes a leap of historical imagination to feel what it must have been like for a black person to confront two drinking fountains—one labeled "White" and the other, probably an inferior facility, labeled "Colored." Every time a white man called a black man "boy," every time that same black man stepped off the sidewalk to let whites pass, and every time he was forced to sit at the back of the bus, the contradiction of his indelibly unequal status in a land that boasted of equal opportunity emerged. The million commonplace gestures and customs of segregation and the enforced poverty added up to a single message for African Americans: You are inferior.

Most of the time, for survival's sake, black people did not complain, but that doesn't mean they didn't notice, and by the mid-1950s, increasing numbers of them stopped looking the other way. It was impossible not to be heartened by the *Brown* decision and other court cases in which African American rights were upheld; it was equally impossible not to be let down when the federal government hesitated to come through with enforcement of its own laws and judicial decisions. The raising of hopes on the one hand and the failure of fulfillment on the other energized many African Americans to mobilize themselves. Their underlying assumption was that, as Americans, they deserved all the rights and privileges of other citizens.

It wasn't as if what has come to be known as the civil rights movement began with the *Brown* decision. Reconstruction itself was part of the quest for civil liberties, citizenship, and voting rights, and many former slaves were deeply involved in postwar politics. Even as the rights they won were abrogated in the late nineteenth and early twentieth centuries—the Supreme Court's 1896 *Plessy versus Ferguson* decision affirmed racial segregation under the "separate but equal" doctrine—African Americans fought back. Ida B. Wells began her decades-long crusade against lynching; scholar and teacher W. E. B. Dubois published *The Souls of Black Folk* and edited *The Crisis*; the National Association for the Advancement of Colored People (NAACP) was founded in 1909, and a decade later, Marcus Garvey launched his "Back to Africa" movement. African Americans gained clout in Congress of Industrial Organizations unions during the 1930s, a handful of black neighborhoods elected their own congressmen, and labor leader A. Phillip Randolph and others pressured the federal government into establishing a Fair Labor Practices Commission. In the 1940s, the NAACP Legal Defense Fund won important cases that chipped away at Jim Crow discrimination, and by the end of that decade, activists secured the desegregation of the armed forces. In an important symbolic step, baseball, the nation's most popular sport, began to integrate.

Image 13.1: An integrated high school in 1957, Washington, D.C.

The landmark *Brown v. Board of Education* Supreme Court decision seemed to herald the onset of school integration, as revealed in this photo of Anacostia High School in Washington, D.C. Resistance, however, proved formidable, especially in the south.

Source: Courtesy Warren K. Leffler, U.S. News & World Report Magazine Photograph Collection, Library of Congress.

The pace of events picked up in the 1950s. For example, several counties in the Mississippi Delta had black majorities without a single registered African-American voter. Mass meetings to organize for voting rights began, thousands of people, mostly from sharecropper families, showed up as the struggle took wing. Parents petitioned for the integration of their local schools so their children could attend longer sessions with better teachers. There was fierce push-back. The "Citizens Councils" organized across the South to resist the dismantling of Jim Crow. Blacks who "got out of line" and threatened "the southern way of life" by organizing or petitioning lost their jobs, homes, and farms. Some were lynched. But the movement continued, and nonviolent direct action became the preferred technique from the Montgomery bus boycott beginning in 1955 through the passage of the Voting Rights Act of 1965. The freedom struggle was led by a remarkable corps of mostly southern black leaders with roots in the Church, some with union ties. Sit-ins, demonstrations, boycotts, civil disobedience, breaking the law, and filling the jails—all this was done without committing violence or retaliating against the aggression of others. This was the essence of nonviolent direct action.

The first dramatic example of such techniques came in Montgomery, Alabama, in December 1955. Mrs. Rosa Parks, a seamstress who had been involved in civil rights organizations, rode the bus home after a long day's work. A white man got on, but she refused to give up her seat to him as law and tradition required. When she was arrested, blacks began a mass boycott of Montgomery's bus system. Local residents like E. D. Nixon, who had been active in the labor movement as a railroad porter, and the new minister in town, twenty-seven-year-old Martin Luther King Jr., freshly graduated from divinity school at Boston University, helped organize and inspire the year-long boycott. The protesters won their point when the Supreme Court ruled that laws forcing blacks to sit at the back of the bus or to give up their seats to whites were illegal. Once again, however, enforcement was slow. In 1957 the push for integrating the schools led to confrontation in Little Rock, Arkansas, where President Dwight D. Eisenhower was forced to use federal troops to enforce the law.

In 1960, the movement took a new turn when four black students from North Carolina Agricultural and Technical College simply sat down at a segregated lunch counter and waited to be served. Whites berated, abused, beat, and then arrested them. For the next few years, sit-ins occurred at public accommodations throughout the South. Protesters requested their rights as citizens and maintained their Gandhian mode of nonviolence; whites responded with increasing levels of bloodshed. Demonstrators were killed and wounded as they registered at previously segregated universities, rode previously segregated buses, and checked into all-white hotels. Boycotts brought local economies to a standstill, massive sit-ins tied up criminal justice systems by filling the jails with protesters, and, above all, evening news images of people protesting peacefully for their rights and being met by police dogs, water cannons, and billy clubs evoked both sympathy and shame. President Kennedy cautiously supported new civil rights legislation before his assassination in late 1963, and the Civil Rights Act of 1964 brought the power of the federal government to bear on the states, dissolving much of the old Jim Crow order.

Yet, as the summer of 1964 approached, the civil rights movement was coming to a crossroads. The right to be served a cup of coffee, to swim in public pools, or even to go to good schools (ten years after the *Brown* decision, southern and northern schools remained largely segregated) were important, but increasingly, the movement was forced to confront issues of politics and power. The 1964 Civil Rights Act guaranteed the right to vote, but there was not much enforcement power in the law. African Americans in the southern states constituted an enormous potential electorate, yet old legal barriers kept them from voting. This ultimate right of citizenship was next on the movement's agenda.

Freedom Struggle leadership had been evolving as well. The NAACP led the way in bringing civil rights cases to courts, especially in the 1950s, but as the movement turned toward nonviolent direct action, other groups with new leaders such as the Southern Christian Leadership Conference (SCLC), led by Martin Luther King Jr., and James Farmer's Congress on Racial Equality (CORE) took center stage. Equally important, in the early 1960s the Student Nonviolent Coordinating Committee (SNCC), emerged, led by John Lewis. SNCC was the most militant of these organizations. Its membership drew heavily on young black southerners, many of whom had grown up poor, had seen the rising tide of white resistance, and were skeptical that integration was the answer. These young activists have been called the Emmett Till Generation, named for the fourteen-year-old Chicago boy who, while visiting relatives in Mississippi in 1955, whistled at a white woman at a crossroads grocery store and was beaten and murdered a few days later by her kin. Till's open-coffin funeral in Chicago attracted tens of thousands of mourners and newspapers around the world covered the trial of his murderers, who were found innocent but later confessed to the crime. In the summer of 1964, aided by northern white college students, the young activists of SNCC began a massive voter registration drive.

The results of those early years were mixed. Local governments were intransigent, acts of violence against African Americans went unpunished, and those sworn to uphold the law often took the side of whites who attacked blacks. On the other hand, Congress passed the Civil Rights Act of 1964, which banned discrimination in public accommodations. The pain and indignity of *legal* apartheid had ended. One year later, President Lyndon Johnson signed the Voting Rights Act of 1965, a law that in not too many years turned Freedom Summer's goal of broad-based enfranchisement into a reality. Since its passage, thousands of African Americans have been elected to political office, including the White House. So those who sacrificed so much for equality brought important changes to the South and even to the North, where residential segregation by custom and law was the norm. There was an important lesson here. Change came slowly, and not because leaders suddenly grew benevolent. The federal laws that emerged out of this era were the result of grass roots democracy, of blood in the streets, of thousands of people organizing over decades to demand change.

INTRODUCTION TO DOCUMENTS 1 AND 2

By 1949, Jackie Robinson was a successful major league athlete, though the crude racism of many fans and players made his path a difficult one. As Chapter 12 documents, these years also brought out America's deepest anxieties about communism. As anti-communist investigations spread across the country, no aspect of American life seemed unaffected. Robinson agreed to testify during House Committee on Un-American Activities hearings regarding communism and minority groups, and this testimony is excerpted in Document 1. Anti-communists worried that bigotry and discrimination made African Americans susceptible to communist appeals, and indeed, the Communist Party held very advanced views on civil rights. Fears of radical subversion were especially acute in the South, where politicians and social elites believed that both labor unions and civil rights organizations sought to overturn white rule.

Years after Jackie Robinson's testimony, in defiance of the *Brown v. Board of Education* decision, Governor Orval Faubus sent the Arkansas State Guard to prevent the entry of nine black students into Little Rock's Central High School. This prompted President Dwight Eisenhower reluctantly to federalize those troops and enforce the students' right to enroll. Earlier, Eisenhower backed a moderate civil rights bill, which was weakened further as it worked its way through Congress, especially by southern Democratic senators. A bill finally passed, and Eisenhower signed it, but its anemic enforcement powers brought much criticism. Eisenhower responded by counseling patience, a word black activists had heard from well-meaning whites for decades. Jackie Robinson's irritation with President Eisenhower is evident in Document 2.

1. SWORN TESTIMONY OF JACK ROOSEVELT ROBINSON (1949)

Mr. Chairman, when the House Committee on Un-American Activities invited me to appear here today and express myself on the subject of your present interest, I answered that I would be glad to do so although it isn't exactly pleasant to get involved in a political dispute when my field of earning a living is as far removed from politics as anybody can possibly imagine. . . .

. . . So you'll naturally ask, why did I stick my neck out by agreeing to be present, and why did I stand by my agreement in spite of advice to the contrary? . . . You can put me down as an expert on being a colored American, with 30 years of experience at it. And just

like any other colored person with sense enough to look around him and understand what he sees, I know that life in these United States can be mighty tough for people who are a little different from the majority—in their skin color, or the way they worship their God, or the way they spell their names. . . .

There are only three major league clubs with only seven colored players signed up, out of close to 400 major league players on 16 clubs.

But a start has been made, and progress goes on, and southern fans as well as northern fans are showing that they like the way things are working. And as long as the fans approve, we're going to keep on making progress, until we go the rest of the way in wiping Jim Crow out of American sports. . . .

The white public should start toward real understanding by appreciating that every single Negro who is worth his salt is going to resent any kind of slurs and discrimination because of his race and he is going to use every bit of intelligence such as he has to stop it. This has got absolutely nothing to do with what Communists may or may not be trying to do. And white people must realize that the more a negro hates communism because it opposes democracy, the more he is going to hate any other influence that kills off democracy in this country—and that goes for racial discrimination in the Army, and segregation on trains and buses, and job discrimination because of religious beliefs or color or place of birth.

And one other thing the American public ought to understand, if we are to make progress in this matter: The fact that it is a Communist who denounces injustice in the courts, police brutality, and lynching when it happens doesn't change the truth of his charges. Just because Communists kick up a big fuss over racial discrimination when it suits their purposes, a lot of people try to pretend that the whole issue is a creation of Communist imagination.

But they are not fooling anyone with this kind of pretense, and talk about "Communists stirring up Negroes to protest," only makes present misunderstanding worse than ever. Negroes were stirred up long before there was a Communist Party, and they'll stay stirred up long after the party has disappeared—unless Jim Crow has disappeared by then as well. . . .

I can't speak for any 15,000,000 people any more than any other one person can, but I know that I've got too much invested for my wife and child and myself in the future of this country, and I and other Americans of many races and faiths have too much invested in our country's welfare, for any of us to throw it away. . . . I am a religious man. Therefore I cherish America where I am free to worship as I please, a privilege which some countries do not give. And I suspect that 999 out of almost any thousand colored Americans you meet will tell you the same thing.

But that doesn't mean that we're going to stop fighting race discrimination in this country until we've got it licked. It means that we're going to fight it all the harder because our stake in the future is so big. We can win our fight without the Communists and we don't want their help.[1]

2. LETTER FROM JACKIE ROBINSON TO PRESIDENT EISENHOWER

MAY 13, 1958

My dear Mr. President:
I was sitting in the audience at the Summit Meeting of Negro Leaders yesterday when you said we must have patience. On hearing you say this, I felt like standing up and saying, "Oh no! Not again."

I respectfully remind you sir, that we have been the most patient of all people. When you said we must have self-respect, I wondered how we could have self-respect and remain patient considering the treatment accorded us through the years.

17 million Negroes cannot do as you suggest and wait for the hearts of men to change. We want to enjoy now the rights that we feel we are entitled to as Americans. This we cannot do unless we pursue aggressively goals which all other Americans achieved over 150 years ago.

As the chief executive of our nation, I respectfully suggest that you unwittingly crush the spirit of freedom in Negroes by constantly urging forbearance and give hope to those pro-segregation leaders like Governor Faubus who would take from us even those freedoms we now enjoy. Your own experience with Governor Faubus is proof enough that forbearance and not eventual integration is the goal the pro-segregation leaders seek.

Image 13.2: Rally at state capitol, Little Rock, 1959.

Federal intervention to integrate Central High School in Little Rock provoked an intense backlash, as seen in this rally at the Arkansas state capitol.

Source: John T. Bledsoe, U.S. News & World Report Photograph Collection, Library of Congress.

In my view, an unequivocal statement backed up by action such as you demonstrated you could take last fall in dealing with Governor Faubus if it became necessary, would let it be known that America is determined to provide—in the near future—for Negroes—the freedoms we are entitled to under the constitution.

Respectfully yours,
Jackie Robinson[2]

INTRODUCTION TO DOCUMENTS 3 AND 4

In one of the closest elections in American history, both Richard Nixon and John F. Kennedy were forced in 1960 to navigate an electorate divided over civil rights. When King was arrested at a sit-in in Atlanta, candidate Kennedy phoned Coretta Scott King to offer his sympathy. Meanwhile, John Kennedy's younger brother, Robert Kennedy, interceded and got King released on bail. King, though grateful, declined to endorse either candidate, surely recognizing the political motivations that might have fueled Kennedy's actions. Kennedy was a cautious ally of civil rights, both before and after his razor-thin election victory in 1961. Jackie Robinson noticed that caution and pressed the newly elected President to back social change more openly (Document 3). Robinson, a Republican, had publicly endorsed Nixon, as did many African Americans who still identified with the party of Lincoln. By 1963, however, Kennedy, along with many other Democrats, became far more supportive of anti-discrimination legislation. Document 4 is taken from the President's special message to Congress, asking for ambitious civil rights legislation to end racial discrimination.

3. LETTER FROM JACKIE ROBINSON TO PRESIDENT KENNEDY

February 9, 1961

My dear Mr. President:

I believe I now understand and appreciate better your role in the continuing struggle to fulfill the American promise of equal opportunity for all.

While I am very happy over your obviously fine start as our President, my concerns over Civil Rights and my vigorous opposition to your election is one of sincerity. The direction you seem to be going indicates America is in for great leadership, and I will be most happy if my fears continue to be proven wrong. We are naturally keeping a wondering eye on what will happen, and while any opposition or criticism may not be the most popular thing when you are leading so well, you must know that as an individual I am interested because what you do or do not do in the next 4 years could have a serious effect upon my children's future.

In your letter to me of July 1, 1960, you indicated you would use the influence of the White House in cases where moral issues are involved. You have reiterated your stand, and we are very happy. Still, we are going to use whatever voice we have to awaken our people. With the new emerging African nations, Negro Americans must assert themselves more, not for what we can get as individuals, but for the good of the Negro masses.

I thank you for what you have done so far, but it is not how much has been done but how much more there is to do. I would like to be patient Mr. President, but patience has caused us years in our struggle for human dignity. I will continue to hope and pray for your aggressive leadership but will not refuse to criticize if the feeling persist that Civil Rights is not on the agenda for months to come.

May God give you the strength and the energy to accomplish your most difficult task.

Respectfully yours,

Jackie Robinson[3]

4. THE WHITE HOUSE SPECIAL MESSAGE ON CIVIL RIGHTS TO THE CONGRESS OF THE UNITED STATES (FEBRUARY 28, 1963)

PRESIDENT JOHN F. KENNEDY

The Negro baby born in America today—regardless of the section or state in which he is born—has about one-half as much chance of completing high school as a white baby born in the same place on the same day—one-third as much chance of completing college—one-third as much chance of becoming a professional man—twice as much chance of becoming unemployed—about one-seventh as much chance of earning $10,000 per year—a life expectancy which is seven years less—and the prospects of earning only half as much.

No American who believes in the basic truth that "all men are created equal, that they are endowed by their Creator with certain unalienable Rights," can fully excuse, explain or defend the picture these statistics portray. Race discrimination hampers our economic growth by preventing the maximum development and utilization of our manpower. It hampers our world leadership by contradicting at home the message we preach abroad. It mars the atmosphere of a united and classless society in which this Nation rose to greatness. It increases the costs of public welfare, crime, delinquency and disorder. Above all, it is wrong.

Therefore, let it be clear, in our own hearts and minds, that it is not merely because of the Cold War, and not merely because of the economic waste of discrimination, that we are committed to achieving true equality of opportunity. The basic reason is because it is right.

The cruel disease of discrimination knows no sectional or state boundaries. The continuing attack on this problem must be equally broad. It must be both private and public—it must be conducted at national, state and local levels—and it must include both legislative and executive action.

In the last two years, more progress has been made in securing the civil rights of all Americans than in any comparable period in our history. Progress has been made—through executive action, litigation, persuasion and private initiative—in achieving and protecting equality of opportunity in education, voting, transportation, employment, housing, government, and the enjoyment of public accommodations.

But pride in our progress must not give way to relaxation of our effort. Nor does progress in the Executive Branch enable the Legislative Branch to escape its own obligations. On the contrary, it is in the light of this nationwide progress, and in the belief that Congress will wish once again to meet its responsibilities in this matter, that I stress in the following agenda of existing and prospective action important legislative as well as administrative measures.

The right to vote in a free American election is the most powerful and precious right in the world—and it must not be denied on the ground of race or color. It is a potent key to achieving other rights of citizenship. For American history—both recent and past—clearly reveals that the power of the ballot has enabled those who achieve it to win other achievements as well, to gain a full voice in the affairs of their state and nations and to see their interests represented in the governmental bodies which affect their future. In a free society, those with the power to govern are necessarily responsive to those with the right to vote.

In enacting the 1957 and 1960 Civil Rights Acts, Congress provided the Department of Justice with basic tools for protecting the right to vote—and this Administration has not hesitated to use those tools. Legal action is brought only after voluntary efforts fail—and, in scores of instances, local officials, at the request of the Department of Justice, have voluntarily made voting records available or abandoned discriminatory registration, discriminatory voting practices or segregated balloting. Where voluntary local compliance has not been forthcoming, the Department of Justice has approximately quadrupled the previous level of its legal effort—investigating coercion, inspecting records, initiating lawsuits, enjoining intimidation, and taking whatever follow-up action is necessary to forbid further interference or discrimination. As a result, thousands of Negro citizens are registering and voting for the first time—many of them in counties where no Negro had ever voted before. *The Department of Justice will continue to take whatever action is required to secure the right to vote for all Americans.*

Experience has shown, however, that these highly useful Acts . . . suffer from two major defects. One is the usual long and difficult delay which occurs between the filing of a lawsuit and its ultimate conclusion. In one recent case, for example, nineteen months elapsed between the filing of the suit and the judgment of the court. In another, an action brought in July 1961 has not yet come to trial. The legal maxim "Justice delayed is Justice denied" is dramatically applicable in these cases.

Too often those who attempt to assert their Constitutional rights are intimidated. Prospective registrants are fired. Registration workers are arrested. In some instances, churches in which registration meetings are held have been burned. In one case where Negro tenant farmers chose to exercise their right to vote, it was necessary for the Justice Department to seek injunctions to halt their eviction and for the Department of Agriculture to help feed them from surplus stocks.

Under these circumstances, continued delay in the granting of the franchise—particularly in counties where there is mass racial disfranchisement—permits the intent of the Congress to be openly flouted.

Federal executive action in such cases—no matter how speedy and how drastic—can never fully correct such abuses of power. It is necessary instead to free the forces of our democratic system within these areas by promptly insuring the franchise to all citizens, making it possible for their elected officials to be truly responsive to all their constituents.

The second and somewhat overlapping gap in these statutes is their failure to deal specifically with the most common forms of abuse of discretion on the part of local election officials who do not treat all applicants uniformly.

Objections were raised last year to the proposed literacy test bill, which attempted to speed up the enforcement of the right to vote by removing one important area of discretion from registration officials who used that discretion to exclude Negroes. Preventing that bill from coming to a vote did not make any less real the prevalence in many counties of the use of literacy and other voter qualification tests to discriminate against prospective Negro voters, contrary to the requirements of the 14th and 15th Amendments, and adding to the delays and difficulties encountered in securing the franchise for those denied it.

An indication of the magnitude of the overall problem, as well as the need for speedy action, is a recent five-state survey disclosing over 200 counties in which fewer than 15% of the Negroes of voting age are registered to vote. This cannot continue. I am, therefore, recommending legislation to deal with this problem of judicial delay and administrative abuse. . . .[4]

Image 13.3: Jackie Robinson and son at March on Washington, 1963

Source: Records of the U.S. Information Agency, Record Group 306, National Archives, Identifier 542024.

INTRODUCTION TO DOCUMENTS 5, 6, AND 7

John F. Kennedy was assassinated November 22, 1963. Three months later, the House of Representatives passed the civil rights bill, and sent it to the Senate. The new president, Lyndon B. Johnson picked up Kennedy's torch, but he faced several powerful opponents in the Senate among southern Democrats. On March 18, 1964 CBS televised a debate between Minnesota Democratic Senator Hubert Humphrey and South Carolina Democrat Strom Thurmond, the latter a longstanding defender of southern segregation and states' rights. Senators Humphrey and Thurmond had clashed publicly fifteen years earlier, back in 1948, when the young Minnesotan led the charge for a strong civil rights plank in the Democratic Party platform, and Thurmond and other southern politicians walked out and formed the States Rights Party. Thurmond ran at the top of the "Dixiecrat" ticket that year, and won thirty-nine electoral votes, from the states of Alabama, Mississippi, Louisiana, and South Carolina. Document 5 is excerpted from a transcript of the 1964 debate. Though both men were Democrats now, the prospect of federal jurisdiction over civil rights divided them. Southern senators sympathetic to Thurmond's position attempted a filibuster to halt the bill's progress. This division over civil rights led southern politicians and many white voters to end their allegiance to the Democratic Party, which stretched back to the American Civil War.

   The civil rights bill became law when supportive Democrats were aided by sympathetic Republicans in ending the southern Democratic filibuster. Just before the Senate voted on the legislation, Georgia Democrat Senator Richard Russell—a close confidant of Lyndon Johnson but ardent opponent of the legislation—reiterated southern concerns about the bill (Document 6). When Russell spoke, the filibuster had gone on for fifty-seven days. Finally, with a few key changes in the legislation, Senate Minority Leader Everett Dirksen and two other Republicans threw their support behind the civil rights bill, ending the two-month talking marathon. Document 7 is Dirksen's address to the Senate.

5. TELEVISED DEBATE BETWEEN HUBERT HUMPHREY (D-MN) AND STROM THURMOND (D-SC), MARCH 18, 1964

Eric Sevareid [moderator]: The U.S. Senate has been debating a motion to take up the civil rights bill and . . . when it does, debate on the merits of the bill developing into a filibuster will begin. Now, Senate rules allow a Senator to talk as long as he wants to, or he's able to, on any question at issue. And when several Senators try to talk a bill to death the resulting filibuster can go on for days, weeks, or even months. For decades Southerners have used the filibuster successfully to defeat or at least to water down civil rights bills. Tonight 19 Southern Senators are ready to try that again. One of them is Senator Strom Thurmond, of South Carolina. Leading the opposition to them is Senator Hubert H. Humphrey, of Minnesota. . . .

SENATOR HUMPHREY: . . . We know that fellow Americans who happen to be Negro have been denied equal access to places of public accommodation—denied in their travels the chance for a place to rest, and to eat, and to relax. We know that one-decade after the Supreme Court's decision declaring school segregation to be unconstitutional that less than 2 percent of the southern school districts are desegregated. And we know that Negroes do not enjoy equal employment opportunities. . . . The time has come for us to correct these evils—and the civil rights bill before the Senate is designed for the purpose. It is moderate—it is reasonable—it is well-designed. It was passed by the House 290 to 130. It is bipartisan.

SENATOR THURMOND: . . . This bill, in order to bestow preferential rights on a favored few who vote en bloc, would sacrifice the constitutional rights of every citizen and would concentrate in the National Government arbitrary powers, unchained by laws, to suppress the liberty of all. This bill makes a shambles of constitutional guarantees and the Bill of Rights. . . . It empowers the National Government to tell each citizen who must be allowed to enter upon and use his property without any compensation or due process of law as guaranteed by the Constitution. This bill would take away the rights of individuals and give to government the power to decide who is to be hired, fired and promoted in private busi-nesses. . . . It is because of these and other radical departures from our constitutional system that the attempt is being made to railroad this bill through Congress without following normal pro-cedures. It was only after lawless riots and dem-onstrations sprang up all over the country that the administration, after 2 years in office, sent this bill to Congress, where it has been made even worse. This bill is intended to increase—to appease those waging a vicious campaign of civil disobedience. The leaders of the demonstrations have already stated that the passage of the bill will not stop the mobs. Submitting to intimida-tion will only encourage further mob violence and to gain preferential treatment. . . . The choice is between law and anarchy. . . .

MR. Sevareid [moderator] . . . Let's [talk about] the public accommodations section of the civil rights bill. . . . This section, if passed, would forbid racial discrimination in hotels and motels, restaurants, theaters and similar places all over the country. . . .

SENATOR THURMOND: This title is entirely a misnomer. It's not public accommodations, it's invasion of private property. This will lead to integration of private life. . . . Under our Constitution a man has a right to use his own private property as he sees fit. The mayor of Salisbury, Md., said that if they had had a law on the books, as we're trying to pass here now, they would not have been able to have desegregated their business. Now, he says they were able to get the business people to do it voluntarily. You can't do some things by law. Some things have got to come in the hearts and minds of people. And we musn't think that we can regiment and control and regulate the lives of people. After all we have a Constitution that guarantees freedom, and we must observe that Constitution, and we don't want to require people to live in involuntary servitude. And I think it is involuntary servitude for a woman of one race to have to give a massage to a woman of another race if she doesn't want to do it.

SENATOR HUMPHREY: May I say, my friend, most respectfully, that many people that have private property do not have full rights to do what they want to do. If you operate . . . a bar, you don't have the right to have juveniles in it. If you oper-ate a restaurant, you don't have a right to have unsanitary conditions . . . I would add this: How is it that this Nation can call upon our colored people . . . to help win us the Olympic contests, to help win our wars, to pay taxes, to do every-thing that a citizen of this country is required to do, but when he wants to come to a hotel and have a night's rest, he's told that he can't come because he's colored.

SENATOR THURMOND: To persons in such a State as Minnesota, it may seem feasible to accomplish total integration of the races. In Minnesota, there are only 7 Negroes per 1,000 persons. It is an entirely different matter, however, where there are 250 to 400 Negroes per 1,000 persons. . . . We have not even mentioned the powers of the Attorney General to bring suits in the field of education. President Johnson led a successful fight in the Senate in 1957 and in 1960 to reject this provision because it was so extreme and unwarranted. Nor have we had time to mention the section which attempts to override the constitutionally reserved right of each State to determine the qualifications of voters. No bill is a civil rights bill if it takes away basic liberties and constitutional rights and guarantees, and replaces them with arbitrary Government powers. . . .

Senator Humphrey: . . . The purpose of this bill is to close a citizen gap in this country that has existed far too long. America has been weakened because we haven't given full opportunity to all of our people and the purpose of this bill is to try to lay down a legal framework within which we can work out our problems peacefully and honorably through law, through courts, rather than through violence and through demonstrations. I happen to believe that the issue before us is the great moral issue of our time and I don't think we can avoid it. . . . I cannot believe that 290 Members of the House of Representatives, 152 Democrats and 138 Republicans, would have voted for this bill if it was as evil as it has been described by my opponent here tonight. . . .[5]

6. SPEECH AGAINST THE CIVIL RIGHTS BILL, (JUNE 18, 1964)

SENATOR RICHARD RUSSELL (D-GA)

Mr. President, the moving finger is writing the final act of the longest debate and the greatest tragedy ever played out in the Senate of the United States. Within a short time, the battle that began on this floor on March 9 will be concluded with the passage of H.R. 7152-a bill bearing the attractive but false title of the Civil Rights Act of 1964.

. . . History may well record this as the last sustained fight to keep inviolate the federal system with its division of powers between the States and the Central Government, and the delicate system of checks and balances between the three branches of our National Government that have been dependent upon respect shown by each branch for the doctrine of the separation of powers between the three equal but coordinate branches. All of the eloquence that has been poured out here in this Chamber this afternoon in behalf of the bill will apply to any piece of proposed legislation that may be brought forward to use the Federal power to enforce absolute conformity of thought and action by every one of our citizens.

. . . I am proud to have been a member of that small group of determined Senators that since the 9th of March has given the last particle of ability and the last iota of physical strength in the effort to hold back the overwhelming combination of forces supporting this bill until its manifold evils could be laid bare before the people of the country. The depth of our conviction is evidenced by the intensity of our opposition. There is little room for honorable men to compromise where the inalienable rights of future generations are at stake. No group of men could have worked harder in a nobler cause. Undismayed and unintimidated by forces marshaling incomparably greater strength than available to us, we have fought the good fight until we were overwhelmed and gagged.

. . . The fact that the great metropolitan press, the radio and television, and other media of communicating news and formulating public opinion strongly support the bill made it all but impossible for us to get our case before the country. They magnified all that was said or done in the emotional appeals for support of the legislation and minimized or omitted the arguments as to its dangers. . . .

It opens up an area of political persecution that is wider than has ever existed before. This bill is not only the greatest delegation of power and authority by the legislative branch to the executive ever seen; it represents an admission of inadequacy and an abdication of responsibility by the national legislature which to all intents and purposes amounts to surrender of any claim to equality with the other two branches of the Government. It is an abandonment by the legislative branch of any defense whatever of the principal doctrine of separation of powers.

This bill would empower the executive branch to reach the long arm of regulation and intimidation into labor unions, business, commerce and industry in many areas into which the Federal power has not heretofore been permitted to intrude.

It places onerous requirements upon all people undertaking to earn a living in the way of reports and recordkeeping, and requires almost weekly obeisance to some bureaucrat in Washington. All of this falls upon the once free enterprise system that is the genesis of our greatness.

It bestows greater powers upon the Attorney General to invade and control the private lives of the American people than has ever been exercised by any other individual in our free system.

It so greatly enlarges the powers of the Federal Government over affairs that, under our constitutional concept, have been the sole concern of States and local governments as to make those governments mere puppets of the gigantic bureaucracy which this legislation strengthens and enlarges.

The bill is a drastic infringement by the Federal Government upon the basic human rights of every American citizen of every race to own and control property honestly gained as well as to be selective in choosing those with whom he wishes to associate.

. . . In all of the sanctimony about protecting the rights of minorities, let us understand fully that the bill is aimed at what has become the most despised and mistreated minority in the country—namely, the white people of the Southern States.

. . . Until we were gagged, we made no secret of the fact that we were undertaking to speak in detail and at length in an effort to get the message across to the American people.[6]

7. SPEECH IN SUPPORT OF CLOTURE AND THE CIVIL RIGHTS BILL (JUNE 1964)

SENATOR EVERETT DIRKSEN (R-IL)

. . . Since the act of 1875 on public accommodations and the Supreme Court decision of 1883 which struck it down, America has changed. The population then was 45 million. Today it is 190 million. In the Pledge of Allegiance to the Flag we intone, "One nation, under God." And so it is. It is an integrated nation. Air, rail, and highway transportation make it so. A common language makes it so. A tax pattern which applies equally to white and nonwhite makes it so. Literacy makes it so. The mobility provided by eighty million autos makes it so. The accommodations laws in thirty-four states and the District of Columbia makes it so. The fair employment practice laws in thirty states make it so. Yes, our land has changed since the Supreme Court decision of 1883.

. . . For many years, each political party has given major consideration to a civil rights plank in its platform. Go back and reexamine our pledges to the country as we sought the suffrage of the people and for a grant of authority to manage and direct their affairs. Were these pledges so much campaign stuff or did we mean it? Were these promises on civil rights but idle words for vote-getting purposes or were they a covenant meant to be kept?

. . . When the New York legislature placed a limit of ten hours per day and six days per week upon the bakery workers in that State, this act was struck down by the U.S. Supreme Court. But in due time came the eight-hour day and the forty-hour week and how broadly accepted this concept is today. Its time had come. More than sixty years ago, [Senator Robert] La Follette thundered against the election of U.S. senators by the state legislatures. The cry was to get back to the people and to first principles. On this Senate floor, senators sneered at his efforts and even left the chamber to show their contempt. But fifty years ago, the Constitution was amended to provide for the direct election of senators. Its time had come. Ninety-five years ago came the first endeavor to remove the limitation on sex in the exercise of the franchise. The comments made in those early days sound unbelievably ludicrous. But on and on went the effort and became the Nineteenth Amendment to the Constitution. Its time had come.

. . . These are but some of the things touching closely the affairs of the people which were met with stout resistance, with shrill and strident cries of radicalism, with strained legalisms, with anguished entreaties that the foundations of the Republic were being rocked. But an inexorable moral force which operates in the domain of human affairs swept these efforts aside and today they are accepted as parts of the social, economic and political fabric of America.

. . . I appeal to all senators. We are confronted with a moral issue. Today let us not be found wanting in whatever it takes by way of moral and spiritual substance to face up to the issue and to vote cloture.[7]

Image 13.4: Leaders of the March on Washington, August 1963

One year after the March on Washington, Congress passed the Civil Rights Act, a direct result of the decades of pressure brought to bear on the federal government. Note how the placards call not just for voting rights and desegregation of schools, but for jobs.

Source: U.S. Information Agency, Record Group 306, National Archives, Identifier 542002.

The Senate passed the Civil Rights Act of 1964 on June 19, 1964, and President Johnson signed the bill into law on July 2. It was by far the most comprehensive and forceful civil rights legislation ever to pass Congress. Document 8 provides highlights from the new law, and Document 9 is excerpted from President Lyndon Johnson's address to the nation.

8. THE CIVIL RIGHTS ACT OF 1964

An Act To enforce the constitutional right to vote, to confer jurisdiction upon the district courts of the United States to provide injunctive relief against discrimination in public accommodations, to authorize the Attorney General to institute suits to protect constitutional rights in public facilities and public education, to extend the Commission on Civil Rights, to prevent discrimination in federally assisted programs, to establish a Commission on Equal Employment Opportunity, and for other purposes.

TITLE I—VOTING RIGHTS

. . . No person acting under color of law shall . . . in determining whether any individual is qualified under State law or laws to vote in any Federal election, apply any standard, practice, or procedure different from the standards, practices, or procedures applied under such law or laws to other individuals within the same county, parish, or similar political subdivision who have been found by State officials to be qualified to vote. . . .

TITLE II—INJUNCTIVE RELIEF AGAINST DISCRIMINATION IN PLACES OF PUBLIC ACCOMMODATION

. . . All persons shall be entitled to the full and equal enjoyment of the goods, services, facilities, and privileges, advantages, and accommodations of any place of public accommodation, as defined in this section,

without discrimination or segregation on the ground of race, color, religion, or national origin. . . .

TITLE III—DESEGREGATION OF PUBLIC FACILITIES

. . . Whenever the Attorney General receives a complaint in writing signed by an individual to the effect that he is being deprived of or threatened with the loss of his right to the equal protection of the laws, on account of his race, color, religion, or national origin, by being denied equal utilization of any public facility which is owned, operated, or managed by or on behalf of any State or subdivision thereof . . . the Attorney General is authorized to institute for or in the name of the United States a civil action in any appropriate district court of the United States against such parties and for such relief as may be appropriate, and such court shall have and shall exercise jurisdiction of proceedings instituted pursuant to this section. . . .

TITLE IV—DESEGREGATION OF PUBLIC EDUCATION

"Desegregation" means the assignment of students to public schools and within such schools without regard to their race, color, religion, or national origin, but "desegregation" shall not mean the assignment of students to public schools in order to overcome racial imbalance. . . . "Public school" means any elementary or secondary educational institution, and "public college" means any institution of higher education or any technical or vocational school above the secondary school level. . . .

TITLE V—COMMISSION ON CIVIL RIGHTS

The Commission shall—

(1) investigate allegations in writing under oath or affirmation that certain citizens of the United States are being deprived of their right to vote and have that vote counted by reason of their color, race, religion, or national origin; which writing, under oath or affirmation, shall set forth the facts upon which such belief or beliefs are based; (2) study and collect information concerning legal developments constituting a denial of equal protection of the laws under the Constitution because of race, color, religion or national origin or in the administration of justice; (3) appraise the laws and policies of the Federal Government with respect to denials of equal protection of the laws under the Constitution because of race, color, religion or national origin or in the administration of justice. . . .

TITLE VI—NONDISCRIMINATION IN FEDERALLY ASSISTED PROGRAMS

. . . No person in the United States shall, on the ground of race, color, or national origin, be excluded from participation in, be denied the benefits of, or be subjected to discrimination under any program or activity receiving Federal financial assistance. . . .

TITLE VII—EQUAL EMPLOYMENT OPPORTUNITY

. . . It shall be an unlawful employment practice for an employer—

(1) to fail or refuse to hire or to discharge any individual, or otherwise to discriminate against any individual with respect to his compensation, terms, conditions, or privileges of employment, because of such individual's race, color, religion, sex, or national origin; or (2) to limit, segregate, or classify his employees in any way which would deprive or tend to deprive any individual of employment opportunities or otherwise adversely affect his status as an employee, because of such individual's race, color, religion, sex, or national origin. . . .[8]

9. PRESIDENT LYNDON B. JOHNSON ADDRESSES THE NATION (JULY 2, 1964)

. . . This is a proud triumph. Yet those who founded our country knew that freedom would be secure only if each generation fought to renew and enlarge its meaning. From the minutemen at Concord to the soldiers in Viet-Nam, each generation has been equal to that trust.

Americans of every race and color have died in battle to protect our freedom. Americans of every race and color have worked to build a nation of widening opportunities. Now our generation of Americans has been called on to continue the unending search for justice within our own borders.

. . . The reasons are deeply imbedded in history and tradition and the nature of man. We can understand—without rancor or hatred—how this all happened.

But it cannot continue. Our Constitution, the foundation of our Republic, forbids it. The principles of our freedom forbid it. Morality forbids it. And the law I will sign tonight forbids it.

That law is the product of months of the most careful debate and discussion. It was proposed more than one year ago by our late and beloved President John F. Kennedy. It received the bipartisan support of more than two-thirds of the Members of both the House and the Senate. An overwhelming majority of Republicans as well as Democrats voted for it.

It has received the thoughtful support of tens of thousands of civic and religious leaders in all parts of this Nation. And it is supported by the great majority of the American people.

The purpose of the law is simple.

It does not restrict the freedom of any American, so long as he respects the rights of others. It does not give special treatment to any citizen.

It does say the only limit to a man's hope for happiness, and for the future of his children, shall be his own ability.

It does say that there are those who are equal before God shall now also be equal in the polling booths, in the classrooms, in the factories, and in hotels, restaurants, movie theaters, and other places that provide service to the public. . . .

We must not approach the observance and enforcement of this law in a vengeful spirit. Its purpose is not to punish. Its purpose is not to divide, but to end divisions—divisions which have all lasted too long. Its purpose is national, not regional.

Its purpose is to promote a more abiding commitment to freedom, a more constant pursuit of justice, and a deeper respect for human dignity.

We will achieve these goals because most Americans are law-abiding citizens who want to do what is right.

This is why the Civil Rights Act relies first on voluntary compliance, then on the efforts of local communities and States to secure the rights of citizens. It provides for the national authority to step in only when others cannot or will not do the job.

This Civil Rights Act is a challenge to all of us to go to work in our communities and our States, in our homes and in our hearts, to eliminate the last vestiges of injustice in our beloved country.[9]

INTRODUCTION TO DOCUMENTS 10, 11, AND 12

The Civil Rights Act forbade many of the practices that kept African Americans from voting in the South such as poll taxes that made it prohibitive to cast a ballot and literacy tests that often contained arcane or bizarre questions. But the new law was light on enforcement mechanisms, prompting southern blacks to continue organizing for the ballot. Mississippi Freedom Summer, 1964, was designed to educate black citizens about politics and help them register to vote. Mississippi was long considered the most recalcitrant southern state, with the ugliest history of lynching. The following documents explain the strategy and rationale for Freedom Summer. Document 10 is from a pamphlet distributed by SNCC in the spring of 1964. It details the conditions of voting rights for blacks in Mississippi. Document 11 is an undated (probably early 1964) summary of SNCC's plans for the Freedom Summer and the reasons for the project. The document is too long to reprint in its entirety; what is left out here goes into great detail about the need to establish "freedom schools," designed to educate black youth in basic literacy skills, and to identify potential young leaders to strengthen the future of the civil rights movement. Document 12 is a memorandum from Robert Moses to the "Friends of Freedom in Mississippi." Moses was head of the Conference of Federated Organizations (COFO), an umbrella group established specifically for Freedom Summer. His memo asks movement leaders to write to President Lyndon Johnson urging protection for civil rights workers. Documents 11 and 12 were circulated among organizers of the movement; they were not for public consumption.

10. SNCC PAMPHLET ON VOTING RIGHTS (1964)

For the first time in United States history colored citizens are organizing across an entire state to overthrow white supremacy. In Mississippi national and local civil rights, civic and church organizations, through the Council of Federated Organizations, are pulling together for the right to demand changes in the Mississippi Way of Life.

At the same time there are whites throughout the state organizing to crush the movement for change. The dominant white supremacy group is known as the White Citizens' Councils, organized by Mississippi's "leading" citizens in 1954 to combat colored voting rights and resist the Supreme Court school decision that same year.

The Citizens' Councils now maintain a firm stranglehold on the governorship, the state legislature and the federal and state courts. They control local and state education throughout most of the state, and dominate the economic base and activity in the state. . . .

In 1890 there were many more colored citizens than white citizens who were eligible to become qualified electors in Mississippi. Therefore, in that year a Mississippi Constitutional Convention was held to adopt a new State Constitution.

Section 244 of the new Constitution required a new registration of voters starting January 1, 1892. This section also established a new requirement for qualification as a registered voter: a person had to be able to read any section of the Mississippi Constitution, or understand any section when read to him, or give a reasonable interpretation of any section. . . .

Under the new registration the balance of voting power shifted. By 1899 approximately 122,000 (82 percent) of the white males of voting age were registered. But only 18,000 (9 percent) of the colored males qualified. Since 1899 a substantial majority of whites of voting age have become registered voters. But the percentage of colored registered voters declined. . . .

On April 22, 1954, the State Legislature again passed a resolution to amend Section 244. This time however, several new qualifications were included in the proposal.

FIRST, that a person must be able to read and write any section of the Mississippi Constitution; and give a reasonable interpretation of the Constitution to the county registrar.

SECOND, a person must be able to demonstrate to the county registrar a reasonable understanding of the duties and obligations of citizenship under a constitutional form of government.

THIRD, that a person must make a sworn written application for registration on a form which would be prescribed by the State Board of Election Commissioners.

FOURTH, that all persons who were registered before January 1, 1954, were expressly exempted from the new requirements. . . .

The burden of the new requirements had to fall on colored citizens because a substantial majority of whites were already registered and therefore exempted from the amendment. Most would still have to apply for registration and therefore have to fulfill the new requirements. In 1954 at least 450,000 (63 percent) of the voting-age whites were registered.

Approximately 22,000 (five percent) of the voting-age colored citizens were registered. With 95 percent of the 472,000 eligible voters white, the proposed amendment to Section 244 was adopted on November 2, 1954. . . .

Without the right to register and vote we cannot take part in any phases of Mississippi's form of republican government.

What recourse do the white supremacists leave Mississippi colored citizens, if they cannot voice their opinions at the polls?[10]

11. PROSPECTUS FOR THE MISSISSIPPI FREEDOM SUMMER (c. 1964)

SNCC

. . . Since 1964 is an election year, the clear-cut issue of voting rights should be brought out in the open. Many SNCC and CORE workers in Mississippi hold the view that Negroes will never vote in large numbers until Federal marshals intervene. At any rate, many Americans must be made to realize that the voting rights they so often take for granted involve considerable risk for Negroes in the South. In the larger context of the national civil rights movement, enough progress has been made during the last year that there can be no turning back. Major victories in Mississippi, recognized as the stronghold of racial intolerance in the South, would speed immeasurably the breaking down of legal and social discrimination in both North and South. . . .

This summer's work in Mississippi is sponsored by COFO, the Council of Federated Organizations, which includes the Student Nonviolent Coordinating Committee (SNCC), the Southern Christian Leadership Conference (SCLC), the Congress of Racial Equality (CORE), and the NAACP, as well as Mississippi community groups. Within the state COFO has made extensive preparations since mid-January to develop structured programs which will put to creative use the talents and energies of the hundreds of expected summer volunteers. . . .

Voter registration workers will be involved in an intensive summer drive to encourage as many Negroes as possible to register. They will participate in COFO's Freedom Registration, launched in early February, to register over 400,000 Negroes on Freedom Registration books. These books will be set up in local Negro establishments and will have simplified standards of registration (the literacy test and the requirement demanding an interpretation of a section of the Mississippi Constitution will be eliminated). Freedom Registration books will serve as the basis of a challenge of the official books of the state and the validity of "official" elections this fall. Finally, registration workers will assist in the campaigns of Freedom candidates who are expected to run for seats in all five of the State's congressional districts and for the seat of Senator John Stennis, who is up for re-election. . . .[11]

12. MEMO TO "FRIENDS OF FREEDOM IN MISSISSIPPI" (1964)

BOB MOSES

RE: MISSISSIPPI FREEDOM SUMMER

Dear Sirs:[12]
I am writing on request of the Executive Committee of the Student Nonviolent Coordinating Committee and in my function as Program Director of the Council of Federated Organizations (COFO).

You are all aware of the summer program COFO is sponsoring in Mississippi this summer. We expect to field over two thousand workers in

Freedom schools, community centers, voter registration drives in every county, and projects in selected white communities. We anticipate up to one thousand volunteers from across the country to join us in this program, including ministers, teachers, lawyers and students.

We have learned through bitter experience in the past three years that the judicial, legislative and executive bodies of Mississippi form a wall of absolute resistance to granting civil rights to Negroes. It is our conviction that only a massive effort by the country backed by the full power of the President can offer some hope for even minimal change in Mississippi.

We have already been accused of launching this project to incite violence and chaos in Mississippi this summer. We have two answers to this charge. For one, violence is prevalent throughout the state; at least six Negroes have been killed by whites in the past three months. And, more important, the responsibility for maintaining law and guaranteeing, at the same time, the right to peaceful protest, must rest, in the final analysis, in the case of Mississippi, with the President of the United States.

The President must be made to understand that this responsibility rests with him, and him alone, and that neither he nor the American people can afford to jeopardize the lives of the people who will be working in Mississippi this summer by failing to take the necessary precautions before the summer begins.

We are writing this letter now to you, to join together as the "Friends of Freedom in Mississippi" to seek a meeting with President Johnson to ask him to do the following things to insure peaceful change in Mississippi this summer.

President Johnson should:

1. Meet in early May with Governor Johnson of Mississippi and extract from Governor Johnson the pledge that he will call together all state and local law enforcement leaders and lay down certain ground rules for the summer. Under these rules the following activities will not only be permitted, but will be protected: peaceful orderly picketing; voter registration; orderly distribution of leaflets; peaceful assembly; freedom of interracial groups to live in the Negro communities and to move around the state without molestation.
2. President Johnson will inform the governor that these are clearly established constitutional rights which the federal government has the responsibility to protect, and that if the governor will not do this, the federal government will. . . .
3. President Johnson should pledge to the committee in advance that he will take these actions if the governor refuses. . . .[13]

INTRODUCTION TO DOCUMENTS 13–16

Nonviolent direct action meant peaceful protest, but everyone involved knew that demonstrations were likely to provoke strong reactions from local authorities. Peaceful, dignified marchers confronting a wall of heavily armed police was dramatic enough. But repeatedly, "peace" officers resorted to clubs, tear gas, water cannons, and mass arrests. One of the most dramatic moments in the civil rights movement came in Selma, Alabama, March 7, 1965. Over 500 people began a march in support of voting rights from Selma to Montgomery. When they crossed the Edmund Pettus Bridge into Dallas County, a phalanx of state troopers and deputy sheriffs began an attack, first shoving demonstrators and then knocking them down and beating them with nightsticks. Newspaper headlines and television footage stirred public outrage. Seventeen people were hospitalized, including SNCC leader John Lewis, who years later became a congressman from Georgia. Document 13 is Lewis's statement to the FBI. Document 14 is an angry letter from a private citizen to the head of the FBI, J. Edgar Hoover. Another private citizen was inspired to describe his opposition to the voting rights bill to Congressman Emmanual Celler of New York, Chairman of the House Judiciary Committee (Document 15). Document 16 is excerpted from the Voting Rights Act of 1965.

13. STATEMENT OF JOHN LEWIS TO THE FBI

Selma, Ala.

March 8, 1965

I, John Robert Lewis, furnish the following signed statement to John H. Lupton and Daniel D. Doyle who have identified themselves as Special Agents of the Federal Bureau of Investigation. I understand that this statement is being taken in connection with an official investigation and might be used in court.

I am twenty-five years of age and reside at 8 ½ Raymond St., Atlanta, Ga. I am National Chairman of Student Nonviolent Coordinating Committee.

On the afternoon of March 7, 1965, I was a leader in a march which was intended to proceed from Selma, Ala. Brown ___ Chapel Church to Montgomery, Ala. I was at the head of the march together with Hosea Williams, an S.C.L.C. Official.

As we approached a point on Highway 80E near the Glass House Restaurant, we were stopped by a row of Alabama State Troopers who were across the highway. A trooper with a megaphone ordered the marchers to disperse or go back to the church. When we stood fast, the troopers moved towards us with night sticks, first pushing us and immediately thereafter charging into the crowd of marchers swinging the night sticks.

I was hit with a night stick and fell to my knees. When I attempted to get up I was struck a second time in the head with a night stick by the same trooper.

At that point, I was engulfed in tear gas which was exploded by the troopers, and I vomited.

To escape the gas I ran to the east of the highway toward the woods. I then proceeded on foot back to Brown___ Chapel Church.

Shortly, thereafter, while addressing a group of marchers at the church, I began to feel severe pain in my head. I therefore, went next door to the church parsonage where I awaited an ambulance which subsequently took me to the Good Samaritan Hospital in Selma.

At no time during the above described incident did I assault or in any way interfere with a law enforcement officer.

I have read the four page statement [sic], and it is true and correct.[14]

14. LETTER FROM ASSONET, MASSACHUSETTS, TO J. EDGAR HOOVER (MARCH 13, 1965)

I would like to hear from you by public press as to whether or not you agree with your F.B.I. agent, Mr. James M. Barbo of Mobile, Ala. that you think the State Troopers acted in the interest of public safety by *tear gassing* Negro marchers last Sunday at Selma, Ala.

I saw a picture on TV of a scene last Sunday night in which men in the uniform of peace officers mounted and deputized officers of sheriffs that trampled, clubbed, bullwhipped and gas bombed prostrate Negroes and their friends, and including women and children because they were trying to exercise their constitutional rights.

It was the most monstrous, brutal thing I've ever seen.

Please also give us some data on Mr. Barbo . . . I think he should be fired immediately.

I think that as a citizen of the U.S. I have a right to ask this. For the record, I am white, Anglo-Saxon and Christian and old. . . .

Yours truly, (Mrs.) A.P.G.[15]

15. LETTER FROM REGO PARK, NEW YORK, TO CONGRESSMAN EMMANUEL CELLER (JULY 9, 1965)

Why do you advocate no literacy tests as a qualification for voting? Is your district so saturated with illiterates that you fear the loss of your seat in Congress at voting time?

Literacy *and good* knowledge of English is required of foreigners immigrating to the United States and seeking their citizenship papers. What's the difference? Why discriminate against this group?

Besides this, how can anyone be sure that unscrupulous politicians won't direct illiterates how to vote—for their own [sake?] by advising them which line to pull the indicators on voting machines or which name to make an "X" alongside on paper ballots of they have no knowledge.

You are taking this too far—I'd appreciate an *answer* to my *questions*.

Mr. C.E.G.[16]

16. THE VOTING RIGHTS ACT OF 1965

AN ACT TO ENFORCE THE FIFTEENTH AMENDMENT TO THE CONSTITUTION OF THE UNITED STATES. . . .

No voting qualification or prerequisite to voting, or standard, practice, or procedure shall be imposed or applied by any State or political subdivision to deny or abridge the right of any citizen of the United States to vote on account of race or color. . . .

Wherever the Attorney General Institutes a proceeding under any statute to enforce the guarantees of the fifteenth amendment in any State or political subdivision the court shall authorize appoint of Federal examiners by the United States Civil Service Commission. . . .

If in a proceeding instituted by the Attorney General under any statute to enforce the guarantees of the fifteenth amendment in any State or political subdivision the court finds that a test or device has been used for the purpose or the effect of denying or abridging the right of any citizen of the United States to vote on account of race or color, it shall suspend the use of tests and devices in such State or political subdivisions as the court shall determine is appropriate and for such period as it deems necessary. . . .

. . . The Civil Service may assign, at the request of the attorney General, one or more persons, who may be officers of the United States, (1) to enter and attend at any place holding an election . . . and (2) to enter and attend at any place for tabulating the votes cast at any election . . . for the purpose of observing whether votes cast by persons entitled to vote are being properly tabulated. . . .

The Congress finds that the requirement of the payment of a poll tax as a precondition to voting (i) precludes persons of limited means from voting . . . (ii) does not bear a reasonable relationship to any legitimate State interest in the conduct of elections, and (iii) in some areas has the purpose or effect of denying persons the right to vote because of race or color. Upon the basis of these findings, Congress declares that the constitutional right of citizens to vote is denied or abridged in some areas by the requirement of the payment of a poll tax as a precondition of voting. . . .

Approved June 6, 1965[17]

POSTSCRIPT

The Civil Rights and Voting Rights Acts are considered the high-water marks of the Freedom Struggle. Just as the Fifteenth Amendment enfranchised the freed slaves, the Voting Rights Act gave the ballot back to African Americans. Yet such gains were fragile. In 2013, the U.S. Supreme Court struck down an essential element of the Act, federal oversight of states that failed to enforce the law. In *Shelby County v. Holder,* the majority ruled that given the progress made in the southern states in the half century since the Voting Rights Act passed in 1965, this section of the law was no longer necessary. The decision opened the way for new franchise restrictions, such as voter identification laws in South Carolina and gerrymandering in Texas that diluted the ballot box power of Latino and black citizens. A federal court in 2017 found Texas to be in violation of the Voting Rights Act, which still retained some of its power to limit voter disfranchisement.

QUESTIONS

1. Why did the issue of civil rights divide Democrats such as Hubert Humphrey from Strom Thurmond and Richard Russell? Why did Thurmond and Russell characterize the civil rights bill as coercive for white southerners?
2. What techniques were used to keep African Americans from voting?
3. What was nonviolent direct action, and how effective was it in advancing civil rights? Was it necessary, in your view, to achieve the gains made in the 1950s and 1960s? Can you envision other techniques that might have also worked to encourage change?
4. Do you consider the civil rights movement a success? Where did it fall short?
5. Why do you think federal intervention in desegregation prompted such resistance in the southern states? Why did civil rights advocates depend so heavily on the federal government?
6. In evaluating the gains made in civil rights, how important was grassroots organizing relative to federal legislation and action?

ADDITIONAL READING

One of the best general introductions to the civil rights movement is Harvard Sitkoff, *The Struggle for Black Equality, 1954–1980* (1981). Also see Juan Williams and Julian Bond, *Eyes on the Prize* (1988). Other important titles include Clayborne Carson, *In Struggle: SNCC and the Black Awakening of the 1960s* (1981); Doug McAdam, *Freedom Summer* (1988); Charles Marsh, *God's Long Summer*

(1997); Charles Payne, *I've Got the Light of Freedom* (1995); and John Dittmer's excellent *Local People* (1995). For good case studies of the movement, see William H. Chafe, *Civilities and Civil Rights: Greensboro, North Carolina, and the Black Struggle for Freedom* (1980); Robert J. Norrell, *Reaping the Whirlwind: The Civil Rights Movement in Tuskegee* (1985); and James T. Patterson, *Brown versus The Board of Education* (2001). For King and his times, see Taylor Branch, *Parting the Waters* (1988), *Pillar of Fire* (1998), and *At Canann's Edge* (2006); and David Garrow, *Protest at Selma: Martin Luther King, Jr., and the Voting Rights Act of 1986* (2015). For a moving oral history by those who participated, see Howell Raines, *My Soul Is Rested* (1977). On the movement after 1964, see William L. Van De Berg, *New Day in Babylon* (1993). For a dramatic account of a key moment, see Raymond Arsenault, *Freedom Riders* (2006). The best documentary remains PBS's *Eyes on the Prize: America's Civil Rights Years, 1954–1965* (1987).

ENDNOTES

1. *Hearings Regarding Communist Infiltration of Minority Groups*, 81st Congress, 1st Session. July 13, 14, and 18, 1949 (Washington, D.C.: Government Printing Office, 1949).
2. White House Central Files, 1953–1961, Dwight Eisenhower Library, Abilene, KS. National Archives Identifier 186627.
3. Jackie Robinson File, Harris L. Wofford Papers, John Kennedy Library.
4. *Public Papers of the Presidents of the United States: John Kennedy, January 1-November 22, 1963* (Washington, D.C.: U.S. Government Printing Office, 1964).
5. Senate *Congressional Record*, March 26, 1964, pp. 6428--6431.
6. Senate *Congressional Record*, June 18, 1964, pp. 14301–14303.
7. Senate *Congressional Record*, June 10, 1964, pp. 11319-13320.
8. The Civil Rights Act of 1964, Record Group 11, National Archives, Identifier 299891.
9. *Public Papers of the Presidents of the United States: Lyndon B. Johnson, 1963-1964* (Washington, D.C.: Government Printing Office, 1965), pp. 842-844.
10. Excerpted from *Baltimore Afro-American*, October 3, 1964. Reprinted courtesy of Afro-American Company of Baltimore City T/A, Afro-American Newspapers.
11. From the Records of the Southern Regional Council, Atlanta, GA, file labeled "1964."
12. The Friends of Freedom in Mississippi included Roy Wilkins, James Farmer, Martin Luther King Jr., James Forman, A. Philip Randolph, Bayard Rustin, John Lewis, Harry Belafonte, James Baldwin, Dick Gregory, Ossie Davis, Marlon Brando, Aaron Henry, Ed King, Robert Spike, Jessie Gray, Larry Landry, Clyde Ferguson, Noel Day, and Ella Baker.
13. From the Records of the Southern Regional Council, Atlanta, GA, file labeled "1964."
14. Statement of John Lewis, March 11, 1965, Classification 44 (Civil Rights) Headquarters Case Files, 1924, 1978, Records of the FBI, Record Group 65, National Archives.
15. Letter to J. Edgar Hoover with response, Classification 44 (Civil Rights) Headquarters Case Files, 1924–1978, Records of the FBI, Record Group 65, National Archives.
16. Records of the U.S. House of Representatives, Record Group 233, National Archives Identifier 595302.
17. "The Voting Rights Act of 1965," August 6, 1965; Record Group 11, National Archives.

CHAPTER 14

VIETNAM: THE TIPPING POINT

HISTORICAL CONTEXT

The United States became involved in Vietnam during the late 1940s, as part of an effort to reign-in communism throughout the world. Members of the Truman administration believed that the way to limit communism and stabilize the region was to help the French reclaim their old colony in Indochina (which the Japanese had seized during World War II), in exchange for a pledge by the French government to join the North Atlantic Treaty Organization (NATO). When the French were soundly defeated in the mid-1950s by a Vietnamese army, the American commitment to controlling Southeast Asia only increased. Rather than see Vietnam "fall" to the communists, the Eisenhower administration scuttled free elections and supported the unpopular, anticommunist regime of Ngo Dinh Diem, which controlled the southern half of the country.

When he took office in 1961, President John Kennedy continued the Cold War policies and strategies of Truman and Eisenhower. He even increased American military involvement in Vietnam, slowly raising troops levels there from 1,000 in January 1961 to 16,000 by November 1963. Vietnam, his policy makers insisted, was the key to all of Southeast Asia. If it "fell," Laos, Cambodia, and Thailand would follow, threatening Japan and Australia. It would be like a line of dominoes: topple the first and the rest would also go down. Keep in mind how powerful Cold War logic had become. China's communist revolution triumphed by 1950, sweeping the world's most populous nation into the "Soviet orbit." The American led war to turn back Communist North Korea's invasion of the south ended in a stalemate in 1953. Communism was indeed a powerful presence in Vietnam. But American foreign policy since Truman tended to see every issue through that lens. At least equally powerful in Vietnam was a nationalist impulse, anti-Chinese, anti-French, and now anti-American, a desire for Vietnamese nationhood, communist or not.

Lyndon Johnson continued the logic inherited from Kennedy: He would not be the first American president to lose a war nor would he preside over a communist victory. Despite the South Vietnamese government's corruption and incompetence; despite his own pledges during the 1964 election not to involve America in a land war in Asia; and despite the lack of international support for the war, he increased American troop levels: 25,000 at the end of 1964; nearly 200,000 one year later, which doubled after another year; 500,000 by the beginning of 1968; and 550,000 before the end of the year. Moreover, these soldiers were no longer "advisers" to South Vietnam, as they had been termed in the Eisenhower–Kennedy years. Now they were initiating combat, while the U.S. Air Force dropped unprecedented numbers of bombs, and the Navy shelled coastal cities. The American military also used new substances such as chemical defoliants to clear away the jungle, and napalm, a flammable jelly that was dropped burning from airplanes and clung to everything it hit. Still, the war was a stalemate. Hundreds of thousands of Vietnamese and tens of thousands of Americans died, farms and jungles became moonscapes, and many American citizens, sensing a gap between official pronouncements and reality-on-the-ground, could not abide what we were doing there. Protests—on college campuses, in churches, on the streets—grew in size and strength during the late 1960s.

No event more clearly showed the difference between official and unofficial versions of the war than the January 31, 1968, Tet Offensive—a massive, coordinated North Vietnamese and Vietcong assault against major cities and towns in South Vietnam (keep in mind that after the French left, Vietnam was divided in two with a North Vietnamese army aided by allies in the south called the Vietcong, opposing the Americans, and an anti-communist South Vietnamese army). The Tet Offensive began shortly after army General William Westmoreland's much-publicized visit to Washington, D.C. An end to the war, Westmoreland had told Johnson and the American people, was in sight; the Vietcong had been overwhelmed, and North Vietnam was suffering terribly. But the Tet Offensive seemed to belie Westmoreland's rosy optimism. And although American forces turned back the offensive, many American civilians no longer fully believed the pronouncements of their leaders. President Johnson realized as much. After Tet, he stopped talking about winning the war; rather he simply wanted it ended.

Two months after the Tet Offensive, on March 16, 1968 in an area designated "Pinkville," units of the U.S. Army's Americal Division assaulted a strip of Quang Ngai province along the South China Sea. Press releases and combat action reports filed in the days after the assault described the confrontation between the U.S. and Vietcong forces as a resounding American victory. Sergeant Jay Roberts, a reporter who covered the assault for the Army's Public Information Department, noted that Americans killed 128 enemy troops and captured enemy weapons and documents. "The combat assault went like clockwork," Lieutenant Colonel Frank Barker, the commander of the task force that conducted the maneuver, told Roberts.

Barker said as much to his superiors in his combat action report, noting that the "operation was well planned, well executed and successful." To be sure, a few civilians in the hamlet of My Lai were caught in the cross fire of the opposing forces, but "the infantry unit on the ground and helicopters were able to assist civilians in leaving the area and in caring for and/or evacuating the wounded."

Newspapers picked up on Roberts's and Barker's comments and printed them in small stories, while General William Westmoreland, commander of U.S. forces in Vietnam, issued an official congratulatory message to Barker. In truth, what had happened in "Pinkville" that March day created hardly any interest. It seemed just the slightest ripple in a very large sea, a minor assault on a minor hamlet far from the center of the action—really nothing important enough to occupy anyone's thoughts.

But the men who took part in the assault stored memories very different from the official one. Some had recorded their thoughts in journal entries and letters. Thomas R. Partsch scribbled in his journal during a water break:

> Mar. 16 Sat. got up at 5:30 left at 7:15 we had 9 choppers. 2 lifts first landed had mortar team with us. We started to move slowly through the village shooting everything in sight children men and women and animals. Some was sickening. The[ir] legs were shot off and they were still moving it was just hanging there. I think the[ir] bodies were made of rubber. I didn't fire a round yet and I didn't kill anybody not even a chicken I couldn't.

That evening, Captain Brian Livingston, a helicopter commander, wrote his wife and expressed his disgust with the operation:

> Well its been a long day, saw some nasty sights. I saw the insertion of infantrymen and were they animals. . . . I've never seen so many people dead in one spot. Ninety-five percent were women and kids. We told the grunts [American soldiers] on the ground of some injured kids. They helped them alright. A captain walked up to this little girl, he turned away took five steps, and fired a volley of shots into her. . . . I'll tell you something it sure makes you wonder why we are here.

Others told friends what they had seen. A month after the attack, Private Charles "Butch" Gruver gave his version of that day to an army buddy named Ronald Ridenhour. Seated in a bar, relaxing with a few bottles of beer, Gruver asked Ridenhour, "Did you hear about Pinkville?" When Ridenhour answered that he had not, Gruver commented, "We went in there and killed everybody." As they drank, more details emerged. Gruver's Charlie Company had gone into My Lai expecting a real fight, but they encountered no hostile Vietcong, only a village full of frightened women, old men, and children, many of whom they herded into small groups for security reasons. But then orders were given to kill the civilians, and some soldiers went on a rampage. There were mass murders, rapes, and torture. It was horrible. Ridenhour could not believe what he was hearing, but Gruver swore it was all true. In the next few months, Ridenhour met and quizzed other soldiers who had been at My Lai. Each confirmed Gruver's tale, adding more details about the terrible day.

So we have two very different versions of the same event, one official, the other unofficial. In an odd way, that had always been the American story in Vietnam. From the start, there had been a confusion between what the American people back home heard about the conflict and what the American soldiers knew was the nasty reality of this war.

My Lai occurred less than two months after the start of the Tet Offensive, and in retrospect, it was a turning point. It took place during a period of low morale and high frustration, a time when many soldiers had lost faith in their mission and questioned why they were fighting and dying. My Lai underscored some of the grim facts of Vietnam, including the nature of the warfare, American attitudes toward the Vietnamese people, the gap between the official pronouncements about the war and the realities on the ground, and the psychological impact of battle. In the following documents, consider these issues and ask yourself about the American aims and actions in Vietnam, and the effect of the war at home. This chapter focuses on the war at this intense moment, from late 1968 through the middle of 1969, when the frustration of battle, and the increasing opposition to the war forced Johnson to reassess not just his policies, but his own position as president.

INTRODUCTION TO DOCUMENTS 1, 2, AND 3

The following documents reveal a range of opinions about the Vietnam War as of early 1968, from strong support to all-out opposition. In Document 1, beloved American writer John Steinbeck conveys his thoughts directly to President Johnson. Both of Steinbeck's sons served in Vietnam, and the author of *Grapes of Wrath* wrote dispatches from the war for *Newsday* from December 1966 to early 1967. By this point, however, increasing numbers of Americans considered Vietnam a mistake. Because of his support for the war, some of Steinbeck's fans believed he had betrayed his reputation as a writer of the American common experience. In Document 2, famed African American athlete Jackie Robinson, whose letters to presidents appear in chapters 11 and 13, again writes to Johnson to explain the important relationship between the struggle in Vietnam and the ongoing fight for Civil Rights at home. It was an agonizing decision for many Civil Rights leaders to oppose Johnson on Vietnam since he had done so much for the Freedom Struggle. Finally, Document 3 is one of many printed anti-draft statements that proliferated in 1967 and 1968, often distributed at recruitment centers to convince young men to reconsider their decision.

1. LETTER FROM JOHN STEINBECK TO PRESIDENT JOHNSON

May 28, 1966

Dear Mr. President:

I am grateful to you for receiving my son and me. It meant a great deal to both of us and I am sure that seeing you reassured him that responsibility is behind him and backing him. He had never been to Washington before. From the plane I took him first to the Lincoln Memorial. He stood for a long time looking up at that huge and quiet figure and then said, "Oh! Lord! We had better be great."

You will understand that I am pleased with this boy and proud. He knows what he wants and must do. He is thoroughly trained to do it. He is proud of his uniform and proud of his country. He goes very soon now, and as you must know, my heart goes with him. And I will ask you, sir, to remember your promise to pray for him.

I know that you must be disturbed by the demonstrations against policy in Vietnam. But please remember that there have always been people who insisted on their right to choose the war in which they would fight to defend their country. There were many who would have no part of Mr. Adams' and George Washington's war. We call them Tories. There were many also who called General Jackson a butcher. Then there were the very many who denounced and even impeded Mr. Lincoln's war. We call them copperheads. . . . I remind you of these things, Mr. President, because sometimes, the shrill squeaking of people who simply do not wish to be disturbed, must be saddening to you. I assure you that only mediocrity escapes criticism.

Again my thanks to you, sir. You gave my boy a pediment of pride, and that a good soldier must have.

As always, faithfully,
John Steinbeck[1]

2. LETTER FROM JACKIE ROBINSON TO PRESIDENT JOHNSON

April 18, 1967

Dear Mr. President:

First, let me thank you for pursuing a course towards Civil Rights that no President in our history has pursued. I am confident your dedication will not only continue, but will be accelerated dependent on the needs of all Americans.

While I am certain your faith has been shaken by demonstrations against the Viet Nam war, I hope the actions of any one individual does not make you feel as Vice President Humphrey does, that Dr. King's stand will hurt the Civil Rights movement. It would not be fair to the thousands of our Negro fighting men who are giving their lives because they believe, in most instances, that our Viet Nam stand is just. There are hundreds of thousands of us at home who are not certain why we are in the war. We feel, however, that you and your staff know what is best and we are willing to support your efforts for a honorable solution to the war.

I do feel you must make it infinitely clear, that regardless of who demonstrates, that your position will not change toward the rights of all people; that you will continue to press for justice for all Americans and that a strong stand now will have great effect upon young Negro Americans who could resort to violence unless they are reassured. . . .

I appreciate the difficult role any President has. I believe, also, yours is perhaps the most difficult any President has had. I hope God gives you the wisdom and strength to come through this crisis at home, and that an end to the war in Viet Nam is achieved very soon.

Again Sir, let me thank you for your domestic stand on Civil Rights. We need an even firmer stand as the issues become more personal and the gap between black and white Americans get wider.

Sincerely yours,
Jackie Robinson[2]

3. DRAFT RESISTANCE LEAFLET (MARCH 28, 1968)

KEEP THIS LEAFLET.

THE PEOPLE INSIDE CAN NOT MAKE YOU THROW THIS AWAY OR KEEP YOU FROM READING IT

What's in the Army for you? What? Not one thing! It's just a way for you to get your ass shot off for the fat bankers and businessmen who run this country. They're the ones this war is being fought for. They want control of Vietnam so they can use its natural resources and cheap labor to make more money. Are you going to get killed so Lockheed can make more money? Money off your blood?

WHEN YOU'RE IN THE ARMY, ASK QUESTIONS AT THE ORIENTATION SESSIONS:

Image 14.1 Noam Chomsky speaking at the New York Town Hall anti-Vietnam draft rally, January 14, 1968

Just days before the Tet Offensive, antiwar activist Noam Chomsky joined others in New York to protest the draft. What does the statement behind Chomsky mean?

Source: Records of U.S. Attorneys, Record Group 118, National Archives, Identifier 7419597.

—If the U.S. is defending freedom in Vietnam, why is it backing Marshall Ky—a corrupt dictator who says his only hero is Adolph Hitler?

—When the Vietnamese were fighting to throw out the French colonialists in 1954, why did the U.S. back the French? Why did the U.S. pay 80 percent of the French war costs?

—Why did the U.S. bring back the rich Vietnamese landlords that the Vietnamese people had thrown out? The big land owners, who don't do any work, force the small farmers to hand over 50% of their crop as rent every year.

—If the Vietnamese people want us in their country, why must we burn their villages and herd them into "pacification" camps (read: concentration camps).

The government is lying to us. It's time to wise up to what kind of war this is. . . .

. . . If we want to put an end to this, *we've all got to stick together* and demand "No Draft for *Anyone* for Unjust Wars" and "U.S. Get Out of Vietnam *Now!*" That's why we refused our student deferments. We think 2-S is a class privilege that the government uses to buy off students and divide them from guys who work.

TALK IT OVER WITH YOUR BUDDIES . . . WHY SHOULD FREE SPEECH AND DEMOCRACY END

WHEN YOU GO INTO THE ARMY? WHY ARE MORE BLACK G.I.'S SENT TO THE FRONT LINES THAN WHITE G.I.'S? WHY DO KIDS FROM RICH FAMILIES GET OUT OF THE DRAFT?

... If you get sent over, remember: don't volunteer for anything, keep your head down, don't fight too hard, and talk to your buddies about the war.

Good luck.
THREE OF YOUR FELLOW INDUCTEES[3]

INTRODUCTION TO DOCUMENTS 4 AND 5

In late January, a series of coordinated attacks by the North Vietnamese Army and the Viet Cong surprised the Americans. Though the Tet Offensive failed to achieve a military victory, it did succeed in eroding American morale even further, both among soldiers on the ground and citizens at home. Just days after Tet ended, President Johnson held a news conference to address the attack, which is excerpted in Document 4. Document 5 is from a telephone conversation between President Johnson and his newly appointed Defense Secretary Clark Clifford in mid-March 1968. Note the degree to which the war was being waged not just in Vietnam, but also against the backdrop of an election year where Johnson himself was challenged by two Democratic rivals, Eugene McCarthy and Robert Kennedy, both of whom opposed the war.

4. PRESIDENTIAL NEWS CONFERENCE

LYNDON JOHNSON

FEBRUARY 2, 1968

THE PRESIDENT: We have known for several months, now, that the Communists planned a massive winter-spring offensive. We have detailed information on Ho Chi Minh's order giving that offensive. . . . We know the object was to overthrow the constitutional government in Saigon and to create a situation in which we and the Vietnamese would be willing to accept the Communist-dominated coalition government.

Another part of that offensive was planned as a massive attack across the frontiers of South Vietnam by North Vietnamese units. We have already seen the general uprising. General Westmoreland's headquarters report the Communists appear to have lost over 10,000 men killed and some 2,300 detained. The United States has lost 249 men killed. The Vietnamese, who had to carry the brunt of the fighting in the cities, lost 553 killed as of my most recent report from the Westmoreland headquarters. . . .

The stated purposes of the general uprising have failed. Communist leaders counted on popular support in the cities for their effort. They found little or none. . . .

QUESTION. Mr. President, does this present rampage in South Vietnam give you any reason to change any assessment that you have made previously about the situation in South Vietnam?

THE PRESIDENT. I am sure that we will make adjustments to what we are doing there.

So far as changing our basic strategy, the answer would be no. . . .

Q. Mr. President, one of the problems people seem to be having in making up their minds on the psychological importance of this goes back to our reports that the Vietcong were really way down in morale, that they were a shattered force.

Now people ask: Well, how, then, can they find the people who are so well-motivated to run these suicide attacks in so many places in such good coordination?

Some people say: Well, that proves they know they are licked and this is their dying gasp. And some people say: Well, it proves that we underestimated their morale. How do you feel, sir?

THE PRESIDENT. I haven't read those reports about underestimating all their morale, and their being out of it, and no more problems, and so forth. . . .

We do think that we have made good progress there. We are for that. We don't want to overplay it or play it in high key. We just want to state it because we believe it is true.[4]

5. TELEPHONE CONVERSATION BETWEEN PRESIDENT JOHNSON AND SECRETARY OF DEFENSE CLIFFORD (MARCH 20, 1968)

CLIFFORD: One very quick item. I had a telephone call from Mac Bundy [former National Security Advisor and speech writer for Kennedy and Johnson] yesterday late in the afternoon. I thought he seemed exceedingly friendly and cooperative. Had no sympathy whatsoever for Bobby [Kennedy's] entry into the race. We had a little talk about the problems of Vietnam. He said he knew we were going through quite a difficult and critical period and made the offer if he could be of any help at all, you only had to let him know and he would be glad to come down and help. Now, I pass it on to you because I thought you might want to consider the advisability—if you thought well of it—of calling him and perhaps asking him to come down. This is a very important speech that has to be written. I spent a couple of hours with Harry McPherson yesterday afternoon and I had the feeling that maybe Mac could be quite useful during this particular period.

PRESIDENT: Yes, I think it would be very good.

I think what we've got to do, too, is to get out of the posture of just being the war candidate that McCarthy has put us in and Bobby is putting us in, the kids [protesters] are putting us in and the papers are putting us in. [New York City mayor John] Lindsay is out advocating rebellions this morning and not responding to the draft and things of that kind. The Mayor urges youth to aid war resistance, and they've got 4-column front-page pictures. Now when the head of the biggest city goes to doing things of that kind, you've got to really look at the picture. . . . Our right hand is going after their jaw with an offense on the war front, but we ought to have a peace front too

Image 14.2 Soldier in Vietnam, 1968.

A sky trooper for the First Calvary Division keeps track of the days left on his tour of duty in Vietnam.

Source: Records of the Office of the Chief Signal Officer, Record Group 111, National Archives, Identifier 531453.

simultaneously and use both fists—not just one, not fight with one hand behind us, so that we can say we are the peace candidate—but we are the true peace candidate. We're not the Chamberlain peace—we're the Churchill peace. We are not the guy that is going to throw in the towel and let them take Athens. We are the Truman who stands up and finally saves Greece and Turkey from the Communists. And that, of course, there is a temporary peace, and if we surrendered, you would have peace until they got their government installed and then by God you'd have a bigger war than ever. . . .

CLIFFORD: . . . Our slogan could very well be—win the peace with honor—and I think we have got to get that thought over. Now I have been giving consideration to offers of de-escalation. I don't know whether they have anything, but if we could begin to start a negotiation toward de-escalation, something to the effect that, now if we could have an agreement with the North Vietnamese, that we would let Hanoi alone if they would let Saigon alone. I don't know that it is very practical, but considering something of that kind, we can't stop, but if there is some program of a gradual de-escalation that the parties could get into, we could then get in a better posture.

. . . We have a posture now in which Kennedy and McCarthy are the peace candidates and President Johnson is the war candidate. Now we must veer away from that and we can do it. What we need is a policy now that is a consistent far-ranging policy, but which we don't have. I think we need a policy of the kind that—say a five-step policy, Mr. President, that we will continue to exert the military pressure. . . . So, as you say, with our right hand we continue to exert the military pressure, then I think we have to have a well thought-out program that we try with our left hand. . . . I think we have to keep in mind that before the [Democratic Party National] Convention, then if not before the Convention, before the election, I think we have to work out some kind of arrangement where we start some kind of negotiation.[5]

INTRODUCTION TO DOCUMENTS 6 AND 7

Events were moving quickly now and mid-March was a pivotal moment for President Johnson. For years he had been advised to enlarge America's military presence in Vietnam. He did so, but more slowly than some critics liked, and they blamed Johnson's cautiousness for the lack of progress in the war. Meanwhile, half a million American troops on the ground and bombing campaigns as intense as any of World War II seemed only to intensify the growing opposition to the war. The Tet Offensive raised the stakes at home, fueling even more protests and dissent. Document 6 is a reflection by Defense Secretary Clifford, who recounts the dilemmas posed by the war and the limitations of American policy. Document 7 is from a televised address Johnson gave to the American people. Faced with antiwar challenges within his own party for the Democratic presidential nomination, Johnson outlined his military strategy and then shocked the nation. What was at stake at this stage in the war? Why did Clifford think the war was hopeless, and why did Johnson make the decision he did?

6. CLARK CLIFFORD ASSESSES HIS EARLY MONTHS AS DEFENSE SECRETARY (MARCH 1968)

In mid-January 1968, President Johnson asked me to serve as Secretary of Defense, succeeding Secretary McNamara, who was leaving to become President of the World Bank. . . .

I took office on March 1, 1968. The enemy's Tet offensive of late January and early February had been beaten back at great cost. The confidence of the American people had been badly shaken. The ability of the South Vietnamese Government to restore order and morale in the populace, and discipline and esprit in the armed forces, was being questioned. At the President's direction, General Earle G. Wheeler, Chairman of the Joint Chiefs of Staff, had flown to Viet Nam in late February for an on-the-spot conference with

General Westmoreland. He had just returned and presented the military's request that over 200,000 troops be prepared for deployment to Viet Nam. These troops would be in addition to the 525,000 previously authorized. I was directed, as my first assignment, to chair a task force named by the President to determine how this new requirement could be met. We were not instructed to assess the need for substantial increases in men and materiel; we were to devise the means by which they could be provided.

My work was cut out. The task force included Secretary Rusk, Secretary Henry Fowler, . . . and other skilled and highly capable officials. All of them had had long and direct experience with Vietnamese problems. I had not. I had attended various meetings in the past several years and I had been to Viet Nam three times, but it was quickly apparent to me how little one knows if he has been on the periphery of a problem and not truly in it. Until the day-long sessions of early March, I had never had the opportunity of intensive analysis and fact-finding. Now I was thrust into a vigorous, ruthlessly frank assessment of our situation by the men who knew the most about it. Try though we would to stay with the assignment of devising means to meet the military's requests, fundamental questions began to recur over and over.

It is, of course, not possible to recall all the questions that were asked nor all of the answers that were given. . . . here are some of the principal issues raised and some of the answers as I understood them:

"Will 200,000 more men do the job?" I found no assurance that they would.

"If not, how many more might be needed—and when?" There was no way of knowing.

"What would be involved in committing 200,000 more men to Viet Nam?" A reserve call-up of approximately 280,000, an increased draft call and an extension of tours of duty of most men then in service.

"Can the enemy respond with a build-up of his own?" He could and he probably would.

"What are the estimated costs of the latest requests?" First calculations were on the order of $2 billion for the remaining four months of that fiscal year, and an increase of $10 to $12 billion for the year beginning July 1, 1968.

"What will be the impact on the economy?" So great that we would face the possibility of credit restrictions, a tax increase and even wage and price controls. The balance of payments would be worsened by at least half a billion dollars a year.

"Can bombing stop the war?" Never by itself. It was inflicting heavy personnel and materiel losses, but bombing by itself would not stop the war.

"Will stepping up the bombing decrease American casualties?" Very little, if at all. Our casualties were due to the intensity of the ground fighting in the South. We had already dropped a heavier tonnage of bombs than in all the theaters of World War II. During 1967, an estimated 90,000 North Vietnamese had infiltrated into South Viet Nam. In the opening weeks of 1968, infiltrators were coming in at three to four times the rate of a year earlier, despite the ferocity and intensity of our campaign of aerial interdiction.

"How long must we keep on sending our men and carrying the main burden of combat?" The South Vietnamese were doing better, but they were not ready yet to replace our troops and we did not know when they would be.

When I asked for a presentation of the military plan for attaining victory in Viet Nam, I was told that there was no plan for victory in the historic American sense. Why not? Because our forces were operating under three major political restrictions: The President had forbidden the invasion of North Viet Nam because this could trigger the mutual assistance pact between North Viet Nam and China; the President had forbidden the mining of the harbor at Haiphong, the principal port through which the North received military supplies, because a Soviet vessel might be sunk; the President had forbidden our forces to pursue the enemy into Laos and Cambodia, for to do so would spread the war, politically and geographically, with no discernible advantage. . . .

"Given these circumstances, how can we win?" We would, I was told, continue to evidence our superiority over the enemy; we would continue to attack in the belief that he would reach the stage where he would find it inadvisable to go on with the war. He could not afford the attrition we were inflicting on him. And we were improving our posture all the time.

I then asked, "What is the best estimate as to how long this course of action will take? Six months? One year? Two years?" There was no agreement on an answer. Not only was there no agreement, I could find no one willing to express any confidence in his guesses. Certainly, none of us was willing to assert that he could see "light at the end of the tunnel" or that American troops would be coming home by the end of the year. . . .

I was more conscious each day of domestic unrest in our own country. Draft card burnings, marches in the streets, problems on school campuses, bitterness and divisiveness were rampant. Just as disturbing to me were the economic implications of a struggle to be indefinitely continued at ever-increasing cost. . . .

I was also conscious of our obligations and involvements elsewhere in the world. There were certain hopeful signs in our relations with the Soviet Union, but both nations were hampered in moving toward vitally important talks on the limitations of strategic weapons so long as the United States was committed to a military solution in Viet Nam. . . .

Also, I could not free myself from the continuing nagging doubt . . . that if the nations living in the shadow of Viet Nam were not now persuaded by the domino theory, perhaps it was time for us to take another look. Our efforts had given the nations in that area a number of years following independence to organize and build their security. I could see no reason at this time for us to continue to add to our commitment. Finally, there was no assurance that a 40 percent increase in American troops would place us within the next few weeks, months or even years in any substantially better military position than we were in then. All that could be predicted accurately was that more troops would raise the level of combat and automatically raise the level of casualties on both sides.

And so, after these exhausting days, I was convinced that the military course we were pursuing was not only endless, but hopeless. . . . Henceforth, I was also convinced, our primary goal should be to level off our involvement, and to work toward gradual disengagement.

. . . Finally, the President, in the closing hours of March, made his decisions and reported them to the people on the evening of the 31st.[6]

7. PRESIDENTIAL ADDRESS (MARCH 31, 1968)

LYNDON B. JOHNSON

Good evening, my fellow Americans:

Tonight I want to speak to you of peace in Vietnam and Southeast Asia.

No other question so preoccupies our people. No other dream so absorbs the 250 million human beings who live in that part of the world. No other goal motivates American policy in Southeast Asia.

. . . Tonight, I renew the offer I made last August— to stop the bombardment of North Vietnam. We ask that talks begin promptly, that they be serious talks on the substance of peace. We assume that during those talks Hanoi will not take advantage of our restraint. . . .

So, tonight, in the hope that this action will lead to early talks, I am taking the first step to deescalate the conflict. We are reducing—substantially reducing— the present level of hostilities.

And we are doing so unilaterally, and at once.

Tonight, I have ordered our aircraft and our naval vessels to make no attacks on North Vietnam, except in the area north of the demilitarized zone where the continuing enemy buildup directly threatens allied forward positions and where the movements of their troops and supplies are clearly related to that threat. . . .

I call upon President Ho Chi Minh to respond positively, and favorably, to this new step toward peace. . . .

Image 14.3 Lyndon Johnson speaks to the nation, March 31, 1968

Confronted with a deepening war, and challenges within his own party, President Johnson outlines a strategy of gradual de-escalation and his decision not to run for re-election.

Source: Yoichi Okamoto, LBJ Presidential Library, Austin, Texas. Photo C9284-35.

. . . We and the other allied nations are contributing 600,000 fighting men to assist 700,000 South Vietnamese troops in defending their little country.

Our presence there has always rested on this basic belief: The main burden of preserving their freedom must be carried out by them—by the South Vietnamese themselves.

. . . In order that these forces may reach maximum combat effectiveness, the Joint Chiefs of Staff have recommended to me that we should prepare to send—during the next 5 months—support troops totaling approximately 13,500 men.

A portion of these men will be made available from our active forces. The balance will come from reserve component units which will be called up for service. . . .

We have no intention of widening this war.

But the United States will never accept a fake solution to this long and arduous struggle and call it peace.

No one can foretell the precise terms of an eventual settlement.

Our objective in South Vietnam has never been the annihilation of the enemy. It has been to bring about a recognition in Hanoi that its objective—taking over the South by force—could not be achieved.

. . . I reaffirm the pledge. . . that we are prepared to withdraw our forces from South Vietnam as the other side withdraws its forces to the north, stops the infiltration, and the level of violence thus subsides. . . .

One day, my fellow citizens, there will be peace in Southeast Asia.

It will come because the people of Southeast Asia want it—those whose armies are at war tonight, and those who, though threatened, have thus far been spared.

Peace will come because Asians were willing to work for it—and to sacrifice for it—and to die by the thousands for it.

But let it never be forgotten: Peace will come also because American sent her sons to help secure it. . . .

With America's sons in the fields far away, with America's future under challenge right here at home, with our hopes and the world's hopes for peace in the balance every day, I do not believe that I should devote an hour or a day of my time to any personal partisan causes or to any duties other than the awesome duties of this office—the Presidency of your country.

Accordingly, I shall not seek, and I will not accept, the nomination of my party for another term as your President.

But let men everywhere know, however, that a strong, a confident, and a vigilant America stands ready tonight to seek an honorable peace—and stands ready tonight to defend an honored cause—whatever the price, whatever the burden, whatever the sacrifice that duty may require. . . .[7]

INTRODUCTION TO DOCUMENTS 8 AND 9

At just the time that Johnson was negotiating the stakes of the war at home, the terrible My Lai massacre occurred abroad. The next two documents present the official versions of the My Lai assault. Sergeant Jay A. Roberts's press release is a sanitized version of what happened. Next, Colonel Oran K. Henderson reports to his superiors on the investigation he conducted concerning an alleged massacre at My Lai. Together they illustrate what was officially reported about the event.

8. PRESS RELEASE (MARCH 17, 1968)

SERGEANT JAY A. ROBERTS

CHU LAI, VIETNAM—For the third time in recent weeks, the Americal Division's 11th Brigade infantrymen from Task Force Barker raided a Viet Cong stronghold known as "Pinkville" six miles northeast of Quang Ngai, killing 128 enemy in a running battle.

The action occurred in the coastal town of My Lai where, three weeks earlier, another company of the brigade's Task Force Barker fought its way out of a VC ambush, leaving 80 enemy dead.

The action began as units of the task force conducted a combat assault into a known Viet Cong stronghold. "Shark" gunships of the 174th Aviation Company escorted the troops into the area and killed four enemy during the assault. Other choppers from the 123d Aviation Battalion killed two enemy.

"The combat assault went like clockwork," commented LTC Frank Barker, New Haven, Conn., the tack force commander. "We had two entire companies on the ground in less than an hour."

A company led by [Captain] Ernest Medina, Schofield Barracks, Hawaii, killed 14 [Viet Cong] minutes after landing. They recovered two M1 rifles, a carbine, a short-wave radio and enemy documents.

9. REPORT OF INVESTIGATION (APRIL 24, 1968)

COLONEL ORAN K. HENDERSON

1. An investigation has been conducted of the allegations cited in Inclosure 1. The following are the results of this investigation. . . .

2. This area has long been an enemy strong hold, and Task Force Barker had met heavy enemy opposition in this area on 12 and 23 February 1968. All persons living in this area are considered to be VC or VC sympathizers by the District Chief. Artillery and gunship preparatory fires were placed on the landing zones used by the two companies. Upon landing and during their advance on the enemy positions, the attacking forces were supported by gunships. By 1500 hours all enemy resistance had ceased and the remaining enemy forces had withdrawn. The results of this operation were 128 VC soldiers KIA. During preparatory fires and the ground action by the attacking companies 20 noncombatants caught in the battle area were killed. Interviews revealed that at no time were any civilians gathered together and killed by US soldiers. The civilian habitants of the area began withdrawing to the southwest as soon as the operation began and within the first hour and a half all visible civilians had cleared the area of operations.

3. The Son Tinh District Chief does not give the allegations any importance and he pointed out that the two hamlets where the incidents is alleged to have happened are in an area controlled by the VC since 1964. [He] reported that the making of such allegations against US Forces is a common technique of the VC propaganda machine.

4. It is concluded that 20 non-combatants were inadvertently killed when caught in the area of preparatory fires and in the cross fires of the US and VC forces on 16 March 1968. It is further concluded that no civilians were gathered together and shot by US soldiers. The allegation that US Forces shot and killed 450–500 civilians is obviously a Viet Cong propaganda move to discredit the United States in the eyes of the Vietnamese people in general and the ARVN soldier in particular.

5. It is recommended that a counter-propaganda campaign be waged against the VC in eastern Son Tinh District.

INTRODUCTION TO DOCUMENTS 10–13

Documents 10 to 13 detail the events on and just before March 16, 1968. In Document 10, Gregory Olson, a member of the platoon that assaulted My Lai, discusses the orders that Charlie Company, under the command of Lieutenant William Calley, was given the day before the My Lai assault. Documents 11 and 12 describe the day of the massacre, illuminating what individual soldiers did and thought. In Document 13, Nguyen Hieu, tells the story from the perspective of a Vietnamese villager who survived the attack. All these documents are from the *Peers Report*—an investigation that collected oral testimony—except for the Calley interview, which is taken from his court martial trial.

10. TESTIMONY OF GREGORY T. OLSEN (1970)

Q: Prior to the assault on My Lai did the Company receive a briefing?

A: Yes the company did. The briefing was given by CPT Medina and I attended the briefing. At the time everybody was down in the dumps, because just previous due to various operations in the past few weeks we had lost about 25 men. Seven of them had been killed and the rest wounded. The briefing was given at LZ Dottie, where CPT Medina, drew a map on the ground and explained the entire procedures. We had instructions to shoot on sight any military age male, running from us, or shooting at us. We were then told, that we are to clear all the people out of the village. He (CPT Medina) did not say anything about the disposition of the people that we had or would clear out of the village. We were told, to destroy all the food supplies and the animals in the area. I do not remember if in the initial briefing we were told to burn all the huts. CPT Medina made the statement that we owed the enemy something. The troops had a feeling that they should revenge their fallen comrades.

Q: Did CPT Medina ever order during the aforementioned briefing to kill all the inhabitants of the village? With all the inhabitants I mean also women and children.

A: Negative. He did not. CPT Medina, was in my opinion an outstanding Commander. He was always concerned with the welfare of his men. Sometimes we did things the hard way, but in the end it was always the best for us. CPT Medina would never have given an order to kill women and children.

Q: Was LT Calley present during the briefing?

A: I assume he was.

Q: Did you attend a briefing on the operation My Lai by LT Calley?

A: I only remember that he told us on which helicopters we were supposed to go on. I do not remember LT Calley giving us a specific briefing on My Lai after CPT Medina had briefed us. I do not remember who my squadleader was during the Pinkville Operation. It is quite a long time ago.

11. TESTIMONY OF HERBERT L. CARTER (1970)

We were picked up by helicopters at LZ Dottie early in the morning and we were flown to My Lai. We landed outside the village in a dry rice paddy. There was no resistance from the village. There was no armed enemy in the village. We formed a line outside the village.

The first killing was an old man in a field outside the village who said some kind of greeting in Vietnamese and waved his arms at us. Someone—either Medina or Calley—said to kill him and a big heavyset white fellow killed the man. I do not know the name of the man who shot this Vietnamese. This was the first murder.

Just after the man killed the Vietnamese, a woman came out of the village and someone knocked her down and Medina shot her with his M16 rifle. I was 50 or 60 feet from him and saw this. There was no reason to shoot this girl. Mitchell, Conti, Meadlo, Stanley, and the rest of the squad and the command group must have seen this. It was a pure out and out murder.

Then our squad started into the village. We were making sure no one escaped from the village. Seventy-five or a hundred yards inside the village we came to where the soldiers had collected 15 or more Vietnamese men, women, and children in a group. Medina said, "Kill everybody, leave no one standing." Wood was there with an M-60 machine gun and, at Medina's orders, he fired into the people. Sgt Mitchell was there at this time and fired into the people with his M16 rifle, also. Widmer was there and fired into the group, and after they were down on the ground, Widmer passed among them and finished them off with his M16 rifle. Medina, himself, did not fire into this group.

Just after this shooting, Medina stopped a 17 or 18 year old man with a water buffalo. Medina said for the boy to make a run for it—he tried to get him to run—but the boy wouldn't run, so Medina shot him with his M16 rifle and killed him. The command group was there. I was 75 or 80 feet away at the time and saw it plainly. There were some demolition men there, too, and they would be able to testify about this. I don't know any other witnesses to this murder. Medina killed the buffalo, too.

Q: I want to warn you that these are very serious charges you are making. I want you to be very sure that you tell only the truth and that everything you say is the truth?

A: What I have said is the truth and I will face Medina in court and swear to it. This is the truth: this is what happened.

Q: What happened then?

A: We went on through the village. Meadlo shot a Vietnamese and asked me to help him throw the man in the well. I refused and Meadlo had Carney help him throw the man in the well. I saw this murder with my own eyes and know that there was no reason to shoot the man. I also know from the wounds that the man was dead.

Also in the village the soldiers had rounded up a group of people. Meadlo was guarding them. There were some other soldiers with Meadlo. Calley came up and said that he wanted them all killed. I was right there within a few feet when he said this. There were about 25 people in this group. Calley said when I walk away, I want them all killed. Meadlo and Widmer fired into this group with his M16 on automatic fire. Cowan was there and fired into the people too, but I don't think he wanted to do it. There were others firing into this group, but I don't remember who. Calley had two Vietnamese with him at this time and he killed them, too, by shooting them with his M16 rifle on automatic fire. I didn't want to get involved and I walked away. There was no reason for this killing. These were mainly women and children and a few old men. They weren't trying to escape or attack or anything. It was murder.

A woman came out of a hut with a baby in her arms and she was crying. She was crying because her little boy had been in front of her hut and between the well and the hut and someone had killed the child by shooting it. She came out of the hut with her baby and Widmer shot her with an M16 and she fell. When she fell, she dropped the baby and then Widmer opened up on the baby with his M16 and killed the baby, too.

I also saw another woman come out of a hut and Calley grabbed her by the hair and shot her with a caliber 45 pistol. He held her by the hair for a minute and then let go and she fell to the ground. Some enlisted man standing there said, "Well, she'll be in the big rice paddy in the sky."

Q: Do you know any witnesses to these incidents?

A: Stanley might have [seen] the one Calley killed. There were a lot of people around when Widmer shot the woman with the baby. I can't definitely state any one person was there, but there were a lot of people around.

I also saw a Vietnamese boy about 8 years old who had been wounded, I think in the leg. One of the photographers attached to the company patted the kid on the head and then Mitchell shot the kid right in front of the photographer and me. I am sure the boy died from the fire of Mitchell.

About that time I sat down by a stack of dying people and Widmer asked me if he could borrow my caliber .45 pistol and finish off the people. I gave him my pistol and he walked in among the people and would stand there and when one would move, he would shoot that person in the head with the pistol. He used three magazines of caliber 45 ammunition on these people. These were men, children, women, and babies. They had been shot by machinegunners and riflemen from Company C, 1/20th Infantry. This was at a T-junction of two trails on the outskirts of the village. I got my pistol back from Widmer and holstered it again.

Image 14.4 John Kerry addresses an antiwar rally, 1971

John Kerry was one of many servicemen who joined Vietnam Veterans Against the War. Speaking here in 1971, Kerry later became a U.S. Senator from Massachusetts, ran for president, then served as Secretary of State Under Barack Obama.

Source: Courtesy Warren K. Leffler, U.S. News & World Report Magazine Photograph Collection, Library of Congress.

Q: How many people do you figure Widmer finished off when he used your pistol?

A: I know he shot some twice, so I figure he shot fifteen or so with my pistol. I know he shot one guy in the head and I imagine that was where he was shooting them all.

Q: What happened then?

A: We went on through the village and there was killing and more killing. I was with Stanley, mainly. I sat down with Stanley and Widmer came up again and asked to borrow my pistol again. I gave it to him. I saw a little boy there—wounded, I believe in the arm—and Widmer walked up close to the kid and shot him with my pistol. Widmer said something like, "Did you see me shoot that son of a bitch," and Stanley said something about how it was wrong. My gun had jammed when Widmer shot the kid. As far as I could tell, the kid died as a result of this gunshot. Then

Widmer gave me my pistol back and walked off. I was trying to clean it when it accident[al]ly went off and I was shot in the left foot. Stanley gave me medical aid and then the medics came. Medina and some of the command group came up and then I was flown out in a helicopter. The next day the medics brought Meadlo into the hospital. He had stepped on a booby-trap and had lost his foot. He said he thought God might be punishing him for what he had done in My Lai. . . .

Q: Did you murder anyone in Vietnam?

A: The only people I killed in Vietnam I killed in combat. I didn't kill any women or kids or unarmed persons at all, ever.

Q: How many people do you think were killed in My Lai?

A: There were more than 100, but I couldn't tell you accurately how many people were killed. I don't believe there were any people left alive.

12. TESTIMONY OF WILLIAM L. CALLEY (1970)

Q: There has been some information disclosed that you heard before the court that you stood there at the ditch for a considerable period of time, that you waited and had your troops organize groups of Vietnamese, throw them in the ditch or knock them in the ditch or pushed them in the ditch, and that you fired there for approximately an hour and a half as those groups were marched up. Did you participate in any such a shooting or any such an event?

A: No, sir, I did not.

Q: Did you at any time direct anybody to push people in the ditch?

A: Like I said, sir, I gave the order to take those people through the ditch and had also told Meadlo if he couldn't move them to "waste them" and I directly—other than that—it was only that one incident. I never stood up there for

any period of time. My main mission was to get my men on the other side of that ditch and get in that defensive position and that's what I did, sir.

Q: Now why did you give Meadlo a message or the order that if he couldn't get rid of them to "waste them"?

A: Because that was my order. That was the order of the day, sir.

Q: Who gave you that order?

A: My commanding officer, sir, Captain Medina, sir.

Q: And stated in that posture, in substantially those words, how many times did you receive such an order from Captain Medina?

A: The night before in the company briefing, the platoon leaders' briefing, the following morning before we lifted off, and twice there in the village, sir. . . .

13. TESTIMONY OF NGUYEN HIEU

Q: What is your name?

A: Nguyen Hieu.

Q: How old are you?

A: Twenty-five years old.

Q: Are you native of Tu Cung?

A: Yes. . . .

Q: . . . Were you in your house on the morning of 16 March 1968 when the Americans came?

A: Yes, I lived there in 1968.

Q: Were you there on the morning of 16 March 1968 when the Americans came?

A: Yes, I was there that morning.

Q: How many other members of your family were there with you in the house that morning?

A: Five.

Q: What did you do when you heard the artillery fire?

A: For the first time early in the morning I heard artillery come in here (indicating) and American helicopters come into here (indicating) on the west side of the village. They came here and they took us from the bunker.

Q: Was the bunker near your house?

A: Yes, right here (indicating).

Q: Did all the members of your family go in the bunker?

A: My mother stayed in the house. I and the children went to the bunker.

Q: How long did you stay in the bunker?

A: About 2 hours.

Q: Did the Americans come near the bunker?

A: Yes, they came into the bunker.

Q: They came into the bunker?

A: Yes.

Q: And did they make you come out of the bunker?

A: When the Americans came to the house my mother came out of house, and the Americans then raped my mother and they shot her.

Q: They shot and raped your mother?

A: Yes, shot and raped my mother. My sister ran out of the bunker and they shot my sister and two children. . . .

Q: How many Americans were there?

A: Two Americans.

Q: Were they Caucasians or Negroes?

A: I saw only one black and one yellow.

Q: One black and one yellow. No white?

A: I saw one black, one yellow, and another I don't know exactly.

Q: Which one raped your mother?

A: The black soldier. . . .

Q: What did the white soldier do while the Negro solider was raping your mother?

A: After they shot my mother, the white soldier checked the house to see that everybody was dead and then he went out. . . .
And later, a second group of Americans came in to burn the house.

Q: Were you the only one that stayed in the bunker?

A: Yes, I stayed alone.

Q: And your sister went out of the bunker and was shot?

A: My sister went out to help my mother and was shot.

Q: Were they all shot right around your house or did they take them some place else and shoot them?

A: They were all shot in the house.

Q: After the soldiers that shot the people left, how long were you in the bunker before the other soldiers came that burned the house?

A: About 40 minutes.

Q: About 40 minutes?

A: Yes.

Q: Did you see the soldiers that burned the house?

A: No, I did not see the Americans that burned the house.

Q: Did they shoot any livestock? Any animals, chickens, pigs?

A: They killed two buffalo.

Q: What did you do after the soldiers left?

A: After the Americans left I buried my mother and sister.

Q: I am sorry that your family was killed like this. Thank you for coming here today to help us.[8]

POSTSCRIPT

Three years after the My Lai massacre, a young war hero gave testimony before the Senate Committee on Foreign Relations. Massachusetts native John Kerry served on a gunboat in the Mekong Delta, and he received the Silver Star, the Bronze Star, and three Purple Hearts for valor. But by 1971, after he left the navy, he was a leader of the antiwar group, Vietnam Veterans Against the War. He told the committee that too many people wanted to avoid the truth: "We saw America lose her sense of morality as she accepted very coolly a My Lai and refused to give up the image of American soldiers who hand out chocolate bars and chewing gum." (Kerry later served as a senator from Massachusetts, then as Secretary of State under President Barack Obama.)

My Lai eventually became shorthand for the hell of war, but it almost escaped the notice of the American people. Chief Warrant Officer Hugh Thompson—who literally put himself between American troops and the Vietnamese and then flew wounded civilians out of the combat zone—kept the case alive by filing a complaint. The military brass, however, preferred to treat My Lai as an unfortunate but inadvertent killing of a dozen or two-dozen civilians. Only when soldier Ronald Ridenhour investigated the story then spread the word did others begin to pay attention. In March 1969, Ridenour wrote to President Nixon, the joint Chiefs of Staff, the State Department, and several congressmen—among whom was Representative Morris Udall, an Arizona Democrat, who pushed for a full investigation.

The case was finally turned over to the Army's inspector general, and as witnesses were interviewed, the enormity of the crime became apparent. By the end of the year, My Lai made the cover of both *Time* and *Newsweek*, and graphic photographs of the massacre filled the pages of *Life Magazine*. The Pentagon appointed a commission headed by three-star General William Peers for a closed-door investigation. The commission interviewed nearly 400 witnesses and produced 20,000 pages of testimony. The Peers Commission recommended action against dozens of soldiers for rape and murder and also singled out several officers for covering up crimes.

Twenty-five men initially were prosecuted, but due to a combination of circumstances, only a few were charged and one tried. The case against Lieutenant William Calley was overwhelming—too many eyewitnesses identified him mowing down dozens of unarmed civilians. Upwards of 500 people died at My Lai. Calley's defense attorney argued that the lieutenant was being made a scapegoat for higher-ups like Captain Ernest Medina. Medina, it was alleged, gave the orders to leave no one alive. But on March 29, 1971, the military tribunal, after deliberating thirteen days, found Calley—and Calley alone—guilty of twenty-two counts of premeditated murder and sentenced him to be confined to prison for life.

Opinion polls indicated that the American public strongly disapproved of the verdict. Many citizens agreed with Calley's attorney that the lieutenant had been made a scapegoat. Days after Calley's sentencing, President Nixon, pending appeals, ordered Calley taken out of confinement and moved to house arrest. Calley's prosecutor, Aubrey Daniel, crusaded against what he considered the political expediency that prevented those who murdered innocent civilians from receiving justice. Nonetheless, William Calley, the only man who served any time at all for the massacre, ended up spending four months in the brig at Fort Benning before he was paroled at the end of 1974.

Calley settled quietly into civilian life in Columbus, Georgia. In 2009, he broke his silence and apologized for the events at My Lai. "There is not a day that goes by that I do not feel remorse for what happened," he told the Kiwanis Club in Columbus. "I feel remorse for the Vietnamese who were killed, for their families, and for the American soldiers involved and their families. I am very sorry." Calley had always maintained that he was just following orders, though the courts did not find Captain Medina or others guilty of issuing such orders. Besides, as one soldier observed at Calley's 2009 press conference, obeying unlawful orders is itself an unlawful act.

As historian Gary Kulik points out, soldiers have not just the right but a duty to disobey such commands. Kulik argues against seeing Calley as a scapegoat, as so many Americans did back in the 1970s. Events like My Lai happen not just because someone gives orders but because everyone else abdicates their legal and moral responsibilities to disobey. "What would it have taken to stop the massacre?" Kulik asks. "There is a simple answer. A morally competent officer willing to tell his superiors that army intelligence was wrong again, there were no armed Viet Cong there, and willing to order a cease fire." Kulik agrees that higher-ups were guilty too, but the principles established after World War II at the Nuremberg Trials affirmed that following orders brought no exoneration for war crimes. Kulik concludes, "It was an atrocity-producing war, that is the way we fought the war, body counts, every dead Vietnamese is a dead Vietcong. There is an ugly underlying truth here, but it is not the whole truth, and even if it were, it would not be exculpatory." War might be hell, but individual soldiers still had moral responsibilities.

Some have complained that the "Vietnam syndrome" makes America skittish about using military force; others think that reluctance to wage war is healthy. Either way, Vietnam is still with us. Forty years after My Lai, for example, at the end of 2009, upon ordering 30,000 fresh troops into Afghanistan, President Obama felt it necessary to explain to the American people in a nationally televised speech his belief that the analogy was not accurate, that the war he inherited in Afghanistan was not like Vietnam. American troops are still there almost a decade later.

QUESTIONS

1. Why did the Vietnam War prove so divisive and controversial on the home front?
2. How were American interests in Vietnam framed by Jackie Robinson, John Steinbeck, and the draft resistance leaflet? Do you see similarities in these assessments?
3. What does the conversation between Defense Secretary Clifford and President Johnson—as well as Clifford's subsequent recollection—tell us about the administration's understanding of Vietnam in 1968?
4. What does the My Lai massacre reveal about the nature of warfare in Vietnam? Do you think My Lai was an isolated case or part of a larger problem?
5. What were President Johnson's aims in the war? Why do you think he failed to persuade a majority of Americans to support his goals?
6. How did the official version of the My Lai assault differ from the soldiers' testimonies? Why were they so different from each other?

ADDITIONAL READING

The literature on the war in Vietnam is extensive, but anyone interested in the nature of the combat and the experiences of the soldiers should read Neil Sheehan, *A Bright Shining Lie* (1988); Christian Appy, *Working-Class War* (1993); Michael Herr, *Dispatches* (1977); Mark Baker, *'Nam* (1982); Stewart O'Nan, *The Vietnam Reader* (1998); and Davis Maraniss, *They Marched into Sunlight* (2003).

Stanley Karrow, *Vietnam: A History* (1999) remains a useful introduction. For the war in a larger historical and diplomatic context, see James S. Olson and Randy Roberts, *Where the Domino Fell: America and Vietnam, 1945–1995* (2008). For the experience of a combat veteran, see Tim O'Brien, *If I Die in the Combat Zone* (1988), and *The Things They Carried* (1990). For a more extended collection of sources related to the massacre, see James S. Olson and Randy Roberts, editors, *My Lai: A Brief History with Documents* (1998). Two fine books on the massacre are Seymour Hersh, *My Lai 4: A Report on the Massacre and Its Aftermath* (1970), and Michael Bilton and Kevin Sim, *Four Hours in My Lai* (1992). On the antiwar movement at home, see Paul Berman, *A Tale of Two Utopias: The Political Journey of the Generation of 1968* (1997); Noam Chomsky, *American Power and the New Mandarins* (1969); and Sherry Gershon Gottlieb, *Hell No, We Won't Go: Resisting the Draft during the Vietnam War* (1991). For a particular individual's role, see Howard L. Bingham and Max Wallace, *Muhammad Ali's Greatest Fight: Cassius Clay vs. The United States of America* (2000). Gary Kulik's comments can be found at the History News Network's Web site for September 28, 2009, at http://hnn.us/articles/117472.html. Films on the war include Oliver Stone, *Platoon* (1986); Francis Ford Coppola, *Apocalypse Now* (1979); and WBGH Boston's documentary *Vietnam: A Television History* (1983).

ENDNOTES

1. White House Central Files, National Archives, Identifier 6207609.
2. White House Central Files, National Archives, Identifier 7329806.
3. Records of the U.S. Attorneys, Record Group 118, National Archives, Identifier 7419639.
4. *Public Papers of the Presidents of the United States: Lyndon B. Johnson, 1968-1969* (Washington: Government Printing Office, 1970).
5. Document 146, in *Foreign Relations of the United States, 1964-1968, Volume VI, Vietnam, January–August 1968.*
6. Clark Clifford, "A Viet Nam Reappraisal: the Personal History of One Man's View and How It Evolved," *Foreign Affairs* (July 1969).
7. *Public Papers of the Presidents of the United States: Lyndon B. Johnson, 1968-69.* Vol. 1, pp. 469–476. Washington, D.C.: Government Printing Office, 1970.
8. Documents 8 through 12 are excerpted from James S. Olson and Randy Roberts, ed., *My Lai: A Brief History with Documents* (New York: Bedford St. Martins, 1998). Testimony from Olsen, Carter, and Nguyen Hieu originally appeared in William Peers, *Report of the Department of the Army, Review of the Preliminary Investigation to the My Lai Incident* (Washington, D.C.: Government Printing Office, 1970).

CHAPTER 15

TURNING LEFT

HISTORICAL CONTEXT

When young black southerners began their boycotts and sit-ins to integrate busses and lunch counters, they started something that reached beyond the civil rights movement. By the late 1960s, as the Vietnam War raged on, Americans took to the streets in protest. Draft-age college students, clergymen, and even Vietnam veterans turned out by the hundreds of thousands. Beyond the antiwar movement, the 1960s launched an experiment in mass, participatory politics. Street demonstrations, protests, and community organizing focused on a range of issues, and activists saw themselves as keepers of America's democratic promise. New groups organized as never before, and "rights consciousness," as some have called it, accompanied the assumption that democracy involves more than mere voting. Social change happened when the excluded—often identified by ethnicity, gender, and sexual orientation—became aware of their plight and asserted themselves. Activists defined themselves as liberal, progressive, or radical, and they are the subject of this chapter.

The new activism was different from the old organizing efforts of the class-based labor movement, which had its roots deep in the nineteenth century and found its greatest triumphs during the Great Depression and its aftermath. In the 1930s, intense work by unionists in America's basic industries led to the formation of the Congress of Industrial Organizations. Massive new unions like the United Auto Workers were legitimated by the Wagner Act of the New Deal, which gave federal sanction to workers' collective bargaining rights for the first time. During the post-World War II era, roughly a third of America's workers belonged to labor unions, and they led the way in setting a rising standard of living for working people that lasted until the end of the 1970s.

But the activism of the 1960s was not primarily motivated by economic justice. An unusual cultural tone pervaded the 1960s. America's affluence and the upbeat rhetoric during the Kennedy and Johnson administrations gave a sense of limitless possibilities. More, a distinct spirituality pervaded many of the era's reforms. The civil rights movement, with its base in the black churches, was the most obvious example. New organizing among Native Americans also gained energy from spiritual sources, as did efforts among Mexican farm workers and by American women. Beyond the specific groups, the era was characterized by remarkably utopian hopes, as if humankind stood at the verge of a social, spiritual, and personal millennium that for centuries had tantalized yet eluded the faithful.

What became known as the counterculture was the era's most obvious manifestation of utopian dreams. The shock troops of the counterculture, the so-called hippies, sought not so much political or economic solutions to American problems but cultural ones. During the 1960s countless youths responded to the call to "turn-on, tune-in, drop-out," an ambiguous phrase that implied leaving behind the world of school, work, and career for a freer life centered on the open expression of impulses and desires, all made easier with recreational drugs such as marijuana and LSD. A very popular book of the era, Charles Reich's *Greening of America,* argued that the counterculture foretold a change of consciousness in America—youths were leading the way toward abandoning the work ethic, the obsession with success, and the destructiveness of American business culture. The phrase "sex, drugs, and rock and roll" implied a hedonism that was real enough, but the counterculture also embodied important ideological commitments. The new order would be founded on communal consciousness, freedom, play, and the sacredness of the natural world; it opposed the 1950s image of "the organization man," or "the man in the gray flannel suit."

The counterculture had its attractions for many youthful Americans, and certainly "hippie" styles quickly entered consumer awareness. Long hair, bell-bottom jeans, and psychedelic displays grew common by the 1970s, long after the numbers of hippies in meccas like the Haight-Ashbury district of San Francisco declined. But equally important, and perhaps more profound than the counterculture, was America's tilt toward the political left. Within the federal government, the Kennedy and Johnson administrations sponsored a range of new programs that extended the old social welfare interventions of the New Deal— civil rights and voting rights laws, Medicare and Medicaid, expanded versions of Aid to Families with Dependent Children and unemployment compensation, equal opportunity programs, the Environmental Protection Agency, the Occupational Safety and Health Administration, and so forth. Such policies and programs did not end with the 1960s but continued long into the 1970s, as the Republican administration of Richard M. Nixon added Affirmative Action, strong new environmental laws, and the Endangered Species Act.

But it was outside of mainstream politics that some of the most interesting developments took place. For example, the long history of women attempting to gain full recognition and equality reignited in the 1960s. A founding document of "second wave feminism" was the unlikely bestseller, Betty Friedan's *The Feminine Mystique* (1963). Friedan, a journalist with experience in the labor movement, asked why it was that after participating broadly in American society and economy during World War II, American women found themselves shunted back into their homes as wives and mothers, caretakers of new postwar suburban households. By "feminine mystique" she meant that women were now valued only for their "sex functions," which in American culture meant traditionally female attributes— beauty, child rearing, nurturance, housekeeping—rather than job skills or creativity. For many women, it was the sense of achievement that came from working in the civil rights or antiwar movements, followed by the frustration of not having their contributions acknowledged by the men who dominated those movements, that led toward feminism.

Two-dozen women founded the National Organization for Women in 1966 to lobby the federal government for enforcement of antidiscrimination laws. From there the movement grew. In 1971, the very first issue of *Ms.* magazine sold over a quarter million copies. Women founded new groups, some of them overtly political, some of them dedicated to "consciousness raising." Like most of the movements of this era, there was no single voice, point-of-view, or organization representing everyone. Many women considered lack of opportunity in the workplace to be the most compelling problem; others focused on inequalities in relationships between men and women; "homemakers" and "career women" sometimes expressed opposing goals. Health issues, daycare, and the cult of beauty all came under scrutiny. Equal opportunity and equal pay remained fundamental concerns of the women's movement, but cultural issues grew increasingly prominent, and often very divisive. Many women believed that laws making abortion a crime must be overturned, and the U.S. Supreme Court agreed in 1973 with the *Roe v. Wade* decision. Despite this ruling, not only has the abortion issue not gone away, positions have become ever more entrenched, dividing Americans along lines of religion, gender, and region.

A new movement also began among Latino Americans. In California's central valley, the United Farm Workers gained unexpected success organizing poor itinerant farm laborers, mostly Mexicans and the children of Mexicans. Inspired in part by the civil rights movement under Martin Luther King Jr. and led by the equally charismatic Cesar Chavez, this AFL-CIO affiliate began with grape pickers in the town of Delano in 1965 and quickly gained converts in California's enormous "factories in the fields." This was no simple union movement, however. The farm workers' rallies took place in both English and Spanish, they borrowed anthems from the civil rights movement like "We Shall Overcome," and they featured banners with the symbolism of an Aztec eagle and of the Virgin of Guadalupe. Chavez received considerable support from other unions like the United Auto Workers, from student groups, and from the Catholic Church. Above all, the farm workers melded their commitment to economic justice with ethnic nationalism, with the recognition that they were mostly of Mexican descent. They made "la causa" and "la huelga" their own. Soon Latino organizing spread beyond the farm workers to urban battles for quality schools in western cities and to other groups, especially Puerto Ricans in New York and Chicago.

The breaking down of the old Cold War consensus—which included increasingly militant protest for African-American equality and growing street demonstrations against the Vietnam War—continued to manifest itself as a rising tide of dissent among other groups. After decades of relative calm, Native Americans began a cycle of protest in the late 1960s and 1970s. New challenges regarding tribal rights and land claims began to enter the courts. More dramatically, a group of nearly 100 Indians from various tribes took over and occupied Alcatraz Island—formerly a federal prison—in the middle of San Francisco Bay, and held it for eighteen months. By 1973, 300 Oglala Sioux, members of a new organization called the American Indian Movement (AIM), occupied Wounded Knee, South Dakota, scene of the massacre where the Plains Wars had ended eighty years before. The American Indian Movement fought FBI and other federal agents to a standoff, and only after more than two months was a truce arranged and the shooting stopped.

Also in the late 1960s came the beginnings of "Gay Power." Homosexual relationships had been long stigmatized and criminalized. In furtive gay hangouts in large cities, gay bashing by straight men and shakedowns by police had been routine for decades. Rather suddenly, it seemed, gays refused to accept this second-class citizenship. The symbolic beginning came in June 1969, at the Stonewall Inn in New York City, where a riot underscored this unwillingness to put up with harassment any more. Equally important, the 1970s became a time for "coming out of the closet," not just for individuals, but for gays as a group with a distinct identity. Now, many believed, was the time to assert themselves, to fight for legislation ending discrimination, and to resist being stigmatized as sick or depraved.

Finally, the "ecology movement," or what is more commonly referred to today as environmentalism, received an enormous push during these years. The Clean Air Act, Clean Water Act, Environmental Protection Agency, and Endangered Species Act garnered broad-based support, but much of the impetus for this legislation came from mass organizing. Twenty million Americans celebrated the first annual Earth Day on April 22, 1970, while rallies, teach-ins, and sit-ins, especially on college campuses, alerted people to ecological dangers. Moreover, environmentalism caused Americans to question the wisdom of constant economic growth and technological progress. The movement pushed the ideas of the early twentieth-century conservation movement—which gave us the national forests and parks—further than ever. Now the focus shifted to dealing with the environmental damage caused by mass production and consumption.

The burst of activism on so many fronts did not simply end with the 1970s. Environmental issues, for example, continue to be a strong presence on the political landscape. The gay rights movement garnered headlines in the twenty-first century, as courts ruled on the subject of same-sex marriage and the political parties staked out positions on the desirability of civil unions. Certainly, by the 1980s, however, with the election of Ronald Reagan and the rightward drift of Congress, the courts, and state governments, Americans in general shifted toward more conservative positions. Progressive, left, or liberal causes found themselves increasingly on the defensive as the century waned. Still, the existence today of a substantial black middle class, the presence of women not just in the workforce but in positions of authority, the fact that we have openly gay communities built on gay political coalitions in major American cities, and the cleaner air and water in our environment are all legacies of earlier activism.

INTRODUCTION TO DOCUMENTS 1, 2, AND 3

Although the rhetoric of the family farm still resonates in American culture, rural life in the post–New Deal era has been dominated by large, consolidated "agribusinesses." California led the way in the creation of "factories in the fields," with massive public works programs bringing water into the enormous Imperial, Sacramento, and San Joaquin Valleys. Farms that grew into hundreds, thousands, even tens of thousands of acres employed a succession of immigrant laborers—Chinese, Japanese, South Asian, Filipino, and especially Mexican. Beginning with World War II, the federal "Bracero" program opened western farms to Mexican nationals explicitly working as migratory, temporary hands. Entire families worked brutal hours for poverty wages. They covered thousands of miles each year, planting and harvesting not only in West but also in midwestern states, riding buses from job to job and living in primitive labor camps. Sometimes they wintered in Mexico and sometimes in California towns like Salinas. But a permanent home, regular schooling for their children, and health care were all impossible dreams.

Cesar Chavez grew up in Arizona on a tiny family farm. The Great Depression made it impossible for his family to pay the taxes they owed, and they were forced into migratory labor when their farm was taken and their home bulldozed. Years later, after struggling with issues of how best to aid farm workers and their families, Chavez joined the union movement, eventually helping to found the United Farm Workers of America (UFW). Towns in California's Central Valley such as Fresno, Merced, Visalia, and Bakersfield were consistently ranked among those with the lowest income in America. Migrants had life expectancies twenty years shorter than the American average, and infant mortality rates that doubled national norms. Their work-related injuries came not just from stoop-labor but also from exposure to highly toxic pesticides and herbicides. In California alone, 100,000 hired farm laborers were children.

After several years of organizing, a 1965 strike of Filipino grape pickers began near Delano. This ignited the UFW's first big organizing drive, which, after a decade of effort, resulted in the signing of collective bargaining agreements between the union and major growers. In Document 1, Cesar Chavez explains the movement and its goals in hearings before the Senate Subcommittee on Labor. Document 2 is the testimony of Dolores Huerta, the vice president of the UFW Organizing Committee of Delano, where the striking began. Note her account of the obstacles that the organizers were up against. Document 3 is from a 1971 talk given by Cesar Chavez on organizing and personal sacrifice.

---

1. TESTIMONY BEFORE THE SENATE COMMITTEE ON LABOR AND PUBLIC WELFARE (APRIL 16, 1969)

CESAR CHAVEZ

My name is Cesar E. Chavez. I am Director of the United Farm Workers Organizing Committee AFL-CIO. . . .

. . . It is indeed a privilege to address this body, so many of whose members have distinguished themselves over the years by their genuine concern for the welfare of farm workers. For this we are grateful. What has impressed us most is your open mindedness, your desire to explore our problems in depth. Unwilling to believe what you have heard or read about the farm worker, some of you have even come to our valley to see for yourselves and experience at first hand our deprivation, our frustration and our struggle for social justice.

First, let me say that we too have been learning. In the no-nonsense school of adversity, which we did not choose for ourselves, we are learning how to operate a labor union. The difficulty of our struggle, together

Image 15.1: Strike against S&W Foods for higher wages during the grape boycott in Long Beach, California

Members of the United Auto Workers and the United Farm Workers marched together in 1966 to support the Grape Boycott. In sunglasses is Larry Itliong, a veteran labor organizer who led the largely Filipino-American farmworkers to strike in Delano, California, for pay to match the federal minimum wage. To Itliong's left is Cesar Chavez, who brought Mexican-American workers into strike a month after it began; by August 1966 the two groups merged to create the United Farm Workers.

Source: Courtesy Walter Reuther Library, Wayne State University.

with the growing possibility of labor relations legislation for agriculture, has led us to challenge again and again the assumption that coverage under the NLRA [National Labor Relations Act] would prove the ultimate salvation of the farm worker. This much is certain. His salvation will not be found in sloganeering. . . .

[L]aws cannot deliver a good union any more than laws can bring an end to poverty. Only people can do that through hard work, sacrifice and dedicated effort.

The end to be achieved, and therefore the starting point of the debate, is the elimination of rural poverty in America. How can the nation, how can Congress help the farm worker close the yawning gap between his own social and economic condition and

that of the other wage earners, even those of comparable skill in other industries such as manufacturing and construction?

Answer? Through strong, effective, well-run unions. The road to social justice for the farm worker is the road of unionization. Our cause, our strike and our international boycott are all founded upon the deep conviction that the form of collective self-help which is unionization holds far more hope for the farm worker than any other single approach, whether public or private. . . .

Repressive legislation is not the answer to strikes during harvest time and boycotts of farm products. The farm worker has learned that his sub-human existence is not inevitable. He has awakened to the realization that something better is possible for himself and his family. Laws are not going to stop strikes and boycotts so long as his honest, law- abiding efforts to improve his condition are met with massive, hostile grower resistance. Such resistance will only feed the fires of his own burning frustration. The best insurance against strikes and boycotts lies not in repressive legislation, but in strong unions that will satisfy the farm worker's hunger for decency and dignity and self-respect. . . .

If we could have our own way, what we would really like to see is a family living wage for every farm worker, a family living income for every family-sized farm owner, and a fair return on investment for every grower, whether he is an employer or not. . . .

Our potential competition appears almost unlimited as thousands upon thousands of green carders pour across the border during peak harvest seasons. These are people who, though lawfully admitted to the United States for permanent residence, have not now, and probably never had, any bona fide intention of making the United States of America their permanent home. They come here to earn American dollars to spend in Mexico where the cost of living is lower. They are natural economic rivals of those who become American citizens or who otherwise decide to stake out their future in this country. . . .

. . . As one looks at the millions of acres in this country that have been taken out of agricultural production; and at the millions of additional acres that have never been cultivated; and at the millions of people who have moved off the farm to rot and decay in the ghettoes of our big cities; and at all the millions

of hungry people at home and abroad; does it not seem that all these people and things were somehow made to come together and serve one another? If we could bring them together, we could stem the mass exodus of rural poor to the big city ghettoes and start it going back the other way; teach them how to operate new farm equipment; and put them to work on those now uncultivated acres to raise food for the hungry. If a way could be found to do this, there would be not only room but positive need for still more machinery and still more productivity increase. There would be enough employment, wages, profits, food and fiber for everybody. If we have any time left over after doing our basic union job, we would like to devote it to such purposes as these.

Thirty-four years ago a nation groping its uncharted course through the seas of the Great Depression faced the threatening storms of social and economic revolution.

The late President Franklin D. Roosevelt met the challenge with the Wagner Act and with other New Deal measures, then considered quite revolutionary, such as Social Security, unemployment insurance and the Fair Labor Standards Act.

While these measures modified the existing capitalistic system somewhat, they also saved the nation for free enterprise.

They did not save the farm worker. He was left out of every one of them. The social revolution of the New Deal passed him by. To make our union possible with its larger hope that the farm worker will have his day at last, there was required a new social revolution.[1]

2. TESTIMONY BEFORE THE SENATE (1969)

DOLORES HUERTA

Mr. Chairman, and members of the committee, we are again glad to be here and present our long, sad story of trying to organize the farmworkers.

. . . As you know, UFWOC has undertaken an international boycott of all California-Arizona table grapes in order to gain union recognition for striking farmworkers. We did not take up the burden of the boycott willingly. It is expensive. It is a hardship on the farmworkers' families who have left the small valley towns to travel across the country to boycott grapes.

But, because of the table grape growers' refusal to bargain with their workers, the boycott is our major weapon and I might say a nonviolent weapon, and our last line of defense against the growers who use foreign labor to break our strikes. . . .

. . . Many farmworkers are members of minority groups. They are Filipino and Mexican and black Americans. These same minority people are on the frontlines of battle in Vietnam. It is a cruel and ironic slap in the face to these men who have left the fields to fulfill their military obligation to find increasing amounts of boycotted grapes in their mess kits.

. . . In addition to the thousands of illegals and green carders being brought in to break the strike in Delano, there are many wetbacks that are being brought to other parts of the State to work, and other parts of the country. . . .

The police harassment against the strikers is unbelievable. We have to say that the police departments and sheriffs' departments are in most cases direct agents of the employers. We have had several hundred arrests. We had one conviction, which was for resisting arrest. All the hundreds of arrests have cost the union a tremendous amount of money in bail and attorneys' fees. . . .

Just Saturday, when 60 melon pickers went out on strike in Lost Hills, there was a picket line, and the sheriff's deputies, David Kaylor and R. M. Osborn, refused to protect our picket line, dragged a striker on the ground and arrested him. We had this picket line; across the street from our picket line was a counterpicket line, which was being conducted by the reactionary groups in Delano. They were shouting things like "Go home, Spic," and saying a lot of four-letter words to the women on the picket line. In fact, the officers went over and shook hands with them, and were conversing with them. The counterpickets opened up a tank of ammonia, and the strikers were getting gagged from ammonia. . . .

Regardless of what may happen to the strikers, they never arrest those who harass strikers and pickets. You have to go to the district attorney's office to try to get a complaint, and the chances of getting complaints are very few and far between. . . .

. . . I don't see that we are going to get any kind of a relief from the courts at all. Even under the national labor relations law, even though we are not covered by the law, the growers are constantly filing unfair labor practices against us, and although they know they can't win them, this takes up the time of our attorneys.

When we try to go to the Government for any kind of help, even for the enforcement of the sanitation laws, the Government turns its head. When we went to a local agent of the Agriculture Department to get information on DDT, our attorney went to the office at 11 o'clock, and by 1 o'clock the growers had an injunction prohibiting us from seeing the records on DDT. . . .

. . . In addition to all of this lack of protection from the police, in addition to the lack of protection from the courts, we also have all of the attempts to break the union. . . .

. . . The growers are willing to spend tremendous amounts of money to try to represent the fact that farmworkers don't want a union, by hiring people like Jose Mendoza, who took a picture with Senator Dirksen to try to prove that the farmworkers don't want a union. They could very easily have paid the workers decent wages with the money they are spending.

They have hired public relations firms to try to prove that we are a violent union, which I think everyone knows we are not.

They are spending an awful lot of money on this campaign. I have heard reports of as high as $5 million a year, they are going throughout the country, buying television and radio time, printing up brochures by the hundreds of thousands, and I want to express something here.

I think we are very, very concerned. We have seen reports of recent incidents of violence that we know are being perpetrated by someone other than ourselves, and these instances of violence make us believe that there is going to be a concerted effort by individuals to create violence either in some of the boycott cities or in some of the areas of California where the strike is now in progress. . . .

So, you can see that the situation is very, very serious. Now, if we look at some of the noises that some of the people that are fighting the union are making, they are talking about violence.

We look at Mr. Baur, who is one of the members of the California Grape & Tree Fruit League, and he is talking about violence.

Mr. Allen Grant, one of Reagan's top men in agriculture in California, is talking about violence. They are trying to create a climate of fear and violence.

We are going to do everything we can to create just the opposite kind of a climate, but I want you to be aware of this, because I think that all of these aspects should be investigated.

We think that this is a deliberate effort to bring violence into the farm labor scene which we know has not been there.

There have been incidents of violence against the union, many of them, and it has taken all that Cesar [Chavez] can do and the rest of the people can do to keep workers nonviolent. . . .

. . . The growers don't have any heart at all. They have all the economic power, the power in hiring and firing. There have been entire crews of workers fired because one person in the crew said something favorable about the union. There are entire crews of workers who were fired because they had Kennedy stickers on the bumpers of their cars. . . .

. . . Gunmen have gone to our offices, taken canceled checks, membership files, and some of these membership files have been used in blacklisting for jobs. . . .

. . . We are not afraid, and we will continue, but we do need some help, and we hope that the committee here will be able to furnish some of it.[2]

3. SPEECH ON MONEY AND ORGANIZING (1971)

CESAR CHAVEZ

What I'm going to say may not make much sense to you. On the other hand, it may make an awful lot of sense. This depends on where you are in terms of organizing and what your ideas are about that elusive and difficult task of getting people together—to act together and to produce something. . . .

We started with two principles: First, since there wasn't any money and the job had to be done there would have to be a lot of sacrificing. Second, no matter how poor the people, they had a responsibility to help the union. If they had $2.00 for food, they had to give $1.00 to the union. Otherwise, they would never get out of the trap of poverty. They would never have a union because they couldn't afford to sacrifice a little bit more on top of their misery. The statement: "They're so poor they can't afford to contribute to the group," is a great cop-out. You don't organize people by being afraid of them. You never have. You never will. You can be afraid of them in a variety of ways. But one of the main ways is to patronize them. You know the attitude; Blacks or browns or farm workers are so poor that they can't afford to have their own group. They hardly have enough money to eat. This makes it very easy for the organizer. He can always rationalize, "I haven't failed. They can't come up with the money so we were not able to organize them."

We decided that workers wanted to be organized and could be organized. So the responsibility had to be upon ourselves, the organizers. Organizing is one place where you can easily get away with a failure. If you send a man to dig a ditch 3 feet by 10 feet, you'll know if he did it or not. Or if you get someone to write a letter, you'll know if he wrote it. In most areas of endeavor, you can see the results. In organizing, it's different. You can see results years later, but you can't see them right away. That's why we have so many failures. So many organizers that should never be organizers go in and muddy the waters. Then good organizers have to come in and it's twice as hard for them to organize.

We knew we didn't have the money. We knew farm workers could be organized and we were going to do it. We weren't going to accept failure. But we were going to make sure that workers contributed to the doing of this organizing job. That has never been done in the history of this country.

We started out by telling workers, "We are trying to organize a union. We don't have money but if you work together it can be done." 95% of the workers we talked to were very kind. They smiled at us. 5% asked us questions and maybe 1% had the spirit and really wanted to do something.

We didn't have any money for gas and food. Many days we left the house with no money at all. Sometimes we had enough gas to get there but not enough to come back. We were determined to go to the workers. In fact at the very beginning of the organizing drive, we looked for the worst homes in the barrios where there were a lot of dogs and kids outside. And we went in and asked for a handout. Inevitably, they gave us food. Then they made a collection and gave us money for gas. They opened their homes and gave us their hearts. And today, they are the nucleus of the union's leadership. We forced ourselves to do this. We kept telling ourselves, "If these workers don't get organized, if we fail, it's our fault not theirs."

Then the question came up, how would we survive? My wife was working in the fields. We used to take the whole family out on Sundays and earn a few dollars to be able to survive the following week. We knew we couldn't continue that way. And we knew that the money had to come not from the outside but from the workers. And the only way to get the money was to have people pay dues.

So we began the drive to get workers to pay dues so we could live, so we could just survive. We were very frank, very open. At a farm worker's convention, we told them we had nothing to give them except the dream that it might happen. But we couldn't continue unless they were willing to make a sacrifice. At that meeting everyone wanted to pay $5.00 or $8.00 a month. We balked and said "No, no. Just $3.50. That's all we need." There were about 280 people there, and 212 signed up and paid the $3.50 in the first month.

Ninety days from that day, there were 12 people paying $3.50. By that time we had a small community. There were 6 of us—four of us working full time. There were a lot of questions being asked. Some said, "They're very poor and can't afford it. That's why they're not paying." And a few of us said, "We're poor too. We're poorer than they are. And we can afford to sacrifice our families and our time. They have to pay."

I remember many incidents when I went to collect dues. Let me tell you just one. I'd been working 12 years with the mentality that people were very poor and shouldn't be forced to pay dues. Keep that in mind. Because that comes in handy in understanding what you go through when you're not really convinced that this is the way it should be.

I went to a worker's home in McFarland, 7 miles south of Delano. It was in the evening. It was raining and it was winter. And there was no work. I knew it. And everyone knew it. As I knocked on the door, the guy in the little two room house was going to the store with a $5.00 bill to get groceries. And there I was. He owed $7.00 because he was one full month behind plus the current one. So I'd come for $7.00. But all he had was $5.00. I had to make a decision. Should I take $3.50 or shouldn't I? It was very difficult. Up to this time I had been saying, "They should be paying. And if they don't pay they'll never have a union." $3.50 worth of food wasn't really going to change his life one way or the other that much. So I told him, "You have to pay at least $3.50 right now or I'll have to put you out of the union." He gave me the $5.00. We went to the store and changed the $5.00 bill. I got the $3.50 and gave him the $1.50. I stayed with him. He bought $1.50 worth of groceries and went home.

That experience hurt me but it also strengthened my determination. If this man was willing to give me $3.50 on a dream, when we were really taking the money out of his own food, then why shouldn't we be able to have a union—however difficult. There had never been a successful union for farm workers. Every unionizing attempt had been defeated. People were killed. They ran into every obstacle you can think of. The whole agricultural industry along with government and business joined forces to break the unions and keep them from organizing. But with the kind of faith this farm worker had why couldn't we have a union? . . .

When you sacrifice, you force others to sacrifice. It's an extremely powerful weapon. When somebody stops eating for a week or ten days, people come and want to be part of that experience. Someone goes to jail and people want to help him. You don't buy that with money. That doesn't have any price in terms of dollars.

Those who are willing to sacrifice and be of service have very little difficulty with people. They know what they are all about. People can't help but want to be near them—to help them and work with them. That's what love is all about. It starts with you and radiates out. You can't phoney it. It just doesn't go. When you work and sacrifice more than anyone else around you, you put others on the spot and they have to do at least a bit more than they've been doing. And that's what puts it together.

These observations tie in directly with the whole question of organizing. Why do we have leaders? We put some people out in the fields and all of a sudden they hit, they click. Everyone's happy with them and they begin to move mountains. With other people there are problems and heartaches. They just don't go. When we look and see what's happening, almost invariably the differences are along the lines of willingness to sacrifice and work long hours.

We didn't start out knowing these things. We have discovered them. During those six years of strike and boycott it never seemed like that much of a struggle. We accepted it as a fact. Now that we're over that big hurdle, we look back and say, "My God. People really sacrificed. And the things that I asked them to do! Did I really ask them to do that much?" I asked them to do it to the maximum and they did it. . . .

INTRODUCTION TO DOCUMENTS 4–8

When Betty Friedan published *The Feminine Mystique*, women's wages were less than three-fifths of those earned by men, and fewer than 10 percent of American professionals—doctors, lawyers, architects, college professors—were women. Increasingly in the late 1960s and into the 1970s, women organized and demonstrated for greater equity on the job. One result was the revival of the Equal Rights Amendment (ERA), which was first proposed in 1923. The amendment's aim was to grant constitutional guarantees of full citizenship to women. Some opponents argued that women were incapable of equality; others feared that that the ERA would abrogate women's protective workplace legislation. Finally, though, in 1972, with both Democrat and Republican backing, the proposed Twenty-Seventh Amendment to the Constitution passed both houses of Congress. But getting ratification from three-quarters of the states was another matter. Thirty-five states—70 percent of the total, just three shy of approval—were on board by 1975. But then the country slowly drifted toward conservatism, and the opposition became better organized. Claims that the amendment jeopardized wives' rights to be supported by husbands, that it opened the door to greater leniency on abortion, and that women might be sent into combat all took their toll. Time ran out on the ratification process before another state mustered the votes in favor of the amendment.

In Document 4, New York City Congresswoman Shirley Chisolm—one of the only women in Congress during the 1960s—argues for the ERA. Document 5 is the amendment itself. Documents 6 is a letter from a citizen in California opposed to the amendment, sent to her representative, Don Edwards, an ERA supporter. Document 7 is an equally passionate letter to Representative Edwards from Liz Carpenter, press secretary to Lady Bird Johnson (President Johnson's widow), supporting the ERA. In Document 8, Gloria Steinem—one of the most visible and important leaders of the women's movement—lays out the types of discrimination women faced and its corrosive effects. Steinem also forcefully argued that the largest goal of the women's cause was creating not just gender equality but also a more humane society. Her testimony before Congress reflects the nationwide attention to the issues around feminism by the early 1970s.

4. EQUAL RIGHTS FOR WOMEN

HON. SHIRLEY CHISHOLM OF NEW YORK,
IN THE HOUSE OF REPRESENTATIVES, MAY 21, 1969

Mr. Speaker, when a young woman graduates from college and starts looking for a job, she is likely to have a frustrating and even demeaning experience ahead of her. If she walks into an office for an interview, the first question she will be asked is, "Do you type?"

There is a calculated system of prejudice that lies unspoken behind that question. Why is it acceptable for women to be secretaries, librarians, and teachers, but totally unacceptable for them to be managers, administrators, doctors, lawyers, and Members of Congress.

The unspoken assumption is that women are different. They do not have executive ability, orderly minds, stability, leadership skills, and they are too emotional.

It has been observed before, that society for a long time, discriminated against another minority, the blacks, on the same basis—that they were different and inferior. The happy little homemaker and the contented "old darkey" on the plantation were both produced by prejudice.

As a black person, I am no stranger to race prejudice. But the truth is that in the political world I have been far oftener discriminated against because I am a woman than because I am black.

Prejudice against blacks is becoming unacceptable although it will take years to eliminate it. But it is doomed because, slowly, white America is beginning to admit that it exists. Prejudice against women is still acceptable. There is very little understanding yet of the immorality involved in double pay scales and the classification of most of the better jobs as "for men only."

More than half of the population of the United States is female. But women occupy only 2 percent of the managerial positions. They have not even reached the level of tokenism yet. No women sit on the AFL-CIO council or Supreme Court. There have been only two women who have held Cabinet rank, and at present there are none. Only two women now hold ambassadorial rank in the diplomatic corps. In Congress, we are down to one Senator and 10 Representatives.

Considering that there are about 3 1/2 million more women in the United States than men, this situation is outrageous.

It is true that part of the problem has been that women have not been aggressive in demanding their rights. This was also true of the black population for many years. They submitted to oppression and even cooperated with it. Women have done the same thing. But now there is an awareness of this situation particularly among the younger segment of the population.

As in the field of equal rights for blacks, Spanish-Americans, the Indians, and other groups, laws will not change such deep-seated problems overnight. But they can be used to provide protection for those who are most abused, and to begin the process of evolutionary change by compelling the insensitive majority to reexamine its unconscious attitudes.

It is for this reason that I wish to introduce today a proposal that has been before every Congress for the last 40 years and that sooner or later must become part of the basic law of the land—the equal rights amendment. . . .[3]

5. THE EQUAL RIGHTS AMENDMENT

Section 1. Equality of rights under the law shall not be denied or abridged by the United States or by any state on account of sex.

Section 2. The Congress shall have the power to enforce, by appropriate legislation, the provisions of this article.

Section 3. This amendment shall take effect two years after the date of ratification.

Image 15.2: Equal rights supporters on a "Relay for the ERA" (1977)

These women were on their way from Seneca Falls, site of the first women's rights convention in 1848, to Houston for a national women's conference in 1977.

Source: Records of Temporary Committees, Commissions, and Boards, Record Group 220, National Archives, Identifier 7452296.

6. CONSTITUENT'S LETTER TO CONGRESSMAN DON EDWARDS

September 9, 1971

Dear Mr. Edwards,

I am writing to voice my opposition to the so-called "Equal Rights Amendment, H.J. Res. 208."

The mal-contents, lesbians and Communists of women's lib main purpose seems to be to downgrade the marvelous vocation of mother-homemaker, have the government play babysitter, and make women feel subservient who aren't competing with men in the business world.

Women, of course, should receive equal pay for equal work, but to make it seem that a woman will find her fulfillment in competing for some traditionally male position just isn't so. Having worked in the personnel field a number of years before taking on the more challenging role of wife-mother-homemaker, I am aware that most men just don't have that exciting a job—many are boring, frustrating, and dead-end.

I feel that if the aims of women's lib are realized it will be a big step down for women. If more women worked for a few years BEFORE marriage, they might come to a greater appreciation of the responsibility involved in rearing a family. From the high rate of crime, venereal disease, drug abuse and suicide among the young, and lack of respect for God and country, it would seem women are failing terribly in their most important job.

Please don't help the women's lib movement, but work toward restoring a higher regard for family life, which would greatly improve our country.

Sincerely,

Mrs. T. Z.[4]

7. LETTER TO CONGRESSMAN DON EDWARDS

September 23, 1971

Dear Congressman,

As you know, through the years women have been stepped upon, wept upon and slept upon. Still we find something in men to love—and I will be glad to say this again to every one of you after the Equal Rights Amendment is passed *without* crippling amendments.

As you know, this issue has been with us since 1920, when women were given the vote. It would have passed by now except for being fogged up by the phony issue of "protective" legislation for women.

It is high time men recognized that some "protective" laws treat women like idiots, and others keep women out of jobs where they'd lift no more than a three-year-old child does.

Don't be fooled by the bugaboos raised by the Amendment's opponents. Women will gladly trade protective laws for some equal pay and equal rights.

I hope very much that you will give this your real support. I have traveled 100,000 miles this past year, and one thing is clear—women are ready for it, the country is ready for it. Won't you be with it?

Sincerely,

Liz Carpenter[5]

Image 15.3: Betty Ford, February 1975

First Lady Betty Ford was an outspoken feminist, a position which many worried would generate opposition among Republican voters. Surviving breast cancer as well as substance addiction, she became a hero to many for her candor and activism.

Source: Courtesy National Archives.

8. STATEMENT OF GLORIA STEINEM, WRITER AND CRITIC (MAY 1970)

My name is Gloria Steinem. I am a writer and editor, and I am currently a member of the policy council of the Democratic committee. And I work regularly with the lowest-paid workers in the country, the migrant workers, men, women, and children both in California and in my own State of New York. . . .

During 12 years of working for a living, I have experienced much of the legal and social discrimination reserved for women in this country. I have been refused service in public restaurants, ordered out of public gathering places, and turned away from apartment rentals; all for the clearly-stated, sole reason that I am a woman. And all without the legal remedies available to blacks and other minorities. I have been excluded from professional groups, writing assignments on so-called "unfeminine" subjects such as politics, full participation in the Democratic

Party, jury duty, and even from such small male privileges as discounts on airline fares. Most important to me, I have been denied a society in which women are encouraged, or even allowed to think of themselves as first-class citizens and responsible human beings.

However, after 2 years of researching the status of American women, I have discovered that in reality, I am very, very lucky. Most women, both wage-earners and housewives, routinely suffer more humiliation and injustice than I do.

As a freelance writer, I don't work in the male-dominated hierarchy of an office. (Women, like blacks and other visibly different minorities, do better in individual professions such as the arts, sports, or domestic work; anything in which they don't have authority over white males.) I am not one of the millions of women who must support a family. Therefore, I haven't had to go on welfare because there are no day-care centers for my children while I work, and I haven't had to submit to the humiliating welfare inquiries about my private and sexual life, inquiries from which men are exempt. I haven't had to brave the sex bias of labor unions and employers, only to see my family subsist on a median salary 40 percent less than the male median salary.

I hope this committee will hear the personal, daily injustices suffered by many women—professionals and day laborers, women housebound by welfare as well as by suburbia. We have all been silent for too long. But we won't be silent anymore.

The truth is that all our problems stem from the same sex based myths. We may appear before you as white radicals or the middle-aged middle class or black soul sisters, but we are all sisters in fighting against these outdated myths. Like racial myths, they have been reflected in our laws. Let me list a few.

That women are biologically inferior to men. In fact, an equally good case can be made for the reverse. Women live longer than men, even when the men are not subject to business pressures. Women survived Nazi concentration camps better, keep cooler heads in emergencies currently studied by disaster-researchers, are protected against heart attacks by their female sex hormones, and are so much more durable at every stage of life that nature must conceive 20 to 50 percent more males in order to keep the balance going. . . .

However, I don't want to prove the superiority of one sex to another. That would only be repeating a male mistake. English scientists once definitively proved, after all, that the English were descended from the angels, while the Irish were descended from the apes; it was the rationale for England's domination of Ireland for more than a century. The point is that science is used to support current myth and economics almost as much as the church was. What we do know is that the difference between two races or two sexes is much smaller than the differences to be found within each group. Therefore, in spite of the slide show on female inferiorities that I understand was shown to you yesterday, the law makes much more sense when it treats individuals, not groups bundled together by some condition of birth. . . .

Another myth, that women are already treated equally in this society. I am sure there has been ample testimony to prove that equal pay for equal work, equal chance for advancement, and equal training or encouragement is obscenely scarce in every field, even those—like food and fashion industries—that are supposedly "feminine."

A deeper result of social and legal injustice, however, is what sociologists refer to as "Internalized Aggression." Victims of aggression absorb the myth of their own inferiority, and come to believe that their group is in fact second class. Even when they themselves realize they are not second class, they may still think their group is, thus the tendency to be the only Jew in the club, the only black woman on the block, the only woman in the office.

Women suffer this second class treatment from the moment they are born. They are expected to be, rather than achieve, to function biologically rather than learn. A brother, whatever his intellect, is more likely to get the family's encouragement and education money, while girls are often pressured to conceal ambition and intelligence, to "Uncle Tom."

I interviewed a New York public school teacher who told me about a black teenager's desire to be a doctor. With all the barriers in mind, she suggested kindly that he be a veterinarian instead. The same day, a high school teacher mentioned a girl who wanted to be a doctor. The teacher said, "How about a nurse?"

Teachers, parents, and the Supreme Court may exude a protective, well-meaning rationale, but limiting the individual's ambition is doing no one a favor. Certainly not this country; it needs all the talent it can get. . . .

Another myth, that children must have full-time mothers. American mothers spend more time with their homes and children than those of any other society we know about. In the past, joint families, servants, a prevalent system in which grandparents raised the children, or family field work in the agrarian systems—all these factors contributed more to child care than the labor-saving devices of which we are so proud.

The truth is that most American children seem to be suffering from too much mother, and too little father. Part of the program of Women's Liberation is a return of fathers to their children. If laws permit women equal work and pay opportunities, men will then be relieved of their role as sole breadwinner. Fewer ulcers, fewer hours of meaningless work, equal responsibility for his own children: these are a few of the reasons that Women's Liberation is Men's Liberation too. As for psychic health of the children, studies show that the quality of time spent by parents is more important than the quantity. The most damaged children were not those whose mothers worked, but those whose mothers preferred to work but stayed home out of the role-playing desire to be a "good mother."

Another myth, that the women's movement is not political, won't last, or is somehow not "serious."

When black people leave their 19th century roles, they are feared. When women dare to leave theirs, they are ridiculed. We understand this; we accept the burden of ridicule. It won't keep us quiet anymore.

Similarly, it shouldn't deceive male observers into thinking that this is somehow a joke. We are 51 percent of the population; we are essentially united on these issues across boundaries of class or race or age; and we may well end by changing this society more than the civil rights movement. That is an apt parallel. We, too, have our right wing and left wing, our separatists, gradualists, and Uncle Toms. But we are changing our own consciousness, and that of the country. Engels noted the relationship of the authoritarian, nuclear family to capitalism: the father as capitalist, the mother as means of production, and the children as labor. He said the family would change as the economic system did, and that seems to have happened, whether we want to admit it or not. Women's bodies will no longer be owned by the state for the production of workers and soldiers; birth control and abortion are facts of everyday life. The new family is an egalitarian family.

Gunnar Myrdal noted 30 years ago the parallel between women and Negroes in this country. Both suffered from such restricting social myths as: smaller brains, passive natures, inability to govern themselves (and certainly not white men), sex objects only, childlike natures, special skills, and the like. When evaluating a general statement about women, it might be valuable to substitute "black people" for "women"—just to test the prejudice at work. And it might be valuable to do this constitutionally as well. Neither group is going to be content as a cheap labor pool anymore. And neither is going to be content without full constitutional rights.[6]

INTRODUCTION TO DOCUMENT 9, 10, AND 11

What today is called the environmental movement has a long history. Theodore Roosevelt was associated in image and in fact with the American West, and he is thought of as the father of the National Park System. The early environmental movement stressed "conservation," managing natural resources efficiently. Over the years, a range of writers, from Henry David Thoreau to John Muir and from Aldo Leopold to Edward Abbey sought a less calculating vision of the environment. Wilderness was not a resource to be mined but humankind's foundation in the natural world.

One book in particular, Rachel Carson's *Silent Spring,* published in 1962, brought environmental issues to the front of Americans' awareness. For years Carson had been writing popular books about the new science of ecology—about the relationships and interdependencies of species with each other. *Silent Spring,* however, did not so much describe the "web of life," as raise in alarming detail the possibility that humankind was slowly poisoning the world. Carson focused especially on the chemical DDT, an unusually effective insecticide used during the postwar era that helped farmers control pests. She revealed that a growing body of research demonstrated the long-term, cumulative effects of such sprays. Simply put, DDT did not break down, did not just float away, it accumulated and made its way up the food chain. *Silent Spring* was the beginning of environmental consciousness for many Americans because it demonstrated so powerfully that the benefits of progress came at an enormous cost—in the case of DDT, poisoning the earth and water. Within a few years, grassroots pressure prompted the federal government under President Nixon to establish the Environmental Protection Agency in 1970. Soon after, Congress passed the Clean Air and Clean Water Acts. States and local communities created their own environmental agencies, while militant activist groups like Green Peace and Earth First pressed hard for change. In 1972, the federal government banned the use of DDT.

Citizen participation took many forms, most spectacularly the first Earth Day on April 22, 1970. The idea of a day devoted to celebrating nature and pondering ecological issues had been around for a while, but an environmentally minded senator, democrat Gaylord Nelson of Wisconsin, took a leading role in garnering political support. Earth "Day" was a series of mass meetings in hundreds of cities and on college campuses across the country. These were a bit reminiscent of the demonstrations against the Vietnam War, with speeches, poetry readings, and music. Above all, the idea was to bring people out, and in fact, roughly 20 million Americans attended the first Earth Day celebrations, providing striking footage on the evening news. Document 9 is text from a January 1970 advertisement for Earth Day, one of many in an enormous if uncoordinated campaign to raise awareness about an issue that few Americans thought about in any serious or sustained way. Messages like this across the country—issued by grassroots organizations through newsletters as well as national media—contributed to the enormous turnout on Earth Day and a lasting shift in environmental awareness. Document 10—also from January 1970—is excerpted from Senator Nelson's speech introducing an ambitious bill to regulate various threats to the environment. Ask yourself how Nelson frames the urgency of the situation, and what he sees as the federal government's role.

While Nelson was developing his bill, students at the University of Michigan were simultaneously organizing their own movement to fight pollution and raise awareness about environmental degradation. Document 11 is an account of the first teach-in at Michigan, just a few weeks before the national Earth Day. It is taken from *Environmental Action,* a newsletter created by the activists. How did they articulate their goals, and what were their strategies to achieve them and enlarge the movement? What differences do you see between Nelson and the students at Michigan? Were they reinforcing Nelson's efforts or advocating something different? What is the relationship of environmentalism to capitalism?

9. EARTH DAY ADVERTISEMENT (JANUARY 1970)

Adisease has infected our country. It has brought smog to Yosemite, dumped garbage in the Hudson, sprayed DDT in our food, and left our cities in decay. Its carrier is man.

The weak are already dying. Trees by the Pacific. Fish in our streams and lakes. Birds and crops and sheep. And people.

On April 22 we start to reclaim the environment we have wrecked.

April 22 is the Environmental Teach-In, a day of environmental action.

Hundreds of communities and campuses across the country are already committed.

It is a phenomenon that grows as you read this.

Earth Day is a commitment to make life better, not just bigger and faster. To provide real rather than rhetorical solutions.

It is a day to re-examine the ethic of individual progress at mankind's expense.

It is a day to challenge the corporate and governmental leaders who promise change, but who short change the necessary programs.

It is a day for looking beyond tomorrow. April 22 seeks a future worth living.

April 22 seeks a future.[7]

10. SENATOR GAYLORD NELSON INTRODUCES AN ENVIRONMENTAL AGENDA FOR THE 1970S (JANUARY 19, 1970)

. . . The mindless pursuit of quantity is destroying—not enhancing—the opportunity to achieve quality in our lives. In the words of the American balladeer, Pete Seeger, we have found ourselves "standing knee deep in garbage, throwing rockets at the moon."

Cumulatively, "progress—American style" adds up each year to 200 million tons of smoke and fumes, 7 million junked cars, 20 million tons of paper, 48 billion cans, and 28 billion bottles.

It also means bulldozers gnawing away at the landscape to make room for more unplanned expansion, more leisure time but less open space in which

to spend it, and so much reckless progress that we face even now a hostile environment.

As one measure of the rate of consumption that demands our resources and creates our vast wastes, it has been estimated that all the American children born in just one year will use up 200 million pounds of steel, 9.1 billion gallons of gasoline, and 25 billion pounds of beef during their lifetimes.

To provide the electricity for our air conditioners, a Kentucky hillside is strip-mined. To provide the gasoline for our automobiles, the ocean floor is drilled for oil. To provide the sites for our second homes, the shore of a pristine lake is subdivided.

. . . It is the laboring man, living in the shadows of the spewing smokestacks of industry, who feels the bite of the "disposable society." Or the commuter inching in spurts along an expressway. Or the housewife paying too much for products that begin to fall apart too soon. Or the student watching the university building program destroy a community. Or the black man living alongside the noisy, polluted truck routes through the central city ghetto.

. . . Man is on the way to defining the terms of his own extinction. . . .

America is one again faced with a crisis that has to do with material things—but it is an entirely different sort of dilemma. In effect, America has bought environmental disaster on a national installment plan: Buy affluence now and let future generations pay the price. Trading away the future is a high price to pay for an electric swizzle stick—or a car with greater horsepower.

. . . What has been missing is the unity of purpose, forged out of a threat to our national health or security or prestige, that we so often seem to have found only during world war.

But there is now, I think, a great awakening underway. We have begun to recognize that our security is again threatened—not from the outside, but from the inside—not by our enemies, but by ourselves. . . .

A freshman college student attitude poll, conducted last fall by the American Council on Education, found that 89.9 percent of all male freshmen believed the Federal Government should be more involved in the control of pollution. And a Gallup poll published in late December found that the control of air and water pollution is fast becoming a new student cause, with students placing this issue sixth on a list of areas where they felt changes must be made. . . .

In short, I believe that today we are at a watershed in the history of the struggle in this country to save the quality of our environment. . . .

A victory will take decades and tens of billions of dollars. Just to control pollution, it will take $275 billion by the year 2000. Although that sounds like a lot of money, it will be spent over the next 30 years and is equivalent to the Defense expenditure for the next 4 years.

More than money, restoring our environment and establishing quality on a par with quantity as a goal of American life will require a reshaping of our values, sweeping changes in the performance and goals of our institutions, national standards of quality for the goods we produce, a humanizing and redirection of our technology, and greatly increased attention to the problems of our expanding population. . . .

American acceptance of the ecological ethic will involve nothing less than achieving a transition from the consumer society to a society of "new citizenship"—a society that concerns itself as much with the well-being of present and future generations as it does with bigness and abundance. . . .

An Environmental Agenda for the 1970's. . . .

The first item I suggest for this agenda will be the introduction of an amendment to the U.S. Constitution which will recognize and protect the inalienable right of every person to a decent environment.

As the second item for an agenda, I propose immediate action to rid America in the 1970's of the massive pollution from five of the most heavily used products of our affluent age. For each of these products, I am convinced that it can be done—with firm Federal action to assure it.

The five areas are: Internal combustion engines, hard pesticides, detergent pollution, aircraft pollution, and nonreturnable containers. . . .

The third item on an agenda . . . should be protecting the right of every citizen to plan his family. The funds and coordination must be made available for conducting necessary research into population problems and providing family planning services.

The fourth item . . . must [include] new channels and forums for public participation, creation of a citizen environmental advocate agency, and creation of an environmental overview committee in Congress. . . .

A national policy on land use must be delineated and implemented that will halt the chaotic, unplanned combination of urban sprawl, industrial expansion, and air, water, land, and visual pollution that is seriously threatening the quality of life of major regions of the Nation.[8]

Image 15.4: Cyclist in front of local environmental center, Humboldt County, California, May 1972

The environmental movement involved not just an ethic of activism, but an interest in reconfiguring the very structure of modern life around grassroots networking and attention to local conditions.

Source: Records of the Environmental Protection Agency, Record Group 412, National Archives, Identifier 543032.

11. "MICHIGAN TEACH-IN FACES SOCIETAL ISSUES" (MARCH 1970)

ENVIRONMENTAL ACTION

In a confrontation with the underlying social, political, and economic issues involved in the environmental movement, the University of Michigan student group ENACT (Environmental Action for Survival) put on one of the largest programs of talk, action and concern yet for their teach-in, March 11–14.

Every major and many minor events were packed with students and citizens from the community of Ann Arbor. ENACT chose the March dates to avoid conflict with the university final exams scheduled the week of April 22.

Fifteen thousand participants In Wednesday's kick off rally heard views ranging from Michigan

Governor Milliken's call for a "clean earth corps" for work on action projects in the state to ecologist Barry Commoner's declaration that "we cannot defer for long a confrontation with the real debt that we owe to nature—the total reorganization of our system of productivity to make it compatible with the ecosystem."

. . . A representative of Black Action Movement on Campus . . . warned against using the environment issue to coopt others from the concerns of the blacks and poor in America.

High school programs abounded during the four-day teach-in with workshops on abortion and population issues, circulation of petitions, and other activities. Women's Liberation conducted some workshops, and disrupted others explaining that "domination of nature by man is the root cause of the ecological crisis" and that "the liberation of woman from her submissive and inferior position in society is essential in changing the relationships of man to his environment."

Dow Chemical President Ted Doan, panelist in a discussion of the root causes of the environmental crisis, faced an evening of heckling and direct questioning about Dow's production of napalm, herbicides used in Vietnam and pesticides used in the United States. Walter Reuther, president of UAW, admitted in the same panel that the world might need fewer automobiles. . . .

Ralph Nader, everybody's lawyer, delivered Saturday afternoon a condemnation of corporate violence, crime, and manipulation of American symbols and bodies. Commenting on the inequities of corporate life, Nader declared that "if an individual cannot relieve himself in the Detroit River, I don't see any reason corporations can be allowed to."

After all the talk, demonstrations by street people, Huron River pollution tours, and a Congressional hearing held in Ann Arbor by the House Subcommittee on Natural Resources and the Environment, the students discussed post-teach-in activities. Co-chairman Doug Scott of ENACT described a strongly-worded letter from the organizing student group to university president Robin Fleming calling for experiments in entirely new forms of life and societal structure.

ENACT demanded specifically that the University of Michigan hold open hearings in the university community on the voting of its 27,538 shares of General Motors stock for the next stockholders meeting May 22 in Detroit. They asked for a student-faculty committee to represent the university at the meeting.

The students also demanded that the university write GM "condemning its arrogant refusal" to submit the proposed corporate policy changes suggested by the Project for Corporate Responsibility and Ralph Nader for stockholders' consideration before the meeting.[9]

POSTSCRIPT

The movements begun in the 1960s and 1970s had far-reaching consequences and lasting results. But as we will see in the next chapter, by 1980 American politics took a decided turn to the right. Beginning with the presidency of Ronald Reagan, conservative ideas and policies clearly had the upper hand. Even in the 1990s, the Clinton administration was most notable for its failure to pass major new legislation, such as a comprehensive health-care bill, and for cutting back on welfare programs like Aid to Families with Dependent Children. It was not until the election of 2008 that a presidential administration seemed to evoke the Great Society of Lyndon Johnson.

With a white mother from Kansas and a black father from Kenya, Barack Obama embodied the diversity championed by the American left. He was raised in the most polyglot American state, Hawaii. He worked on Chicago's south side as an organizer before attending Harvard Law School, where he was elected editor of the *Law Review*. Obama returned to the South Side and married the great granddaughter of former slaves, Michelle Robinson, a successful Princeton-educated attorney from a black working-class family. His brief career in the U.S. Senate clearly identified Obama as a liberal.

In his first year as president, Obama's support for a major expansion of federal jobs programs, comprehensive health-care reform, and regulation of the financial industry signaled a more progressive administration than in recent decades. Certainly, Obama's Inaugural address on January 20, 2009, coming as it did after years of the unpopular Iraq War and at the beginning of a major recession suggested the expansive vision of earlier times:

> . . . Everywhere we look, there is work to be done. The state of the economy calls for action, bold and swift, and we will act—not only to create new jobs, but to lay a new foundation for growth. We will build the roads and bridges, the electric grids and digital lines that feed our commerce and bind us together. We will restore science to its rightful place, and wield technology's wonders to raise health care's quality and lower its cost. We will harness the sun and the winds and soil to fuel our cars and run our factories. And we will transform our schools and colleges and universities to meet the demands of a new age. . . .
>
> Now there are some who question the scale of our ambitions, who suggest that our system cannot tolerate too many big plans. Their memories are short. For they have forgotten what this country has already done, what free men and women can achieve when imagination is joined to common purpose, and necessity to courage. . . .
>
> Nor is the question before us whether the market is a force for good or ill. Its power to generate wealth and expand freedom is unmatched, but this [economic] crisis has reminded us that without a watchful eye, the market can spin out of control—that a nation cannot prosper long when it favors only the prosperous. The success of our economy has always depended not just on the size of our Gross Domestic Product, but on the reach of our prosperity, on the ability to extend opportunity to every willing heart—not out of charity, but because it is the surest route to our common good. . . .
>
> . . . We know that our patchwork heritage is a strength, not a weakness. We are a nation of Christians and Muslims, Jews and Hindus, and non-believers. We are shaped by every language and culture, drawn from every end of this earth; and because we have tasted the bitter swill of civil war and segregation, and emerged from that dark chapter stronger and more united, we cannot help but believe that the old hatreds shall someday pass, that the lines of tribe shall soon dissolve, that as the world grows smaller, our common humanity shall reveal itself, and that America must play its role in ushering in a new era of peace. . . .[10]

Donald Trump followed Obama to the Presidency in 2017. Trump's campaign against Democrat Hillary Clinton and the first weeks of his administration indicate yet another turn to the right, including major budget cuts for social programs, an emphasis on national security, and highly restrictive new immigration rules. Equally important, Trump won his election with the slogan, "America First," rejecting Obama's embrace of globalization and cosmopolitanism.

QUESTIONS

1. Why did Cesar Chavez and Dolores Huerta think unionizing farm workers was necessary? Might the farmworkers have been sympathetic to the environmental movement, and vice versa?
2. Do you think Cesar Chavez's ideas about personal sacrifice applies to all organizing? What did Huerta and Chavez seek from the federal government?
3. What did Gloria Steinem mean by saying that women's liberation would free men too? Was she simply making a rhetorical point, or was this statement part of her larger vision of the future?
4. Given the relative simplicity of the Equal Rights Amendment, why do you think it sparked opposition strong enough to effectively defeat the measure? Do the arguments of women like Liz Carpenter and Gloria Steinem seem relevant today?

5. Why, according to Senator Nelson and the early Earth Day activists, was there a need for Earth Day? Who were their targets, and who might have been their natural and political allies?

6. Are the issues covered here—workers' rights, women's rights, and the protection of the environment—part of a larger ideology, or is there little overlap or even antagonism between them? Do you see any relevant connection between the activists of this era and the Progressives of the early twentieth century?

ADDITIONAL READING

The literature on the 1960s and 1970s is enormous, but some good titles include Todd Gitlin, *The Sixties: Years of Hope, Days of Rage* (1987); Maurice Isserman, *If I Had a Hammer: The Death of the Old Left and the Birth of the New* (1987); G. Calvin Mackenzie and Robert Weisbrot, *The Liberal Hour: Washington and the Politics of Change in the 1960s* (2009); and Bruce J. Schulman, *The Seventies: The Great Shift in American Culture, Society, and Politics* (2002). Other works include James Miller, *"Democracy Is in the Streets": From Port Huron to the Siege of Chicago* (1987), and David Farber, *Chicago '68* (1987). On the women's movement, a now-classic work is Sara Evans, *Personal Politics: The Roots of Women's Liberation in the Civil Rights Movement and the New Left* (1979). Also see Alice Echols, *Daring to Be Bad: Radical Feminism in America, 1967–1975* (1989). On the farm workers' movement, see Marshall Ganz, *Why David Wins* (2009); Frederick John Dalton, *The Moral Vision of Cesar Chavez* (2003); and Randy Shaw, *Beyond the Fields* (2008). On the environmental movement, see Adam Rome, *The Genius of Earth Day: How a 1970 Teach-In Unexpectedly Made the First Green Generation* (2014); Benjamin Kline, *First Along the River* (2007); Thomas Jundt, *Greening the Red White and Blue* (2014); and Edward Abbey's novel, *The Monkey Wrench Gang* (1976). Other important works on the era include Alexander Bloom, ed., *Longtime Gone: Sixties America Then and Now* (2001); James J. Farrell, *The Spirit of the Sixties* (1997); Martin Duberman, *Stonewall* (1993); William Cronon, *Uncommon Ground* (1995); Beth Bailey and David Farber, *America in the Seventies* (2004). For films, see *Berkeley in the 60's* (1990), *The Fight in the Fields* (1997), and *An Inconvenient Truth* (2006).

ENDNOTES

1. U.S. Senate Subcommittee on Migratory Labor, *Hearings on Agricultural Labor Legislation*, 91st Congress, 1st Session, April 16, 1969.

2. Hearings on Migrant and Seasonal Worker Powerlessness, July 15, 1969 (Washington, D.C.: Government Printing Office, 1970).

3. House *Congressional Record*, Extensions of Remarks, E4165-6, May 21, 1969.

4. Records of the U.S. House of Representatives, Record Group 233, National Archives, Identifier 24824228.

5. Records of the U.S. House of Representatives, Record Group 233, National Archives, Identifier 24224217.

6. Subcommittee on Constitutional Amendments of the Senate Committee on the Judiciary, May 5, 6, and 7, 1970. 91st Congress, 2nd Session.

7. Gaylord Nelson Collection, Wisconsin Historical Society.

8. Senate *Congressional Record*, 116th Congress, pp. 81–85.

9. *Environmental Action*, v.1 n.6 (March 26, 1970), p. 2. Courtesy of the Gaylord Nelson Collection, Wisconsin Historical Society.

10. President Barack Obama, Inaugural Address, January 21, 2009.

CHAPTER 16

TURNING RIGHT

HISTORICAL CONTEXT

Two of the most frequently used but also slippery words in English are *liberal* and *conservative*. Both are used as nouns and adjectives. Each word implies a political position as well as a way of life. Watch political talk shows and you will come away convinced that liberals are Democrats who support activist government; racial, gender, and gay rights; freedom of choice in the abortion debate; and the belief that wealthy businessmen probably have something to hide. Conservatives, on the other hand, are portrayed as Republicans who advocate small government; believe that racial, gender, and gay rights issues mask other agendas; oppose abortion; and argue that wealthy businessmen create jobs and wealth that benefit all Americans. More negatively, liberals are depicted as gullible idealists who throw away federal money and conservatives as tightfisted and heartless advocates of the rich and powerful. In reality, Democrats in recent years have been almost as pro-business as Republicans, and Republicans have voted for big federal budgets almost as consistently as Democrats. Moreover, the very terms *liberal* and *conservative* have not always meant the same thing; over the last 250 years their meanings have changed radically.

Ambrose Bierce, a turn-of-the-twentieth-century writer noted for his sardonic humor, defined *conservative* in his *Devil's Dictionary* as "A statesman who is enamored of existing evils, as distinguished from a Liberal, who wishes to replace them with others." Bierce was right—the idea of inherent, recognizable evil is part of traditional conservatism. In its modern form, the term *conservative* is as much a product of the French Revolution as the idea of liberty, equality, and fraternity. For many thinkers and writers in England and the United States, the French Revolution came to symbolize the excesses of freedom, the idea that if people were cut loose from traditions, chaos and anarchy would result. In England, Edmund Burke, often called the father of modern conservatism, believed that social and political stability rested on a foundation of traditions and time-proven institutions. Change, he maintained, should be slow and incremental. He detested grand, utopian ideas, asserting that imperfect people could never create a perfect society and that radical change would always end in disaster. At best, humans can find a modicum of order, justice, and freedom, but they can never create a society free from evil, suffering, and inequality. This, conservatives argue, has been the mistake of all social and political revolutions, from the French and Russian to the Chinese and Cuban.

The ideas of Burke found their way into the U.S. Constitution, the Bill of Rights, the *Federalist Papers*, and many state constitutions. But in the United States, liberalism also had powerful advocates. Where conservatives placed faith in God, distrusted human nature, and feared too much democracy, liberals tended to deemphasize religion, believed in the goodness of people, and reveled in certain kinds of freedom. At least in the nineteenth century, it was a strong central government that liberals feared. Thomas Jefferson's notion that "the government that governed least governed best" captured this fear. Many liberals maintained that their distrust of a strong government has a basis in economic fact. They adhered to the economic ideas of Adam Smith, articulated in his influential book *The Wealth of Nations* (1776). Smith was a proponent of economic freedom, arguing that a marketplace freed from interference functioned most efficiently. Free people making free choices promoted economic well-being. An "invisible hand" guided free markets to maximize social good, Smith observed, and archaic customs and governmental meddling created more problems than they solved.

In the nineteenth century, the primary battleground for liberals and conservatives was the marketplace. Jefferson's and Andrew Jackson's Democratic Party generally supported the "laissez-faire" principle that the government should stay out of the economy. Alexander Hamilton's Federalist Party, followed by Henry Clay's Whig Party and Abraham Lincoln's Republican Party, countered with proposals for a more activist federal government. Hamilton, Clay, and Lincoln consistently supported a national bank, protective tariffs, and federally funded internal improvements. By 1912 the Republican Party was clearly the party of a strong central government; it had created a national bank, legislated protective tariffs and internal improvements, and established the principle that the federal government had the right to regulate business activity. The Democratic Party, which only managed to elect two presidents between 1860 and 1932, generally supported a weaker federal government with more limited powers. In short, the conservative position tended to be more government and the liberal position less government.

In the late-nineteenth century and the first half of the twentieth century, however, other issues began to complicate the liberal–conservative debate. The arrival of millions of immigrants, the spread of labor unrest, the growth of cities, the increasing awareness of racial inequalities, and a host of other social problems disturbed many Americans. Severe depressions in the 1890s and 1930s and violent revolutions in Russia and Mexico raised the specter of social and political convulsions. During the Great Depression, President Franklin Roosevelt and his Democratic coalition made an ideological about-face. Roosevelt abandoned the laissez-faire ideas of nineteenth-century Democrats and embraced an activist government. In an effort to preserve capitalism and democracy—to prevent radical social and political upheaval—he expanded programs designed to promote social justice. Out of his presidency came the idea of an American welfare state. His party became the agent of activism, regulating economic activity and promoting social welfare.

From the 1930s through the 1960s, conservatism floundered through an identity crisis, as Roosevelt's New Deal set the course of American politics. The New Deal was followed by Harry Truman's Fair Deal, John F. Kennedy's New Frontier, and Lyndon Johnson's

Great Society. The Democratic Party became identified with federal programs that fostered social justice, racial advancement, and gender equality. It promoted itself as the advocate for the poor and disfranchised, the safeguard against the powerful and the greedy. Even Dwight Eisenhower, the single Republican president between 1932 and 1968, spoke the language of liberalism. Rather than reject the legacy of FDR, he accepted it. Eisenhower said he was a conservative, "but an extremely liberal conservative," and defined his political philosophy as "dynamic conservatism." Under Eisenhower, for example, America fought a war in Korea and undertook an enormous infrastructure project, the Interstate Highway System. By the end of the 1950s, traditional conservatives seemed out of step with the march of the times.

But it wasn't as if conservative ideas had disappeared. Two writers enjoyed great popularity in the immediate postwar years: William F. Buckley, founder of the *National Review*, and Ayn Rand, who wrote novels about heroic individualists who increased social good by concentrating on personal aggrandizement. Then in the early 1960s conservatives found a new voice and a fresh agenda. Barry Goldwater, the Republican senator from Arizona, had no interest in Eisenhower's dynamic conservatism. America's problem, he said, was too much government, not too little. In *The Conscience of a Conservative* (1960), Goldwater articulated a new conservative agenda. He was committed to "achieving the maximum amount of freedom for individuals that [was] consistent with the maintenance of social order." His enemy was the burgeoning federal bureaucracy, "a Leviathan, a vast national authority out of touch with the people, and out of control." He absolutely rejected the legacy of the New Deal, the politics of subsidies, price supports, closed union shops, and special interest legislation, all administered from Washington, D.C. "I have little interest in streamlining government or making it more efficient, for I mean to reduce its size," he wrote. "I do not undertake to promote welfare, for I propose to extend freedom. My aim is not to pass laws, but to repeal them." Ironically, Goldwater conceived of a modern alternative to New Deal liberalism that expanded on Jefferson's distrust of a distant and unchecked federal government. Between 1960 and 1964, Goldwater's thin manifesto sold 3.5 million copies, and although voters rejected him by a landslide in the 1964 presidential race, his message found a large audience. Goldwater's book became, as conservative writer Patrick Buchanan observed, "our new testament; it contained the core beliefs of our political faith. . . . We read it, memorized it, quoted it. . . . For those of us wandering around in the arid desert of Eisenhower Republicanism, it hit like a rifle shot."[1]

The Conscience of a Conservative inspired modern conservatism. But the conservative movement, like the liberal movement, was a broad-based coalition of groups with different agendas. Republican politicians such as Ronald Reagan and Newt Gingrich championed Goldwater's demands for fiscal restraint, lower taxes, deregulation, welfare cuts, and reduced bureaucracy. Yet they also advocated an expanded military budget. Southern conservatives resented such federal actions as desegregation and "forced" busing, but they worked hard to keep and expand New Deal agricultural subsidies, and to bring home new dollars for the burgeoning aerospace industry. Religious conservatives questioned the Supreme Court's ruling on abortion, prayer in schools, and other social issues, yet they had no problem invoking federal power to enforce their social agenda. Western conservatives

Image 16.1: Lyndon Johnson and Richard Nixon meet at the White House on Inauguration Day, 1969

Nixon's victory marked an important moment in the fragmentation of the liberal coalition that had achieved enormous legislative victories under Lyndon Johnson.

Source: LBJ-WHPO (White House Photo Office Collection), National Archives, Identifier 2803422.

demanded state control of federally held western lands and relief from federal restrictions on logging and extraction industries, though they lobbied for federal aid to cattle ranchers. Libertarians simply wanted more freedom from government interference. Uniting these ideological strands was a grassroots movement, particularly strong in the Sunbelt, intent on cutting taxes, diminishing state power, and pushing the Republican Party to the right.

Although Lyndon Johnson soundly defeated Barry Goldwater in 1964, the Republican Party gained ground steadily in the late 1960s and in the 1970s. Richard Nixon, although a centrist Republican himself, capitalized on America's racial backlash and demographic shifts. Goldwater demonstrated that the South and West were receptive to his message, and once president, Nixon courted those sections of the country. During the 1970s, an increasing number of white southerners and working-class Catholics—traditionally Democratic loyalists—voted Republican. In addition, the shift in the population to the Sunbelt added to the political strength of the Republican Party. As president, Nixon extended some of the policies of Lyndon Johnson, signing new civil rights, environmental, and social welfare legislation, but with the election of Ronald Reagan in 1980, the conservative revolution was in full swing.

In the last thirty years, the conservative movement has fashioned an alternative to the welfare state. Certainly, what Roosevelt began has not disappeared, but it no longer stands unquestioned. The elections of Ronald Reagan, George Bush, and George W. Bush—and at least equally important, the shift to the right in Congress—demonstrate the vitality of the conservative ideas. Even the Democrat Bill Clinton cut major welfare programs and pushed policies that encouraged globalization and deregulation of capitalist markets, revealing the triumph of conservatism at the end of the twentieth century. The following documents give a sampling of conservative ideas about political philosophy, the economy, foreign policy, religion and the state, and cultural values.

INTRODUCTION TO DOCUMENTS 1 AND 2

Central to understanding modern American conservatism is Barry Goldwater's brief book *The Conscience of a Conservative*. Franklin Roosevelt's New Deal cast a long shadow. Most mainstream Democrats and Republicans in the 1950s accepted the legacy of the New Deal. They generally agreed on the role government should play in regulating the economy, restraining business, allowing workers to form unions, and providing at least modest help to those in need. They did not view the growth or power of the central government with alarm, believing it was an agent of good for the majority of Americans.

Goldwater challenged these notions. He argued that federal power grew in inverse relationship to economic freedom and individual liberty. For Goldwater, the government in Washington, D.C., was not the solution but the problem. He proposed not to reaffirm and extend the New Deal policies but to eradicate them. Running for the presidency on the Republican ticket in 1964, he promised, "I will not change my beliefs to win a vote. I will offer a choice, not an echo." Lyndon Johnson thrashed Goldwater in the 1964 presidential election, winning one of the greatest electoral victories in history, but the ideas Goldwater espoused energized the conservative movement. Document 1 comes from Chapter 2 of *The Conscience of a Conservative*. Taking issue with both Democrats and Republicans, Goldwater calls for significant changes in the very nature of government.

Goldwater's stand inspired many. Acolytes organized the Young Americans for Freedom in 1960, articulating their position in what came to be called The Sharon Statement, found in Document 2. In 1962, the Young Americans for Freedom organized a massive rally for Goldwater—two years before his presidential campaign—in New York's Madison Square Garden, hoping to amplify his message and political following.

1. FROM *THE CONSCIENCE OF A CONSERVATIVE* (1960)

BARRY GOLDWATER

"THE PERILS OF POWER"

The New Deal, Dean Acheson [Secretary of State under Harry Truman] wrote approvingly in a book called *A Democrat Looks At His Party,* "conceived of the federal government as the whole people organized to do what had to be done." A year later Mr. [Arthur] Larson [who held various positions in the Eisenhower Administration] wrote *A Republican Looks At His Party,* and made much the same claim in his book for Modern Republicans. The "underlying philosophy" of the New Republicanism, said Mr. Larson, is that "if a job has to be done to meet the needs of the people, and no one else can do it, then it is the proper function of the federal government."

Here we have, by prominent spokesmen of both political parties, an unqualified repudiation of the principle of limited government. There is no reference by either of them to the Constitution, or any attempt to define the legitimate functions of government. The government can do whatever *needs* to be done; note, too, the implicit but necessary assumption that it is the government itself that determines *what* needs to be done. We must not, I think underrate the importance of these statements. They reflect the view of a majority of the leaders of one of our parties, and of a strong minority among the leaders of the other, and they propound the first principle of totalitarianism: that the State is competent to do all things and is limited in what it actually does only by the will of those who control the State.

It is clear that this view is in direct conflict with the Constitution which is an instrument, above all, for *limiting* the functions of government, and which is as binding today as when it was written. But we are advised to go a step further and ask why the Constitution's framers restricted the scope of government. Conservatives are often charged, and in a sense rightly so, with having an overly mechanistic view of the Constitution: "It is America's enabling document; we are American citizens; therefore," the Conservatives' theme runs, "we are morally and legally obliged to comply with the document." All true. But the Constitution has a broader claim on our loyalty than that. The founding fathers had a *reason* for endorsing the principle of limited government; and this reason recommends defense of the constitutional scheme even to those who take their citizenship obligations lightly. The reason is simple, and it lies at the heart of the Conservative philosophy.

Throughout history, government has proved to be the chief instrument for thwarting man's liberty. Government represents power in the hands of some men to control and regulate the lives of other men. And power, as Lord Acton said, *corrupts* men. "Absolute power," he added, "corrupts absolutely."

State power, considered in the abstract, need not restrict freedom: but absolute state power always does. The *legitimate* functions of government are actually conducive to freedom. Maintaining internal order, keeping foreign foes at bay, administering justice, removing obstacles to the free interchange of goods—the exercise of these powers makes it possible for men to follow their chosen pursuits with maximum freedom. But note that the very instrument by which these desirable ends are achieved *can* be the instrument for achieving undesirable ends—that government can, instead of extending freedom, restrict freedom. And note, secondly, that the "can" quickly becomes "will" the moment the holders of government power are left to their own devices. This is because of the corrupting influence of power, the natural tendency of men who possess *some* power to take unto themselves *more* power. The tendency leads eventually to the acquisition of *all* power—whether in the hands of one or many makes little difference to the freedom of those left on the outside.

Such, then, is history's lesson, which Messrs. Acheson and Larson evidently did not read: release the holders of state power from any restraints other than those they wish to impose upon themselves, and you are swinging down the well-travelled road to absolutism.

The framers of the Constitution had learned the lesson. They were not only students of history, but victims of it: they knew from vivid, personal experience that freedom depends on effective restraints against the accumulation of power in a single authority. And that is what the Constitution is: *a system of restraints against the natural tendency of government to expand in the direction of absolutism.* We all know the main components of the system. The first is the limitation of the federal government's authority to specific, delegated powers. The second, a corollary of the first, is the reservation to the States and the people of all power not delegated to the federal government. The third is a careful division of the federal government's power among three separate branches. The fourth is a prohibition against impetuous alteration of the system—namely, Article V's tortuous, but wise, amendment procedures. . . .

The system of restraints has fallen into disrepair. The federal government has moved into every field in which it believes its services are needed. The state governments are either excluded from their rightful functions by federal preemption, or they are allowed to act at the sufferance of the federal government. Inside the federal government both the executive and judicial branches have roamed far outside their constitutional boundary lines. And all of these things have come to pass without regard to the amendment procedures prescribed by Article V. The result is a Leviathan, a vast national authority out of touch with the people, and out of their control. This monolith of power is bounded only by the will of those who sit in high places. . . .

How did it happen? How did our national government grow from a servant with sharply limited powers into a master with virtually unlimited power?

In part, we were swindled. There are occasions when we have elevated men and political parties to power that promised to restore limited government and then proceeded, after their election, to expand the activities of government. But let us be honest with ourselves. Broken promises are not the major causes of our trouble. *Kept* promises are. All too often we have put men in office who have suggested spending a little more on this, a little more on that, who have proposed a new welfare program, who have thought of another variety of "security." We have taken the bait, preferring to put off to another day the recapture of freedom and the restoration of our constitutional system. We have gone the way of many a democratic society that has lost its freedom by persuading itself that if "the people" rule, all is well. . . .

I am convinced that most Americans now want to reverse the trend. I think that concern for our vanishing freedoms is genuine. I think that the people's uneasiness in the stifling omnipresence of government has turned into something approaching alarm. But bemoaning the evil will not drive it back, and accusing fingers will not shrink government. *The turn will come when we entrust the conduct of our affairs to men who understand that their first duty as public officials is to divest themselves of the power they have been given.* It will come when Americans, in hundreds of communities throughout the nation, decide to put the man in office who is pledged to enforce the Constitution and restore the Republic.[2]

2. THE SHARON STATEMENT: FOUNDING PRINCIPLES OF THE YOUNG AMERICANS FOR FREEDOM (1960)

In this time of moral and political crises, it is the responsibility of the youth of America to affirm certain eternal truths.

We, as young conservatives, believe:

That foremost among the transcendent values is the individual's use of his God-given free will, whence derives his right to be free from the restrictions of arbitrary force; That liberty is indivisible, and that political freedom cannot long exist without economic freedom;

That the purpose of government is to protect those freedoms through the preservation of internal order, the provision of national defense, and the administration of justice;

Image 16.2: Rally sponsored by the Young Americans for Freedom in support of the Vietnam War, 1969

The activism evident in the Young Americans for Freedom reveals that the 1960s and 1970s was a time of grassroots organizing on both the political left and right.

Source: Courtesy Special Collections, University of Massachusetts at Amherst.

That when government ventures beyond these rightful functions, it accumulates power, which tends to diminish order and liberty;

That the Constitution of the United States is the best arrangement yet devised for empowering government to fulfill its proper role, while restraining it from the concentration and abuse of power;

That the genius of the Constitution—the division of powers—is summed up in the clause that reserves primacy to the several states, or to the people, in those spheres not specifically delegated to the Federal government;

That the market economy, allocating resources by the free play of supply and demand, is the single economic system compatible with the requirements of personal freedom and constitutional government, and that it is at the same time the most productive supplier of human needs;

That when government interferes with the work of the market economy, it tends to reduce the moral and physical strength of the nation; that when it takes from one man to bestow on another, it diminishes the incentive of the first, the integrity of the second, and the moral autonomy of both;

That we will be free only so long as the national sovereignty of the United States is secure; that history shows periods of freedom are rare, and can exist only when free citizens concertedly defend their rights against all enemies;

That the forces of international Communism are, at present, the greatest single threat to these liberties;

That the United States should stress victory over, rather than coexistence with, this menace; and

That American foreign policy must be judged by this criterion: does it serve the just interests of the United States?[3]

INTRODUCTION TO DOCUMENT 3

Phillis Schlafly was a strong backer of Goldwater's bid for the presidency in 1964, and she especially liked his fierce anticommunism and his stand against big government. A constitutional lawyer and conservative activist, Schlafly ardently opposed the more liberal candidate for the Republican nomination, Nelson Rockefeller. By the 1970s, Schlafly became a leader in another branch of conservatism, writing strongly worded polemics against what she perceived to be the misguided nature of feminism. She argued that those who supported abortion and the Equal Rights Amendment failed to understand the unique differences between women and men and aimed to erode the special privileges that women had in a more traditional society. In *The Power of the Positive Woman* (1977), excerpted in Document 3, she argues that feminists threatened a social order built on difference and hierarchy, complementary roles between men and women. Where does she fundamentally part ways with the feminists you read in the prior chapter? In your opinion, does she accurately portray the cause of feminism in the early 1970s? How is her understanding of empowerment different from those depicted in the last chapter?

3. *THE POWER OF THE POSITIVE WOMAN* (1977)

PHYLLIS SCHLAFLY

... For a woman to find her identity in the modern world, the path should be sought from the Positive Women who have found the road and possess the map, rather than from those who have not. In this spirit, I share with you the thoughts of one who loves life as a woman and lives life as a woman, whose credentials are from the school of practical experience, and who has learned that fulfillment as a woman is a journey, not a destination. . . .

The first requirement for the acquisition of power by the Positive Woman is to understand the differences between men and women. Your outlook on life, your faith your behavior, your potential for fulfillment, all are determined by the parameters of your original premise. . . .

The women's liberationist . . . is imprisoned by her own negative view of herself. . . . Someone—it is not clear who, perhaps God, perhaps the "Establishment," perhaps a conspiracy of male chauvinist pigs—dealt women a foul blow by making them female. It becomes necessary, therefore, for women to agitate and demonstrate and hurl demands on society in order to wrest from an oppressive male-dominated social structure the status that has been wrongfully denied to women through the centuries. . . .

Confrontation replaces cooperation as the watchword of all relationships. Women and men become adversaries instead of partners. . . . Within the confines of the women's liberationist ideology, therefore, the abolition of this overriding inequality of women becomes the primary goal.

This goal must be achieved at any and all costs. . . . Women must be made equal to men in their ability *not* to become pregnant and not to be expected to care for babies they may bring into the world. This is why women's liberationists are compulsively involved in the drive to make abortion and child-care centers for all women, regardless of religion or income, both socially acceptable and government-financed. . . .

Finally, women are different from men in dealing with the fundamentals of life itself. Men are philosophers, women are practical, and 'twas ever thus. Men may philosophize about how life began and where we are heading; women are concerned about feeding the kids today. . . . Women don't take naturally to a search for the intangible and the abstract. . . . Where man is discursive, logical, abstract, or philosophical, woman tends to be emotional, personal, practical, or mystical. Each set of qualities is vital and complements the other.[4]

INTRODUCTION TO DOCUMENT 4

Conservatives endorsed traditional families, limited government, and free enterprise. Businessmen and politicians like Goldwater believed that the federal government's growing power to tax and regulate threatened free enterprise and even took America down the road to communism. In 1971, Lewis Powell Jr., chairman of the Education Department at the U.S. Chamber of Commerce, wrote a strongly worded memo about the road ahead. Powell perceived threats

Image 16.3: STOP ERA rally in front of the White House, February 4, 1977

Phyllis Schlafly became an icon of the conservative movement by leading the charge against the ERA. "Stop Taking Our Privileges" (STOP) captured the concern that the women's movement aimed to fundamentally challenge women's roles and family responsibilities.

Source: Courtesy Warren Leffler, Prints and Photographs Division, Library of Congress.

to free enterprise on college campuses and in the media. Powell's memo was a call to arms for businessmen to fight back. He urged them to organize, to take cues from the social and political activists that you read about in the last chapter. Powell's memo was highly influential. Between 1974 and 1980 the Chamber of Commerce doubled its membership, and business grew more vocal against government regulation. Businessmen lobbied Washington as never before, engaged public relations firms to promote favorable policies, and contributed enormous resources to candidates and political organizations. Powell's memorandum to the Chamber is Document 4; just a few months after he wrote it, he was appointed to the U.S. Supreme Court by President Richard Nixon.

4. CONFIDENTIAL MEMORANDUM: ATTACK ON AMERICAN FREE ENTERPRISE SYSTEM (AUGUST 23, 1971)

LEWIS POWELL JR.

DIMENSIONS OF THE ATTACK

No thoughtful person can question that the American economic system is under broad attack. This varies in scope, intensity, in the techniques employed, and in the level of visibility.

There always have been some who opposed the American system, and preferred socialism or some form of statism (communism or fascism). Also, there always have been critics of the system, whose criticism has been wholesome and constructive so long as the objective was to improve rather than to subvert or destroy.

But what now concerns us is quite new in the history of America. We are not dealing with episodic or isolated attacks from a relatively few extremists or even from the minority socialist cadre. Rather, the assault on the enterprise system is broadly based and consistently pursued. It is gaining momentum and converts.

SOURCES OF THE ATTACK

The sources are varied and diffused. They include, not unexpectedly, the Communists, New Leftists and other revolutionaries who would destroy the entire system, both political and economic. . . . But they remain a small minority, and are not yet the principal cause for concern.

The most disquieting voices joining the chorus of criticism, come from perfectly respectable elements of society: from the college campus, the pulpit, the media, the intellectual and literary journals, the arts and sciences, and from politicians. . . .

Moreover, much of the media—for varying motives and in varying degrees—either voluntarily accords unique publicity to these "attackers," or at least allows them to exploit the media for their purposes. This is especially true of television, which now plays such a predominant role in shaping the thinking, attitudes and emotions of our people.

One of the bewildering paradoxes of our time is the extent to which the enterprise system tolerates, if not participates in, its own destruction.

TONE OF THE ATTACK

. . . Although New Leftist spokesmen are succeeding in radicalizing thousands of the young, the greater cause for concern is the hostility of respectable liberals and social reformers. It is the sum total of their views and influence which could indeed fatally weaken or destroy the system. . . .

Perhaps the single most effective antagonist of American business is Ralph Nader who—thanks largely to the media—has become a legend in his own time and an idol of millions of Americans. . . . A frontal assault was made on our government, our system of justice, and the free enterprise system by Yale professor Charles Reich in his widely publicized book: "The Greening of America," published last winter. . . .

THE APATHY AND DEFAULT OF BUSINESS

What has been the response of business to this massive assault upon its fundamental economics, upon its philosophy, upon its right to continue to manage its own affairs, and indeed upon its integrity?

The painfully said truth is that business, including the boards of directors and the top executives of corporations great and small and business organizations at all levels, often have responded—if at all—by appeasement, ineptitude and ignoring the problem. There are, of course, many exceptions to this sweeping generalization. But the net effect of such response as has been made is scarcely visible.

In all fairness, it must be recognized that businessmen have not been trained or equipped to conduct guerrilla warfare with those who propagandize against the system, seeking insidiously and constantly to sabotage it. The traditional role of business executives has been to manage, to produce, to sell, to create jobs, to make profits, to improve the standard of living, to be community leaders, to serve on charitable and educational boards, and generally to be good citizens. They have performed these tasks very well indeed. . . .

What specifically should be done? . . . A significant first step by individual corporations could well be the designation of an executive vice president . . . whose responsibility is to counter—on the broadest front—the attack on the enterprise system. The public relations department could be one of the foundations assigned to this executive. . . .

But independent and uncoordinated activity by individual corporations, as important as this is, will not be sufficient. Strength lies in organization, in careful long-range planning and implementation, in consistency of action . . . and in the political power available only through united action and national organizations. . . . The role of the National Chamber of Commerce is therefore vital.

THE CAMPUS

The assault on the enterprise system was not mounted in a few months. . . . There is reason to believe that the campus is the single most dynamic source. The social science faculties usually include members who are unsympathetic to the enterprise system. . . . Such faculty members need not be in a majority. They are often personally attractive and magnetic; they are stimulating teachers, and their controversy attracts student following; they are prolific writers and lecturers; they author many of the textbooks; and they exert enormous influence—far out of proportion to their numbers—on their colleagues and in the academic world. . . .

EQUAL TIME ON THE CAMPUS

The Chamber should insist upon equal time on the college speaking circuit. . . .

The two essential ingredients are (i) to have attractive, articulate and well-informed speakers; and (ii) to exert whatever degree of pressure—publicly and privately—may be necessary to assure opportunities to speak. The objective always must be to inform and enlighten, and not merely to propagandize.

THE NEGLECTED POLITICAL ARENA

In the final analysis, the payoff . . . is what government does. Business has been the favorite whipping boy of many politicians for many years. But the measure of how far this has gone is perhaps best found in the antibusiness views now being expressed by several leading candidates for President of the United States. . . .

One does not exaggerate to say that, in terms of political influence with respect to the course of legislation and government action, the American business executive is truly the "forgotten man."

Current examples of the impotency of business, and of the near-contempt with which businessmen's views are held, are the stampedes by politicians to support almost any legislation related to "consumerism" or to the "environment." . . .

As unwelcome as it may be to the Chamber, it should consider assuming a broader and more vigorous role in the political arena.

NEGLECTED OPPORTUNITY IN THE COURTS

Perhaps the most active exploiters of the judicial system have been groups ranging in political orientation from "liberal" to the far left.

The American Civil Liberties Union is one example. It initiates or intervenes in scores of cases each year, and it files briefs *amicus curiae* in the Supreme Court in a number of cases during each term of that court. Labor unions, civil rights groups and now the public interest law firms are extremely active in the judicial arena. Their success, often at business' expense, has not been inconsequential.

This is a vast area of opportunity for the Chamber, if it is willing to undertake the role of spokesman for American business and if, in turn, business is willing to provide the funds. . . .

We in America already have moved very far indeed toward some aspects of state socialism, as the needs and complexities of a vast urban society require types of regulation and control that were quite unnecessary in earlier times. . . . But most of the essential freedoms remain: private ownership, private profit, labor unions, collective bargaining, consumer choice, and a market economy in which competition largely determines price, quality and variety of the goods and services provided the consumer.

In addition to the ideological attack on the system itself...its essentials also are threatened by inequitable taxation, and—more recently—by an inflation which has seemed uncontrollable. But whatever the causes of diminishing economic freedom may be, the truth is that freedom as a concept is indivisible. As the experience of the socialist and totalitarian states demonstrates, the contraction and denial of economic freedom is followed inevitably by governmental restrictions on other cherished rights. It is this message, above all others, that must be carried home to the American people.

L.F.P., Jr.[5]

INTRODUCTION TO DOCUMENT 5

For conservatives, revolutionary movements that overthrow traditions, radically change governments, or challenge religious authority are deeply suspect. Ronald Reagan viewed the Soviet Union as just such a revolutionary movement. For him the Cold War was not just a geopolitical battle between two superpowers; it was a contest between good and evil. Once again Reagan followed Goldwater's thinking. Goldwater argued that the Truman and Eisenhower administrations underestimated the Soviet Union's will to conquer. Such an enemy cannot be managed, Goldwater argued. Reagan accepted such a Manichean vision of the world. In a speech before the National Associations of Evangelicals, a conservative Christian organization, Reagan introduced the notion of the "evil empire." For Reagan, foreign policy was not merely a matter of power but also a moral endeavor.

5. RUSSIA AS AN "EVIL EMPIRE" (1983)

PRESIDENT RONALD REAGAN

During my first press conference as President, in answer to a direct question, I pointed out that, as good Marxist-Leninists, the Soviet leaders have openly and publicly declared that the only morality they recognize is that which will further their cause, which is world revolution. I think I should point out I was only quoting Lenin, their guiding spirit, who said in 1920 that they repudiate all morality that proceeds from supernatural ideas—that's their name for religion—or ideas that are outside class conceptions. Morality is entirely subordinate to the interests of class war. And everything is moral that is necessary

Image 16.4: Ronald Reagan in the White House, undated

Ronald Reagan's winning style and strong anti-Communist convictions drew a large following, swaying many former Democrats to the Republican Party.

Source: Courtesy Carol M. Highsmith Archive, Library of Congress.

for the annihilation of the old, exploiting social order and for uniting the proletariat. . . .

This doesn't mean we should isolate ourselves and refuse to seek an understanding with them. I intend to do everything I can to persuade them of our peaceful intent, to remind them that it was the West that refused to use its nuclear monopoly in the forties and fifties for territorial gain and which now proposes 50-percent cut in strategic ballistic missiles and the elimination of an entire class of land-based, intermediate-range nuclear missiles.

At the same time, however, they must be made to understand we will never compromise our principles and standards. We will never give away our freedom. We will never abandon our belief in God. And we will never stop searching for a genuine peace. . . .

Yes, let us pray for the salvation of all of those who live in that totalitarian darkness—pray they will discover the joy of knowing God. But until they do, let us be aware that while they preach the supremacy of the state, declare its omnipotence over individual man, and predict its eventual domination of all peoples on the Earth, they are the focus of evil in the modern world. . . .

So, I urge you to speak out against those who would place the United States in a position of military and moral inferiority. . . . I urge you to beware the temptation of pride—the temptation of blithely declaring yourselves above it all and label both sides equally at fault, to ignore the facts of history and the aggressive impulses of an evil empire, to simply call the arms race a giant misunderstanding and thereby remove yourself from the struggle between right and wrong and good and evil.

I ask you to resist the attempts of those who would have you withhold your support for our efforts, this administration's efforts, to keep America strong and free, while we negotiate real and verifiable reductions in the world's nuclear arsenals and one day, with God's help, their total elimination.

While America's military strength is important, let me add here that I've always maintained that the struggle now going on for the world will never be decided by bombs or rockets, by armies or military might. The real crisis we face today is a spiritual one; at root, it is a test of moral will and faith. . . .

. . . I believe we shall rise to the challenge. I believe that communism is another sad, bizarre chapter in human history whose last pages even now are being written. I believe this because the source of our strength in the quest for human freedom is not material, but spiritual. And because it knows no limitation, it must terrify and ultimately triumph over those who would enslave their fellow man.

For in the words of Isaiah: "He giveth power to the faint; and to them that have no might He increased strength. . . . But they that wait upon the Lord shall renew their strength; they shall mount up with wings as eagles; they shall run, and not be weary. . . ."

Yes, change your world. One of our Founding Fathers, Thomas Paine, said, "We have it within our power to begin the world over again." We can do it, doing together what no one church could do by itself.

God bless you, and thank you very much.[6]

INTRODUCTION TO DOCUMENT 6

Fundamentalist Christians have become a bulwark of conservative politics. They have advocated and fought for a series of social, political, and moral positions, from antiabortion legislation and the right to school prayer to balanced budgets and defense spending. Conservative Christians have used mass media, particularly television, to preach their message and have proven particularly adept at forming grassroots organizations. They have decided the outcomes of many elections, especially when "cultural" issues—gay rights, evolution versus creationism, as well as abortion and school prayer—became salient. Marion Gordon "Pat" Robertson, founder and chairman of the Christian Broadcasting Network (CBN), was one of the most powerful conservative Christian voices in the second half of the twentieth century. A son of a congressman and senator, a marine during the Korean War, and the author of numerous books, Robertson was known to his viewers for his warm smile and his iron opinions. In 1988, at the end of Ronald Reagan's term, he made a bid for the presidency. In the following speech, he summarized what he and other conservative Christians believed was wrong—and right—about America. When his candidacy faltered, he endorsed the Republican candidate George Bush.

6. PAT ROBERTSON LAUNCHES HIS PRESIDENTIAL BID, CONSTITUTION HALL (SEPTEMBER 17, 1986)

On September 17, 1787, just 199 years ago today, 391 men meeting in solemn assembly at Independence Hall in Philadelphia voted their approval of a document drafted on behalf of the people of the United States to "form a more perfect union, establish justice, insure domestic tranquility, provide for the common defense, promote the general welfare, and secure the blessings of liberty to ourselves and our posterity." . . .

A vision was born on this date of a nation united—a nation whose official motto was E Pluribus Unum—out of many one. The vision born on September 17 was of one nation—under God—with liberty and justice for all. . . .

Our First President who had presided over the Constitutional Convention in his farewell address declared, "Reason and experience forbid us to expect public morality in the absence of religious principal."

Our Second President, John Adams, whose wisdom was key to the drafting of our Constitution said, "We have not government armed with power capable of contending with human passions unbridled by morality and religion. Our Constitution was made only for a moral and religious people. It is wholly inadequate to the government of any other."

And our Third President, Thomas Jefferson, the author of our Declaration of Independence, gave us solemn warning, "And can the liberties of a nation be thought secure, when we have removed their only firm basis—a conviction in the minds of the people that these liberties are the gift of God? And they are not to be violated but with His wrath."

WARNINGS DISREGARDED

Yet despite these warnings, we have permitted during the past 25 years an assault on our faith and values that would have been unthinkable to past generations of Americans. We have taken virtually all mention of God from our classrooms and textbooks. Using public funds we have begun courses in so called "values clarification" which tend to undermine our historic Judeo-Christian faith. We have taken the Holy Bible from our young and replaced it with the thoughts of Charles Darwin, Karl Marx, Sigmund Freud, and John Dewey. A small elite of lawyers, judges, and educators have given us such a tortured view of the establishment of religion clause of the First Amendment to our Constitution that it has been called by one United States Senator "an intellectual scandal."

Instead of absolutes, our youth have been given situational ethics and the life centered curriculum. Instead of a clear knowledge of right and wrong, they have been told "if it feels good do it." Instead of

self-restraint they are often taught self-gratification and hedonism.

WHAT WE HAVE PAID

Our motion pictures, our television, our radio, our youth concerts, with a few outstanding exceptions, seem to have a single message—God is out, casual sex, infidelity and easy divorce, the recreational use of drugs, and radical lifestyles are in. . . .

There are 1,000,000 illegitimate pregnancies to unwed teenagers every year in our country. Of these, 400,000 babies are aborted—yet 600,000 babies are born each year to youngsters hardly old enough to be away from their parents. In the black community, according to a CBS report, 60% of all births are to women without a man in residence.

On the darker side of society an estimated 1/4 of all our children are sexually assaulted while they are growing up, and each year between 1.2 and 1.5 million teenagers are either runaways or throwaways. And to match our new sexual freedom this year there will be an estimated 8.6 million new cases of venereal disease in our country, and the dread incurable killer AIDS may have already infected 1,000,000 Americans.

Our schools, with what is called "progressive education," have become progressively worse. We have in our society 27 million functional illiterates. Each year we add 2.3 million to their number. Instead of being the most literate nation on earth, we rank number 14 among the developed nations in literacy and we are falling fast.

WHAT THE LIBERAL ELITE SAY

Now in 1986 the same liberal elites that gave us the problem deny the cause and tell us that this is a problem for government. Ladies and gentlemen, what we are facing is not a governmental problem, it is a moral problem.

Human cruelty, human selfishness, alcoholism, drug addiction, and sexual promiscuity will always bring poverty and the disintegration of society. The answer for us does not lie in institutionalizing aberrant behavior—whether that behavior is substance abuse or sexual perversion. And certainly the answer does not lie in once again penalizing the productive sector of our society with high taxes and wasteful spending.

. . . We must guarantee

1. New tougher discipline in drug and alcohol free schools. For our children and grandchildren we will eliminate once and for all from our land the mob supported drugs and pornography which is destroying and debasing their dream of the future.
2. We will insure to them a return to a basic broad based phonics approach to reading. Our children must learn basic language and basic math.

They must know the facts of history—the facts of geography—the facts of science. The "progressive education" advocated by John Dewey and his followers is a colossal failure and must be abandoned.

3. For our children's and grandchildren's sake we must insure that control of education is returned to their parents and caring teachers in local communities, and taken away from a powerful union with leftist tendencies.
4. There can be no education without morality, and there can be no lasting morality without religion. For the sake of our children, we must bring God back to the classrooms of America![7]

INTRODUCTION TO DOCUMENT 7

Reagan's two-term presidency was followed by that of his vice president, George H. W. Bush. After just one term in 1992, however, Bush faced a rival within his own party for the presidential nomination, Patrick Buchanan. Buchanan had worked for Presidents Nixon and Reagan but found George Bush too liberal for his taste on issues such as taxation and immigration. Buchanan won a substantial minority of the primary vote but ultimately failed to win the Republican nomination and threw his support behind Bush. Perhaps most significant is Buchanan's style of conservatism: populist, defiant, antiestablishment, nationalistic, and unabashedly antiliberal. Document 7 is a portion of Buchanan's concession speech after the Republican primaries in 1992. He began with an attack on the Democrats and their recently completed convention.

7. PATRICK BUCHANAN'S CONCESSION SPEECH (1992)

. . . Like many of you last month, I watched that giant masquerade ball at Madison Square Garden—where 20,000 radicals and liberals came dressed up as moderates and centrists—in the greatest single exhibition of cross-dressing in American political history.

One by one, the prophets of doom appeared at the podium. The Reagan decade, they moaned, was a terrible time in America; and the only way to prevent even worse times, they said, is to entrust our nation's fate and future to the party that gave us McGovern, Mondale, Carter and Michael Dukakis.

No way, my friends. The American people are not going to buy back into the failed liberalism of the 1960s and '70s—no matter how slick the package in 1992. . . .

Mr. Clinton, however, has a different agenda.

At its top is unrestricted abortion on demand. When the Irish-Catholic governor of Pennsylvania, Robert Casey, asked to say a few words on behalf of the 25 million unborn children destroyed since Roe v. Wade, he was told there was no place for him at the podium of Bill Clinton's convention, no room at the inn.

Yet a militant leader of the homosexual rights movement could rise at that convention and exult: "Bill Clinton and Al Gore represent the most pro-lesbian and pro-gay ticket in history." And so they do.

Bill Clinton supports school choice—but only for state-run schools. Parents who send their children to Christian schools, or Catholic schools, need not apply.

Elect me, and you get two for the price of one, Mr Clinton says of his lawyer-spouse. And what does Hillary believe? Well, Hillary believes that 12-year-olds should have a right to sue their parents, and she has compared marriage as an institution to slavery—and life on an Indian reservation.

Well, speak for yourself, Hillary.

Friends, this is radical feminism. The agenda Clinton & Clinton would impose on America—abortion on demand, a litmus test for the Supreme Court, homosexual rights, discrimination against religious schools, women in combat—that's change, all right. But it is not the kind of change America wants. It is not the kind of change America needs. And it is not the kind of change we can tolerate in a nation that we still call God's country.

My friends, this election is about much more than who gets what. It is about who we are. It is about what we believe. It is about what we stand for as Americans. There is a religious war going on in our country for the soul of America. It is a cultural war, as critical to the kind of nation we will one day be as was the Cold War itself. And in that struggle for the soul of America, Clinton & Clinton are on the other side, and George Bush is on our side. And so, we have to come home, and stand beside him.

My friends, in those 6 months [during the primaries], from Concord to California, I came to know our country better than ever before in my life, and I collected memories that will be with me always.

There was that day long ride through the great state of Georgia in a bus Vice President Bush himself had used in 1988—a bus they called Asphalt One. The ride ended with a 9:00 PM speech in front of a magnificent southern mansion, in a town called Fitzgerald.

There were the workers at the James River Paper Mill, in the frozen North Country of New Hampshire—hard, tough men, one of whom was silent, until I shook his hand. Then he looked up in my eyes and said, "Save our jobs!" There was the legal secretary at the Manchester airport on Christmas Day who told me she was going to vote for me, then broke down crying, saying, "I've lost my job, I don't have any money; they've going to take away my daughter. What am I going to do?"

My friends, even in tough times, these people are with us. They don't read Adam Smith or Edmund Burke, but they came from the same schoolyards and playgrounds and towns as we did. They share our beliefs and convictions, our hopes and our dreams. They are the conservatives of the heart.

They are our people. And we need to reconnect with them. We need to let them know we know they're hurting. They don't expect miracles, but they need to know we care.

There were the people of Hayfork, the tiny town high up in California's Trinity Alps, a town that is now under a sentence of death because a federal judge has set aside 9 million acres for the habitat of the spotted owl—forgetting about the habitat of the men and women who live and work in Hayfork. And there were the brave people of Koreatown who took the worst of the LA riots, but still live the family values we treasure, and who still believe deeply in the American dream.

Friends, in those wonderful 25 weeks, the saddest days were the days of the bloody riot in LA, the worst in our history. But even out of that awful tragedy can come a message of hope. Hours after the violence ended I visited the Army compound in south LA, where an officer of the 18th Cavalry, that had come to rescue the city, introduced me to two of his troopers. They could not have been 20 years old. He told them to recount their story.

They had come into LA late on the 2nd day, and they walked up a dark street, where the mob had looted and burned every building but one, a convalescent home for the aged. The mob was heading in, to ransack and loot the apartments of the terrified old men and women. When the troopers arrived, M-16s at the ready, the mob threatened and cursed, but the mob retreated. It had met the one thing that could stop it: force, rooted in justice, backed by courage.

Greater love than this hath no man than that he lay down his life for his friend. Here were 19-year-old boys ready to lay down their lives to stop a mob from molesting old people they did not even know. And as they took back the streets of LA, block by block, so we must take back our cities, and take back our culture, and take back our country.

God bless you, and God bless America.[8]

INTRODUCTION TO DOCUMENT 8

Conservatives held the White House under Reagan and Bush, but the election of Bill Clinton in 1992 ushered a new group into power—men and women who disagreed with conservatives about the role of government in the economy and society. Though a centrist Democrat, Clinton certainly believed in many traditional Democratic policies that clashed with the ideas of conservative Republicans in the House of Representatives and the Senate. During the 1994 elections, Republican Congressman Newt Gingrich proposed a plan that combined many of conservatives' favorite economic, political, social, and cultural themes. As such, it was an extension of the ideas of Barry Goldwater. The "Contract with America" helped the Republicans regain control of both houses of Congress in 1994, with Gingrich becoming Speaker of the House. The entire plan was never enacted, and Clinton was reelected president two years later in 1996. However, the Contract with America became a statement of conservative positions and a template for Republican policymakers well into the twenty-first century.

8. CONTRACT WITH AMERICA (1994)

CONGRESSMAN NEWT GINGRICH

As Republican Members of the House of Representatives and as citizens seeking to join that body we propose not just to change its policies, but even more important, to restore the bonds of trust between the people and their elected representatives.

That is why, in this era of official evasion and posturing, we offer instead a detailed agenda for national renewal, a written commitment with no fine print.

This year's election offers the chance, after four decades of one-party control, to bring to the House a new majority that will transform the way Congress works. That historic change would be the end of government that is too big, too intrusive, and too easy with the public's money. It can be the beginning of a Congress that respects the values and shares the faith of the American family. . . .

. . . Within the first 100 days of the 104th Congress, we shall bring to the House Floor the following bills, each to be given full and open debate, each to be given a clear and fair vote and each to be immediately available this day for public inspection and scrutiny.

1. THE FISCAL RESPONSIBILITY ACT

   A balanced budget/tax limitation amendment and a legislative line-item veto to restore fiscal responsibility to an out-of-control Congress, requiring them to live under the same budget constraints as families and businesses.

2. THE TAKING BACK OUR STREETS ACT

   An anti-crime package including stronger truth-in-sentencing, "good faith" exclusionary rule exemptions, effective death penalty provisions, and cuts in social spending from this summer's "crime" bill to fund prison construction and additional law enforcement to keep people secure in their neighborhoods and kids safe in their schools.

3. THE PERSONAL RESPONSIBILITY ACT

   Discourage illegitimacy and teen pregnancy by prohibiting welfare to minor mothers and denying increased AFDC for additional children while on welfare, cut spending for welfare programs, and enact a tough two-years-and-out provision with work requirements to promote individual responsibility.

4. THE FAMILY REINFORCEMENT ACT

   Child support enforcement, tax incentives for adoption, strengthening rights of parents in their children's education, stronger child pornography laws, and an elderly dependent care tax credit to reinforce the central role of families in American society.

5. THE AMERICAN DREAM RESTORATION ACT

   A $500 per child tax credit, begin repeal of the marriage tax penalty, and creation of American Dream Savings Accounts to provide middle class tax relief.

6. THE NATIONAL SECURITY RESTORATION ACT

   No U.S. troops under U.N. command and restoration of the essential parts of our national security funding to strengthen our national defense and maintain our credibility around the world.

7. THE SENIOR CITIZENS FAIRNESS ACT

   Raise the Social Security earnings limit which currently forces seniors out of the work force, repeal the 1993 tax hikes on Social Security benefits and provide tax incentives for private long-term care insurance to let Older Americans keep more of what they have earned over the years.

8. THE JOB CREATION AND WAGE ENHANCEMENT ACT

   Small business incentives, capital gains cut and indexation, neutral cost recovery, risk assessment/cost-benefit analysis, strengthening the Regulatory Flexibility Act and unfunded mandate reform to create jobs and raise worker wages.

9. THE COMMON SENSE LEGAL REFORM ACT

   "Loser pays" laws, reasonable limits on punitive damages and reform of product liability laws to stem the endless tide of litigation.

10. THE CITIZEN LEGISLATURE ACT

    Further, we will instruct the House Budget Committee to report to the floor and we will work to enact additional budget savings, beyond the budget cuts specifically included in the legislation described above, to ensure that the Federal budget deficit will be less than it would have been without the enactment of these bills.

Respecting the judgment of our fellow citizens as we seek their mandate for reform, we hereby pledge our names to this Contract with America.

POSTSCRIPT

In the years before World War II, the foreign policy outlook of many conservative Republicans was deeply isolationist. Their strong desire to avoid unnecessary foreign entanglements resumed for a while after the fighting ended, even as the Cold War heated up. Senator Robert Taft of Ohio, "Mr. Republican," as he was known, exemplified this strain in conservative thought. But conservatism gradually became more closely associated with activist foreign policy. Despite his skepticism of the federal government, Barry Goldwater advocated a muscular military stance against communism, as did President Nixon ten years after the publication of *The Conscience of a Conservative*. President Reagan continued this expansion of military commitments. By the new century, the Presidency of George W. Bush embraced a wide-ranging engagement with the world, including two wars and "nation building" in the Middle East as a response to the 2001 terrorist attacks on the World Trade Center in New York City. Though the Cold War had ended ten years earlier, metaphors of diabolical, merciless, rapacious evil continued, and so did the Manichean view of the world and the sense of America was under siege. President Bush told the nation,

. . . What we have found in Afghanistan confirms that, far from ending there, our war against terror is only beginning. Most of the 19 men who hijacked planes on September the 11th were trained in Afghanistan's camps, and so were tens of thousands of others. Thousands of dangerous killers, schooled in the methods of murder, often supported by outlaw regimes, are now spread throughout the world like ticking time bombs, set to go off without warning. . . .

Our nation will continue to be steadfast and patient and persistent in the pursuit of two great objectives. First, we will shut down terrorist camps, disrupt terrorist plans, and bring terrorists to justice. And, second, we must prevent the terrorists and regimes who seek chemical, biological or nuclear weapons from threatening the United States and the world. . . .

Iran aggressively pursues these weapons and exports terror, while an unelected few repress the Iranian people's hope for freedom.

Iraq continues to flaunt its hostility toward America and to support terror. The Iraqi regime has plotted to develop anthrax, and nerve gas, and nuclear weapons for over a decade. This is a regime that has already used poison gas to murder thousands of its own citizens—leaving the bodies of mothers huddled over their dead children. . . .

States like these, and their terrorist allies, constitute an axis of evil, arming to threaten the peace of the world. By seeking weapons of mass destruction, these regimes pose a grave and growing danger. They could provide these arms to terrorists, giving them the means to match their hatred. They could attack our allies or attempt to blackmail the United States. In any of these cases, the price of indifference would be catastrophic. . . .

I will not wait on events, while dangers gather. I will not stand by, as peril draws closer and closer. The United States of America will not permit the world's most dangerous regimes to threaten us with the world's most destructive weapons.

Our war on terror is well begun, but it is only begun. This campaign may not be finished on our watch—yet it must be and it will be waged on our watch. . . .[9]

Claiming that Iraq was building chemical and nuclear "weapons of mass destruction," the United States invaded that country in 2003. The war lasted nearly a decade, with hundreds of thousands of Iraqis dead, hundreds of thousands more injured or displaced, and nearly 5,000 Americans killed. The long-term costs to the United States are estimated at between $2 trillion and $3 trillion. After the war, the Middle East was as unstable as ever, new strains of terrorism evolved. No weapons of mass destruction were ever found.

QUESTIONS

1. Do you think conservative views on foreign policy necessarily reinforce conservative domestic ideals, or are these two sets of beliefs sometimes contradictory? More generally, do you find conservative thinking to be consistent, or has it changed with time and circumstances?
2. Compare the messages between the insurgent Republicans, Pat Robertson and Patrick Buchanan. Do they share rhetoric, goals, and visions for America's political future? Compare Robertson and Buchanan with Reagan; do they differ much?
3. Why would the Religious Right support the Republican Party more than the Democratic Party or some third-party movement? What role does religious ideology play in modern conservatism?
4. Do you see similarities between Lewis Powell's agenda and that of Pat Robertson and George W. Bush, or do they express fundamentally different messages and goals?
5. How is Newt Gingrich's Contract with America a fundamentally conservative document?
6. Contrast the underlying political philosophy expressed in Chapter 15 with that of this chapter.

ADDITIONAL READING

A very good introduction to the history of modern conservative thought is Russell Kirk, ed., *The Portable Conservative Reader* (1982). Rowland Berthoff, *An Unsettled People: Social Order and Disorderin American History* (1971) presents a conservative interpretation of American history. Recent works on conservatism include Jennifer Burns, *Goddess of the Market: Ayn Rand and the American Right* (2009); Michael Kazin, *The Populist Persuasion* (1995); Lisa McGirr, *Suburban Warriors: The Origins of the New American Right* (2001); Dan T. Carter, *The Politics of Rage* (1995); John Andrew, *The Other Side of the Sixties* (1997); Mary C. Brennan, *Turning Right in the Sixties* (1995); Kim Phelps-Fein, *Invisible Hands: The Making of the Conservative Movement from the New Deal to Reagan* (2009); Harvey Kaye, *The Powers of the Past* (1992); Elizabeth Tandy Shermer, *Barry Goldwater and the Remaking of the American Political Landscape* (2013); and Michelle Nickerson, *Mothers of Conservatism* (2014). Also see Lee Edwards, *The Conservative Revolution: The Movement That Remade America* (1999); Robert Alan Goldberg, *Barry Goldwater* (1995); and George Will, *The Woven Figure: Conservatism and the American Fabric* (1997). For histories of the movement written by one of its chief intellectual inspirations, see Irving Kristol, *Neoconservatism: The Autobiography of an Idea* (1995) and *The Neoconservative Persuasion* (2011). On the youth movement, see Gregory L. Schneider, *Cadres for Conservatism: Young Americans for Freedom and the Rise of the Contemporary Right* (1998). On the antiwar strain of American conservatism, see Bill Kaufman, *Ain't My America (2008)*. Other works include Robert Brent Toplin, *Radical Conservatism* (2006); Ronald Story and Bruce Laury, eds. *The Rise of Conservatism in America* (2007); and Gregory Schneider, *Conservatism in America since 1930* (2003).

ENDNOTES

1. Patrick Buchanan "Introduction," in *The Conscience of a Conservative*, by Barry Goldwater (New York: MFJ Books, 1990).
2. Barry Goldwater, *The Conscience of a Conservative* (Princeton, NJ: Princeton University Press, 2007, originally published 1960).

3. The Sharon Statement, September 1960, by the Young Americans for Freedom, Sharon, Connecticut.

4. Phyllis Schlafly, *The Power of the Positive Woman* (New Rochelle, NY: Arlington House Press, 1977).

5. Lewis F. Powell Jr. Papers, Box 127, Folder 15; Powell Archives, Washington and Lee University School of Law, Lexington, VA.

6. *Public Papers of the Presidents of the United States: Ronald Reagan, 1985*, v.1 (Washington, D.C.: Government Printing Office, 1988).

7. Pat Robertson, speech, found at http://www.patrobertson.com.

8. Pat Buchanan, speech to the Republican National Convention, 1992.

9. George W. Bush, State of the Union Address, January 2002.